By the Same Author

PRESENT PERSPECTIVES

Present
Perspectives

CRITICAL WRITINGS

Robert
Craft

 Alfred A. Knopf   New York   1984

THIS IS A BORZOI BOOK
PUBLISHED BY ALFRED A. KNOPF, INC.

Most of the essays have been previously published in the *New
York Review of Books*, the *Atlantic*, the *New Republic*, the
Observer, and the Washington *Post*. Grateful acknowledgment
is made to UMI Research Press for permission to reprint
Robert Craft's preface to Asaf'yev's *A Book about Stravinsky*,
copyright © 1982 by Richard French.

Letters and other copyrighted material from the Stravinsky
Archives are published by kind permission of the Paul Sacher
Foundation.

Library of Congress Cataloging in Publication Data
Craft, Robert. Present perspectives, critical writings.
1. Music—Addresses, essays, lectures. I. Title.
MI.60.C92 1984   780   82-48886
ISBN 0-394-53073-X

Manufactured in the United States of America
First Edition

VERA ARTUROVNA STRAVINSKY

d. September 17, 1982

. . . that fair field of Enna, where Proserpine
Gathering flowers, herself a fairer flower
                                        Milton

        . . . rimembri ancora
        Quel tempo della tua vita mortale,
        Quando beltà splendea
        Negli occhi tuoi ridenti . . .
                            Leopardi

Contents

viii   *Contents*

Acknowledgments

I thank the editors of the *New York Review of Books* for permission to reprint the following pieces, which first appeared there: "Josquin's Ars Perfecta," February 23, 1978; "Too Little Waugh," March 9, 1978; "Evviva Vivaldi!," March 23, 1978; "Light on Lasso," May 4, 1978; "From the Vedas to Wagner (and Beyond)," March 22, 1979; "Testaments from Shostakovich and Prokofiev," January 24, 1980; "An 'Unheard-of Intensity,' " November 20, 1980; "Schoenberg and Dika," December 18, 1980; "Liszt's Letters to Baroness von Meyendorff," February 5, 1981; "What 'R.' Wrought," April 16, 1981; "Shadow and Substance," September 24, 1981; "Virgil Thomson," February 4, 1982; "La Grande Mademoiselle," May 27, 1982; "Stravinsky: A Centenary View," June 10, 1982; "Keeping Up with Mr. B.," August 12, 1982. Parts of "Excerpts from a Diary" were also published in the *New York Review of Books*, November 24, 1977, August 17, 1978 ("On T. S. Eliot's Criticism of Prose Fiction"), and March 17, 1983, while another section appeared in the *Observer* (London), April 4, 1982, and still another in the *New Republic*, October 3, 1983. "Diaghilev: Genie of the Ballets Russes" first appeared in the Washington *Post*, October 7, 1979. "Asaf'yev and Stravinsky" is the preface to Asaf'yev's *Book about Stravinsky*, published by UMI

Research Press, Ann Arbor, Michigan, 1982. The *Atlantic Monthly* published "Influence or Assistance?," December 1982, and "In Search of Mozart," April 1983.

I wish to thank Robert Silvers and Barbara Epstein for their work on the essays that originally appeared in the *New York Review of Books*. For numerous improvements throughout this book, thanks are due to Elbert Lenrow, Lawrence Morton, and Phyllis Crawford. I am especially grateful to Malcolm Brown for his translation of Prokofiev's letters concerning Stravinsky and Boris Asaf'yev, and to Mme Lucia Davidova, an expert in deciphering Stravinsky's Russian script, for her translations of his marginalia in the Asaf'yev essay. At Knopf I wish to thank Robert Gottlieb for the task of choosing the contents of this book, and Eva Resnikova for countless corrections and suggestions in matters of substance as well as of style.

PRESENT PERSPECTIVES

What "R." Wrought

The phenomenon of Richard Wagner has been recounted, analyzed, and discussed in such abundance that it would seem as if the end must be somewhere in sight. Instead, the publication of Cosima Wagner's *Diaries*[1] during the centenary (1976) of the first performance of *Der Ring des Nibelungen* has provoked an entirely new interest in the man, though more from historians than from musicians. Books such as Dr. L. J. Rather's *The Dream of Self-Destruction: Wagner's "Ring" and the Modern World*[2] radically readjust the emphasis, to the extent of describing many of Wagner's prose writings as "works of art" and referring to his "greatness as a theoretician in the realm of the sociology of knowledge." Cosima's *Diaries*, however, and in lesser, because shorter, measure *The Diary of Richard Wagner: The Brown Book*,[3] have claimed the attention of the world and therefore demand prior examination.

1. *Cosima Wagner's Diaries, Vol. II: 1878–1883*, edited and annotated by Martin Gregor-Dellin and Dietrich Mack; translated, with an introduction, postscript, and additional notes by Geoffrey Skelton (New York, 1978).
2. *The Dream of Self-Destruction: Wagner's "Ring" and the Modern World*, by L. J. Rather (Baton Rouge, La., 1979).
3. *The Diary of Richard Wagner: The Brown Book, 1865–1882*, presented and annotated by Joachim Bergfeld, translated by George Bird (New York, 1980).

To consider Wagner's own book first, the sixty or so entries date from August 1865 to the spring of 1882. Before a separation from Wagner, Cosima gave him a calfskin notebook so that he might record material which she could read later. About a third of the poems, essays, *pensées*, reminiscences, and sketches for dramatic works that make up the "diary" are now published for the first time. But these heretofore unknown items are disappointing. Wagner equates the nonequatable:

Beeth. = Schopenhauer: his music, translated into concepts, would produce that philosophy.

Wagner's megalomania, however, would seem to warrant psychiatric attention:

I shall set up full court. . . . I shall no longer concern myself with anything directly. . . . Then things shall proceed as at Versailles under Louis XIV. . . . The world I cannot shape I must merely forget.

(Many of his remarks in Cosima's *Diaries* begin with the phrase "If I were emperor . . .")

For this reader, the most interesting sections in *The Brown Book* are the "Annals," embryonic fragments of the autobiography intended for Wagner's benefactor, King Ludwig II of Bavaria, written not in grammatical form but as if in free association. The finished product, unlike the "Annals," had to be doubly tailored, first for Cosima, to whom Wagner dictated the text, second for the ingenuous and deeply illusioned young monarch. In these preliminary jottings, Wagner's belief in astrology is evident—he attributes his inability to write for two months to a "bite from Leo"—and his love of animals, as when he remembers a farewell scene on a Rhine bridge by the presence of "a tired donkey." (He once risked his life to save his dog.) He was fond of lepidoptera, too, and purchased a collection in Naples.

As for the processes of memory, Wagner recalls events and their chronology in connection with the weather, with menus, and with his health and moods. These stream-of-consciousness "Annals" also show how thoroughly pragmatic was the great spinner of fantasies. But though he notes the dates of important dreams, he does not spell out the contents as Cosima does for him in her *Diaries*, where, in fact, they offer the most important clues to the man. Most of his dreams were about women, including his first wife, Minna; Cosima (again and again); and his mother, whom he sees as attractive, young, and "elegant." But Wagner on the relationship between dreams and musical creativity is a subject for a book, whose sequel might be a compilation from his own incredibly prolific dream life.

The Brown Book helps to convict Wagner of a shocking duplicity. A married man, he became the lover (in November 1863) of the twenty-four-years-younger Cosima von Bülow, wife of his friend and apostle, and swore eternal fidelity to her. Wagner then invited Mathilde Maier, a handsome woman also much younger than himself, to share his home on the Starnberger See. One wonders what would have happened if Mathilde, believing his vow—"I've never had anyone else in mind to fill your place"—had accepted his invitation of June 25, 1864, to become the "mistress" of this residence, since, only four days later, not Mathilde but Cosima arrived, without her spouse. Undaunted, Wagner sent to Mathilde a masterpiece of *volte-face*, whose follow-up letter belongs in an anthology of the Great Deceivers:

> You would now find me in a frame of mind where I would not be able to accept any sacrifice that would be offered. . . . Your coming *now* would be a source of totally insupportable torments to my heart. . . .

The composer continued to correspond with Mathilde, and Herr Bergfeld, the editor of *The Brown Book*, says that in these letters Wagner is "touching and considerate . . . a reproof to those who like to regard him as a callous egotist"—as if it were not apparent that by underscoring the word "now," Wagner is keeping the door open in the event that his affair with Cosima does not work out. As some of the newly published material in *The Brown Book* reveals, despite the attempts of Eva, Cosima's daughter, to eradicate the relevant passages, Cosima failed to hide her jealousy of Mathilde. Cosima's *Diaries* mislead the reader, mentioning the "anniversary of my arrival in Starnberg" in an 1878 entry dated June 21, eight days earlier, while further on, she identifies Starnberg as the place "where it all started," though as scholars have now established, "it" had started seven months before.

Cosima's *Diaries* were made available to some biographers during her lifetime, and the books contain little that was not already known. Perhaps for this reason, the long-delayed publication has received less attention from musicologists than from specialists in modern German history who have regarded them as representative documents of their period (1869–83). Peter Gay, for one, has established attitudes toward them and their author (see his articles in the *TLS*, January 28, 1977, and March 24, 1978) that have already been adopted by others, including George Marek in his *Cosima Wagner*.[4] Mr. Gay's appraisal of Cosima's character —"clever and obtuse, learned and ignorant, snobbish and humble"—is generally fair, except for his description of her devotion to Wagner as horrifyingly masochistic. Surely the word does not fit such an obvious labor of love, which, if it were anything else, probably could not have been accomplished at all. To be sure, Cosima was creating an identity for herself and a well-defined place in history, but this does not diminish her achievement: for better or for worse, she has left a morning, noon, and night record of the last fourteen years in the life of one of the greatest composers.

Volume II chronicles every aspect of Wagner's last five

4. *Cosima Wagner*, by George R. Marek (New York, 1981).

years: his work on *Parsifal;* his health (often noted several times a day); his dreams; his reading and his writing; his theories and his ideas; his tempers, affections, and sensations; his observations on his own music as well as on that of other composers (especially Beethoven and Bach); his comments on political events (above all those in Bismarck's Germany); and his opinions on a scarcely believable range of subjects. Cosima also records their travels, the visits of friends and relatives (including Liszt, her not-all-that-welcome father), and the routine of life.

Central to the book are the creation and first performance of *Parsifal.* Cosima has preserved not only "R." 's thoughts about the drama, and the inception of musical ideas (themes, intervals, chordal progressions, ideas for the orchestration), but also discussions about the question of possible profanity in applauding after the "sacramental" ending of Act I. To some extent Wagner's creative processes can be followed in Cosima's logbook of their outward manifestations, but she never goes far enough, telling us that Wagner showed her a sketch on which he had written the word "bad," but not revealing in what way, or ways, he found the draft wanting. Similarly, when she writes that "R. comes to the subject of Bach's fugues, in most of which there is hardly ever a modulation . . . ," she does not clarify the remark. By ordinary definitions, modulations occur in Bach's shortest fughettas; but Wagner's terminology elsewhere in the *Diaries* suggests that he means an episode of a certain length in a related key. Cosima, as an educated musician, could have resolved such ambiguities.

For this reviewer, the book exasperates more often than it satisfies. Cosima's main shortcoming as a diarist is her inability to distinguish between what was and what was not worth recording, and her egotism in recording everything is the reader's first annoyance. Few people can afford to take the time to work their way through the book, yet the valuable and the trivial may be inseparable, an abridged edition an impossibility. (The London *Sunday Times* asked a friend of this reviewer to select eight hundred words for serialization!)

The *Diaries* must also irritate readers who do not like to go from one pronouncement to another with never a question that anything "R." says could possibly be wrong. Nor does Cosima pursue the reasoning behind "R." 's conclusions. If, as he says, "Schumann and Hölderlin are mediocrities," what are the criteria for mediocre, apart from, in the case of Schumann's music, the absence of "a single melody" discernible as such to Wagner? When he dismisses a book by Nietzsche that he has not read because of its "pretentious ordinariness," the composer plainly believes that his artistic and intellectual superiority absolve him from the obligation to justify his judgments. But then, Wagner can be condescending to God. Cosima writes:

> I hear R. saying in his dreams, "If He created me, who asked Him to? And if I am made in His image, the question remains whether I am pleased about that?"

Other irritations in the *Diaries* include Cosima's habit of quoting "R." 's every endearment—"You are the most beautiful of all"; "You are the personification of all inspirations"; *"J'aimerais toujours ma Cosima"*—and of suppressing her own views in favor of Wagner's. These cannot have coincided on every question, if only because of the difference between her aristocratic and Wagner's petit-bourgeois background. For one example, she had some knowledge of painting and Wagner none at all, yet she preserves his most fatuous dicta on this art, writing that "R. finds the Jewish element predominant" in, of all places, the Sistine Chapel. For another, although her command of English far outstripped his, she nevertheless took down his ridiculous remark that a "German can only regard that language as a dialect." Here are instances of the need for selectivity.

George Marek's *Cosima Wagner* includes a useful critique of the *Diaries* that points out the discrepancies between her versions and other people's, as well as confirmations and corrections. Cosima is "honest with herself" in her book, he believes, perhaps on the grounds that only a great fictionalist could have fabricated at such length. Yet even her first entry concerning the relationship with Wagner is patently false: "I have not sought after or brought it about myself: Fate laid it on me." The truth is that she took matters into her own hands, abandoning a dull husband (and their children) for the most exciting man in the artistic world—all perfectly understandable in straightforward terms, without her blaming Fate.

Furthermore, the saccharine view of her marriage to Wagner, and his constant declarations of love, protest too much. An entirely faithful, ever-adoring Wagner is simply not realistic and *was* not true. No one expects to find Cosima reporting on her husband's infatuation with young Judith Gautier, of course, yet the omission of the whole episode can hardly be called "honest." Nor would many of us want to have Wagner's talk in unexpurgated form, since the collected letters, now appearing that way, show that he was scurrilous and, especially, scatological.

Finally, was Cosima's motive in writing the idolatrous "Book of 'R.'" simply the instruction of her children, as she said, or were self-immortalizing and the enlightenment of posterity also involved? This is not to accuse her of false-image making; on the contrary, her hour-by-hour view of "R." inevitably results in a more "human," if only because more intimate and fuller, portrait of him than any other, besides which a diary is understood to be totally biased. Nevertheless, the value of the book would be greatly increased by the addition of a neutral account of certain events and situations, printed in the margins, like *The Annotated Sherlock Holmes*. In lieu of this, the *Diaries* should be read together with two or three of the more recent biographies, a project for a round-the-world cruise.

Marek says that Cosima never criticized Wagner's work, citing King Mark's show-stopping speech—in the wrong sense —in *Tristan* as an instance where intervention on her part might have been beneficial. But Cosima *did* criticize. Wagner followed her advice not to introduce some important new lines,[5] which she thought "rather artificial," in Brünnhilde's scene at the end of *Götterdämmerung.* Cosima prevailed, too, when Wagner wanted to cut some of Hans Sachs's final scene. Yet on the whole she seems to have held her sometimes keen critical sense in abeyance during Wagner's lifetime. Afterward, she wrote to Prince Ernst zu Hohenlohe-Langenburg of a theatrical work of his: "In a play one needs the tangible, the conflict of passions: symbolism cannot be the mainspring." (A pity the prince was not Hugo von Hofmannsthal!) And to this same friend she observed of Strauss's *Death and Transfiguration:* "Its ideas are jejune, its technical mastery sovereign."

The principal obstacle for a biographer of Cosima is that when Wagner is present the spotlight inevitably follows him. The bulk of Marek's book, therefore, is simply another life of Wagner, with only a few novel hypotheses. One of these is that Cosima may not have been sexually satisfied by Bülow, but certainly was by Wagner. Surely something should have been added here on the subject of father and daughter figures, especially since Cosima had been neglected by her parents and dumped in boarding schools, while Wagner was still childless at the age of fifty-one.

Marek also believes that "no overt homosexual components [*sic*] influenced [King Ludwig's] love for the composer." Wagner wasn't Ludwig's "type," Marek says, and he cautions us that the rapturous language of the correspondence was no more than "characteristic of the age." Another of its characteristics, however, was the taboo surrounding the subject. If the king had the tendency, and if it were understood, would anyone dare attribute it to a royal personage? Obviously Wagner, who had an overtly homosexual admirer, Karl Ritter, was fully aware of Ludwig's proclivities. Glase-

5. See *I Saw the World End: A Study of Wagner's "Ring,"* by Deryck Cooke (New York, 1979).

napp, the composer's early biographer, tells us that he had an uncanny instinct for uncovering other people's "weaknesses," which encourages the suspicion that he exploited Ludwig in this one, too.

Marek's portrait of Cosima, pre-Wagner, should be read before the *Diaries*, since it supplies the background necessary for understanding her future behavior.[6] We are told, for example, that Cosima was anti-Semitic before she knew Wagner, but not given the origins of her prejudice—which would be important to know. Such historians as Peter Gay and Gordon Craig have filled almost half of their reviews of the *Diaries*, Volume II, with discussions of this subject, and Marek estimates that a defamation occurs every four pages.

Marek has little to say about the forty-seven years remaining to Cosima after Wagner's death, and almost nothing concerning her final, twenty-four years of ill health. After a period in seclusion, she realized that her mission was to continue the Bayreuth Festival, and at no time during her directorship, 1886–1906, was she merely a figurehead. Not only did she choose the conductors, but she also supervised their performances. And as stage director, she dictated every movement of the singers, even acting out their parts for them. She was present at all rehearsals, ruling on everything and no doubt insisting "This is the way the *Meister* wanted it!"—to the annoyance of all. We learn with surprise that she went so far as to edit the music, inserting dynamic markings, deciding on tempos, reducing the number of strings in one place (in order to increase the audibility of the words), and even deleting a cymbal crash, which was restored by Toscanini, who had memorized the score. She was succeeded by her son, Siegfried, a likable but sad figure, who wrote undistinguished music, married (at age forty-six) an English termagant who was to become Hitler's bosom friend, and died in the same year as his mother.

6. Unfortunately, the chapter on her youth does not quote from the one hundred and fifty letters, 1850–62, between Liszt, Cosima, and her sister, Blandine, now at the University of Texas.

Theodor Adorno's *In Search of Wagner*[7] suffers from the pressure of political events of the time the book was written, the late 1930s. Another drawback of this belated English version is its excruciating vocabulary ("bourgeoisified," "technocization," etc.) and tortuous sentences:

The secondary triads (some of which are tonicized by local modulation), or put simply, the fresh notes of the lower voice are saved up for the consequent which has to make do with the same material as the antecedent. . . .

But why not "put simply" in the first place whatever one wishes to say, except that in this case the "simplifying" adds to the bewilderment?

The book contains astute observations, nevertheless, especially in connecting Wagner the man to his music. "Wagner's lack of character . . . leads deeply into the center of his work," Adorno argues, giving as an example "the absence of tension in Wagner's harmony as it descends from the leading note and sinks from the dominant into the tonic." Further, Wagner's sentimentality and his appeals for sympathy are "represented by Siegmund, the restless wanderer," who uses his self-pity to acquire "a woman and a weapon." And Adorno links the *longueurs* of the operas with the "uncontrollable loquacity" about which the composer's first wife complained. The book is also worth reading on such matters as Wagner's substitution of repetition for development, his inability to make the idea speak through the action—therefore relying on the narrative, and bringing the dramas to standstills—and his conception of the music "entirely from the conductor's point of view," which explains why almost all of *Lohengrin* is "written in regular time."

L. J. Rather's *The Dream of Self-Destruction: Wagner's "Ring" and the Modern World*, a book that should cause a

---

7. *In Search of Wagner*, by Theodor Adorno, translated by Rodney Livingstone (New York, 1981).

shift in our attitudes toward Wagner, is the most impressive interpretative study of his ideas that this reviewer has encountered. That the author is a professor of medicine at Stanford, and has also written *The Genesis of Cancer,* must be mentioned, if only because his discussion of Schopenhauer's neurophysiological approach to perception in the light of modern experiment is alone worth the price of the volume. In an article that can touch on only a few salient features of several books, it is impossible even to summarize Dr. Rather's main theses: the relationship between Jewish ethnocentricity and nineteenth-century theories of Nordic supremacy; Wagner's use of the *Oedipus* trilogy as a model for the *Ring;* and Wagner's discovery of the self-destructive tendency in the unconscious, as well as of the necessity—Freud's future task—of making the unconscious conscious. Dr. Rather's range of reference in connection with these subjects is breathtaking: the Torah to Walter Benjamin, the Kabbalists to Otto Rank and Erich Fromm, Solomon ben Isaac to Wittgenstein.

Sorting out received notions, Dr. Rather maintains that the "myth of Jewish racial purity and supremacy," as set forth by Heine and Disraeli, provided the model for such advocates of the Aryan kind as Gobineau and Houston Stewart Chamberlain. Gobineau seems to have attributed everything of value to the Aryans, as Disraeli, a decade before him, had done with the Jews. The argument of Gobineau and Chamberlain is that by forbidding proselytism, the Talmud guaranteed "physical descent."

So, too, Marx's anti-Semitism—and he believed that Christendom in his time had become Judaized—is based on his "erroneous identification of the Jewish idea with the spirit of modern capitalism." As Dr. Rather explains him, Marx meant that "money power . . . rules Europe, *not* 'ethnic' Jews . . . the power of Rothschild and other Jewish bankers notwithstanding." Wagner could have said the same, Dr. Rather thinks, and he cites Yehuda Cohen's argument against the ban on Wagner's works in Israel, namely, that the composer's "final solution," assimilation, "completely contradicts" the

racist doctrine of the Nazis. (The present reviewer has reservations on the issue of Wagner and Nazism, for example, in
connection with the Ku Klux Klan element in *Parsifal*. As
Adorno writes, "The glorified blood-brotherhood of *Parsifal*
is the prototype of the sworn confraternities of the secret
societies and Führer-adorers. . . ." But this is a subject for
another piece.)

"Why do human beings anticipate an end of the world,"
Kant asked, "and just why a terrible end?" Wagner, who
opposed the misuse of science and denounced European
rearmament, pondered the same question: was some blind
destructive force in human beings determined to bring on a
final *Götterdämmerung* for the whole human race? And, by
way of Schopenhauer, Wagner's conclusion anticipates
Freud's (in *Civilization and Its Discontents*), that the "life
force is really a force of death." As Wagner, the Feuer-
bachian optimist, conceived the *Ring*, Erda, in *Das Rhein-
gold*, warns Wotan of the destruction of the gods unless the
Ring (i.e., the gold) is returned to nature, at the bottom of
the Rhine. But this implies that if the Ring *were* returned,
the gods could save themselves. Later, under the influence of
Schopenhauer, Wagner's earth-mother prophesies inevitable
doom for the gods and all creation, period.

The most interesting of Dr. Rather's inquiries is the one
that has been lying directly under our noses: the relationship
between the *Ring* and Wagner's analysis of the Oedipus
legend in Sophocles' trilogy. In 1851, five years before the
birth of Freud, Wagner wrote that the Oedipus myth is "always true" and "inexhaustible for all times." Oedipus, not
knowing his father, Laius, kills him without discovering his
identity, and Siegfried kills Wotan the same way. Other parallels are found between the incestuous unions of Oedipus and
Jocasta, and Siegmund and Sieglinde, and between Siegfried
and Antigone and Brünnhilde as the children of unlawful
marriages. Wagner's analysis of the Greek myth centers on
the generation of Antigone and her brothers, Polynices and
Eteocles, who kill each other, after which Creon becomes king

and decrees that the body of Polynices cannot be buried. Antigone defies Creon and is buried alive; then Creon's son, who loves her, commits suicide.

For Wagner, this act of Creon's son is that of the symbolic self-destruction of the state, a destruction caused by a free human being, in the name of true morality, opposing the corrupt morality of government. The state has become the monster that must be destroyed and replaced by a just society. Antigone-Brünnhilde is Wagner's goddess of revolution, the one who destroys and redeems. Wagner adds that even if the Thebans had known of Laius's disregard of Pythia's prediction (that he would be killed by his son), they would have accepted the situation for the sake of peace and order. Thus true morality has been impeded by "corrupted custom," and natural human morality usurped by the conventional morality of the state.

Robert Hartford's anthology of descriptions of the Bayreuth Festival, 1876–1914,[8] is an entertaining book that should appeal to anyone who has ever attended the Festival or plans to do so. The texts—letters, critical notices—also provide good reasons to stay away for "those who have no wish to set foot within a hundred miles of the place," as Hartford writes. The accounts of the first festival are the most enjoyable. Among them, Edvard Grieg's should be singled out for its charm and still-valid criticism:

> Wagner's special ability to describe scenes such as occur in *Rheingold* causes the spectator to be carried away by the effects and to forget the lack of drama in them.

But the sense of presence and excitement is best conveyed in Tchaikovsky's report of the arrival of the emperor at the

8. *Bayreuth: The Early Years*, compiled, edited, and introduced by Robert Hartford (New York, 1981).

Bayreuth railroad station, August 12, 1876, the day before
the festival began:

First some brilliant uniforms passed by, then the musicians
of the Wagner Theater. . . . Next followed the interesting
figure of the "Abbé" Liszt, with the fine characteristic
head I have so often admired in pictures; and lastly, in a
sumptuous carriage, the serene old man, Richard Wagner,
with his aquiline nose and the delicately ironic smile. . . .
A noisy "Hurrah" resounded from thousands of throats as
the train entered the station. The old emperor stepped into
the carriage awaiting him and drove to the Palace. Wagner,
who followed in his wake, was greeted by the crowds with
as much enthusiasm as the emperor. What pride, what over-
flowing emotions must have filled at this moment the heart
of that little old man who, by his energetic will and great
talent, has defied all obstacles to the final realization of his
artistic ideals. . . .

Liszt's Letters to
Baroness von Meyendorff

Liszt's newly published letters to Baroness Olga von Meyendorff[1] are a welcome surprise. Far superior to the composer's other writings, these deserve a place on the much-less-than-five-foot shelf of absorbing correspondence by the great composers. The book alters the received notions of Liszt's character and personality, and wholly reverses the portrait of his later years as drawn in Ernest Newman's anti-hagiography. Mr. Waters surmises that the letters "must have slipped out of the hands" of the last of the baroness's four sons in 1933, since they landed on the podium at Sotheby's in April 1934. Newman noted this but presumably did not read the letters; otherwise he would have been obliged to make substantial revisions in his book on the composer, published later the same year.

The only Olga in Newman's biography is Janina, the young "Cossack" countess, whom Liszt had seduced and who, in 1871, pursued the sixty-year-old composer from New York

---

1. *The Letters of Franz Liszt to Olga von Meyendorff, 1871–1886,* translated by William R. Tyler, introduction and notes by Edward N. Waters (Washington, D.C., 1979).

to Rome, and from there, pistol-packing, to Budapest. Re-
buffed, and smarting from the humiliation, she avenged herself in two unreadable books, among the many by women
who had known Franz Liszt. The story of the Baroness von
Meyendorff could not offer greater contrast, for though the
relationship of this attractive young widow to Liszt can only
be assumed by his behavior patterns, she never broke her
silence about him.

Although Newman gives too much space to the Olga
Janina episode, it must be admitted that, apart from Byron,
Liszt is the only major nineteenth-century artistic figure
whose love life alone has provided sufficient material for a
full-length "scholarly" study.[2] In one of the letters to
Baroness von Meyendorff, he both acknowledges this aspect
of his reputation and indicates his disgust with it: "Other
interpretations of my very short stays in Venice and Vienna
are of the *saucy* variety, which I don't much care for."

Until the appearance of the present book, Liszt was
thought to be vain, duplicitous, and, above all, a showman,
given to the tawdry and bombastic in life as in art. His motives in his religious career—he entered the Franciscan order
in 1857 and became an abbé in Rome in 1865—were held
suspect. Moreover, he was accused of consorting exclusively
with the titled and rich, and charged with exploiting his
magnetism for women. The Meyendorff letters, at least in
regard to the later years, belie all but the last two of these
faults, along with various others unmentioned.

Here Liszt is never shallow, and he emerges as genuinely
modest ("opinions . . . are free and I make no claim whatever to imposing mine on anyone"; "[the bust of me] is
larger than life and I hope more successful than the original"), as well as sincere in his religious convictions ("I intend to . . . endure for some time yet on this earth, [but] if I
am wrong, no matter. I am quite ready to obey elsewhere the

2. *Liszt und die Frauen*, by La Mara (Leipzig, 1911).

Father of Mercy"). He is commonsensical ("The fact that certain polite customs are merely a convention does not prevent me from approving of them"); wise ("Truth is a great flirt"); honest with himself and others ("I go on existing with deepest repentance and contrition for having formerly ostentatiously violated the Ninth Commandment"); and he understands human nature ("In order to punish [Janina], I am not going to get angry").

Most unexpected in a so-called snob is a humanitarian Liszt, much moved by Kropotkin's account of the treatment of political prisoners in Siberia, and strongly opposed to Baroness von Meyendorff's support of the death penalty, which he terms "an abominable social crime . . . It is obvious that we are all more or less guilty, deranged or crazy, but it does not follow that we ought to be guillotined"—so writes the ardent royalist who respected the Count of Chambord's claims to the French throne.

Neither the translator nor the author of the introduction and notes offers any information as to the whereabouts of the letters between Sotheby's in 1934 and Dumbarton Oaks in 1970, where Liszt's great-granddaughter saw them, and, according to Mr. Waters, "pleaded" that they be published. Mr. Waters finds it noteworthy that this lady, from Liszt's French line of descent, spoke "remarkable English" (in what way remarkable?), though the translator, Mr. Tyler, conversed with her "in characteristically rapid and fluent French." (Is this bilingualism unusual?) But Mr. Waters is easily amazed, observing that "gossip was as rife [in Liszt's day] as it is now," and actually explaining Liszt's bad pun about a prelate who is more *ultra-mondain* than *ultramontain*. Mr. Waters further quotes the composer's descendant: "never . . . have I ever heard anyone speak more perfect French [than Mr. Tyler]. You must see that he translates those letters." This provokes Mr. Waters to an exclamation— "the die was cast"—but does not induce him to provide any explanation as to why the letters were not published first, or ever, in the original French, the favored language (as the present reviewer observed on many occasions) of the chatelaine of Dumbarton Oaks, Mildred Bliss, herself.

In any event, the quality of the translator's French is less important in this task than that of his English, which, in Mr. Tyler's case, is marred by internal rhymes ("hardly conducive to effusiveness," "pending finding people . . .") and horrible anachronisms (imagine Liszt mentioning a "lifestyle" and referring to "phony" princesses).

The reader is also curious about the Baroness von Meyendorff's mother tongue. Was it Russian or Polish—she was born (1838) Princess Gorchakova[3] of Warsaw—and was her second language French or German? Liszt's daughter Cosima Wagner says that the lady "obstinately" spoke the former, but Wagner's wife disliked both French and the Baroness von Meyendorff. Since the latter's husband was ambassador to the court of Weimar, she must have used German regularly, but her second language may well have been Italian: in one letter Liszt advises her to read the eight-volume Italian edition of *The Modern Jesuit*.

Messrs. Waters and Tyler do not refer to the fate of the Baroness Olga's side of the correspondence. True, Liszt wrote to her, December 15, 1881: "The best way not to expose letters to the indiscretion of others is to burn them immediately after reading them, as I shall do with yours henceforth." Yet four-fifths of the contents of his collection antedate the resolution. Was a search instituted for her pre-1882 letters? It must be admitted that a knowledge of her that is limited to inferences from the composer's letters leaves many unanswered questions.

Felix von Meyendorff, the baroness's husband and a nephew of the Russian ambassador to Berlin, died suddenly in 1871 (at age thirty-six). Liszt had known Olga when she was in her early twenties, but they seem not to have cor-

---

3. This is the spelling adopted by the editors of Cosima Wagner's diaries. Mr. Waters writes the name "Gortschakoff."

responded before her widowhood. Except for Mr. Waters's description of her portrait ("an enchanting face" combining "intelligence and pulchritude"), most references to her are uncomplimentary. Amy Fay, Liszt's American pupil, states that "the haughty countess" is "not pretty" and her "arrogance piques all Weimar." Cosima, her elder, found her "very unpleasant . . . cold and repelling," and in the later diaries simply records "Frau von M.'s" arrival, presence, and departure, making no mention of the letter received from her after the death of Cosima's mother. Yet at Liszt's funeral, Cosima and Baroness Olga rode in the same carriage.

To some extent, Liszt's letters bear out the judgments of his daughter and Miss Fay. Olga's insistent inquiries concerning his health plainly irritate him, and he writes that, since fireworks are customary on John the Baptist's feast day, he intends to burn the whole file of her "objurgations and minatory ukases." Why, then, did he continue to write? Obviously because "Frau von M." was a woman of exceptional intellect, well read, and interested in the new ideas of the age: the correspondents discuss such matters as "the positivism of M. Comte" and the theories of Fourier, whose lectures Liszt had attended in 1832 in Paris, but whose "oratorical talent, like his style, left much to be desired. He spoke easily and glibly. . . ." Furthermore, the baroness was a knowledgeable musician—Liszt played the complete *Ring of the Nibelung* for her—and an excellent pianist; shortly before his death, he wrote to her that "among the best of my memories is that of playing four-hands with you." She died in obscurity in Rome, in 1926, an untapped source for historians of the great age of Bayreuth; it is regrettable that, unlike Willa Cather and Flaubert's niece, she had no good writer to listen to her fascinating story.

The correspondence, beginning as it did in the year of the Olga Janina scandal, must have afforded Liszt an agreeable contrast to that harrowing experience. Yet after becoming an abbé he does not appear to have been more reclusive or less worldly, remaining fond of whist, which he played with Wagner, relishing oysters washed down with Yquem, and indulging a passion for Forti Napolitani—*not* Cavour—cigars. He enjoyed his domestic life in Rome, where he kept two cats, and at Frascati, where in fine weather he dined on the terrace. But he also liked society and being a guest of Duke Caetani at Sermoneta, as well as of other aristocrats in their palazzi. Eventually Rome became too hectic—"Crossing the Piazza de Spagna is no fun for me"—and he spent more time in Bayreuth. Even in the late years he was almost constantly traveling—Venice, Vienna, Budapest, Munich, Weimar, Bayreuth.

In music, the abbé tried to restrain an impulse to write secular and even frivolous pieces, and, in a letter of February 1873, he says that though practicing "abstention from desires," he has turned out variations on some Schubert waltzes "of which the French title is *Le Désir.*" But composition demands a great effort of him. Commenting on an author who is plagued by questions of punctuation and grammar "to the point of banning identical consonants at the beginning of sentences," the composer remarks that "in music I suffer from analogous torments." What interests him most in Zola's study of Flaubert is the latter's

> lengthy method of work. . . . I know similar [tortures] in music. This or that chord, or even pause, have cost me hours and numerous erasures. Those who know the meaning of *style* are prey to [this].

Near the end of his life he writes that "for Christmas I wanted to give myself a big negative present, that of writing no more music."

Liszt is at his most caustic in passages about musicians. Referring to one of them, he warns Baroness Olga to "overlook a certain prolixity on the subject of his friendship for me." Liszt ridicules not only the "young matadors of the piano," but also those of the violin, as when he says of Sarasate:

How can one thus climb on the very first page to the higher octave like squirrels or acrobats, and then go down rapidly to the lower strings, then climb and fall again, then finally swoon on a most trivial cadenza?

The abbé criticizes the "faltering rhetoric" of the man who said: "I don't want to disappear like a lamp going out, but like a setting star," since "the public is sometimes interested in rising stars, but not in setting [ones]." And Liszt delights in repeating Berlioz's rejoinder to the person who asked if one of Beethoven's last quartets had given him pleasure: "Do you think that I listen to music for pleasure?"

The Meyendorff letters further document the unprecedented catholicity of Liszt's musical tastes. It pleases him that an audience has given a warm reception to two movements of Tchaikovsky's Second Symphony, "as I more or less imposed this work on the program." The Verdi quartet, in the abbé's estimation, is "a more attractive piece than many renowned classical compositions, and just as carefully composed." Of other contemporaries, he is chilly to Brahms, though not mean, as Wagner was; fair to Gounod and Massenet; respectful to Bizet, though the music of *Carmen* is "of a kind which is most successful in Paris." The championship of Sgambati is evident throughout the letters and remains inexplicable. The last two Mozart symphonies, Liszt writes, are superior to any of those by Haydn, which "I admire . . . as long as I don't have to hear them often."

One of Liszt's criticisms might have been intended for Webern, or for a style attributed to him and much abused today: "To reduce music to single sounds, to isolate the features of a beloved person . . . away with this method." But if Liszt had actually heard this music of a century later, would he still have thought that "silence suffices for a well-brought-up audience to express its disapproval"? Curiously, while he is inspired by the grandiose—in the Cathedral of Ratisbon he "dreamed . . . of a music which I know not how to write"— he professes not to like the trumpet and trombone, and turns his bias, conspicuous by its absence in much of his own music, into a rule of social behavior: "I like mutes when it is a matter of giving advice: they do not impair accuracy of pitch, and, save for exceptional cases, it is better to be restrained than noisy."

The music of Richard Wagner is one of the main subjects of the letters, and though Liszt hints that his "conviction and zeal" are tempered with reservations, and if he sins "out of excessive admiration for Wagner, it is not for lack of awareness of what his adversaries think," Liszt's "passionate admiration for [Wagner's] genius continues to increase. . . . King Louis of Bavaria and my daughter have the right perspective—adoration." For many readers, the references to Wagner will be the high points of the book, especially the glimpses of him in Venice two months before his death, and the following early reference to *Parsifal:*

> I reread this most highly sublime work, first in my room without a piano, and yesterday we went through the last part of the third act with Wagner; he singing and I accompanying. . . . I know nothing comparable in music.

Liszt's appreciation of literature is remarkable in a musician. He himself is an artist with words, with an epistolary style that is felicitous but never florid. He reads Renan—unusual in itself for a man of the cloth—not only for content but also because the author of *La Vie de Jésus* "introduces nuances in good French." The style of Nietzsche, on the other hand, dazzles more than his books enlighten: "How can I become converted to the man created by Schopenhauer, or to the man of Goethe and of Rousseau?" The abbé's scope is stunning: Pascal and Zola, Joseph de Maistre and Maupassant, Leopardi and Hugo, Sainte-Beuve and Taine, Turgenev and Tolstoy (whom Liszt knew in Weimar), George Sand—in whose letters to Flaubert the composer finds a "touch of genius"—and Flaubert himself, whose *Temptation of St. Anthony* holds Liszt in thrall.

Benjamin Constant, Gregorovius, Ségur (*The History of Russia*), and the Book of Job are discussed side by side. A piece by Alexandre Dumas and a passage in Heine's *Memoiren* are condemned for their facetiousness, while Liszt scores La Rochefoucauld for reducing all feelings to *amour-propre*. The abbé is even familiar with Voltaire, borrowing his word *folliculaires* in reference to the "scribblers of the press," and apparently adapting his aphorism "*Le superflu, chose très nécessaire*" in "Let us continue to talk about minor matters: altogether they make up roughly two-thirds of life; to neglect them is a fault which does harm." One wonders when the composer found time to read his breviary.

Liszt's life as an abbé is surely atypical. He attends the Russian Orthodox Christmas service for the sake of Olga von Meyendorff, and at the Eastern Church Easter, he greets her with "*Khristos Voskres.*" Reporting on a private audience with the pope, Liszt mentions that "while telling me about the present trials of the church," and "developing admirably a text of St. Paul, Pius IX was not above commenting on Roman aristocrats and society figures." The concept of the "Holy Roman Democracy" mystifies the abbé, who says that the one bright point in this "Vaticanist Philippic is the phrase 'For the world to live, it needs the Eucharist.'" Nevertheless, Liszt observes the religious life—"I returned on December 23 and shall stay until mid-January in meditation and prayer"—and no matter what he says or does, his faith is unassailable. "I am extremely tired of living," he writes. "But I believe that God's Fifth Commandment also applies to suicide." Meanwhile, "To serve well is the main thing in this world—while awaiting a better one."

The Abbé Liszt's quarters in Rome, in the priory of Santa Francesca, where he was cared for by Olivetan Fathers, overlooked the church of Saint Francis, as well as, most appropriately, its foundations, the ruins of the Temple of Venus.

Schoenberg and Dika

In September 1938, a precocious girl of fourteen and her mother, leaving father and husband at home in East Lansing, Michigan, boarded a train bound for Los Angeles. The child had been admitted not only to UCLA, but also to its composition classes taught by Arnold Schoenberg.

Three years earlier, eleven-year-old Dika Newlin had written a piece of music that attracted the attention of professionals, among them the conductor Vladimir Bakaleinikoff, who, after a spell in film music in Hollywood, returned to Michigan convinced that Schoenberg was the supreme teacher of composition. At this time, anyone advising a young student such as Dika would in all likelihood have recommended Nadia Boulanger or Hindemith, the Curtis Institute or the Eastman School. Bakaleinikoff insisted that the girl go to Schoenberg, and that any sacrifice was worth the goal. The steps by which this was attained do not require recounting here. Sufficient to say that the diaries kept by young Dika about her association with the master contain the only intimate views of Schoenberg the man yet published, as well as the first detailed account of his teaching in the American period. For this reason, Ms. Newlin's *Schoenberg Remembered*[1] will be read by generations to come.

1. *Schoenberg Remembered: Diaries and Recollections, 1938–1976* (New York, 1980).

On one level, the book is a chronicle of classroom events and reports on the author's progress. But the main interest is in a drama: a battle of two giant egos. Something of Schoenberg's has long been known from other sources, but never so closely observed as by Ms. Newlin: it takes one to know one. The enduring value of her diaries lies in the glimpses they offer of Schoenberg's sessions in musical analysis, which serve Ms. Newlin as a *theatricum anatomicum* for analyzing Schoenberg, and from which she quickly emerges as a kind of challenger. In one corner of the ring was the sixty-five-year-old world-champion composer and musical revolutionary— though not yet recognized as such by the world of music in general, which was and still is ignorant of his works. In the opposite corner stands the contender, the fourteen-year-old kiddy-composer who intends to take the great man's measure in her diary, providing, it may be, the only three-dimensional portrait of him to survive.

In some ways the contestants were well matched. For one thing, their self-esteem is relatively equal: "All the local lights present were making much of him, and of me, too . . . ," Ms. Newlin writes. For another, neither has even the semblance of a superego in the accepted meaning of the term —though Schoenberg requires none, thanks to his exceptional endowment of intuitive, and perhaps even psychic, powers. Then, too, both combatants are peculiarly able to arouse feelings of guilt, though their stratagems for this are not always successful on each other. ("Probably I should not go to him," Dika writes, after a spat, "but will do so this time to give him a chance to redeem himself"; and, "I had prepared for [the oral exam] by making myself up to look interestingly ill.") Finally, though the aspiring composer worships the renowned master, she nevertheless possesses a mind of her own, and speaks it in her diaries on almost everything Schoenberg says or does. Thus, in spite of areas of agreement —"Schoenberg and I shared this taste," the fifteen-year-old writes on one occasion—there are vast differences: "He thinks Verdi is a great composer. I do not concur."

Although Ms. Newlin might see the matter differently, Schoenberg emerged the winner; at the end of her third year, he did not invite her to return, this despite her triumph in the award of a University Fellowship ("I was the indubitable first out of 142 applicants"). On the night of the performance of her string quartet, June 6, 1941, she had "thought of staying away, to give Uncle Arnold a well-deserved punch, but [I] let my better nature get ahead of me." This cherubic side directed her to sit "in the back of the auditorium by myself, and [wear] a hat with a veil, so he got scared for fear that I'd left town without bidding him a fond farewell! . . . He refrained from insulting anybody all evening. . . ." Perhaps Ms. Newlin should have titled her book, as she once put it, "the story of Schoenberg *in my life.*"

Apart from the two principals in the ego department, the only others of any importance in the cast of characters are Schoenberg's family and dog, and Leonard Stein, the composer's assistant, who, though not listed in the index, appears throughout, frequently as the focal point of one disaster or another:

> We played it splendidly, to my mind. Stein skipped a few beats, but not so that you'd notice it. . . .

> Stein broke a record today by bringing one measure of orchestration. Uncle Arnold had to spend nearly the whole hour explaining what was wrong with it. He wrote 12 p's over it and crossed out all the notes. . . .

The author's classmates provide little more than a backdrop. Apparently, a similar relationship existed in East Lansing, where young Dika was secretly given high-school entrance exams after only three years of grade school, her "diminutive presence" having angered her classmates' parents, who "feared that I might give their children an 'inferiority complex' "! (Ms. Newlin adds, characteristically, "It wasn't the last time I would be perceived as a threat. . . .") It follows that at UCLA she was soon doing more work than the other members of Schoenberg's classes ("I had to present my variations. . . . I brought the number up to seven; no one else had more than three"), that she received his highest marks, and was invited to become a private pupil. Whatever the effects of her brilliance and domineering personality on her faceless fellow students, *they* are mentioned only because of their poor showings: "Y. was slow on the uptake," and as for Miss E.,

> I might have commented that Schoenberg wouldn't get music out of *her* manuscripts, but confined myself to saying that, as much as I remembered, we had not handed in our variations on that day. At that, I think she would like to have killed me!

On one occasion Schoenberg berated Ms. Newlin for the sloppiness of her writing:

> "No more, Miss Newlin, no more. There's no use, I cannot help you. I cannot read one word of these hieroglyphics. . . . I absolutely refuse to look at your music so long as it is like this. You *must* write a clear manuscript. Why you not write like Miss Temple, hm?"

Whereupon Ms. Newlin describes Miss Temple as "a neat but untalented student," and, a few days later, in another class, remarks that "Schoenberg did not look at our work today. A cursory look at Miss Temple's current masterpiece got him shuttled off to a discussion of chorale harmonization. . . ."

At times, the classroom of advanced composition students could be mistaken for a kindergarten. Here is a scene from "Structural Functions":

> When he asked me to describe the codettas and retransition [in the first section of the first Razumovsky Quartet], I did so in this way: "The retransition begins in measure

98." That didn't seem to satisfy him; he asked several others for the answer, but didn't seem to be satisfied with theirs, either. Finally, he asked, . . . "Why . . . do you not see that the codettas end in measure 97 and not in measure 98?" "But that's what Miss Newlin said!" shouted Abraham. . . . "But you did not say this! . . . You said that the codettas end in measure 98!" "I did not! . . . I said the retransition began in 98! . . ." "Mr. Stein, . . . did I misunderstand her? Did she say this? Now, don't become embarrassed; tell me frankly if she said it, for I might have misunderstood her!" "Well," muttered Stein, "all I heard was 98." (He has to keep his job, you know!) "Mr. Abraham, . . . did she say it? Swear to tell the truth, the whole truth, and nothing but the truth! . . . Say yes or no!" "YES!" (chorus of assent from the whole class). "And I still say she did not say it!" [from Schoenberg].

At this point, one of Ms. Newlin's positive attributes should be mentioned. She became fanatically devoted to Schoenberg's artistic principles, and to his music, in much the same way that Berg and Webern had three decades before her. But her horizons expanded far less in the direction of the music of these earlier pupils than in that of Bruckner and Mahler. At twenty-three, Dika Newlin published a classic study of Schoenberg and these two predecessors, the first in English to exhibit a profound knowledge of their interconnections and of the subject as a whole. Shortly after that (1947) she translated René Leibowitz's *Schoenberg et son école*[2] (i.e., Berg and Webern), which became one of the most influential books in American musical life in the early 1950s.

The most troublesome aspect of *Schoenberg Remembered* is in the question of genre. Practically all of the book is in diary form, yet much of it reads like a memoir. In her foreword, Ms. Newlin asserts that, apart from using pseudonyms

2. *Schoenberg and His School* (New York, 1949).

and initials to protect people's identities—such as "St." for Schoenberg's assistant!—and normal English spelling for the composer's pronunciation, "the diaries are as I originally wrote them." Yet at the end of the volume she refers to her work of "editing . . . for the reader of the present day." These editorial additions and changes are voluminous, however, and they require demarcation by italics, brackets, footnotes, typeface, or other means. For instance, after only nine entries, she writes of Schoenberg's "character (Which I never did admire, by the way. I always thought him mean. . . .)." This, transparently, is a conclusion of a later date, and not, as the entry begins, an observation of "this afternoon." So, too, in the phrase already quoted in this review referring to Ms. Newlin's fellow student Miss E., "as much as I remembered," why is the verb in the past tense, when the action is in the present, and would Ms. Newlin be likely to forget what she had said only a few hours before? Moreover, are "by the way" and "you know" diarists' expressions—except in unusual cases such as that of Anne Frank? And who is the addressee in such questions as "Did you ever hear of such a mix-up in your life?"

More important, the reader is utterly confused by the language of the diaries, in which, on the one hand, the fifteen-year-old writes such a sentence as "After any prolonged period of highly concentrated and alembicated happiness, a corresponding period of depression should occur . . . ," and, on the other, refers to Schoenberg as "Nuncie," "Schoenie," "Arnelie," "a scream," "goofy," "loopy," and calls his home "the dear old loony-bin." (Interestingly, Ms. Newlin makes Schoenberg sound more Japanese than I, at any rate, remember him. "Ah so," he says, and "This all the same," "This fine," as if he only rarely used verbs.) Furthermore, in 1940, such expressions as "I trow" and the "latest wrinkle" are anachronistic—from opposite time zones. But these questions aside, Ms. Newlin *is* responsible for writing that she acknowledges to be of recent vintage—"To whoever would listen he would talk . . ."; various libraries were "handy hideouts for peaceful proofreading, far from frenetic felinity"; "Uncle Arnold was infernally diabolical"—and this is puzzling. How can an intellectual and multilingual woman write this way? Is it an example of Eliot's famous contrast, with reference to Thomas Carlyle, between intellect and intelligence?

Withal, nearly every page contains illustrations of Schoenberg's deserved reputation as a great teacher. This lies, above all, in his philosophy. He says of a colleague, "All he must do is teach what he knows; this easy; what I do, I teach the student what *he* must know; and this hard." Ms. Newlin observes that, for Schoenberg,

> . . . a rule is like a law of nature, and admits of absolutely no exceptions. Hence, he gives us but few rules . . . but much advice. This latter is not meant to be followed slavishly, but rather to develop our ear so that we can use our own judgment. . . . He sees no sense in teaching us to write . . . in the . . . "Palestrina style."

Here is the essence of Schoenberg's approach. For him it was absurd to learn to duplicate music of an unrepeatable past. He obliged his students to become self-reliant with an understanding of music from the inside, and to think creatively— rather than academically, in, say, a "scholarly," and perfectly sterile, argument on sonata form.

To mention only three instances of Schoenberg's pedagogy touched on in the book, Ms. Newlin paraphrases him on the subject of too-rapid emotional change since the time of Beethoven, resulting from the traditional use of the major key for the subordinate theme in a minor-key piece. As an example of this weakness of "turning too quickly from clouds to sunshine," Schoenberg mentions Brahms's C-minor Quartet. But surely the key does not necessarily define the mood; Schubert, for one, can be as sad in the major as in the minor.

The second point shows Schoenberg's acuity in making distinctions, in this case between "modern" thematic counterpoint and an earlier kind based on motifs. Contrapuntal art, in his immediate background as well as in his own work, consists in combining two or more themes in as many ways as possible, whereas in the older counterpoint all of the voices are strictly derived from the given motif.

The final point will surprise many, including musicians. Schoenberg, Ms. Newlin says, "doesn't believe in teaching harmony and composition concurrently," harmony being so complex a subject that to learn it while composing would require too much time. What, then, is the student composer's harmonic language? Schoenberg, self-taught in this regard, evidently thought that others should follow his example. But the question of the harmonic dimension in his own so-called twelve-tone theory of it cannot be said to offer an entirely satisfactory explanation.

The book is more informative about the quirks of Schoenberg's mind outside music than in it, and about the idiosyncrasies of his personality and character. Unfortunately, Ms. Newlin directs us to what she considers to be his best remarks and most eccentric behavior, while virtually ignoring the truly revealing statement or story. Thus she introduces as a "terribly funny incident"—albeit wholly lacking in mirth for this reviewer—the composer's attempt to mend a chair with a loose seat, ending in an accident of a splinter in his finger: "He screamed and yelled bloody murder, made the most terrifying faces, and pulled . . . until the blood came." She also cites as "typically Schoenbergian naïveté" the composer's "exclamation" one day, "in a voice replete with childish joy and wonderment," "Oh look, it rains! Is it not wonderful?" In what way is this observation either Schoenbergian or naïve? Yet a deeply revealing incident, the story of Schoenberg's temporarily runaway dog, Roddie, is passed over lightly. The composer's reaction is indicative of his unparalleled self-centeredness. Not considering that all dogs have natural urges, and, at one time or another, take off on their own, Schoenberg was ready to give the animal away. As Ms. Newlin explains, "he won't have a dog that is so disloyal."

The author also seems not to have comprehended one of

Schoenberg's most famous witticisms. According to her, "he admitted having made . . . errors . . . in the *Gurre-Lieder*, where he wrote low B's for the 'cello and viola" (actually one low B in the third division of cellos at 100). But the story is that when someone observed to him that he had written a non-existent note in the final tutti in that work, he riposted: "Leave it out: we won't hear it anyway."

The reader can decide for himself if "cruel" is a justified adjective to describe many of Schoenberg's remarks to his students, and perhaps it is unfair to extract examples from the context of the book as a whole. Yet it must be remembered that Schoenberg, at the summit of his art, was obliged, in one class, to teach as many as thirty-six pupils, of whom few, if any, could have been qualified to receive the instruction he was able to impart. Another consideration, also overlooked by the author, is that, all his life, the composer himself had been harshly abused, and this did not thicken his epidermis; in one sense, he was giving back what he had received. Certainly it was ungracious of him to say to a pupil who claimed to have thought of a "soaring" melody, "You mean, perhaps, snoring," yet to Schoenberg this was simply a joke. But at times he does seem to be truculent with both Leonard Stein, the "harassed" and "docile" as Ms. Newlin calls him, and herself. One day when Mr. Stein appears with no work and gives the excuse that he has been moving, Schoenberg quips, "I think you've been moving all year." And to Ms. Newlin he says that "the judges know so little that they will surely give the prize to someone like you, or to one who knows even less, if this is possible."

A few mistakes should be corrected if the book is reprinted. Ms. Newlin gives the wrong title for Schoenberg's Opus 34 (see p. 207) and says of this music that it "was not really for the movies, but only symbolically." (Only symbolically *what?*) And when Ms. Newlin repeats Schoenberg's story about the man who shouted, after a performance of *Pierrot Lunaire*, "Not a single triad," she neglects to mention that the very end of the work, the part that the listener would

be most likely to remember, contains several of them. Earlier
(p. 155) she writes that

> Stravinsky attended the dress rehearsal of *Pierrot Lunaire*
> on October 9, 1912. He was deeply impressed, and dis-
> cussed the work with Ravel . . . early in 1913. The fruits
> of this discussion were Ravel's Mallarmé songs and Stravin-
> sky's Japanese songs.

In truth, Stravinsky was in Russia on October 9, 1912, and by
that date had already sketched two of his *Three Japanese
Lyrics*. He first heard *Pierrot* on December 8, 1912, and did
not see Ravel until almost four months later.

Schoenberg Remembered is an invaluable history of a Los
Angeles that is now all but buried. This reviewer, who knew
all of the places and most of the people that the author
mentions, read the book with unanticipated nostalgia. Here
are Peter Yates's Evenings on the Roof—the Schindler house
on the same street as the Stravinskys' Russian church—and
the rehearsal orchestra made up of film-studio musicians,
which was conducted by both Stravinsky and Schoenberg
(and, for that matter—*horribile dictu*—by this reviewer,
too, who remembers Alma Mahler and Bruno Walter listening to him rehearse *Petrushka* and Haydn's Symphony No.
31). And here on page after page are Klemperer, Krenek,
and many other fascinating musicians, though none more
so than the subject of the book, of whom it may be said, as
Ms. Newlin quotes him on J. S. Bach, he had an "infinite
knowledge of the biology of tone."

Dika Newlin taught at Syracuse University and Drew University, after which she became the head of the music department at North Texas State University. She is active as a
composer and performer, as well as a teacher, and the list of
her writings is formidable.

An "Unheard-of Intensity"

It is not only the fate of this poor man,
exploited and tormented by *all the world*, *that*
touches me so closely, but also the unheard-of
intensity of mood of the individual scenes.

ALBAN BERG to ANTON WEBERN,
August 19, 1918

After *Wozzeck* had won comparatively wide acclaim, Berg stated that "the social problems of the opera by far transcend the personal destiny of Wozzeck." But surely Berg was too great an artist to believe this and not to recognize that the tragedies of Wozzeck, Marie, and their illegitimate child far transcend sociology. Even on this level the composer does not do justice to his achievement, since the opera indicts not a particular society, but the *condition humaine;* the tormentors—the harebrained Captain, sadistic Doctor, bullying Drum Major—are also victims, prisoners of their circumstances and personalities, and, as such, more pathetic than evil. The subjects of universal drama are not theses and philosophies but human beings.

Opera can reveal contradictions between a character's words and thoughts in a way not possible in spoken drama, a resource that Berg fully exploits. Yet critical commentaries on *Wozzeck* tend to overemphasize the importance of its ironies, apart from the principal one of Wozzeck himself, who has the lowest status and the greatest power of feeling. A larger aspect of both the opera and Büchner's play, on which it was based, is the portrayal of incomprehension. Understood by no one, Wozzeck is thought to be mentally unbalanced, even when, with perfect sanity, he says of his child, "The good Lord's not going to look down on the poor worm just because nobody said 'amen' before he was made." The conventional mind of the Captain cannot appreciate the logic and humanity of this. No wonder that, in another dimension, Wozzeck is talking only to himself, as when he cries out, Lear-like, "Why doesn't God put out the sun?"

Berg's genius is nowhere more manifest than in his musical realization of Büchner's characters. The plot is secondary, a tale of infidelity, vengeance, and retribution that begins only when the opera is almost one-third over. Partly for this reason, the classical three-act formula, exposition-development-catastrophe, does not fit a play made up of disconnected scenes, dependent on juxtaposition rather than development, and cumulative in effect. The unprecedented economy and concentration of each scene—the play contains nearly twice as many as the opera—preclude the standard processes of elaboration.

George Perle remarks in his perceptive new study of *Wozzeck*[1] that "it was the nature of the composer rather than the nature of his subject that led Berg to impose order . . . through the rigorous formal framework that governs the work as a whole." In truth, both natures coalesce in this perfect unification of music and subject, and to transform Büchner's detached episodes into opera clearly required a musical structure, if not the autonomous one that Berg provided. He told Webern of being "tempted" by the idea of "combining scenes through orchestral interludes." Eventually these were to function not only as links and transitions, but also—and in

---

1. *The Operas of Alban Berg, Vol. I: "Wozzeck,"* by George Perle (Berkeley, Calif., 1980).

this the opera far outstrips the play—to heighten the tensions of preceding scenes and the contrasts with succeeding ones. Each interlude is a high point in the opera.

Danton's Death, the political pamphlet *Der hessische Landbote* (attacking tyranny in his native Hesse), and the doctoral thesis *The Nervous System of the Barbel* (written in French) were the only works by Georg Büchner to be published in his twenty-three-year lifetime. Shortly after his death, in 1837, *Leonce and Lena* and *Lenz*, a prose fragment, appeared in a periodical, and in 1850, Dr. Ludwig Büchner, Georg's brother and the author of a popular book on "freethinking" philosophy, published the *Nachgelassene Schriften*. But this volume included neither *Pietro Aretino*, the last completed play, now presumed to be lost, nor *Woyzeck*,[2] which survived only in preliminary drafts and sketches. Though the play was published in 1870, *Woyzeck* was not performed until 1914, in Munich. In the following year, Berg saw it in Vienna; also in 1914, Hugo Bieber discovered that Büchner had based the story on the life of Johann Christian Woyzeck, executed in Leipzig in 1824 after two examinations to determine his mental competence. The doctor who performed these, Clarus, later published a paper on his findings in a medical journal to which Büchner's father was a contributor. Johann Woyzeck evidently suffered from delusions, and some of the things he said, as repeated by Clarus, were incorporated into Büchner's play.

Berg decided to compose the opera as soon as he saw the play, but World War I intervened, and in 1915 he was conscripted. The score was completed in 1922, but the first performance did not take place until December 1925, in Berlin. One other early production—1927, in Leningrad—must be mentioned, both because the Russian text was by Mikhail Kuzmin, and because a performance of this greatest modern opera in the USSR today would be scarcely conceivable.

2. Berg used the diphthong spelling at first, then chose the one that is easier for singers to pronounce. "Woyzeck" is possibly a Polish name and would for this reason contribute to the character's alienation in a German town.

In a staging of the opera at the 1980 Edinburgh festival, Büchner's word *"pissen"* in the Doctor's scene was employed instead of Berg's word *"husten"* (cough). The restoration is not merely of a detail, but of the meaning of an entire episode; the Doctor, having sought to prove that "the bladder muscle is subordinate to the will," intended to do a urinalysis. *"Pissen,"* moreover, immediately indicates that the Doctor treats Wozzeck as an experimental dog. The words that Berg substituted, "I saw it, Wozzeck, you coughed in the street, barked like a dog," not only are meaningless—coughing in the street being in no way unusual—but rob the scene of its purpose. Although the bowdlerization was probably inevitable in the Vienna of 1919, would the same have been true of the Berlin of Brecht and Weill, where, by the end of the 1920s, *Wozzeck* had become a success? One wonders why Berg did not make the change himself at the later date, especially since the published score optionally retains the word *"Altweiberfurz,"* which has no significance in the drama. Yet in Britain, as late as the 1960s, Büchner's play, which contains such handy scatological locutions as *"Arschloch,"* could "only be performed in public with certain modifications approved by the Lord Chamberlain."

Mr. Perle is absorbing on these and other textual amendments, and especially on the contributions of Karl Emil Franzos, "the Galician-Jewish novelist who first deciphered the faded and almost illegible manuscripts." Franzos must be credited not only with transcribing, editing, and publishing the play, but, first of all, with discovering it—in 1875, among the papers sent to him by Ludwig Büchner. The dramatist's brother, who had read as much of the text as he could make out, was convinced that because of "cynicisms" and "trivialities" it could not be of much value. Franzos's 1879 edition is not without errors and misunderstandings, but, as Mr. Perle concludes, "the historical and textual investigations" of modern scholars are on the whole "more damaging than Franzos's mistakes. . . . After forty years of critical research, we are brought back to Franzos's conception of the dénouement," concerning which Büchner's intentions are unknown. No less remarkable are the many additions by Franzos that are worthy of Büchner and enhance the play. In fact, what may be its best-known line, *"Du! Dein Mutter is tot!,"* which one of the children says to Wozzeck's infant son in the final scene, is actually the contribution of Franzos.

So, too, Wozzeck's exclamation *"Ach, Marie!"*—a significant slip from his unconscious, which the Doctor on his *a priori* path fails to notice—is Franzos's interpolation, along with several improvements in the drowning scene, including the repetition of Wozzeck's cry "Murderer, murderer" from the end of the second scene in the act. The hobbyhorse that Marie's child rides in the final scene was also Franzos's idea. As for his mistakes, the most serious was his exclusion of the Idiot's appearance before the scene in the Tavern Garden, thus making his entry there *ex machina,* and his vision of blood gratuitous. This incident remains the weakest in the opera.

Berg used Franzos's edition, but in Acts I and II followed the order of the scenes in Paul Landau's 1909 version, which reverses Büchner's first two scenes—opening with the one in the fields rather than with that of Wozzeck shaving the Captain. Most productions of the play now follow Büchner, though Jean Jourdeuil, who translated the version used in Paris in 1980, points out the disadvantages of placing either scene first: "To start with the Captain/Wozzeck is to place the emphasis of the play on the oppression of Wozzeck, but to begin with the scene in the fields is to make of the work a *fait divers."* Berg, having made the *"wir arme Leut'"* ("we poor people") theme primary, had to begin the opera with the Captain scene. And in respect of musical dynamics, the extended and deepened portrait of Wozzeck in the field could only follow the comparatively limited one in the scene with the Captain. Here, in Scene 2, Wozzeck is with an equal, his companion Andres, whose normality provides a radical contrast to Wozzeck's wild visions. Mr. Perle quotes the critic Margaret Jacobs:

The fire and thunder of the storm bring to [Wozzeck's] mind the images of the Apocalypse. . . . His hallucinations have all the terror . . . of weird folk-superstition, and in his inarticulateness before the Doctor he can only give to all these unintelligible, irrational and fearful things the name, *"die doppelte Natur."*

The field scene, too, best demonstrates the truth of Ms. Jacobs's observations that Wozzeck's words are "tersely allusive, not explanatory." With Andres, Wozzeck sees toadstools. Then, two scenes later, he remarks to the Doctor: "The toadstools . . . Circles, figures, if one could read them!" Mr. Perle calls such recurrences "verbal *Leitmotive*," a new but henceforth indispensable term in the analysis of this as well as of other operas.

Berg's own textual emendations testify to his theatrical imagination as well as to his exceptional literary sensitivity. In the street scene, when Wozzeck is taunted about Marie's infidelity, the stage direction is the composer's: The Doctor beats time with his umbrella, imitating the Drum Major with his baton. Not surprisingly, Berg devised verbal correspondences, just as he did musical ones; an example is his repetition in the phrase *"Langsam, Wozzeck, langsam."* Still other alterations were necessary because he omitted scenes included by Franzos, and references to them had to be deleted.

Wisely, Berg corrected the Franzos text in the tavern scene, when, after murdering Marie, Wozzeck tries to immerse himself in the crowd of merrymakers. In his "desperate attempt to escape from his own identity . . . he sings another man's song," that of his comrade Andres from the opera's second scene. Franzos attributed this repetition to oversight and provided new words, but Berg, perceiving the relevance of Büchner's lines, and the irony in their suggestion of a faithless woman, retained the original. Here, remarking on Wozzeck's "assumption of the Drum Major's manner" in saying "I'd like a fight today, a fight," thereby pathetically echoing the man who has humiliated and destroyed him, Mr. Perle uncovers a musical reference to one of Marie's leitmotifs, and connects it to "the sudden obtrusion of thoughts which Wozzeck has come here to escape." Finally, the reader learns to think of the scene, of "the stage piano's Polka . . . and Margret's song, accompanied only by the stage piano . . . [as] musical parentheses in which the 'real' music on the stage [represents] that outer world in which the murderer Wozzeck seeks refuge from his own . . . identity. . . ."

Mr. Perle writes that "the musical coherence of the opera, independent of the staged events, reflects an objective order whose irrelevance to the subjective fate of Wozzeck poignantly emphasizes his total isolation in an indifferent universe." On one level, however, the music relates very literally to the action, moving upward or downward according to the words' suggestion, screaming with Marie when Wozzeck stabs her, and whispering with him in his aside, "When the morning dew falls, you won't feel the cold." The music mimics real noises, too—croaking frogs, snoring soldiers in their barracks—with a degree of verisimilitude that makes them identifiable even without the stage picture. "Real," too, are the popular forms, the march, lullaby, and waltz, no matter how untraditional some of the harmonic ingredients.

In the opera's subterrain, Berg has erected a complex of musical symbols and analyses that are dependent on "learned" and often remote conventions. Thus the Doctor's scene is a passacaglia, an "academic" and an "old" form suitable to represent an educated man who knows Latin and quotes Pliny. (Was Pliny's *"Natura nusquam magis est tota quam in minimis"* in Büchner's mind when he wrote the line about the circles and rings in toadstools?) The passacaglia also serves to connect the Doctor with science, for the theme employs the twelve pitches of the chromatic scale, as Strauss had done in the "science" section of *Also sprach Zarathustra.* Thus the form is an overall symbol for an entire scene. At the same time, Berg has created many small musical analogues for the notion of an *idée fixe.* According to the Doctor, Wozzeck suffers from this malady, but Mr. Perle demonstrates how the music "tells us," by association, that the more seriously afflicted of the two characters is the Doctor himself. When he says, "Cultivate your obsession," the words are accompanied by "a three-part canon on an *ostinato* motive," and when he exults, *"Oh! meine Theorie!,"* the music is a six-part canon "culminating in a verticalized segment of the cycle of perfect fourths . . . [which,] since it is generated by a single interval, can 'stand' for the Doctor's monomaniacal obsession." The reader may wonder why a repeated note or chord would not be a more apt metaphor for the aberration. But Berg's mind worked differently.

Mr. Perle traces the composer's mental processes at their most ingenious in the music accompanying Wozzeck's reference to Marie's adultery with the Drum Major: "It must stink enough to smoke the angels out of heaven." Here, four instruments play simultaneously ascending figures in regular patterns starting from the same note, one of them a chromatic scale, the second a whole-tone scale, the other two sequences of, respectively, minor and major thirds. A fifth part, the solo violin, "representing the odor of Marie's sin rising to heaven," spoils these perfect designs "in its weaving and irregular ascent and in its interpolation of a 'wrong' note into each of the simultaneities"—an example of Walter Pater's "getting as many pulsations as possible into the given time."

Proceeding from the most obscure to the most obvious of such devices, in the opera's final interlude, or orchestral epilogue, catharsis and tonality are identified, willy-nilly. Did Berg anticipate philistine comment concerning this phenomenon? In any event, the audience's feeling of recognition and relief at the beginning of the D minor is almost tangible, even today. Mr. Perle ignores the matter, no doubt because he does not regard this symphonic peroration as an integral part of the drama, but also, perhaps, because he considers such questions to be beneath the book's intellectual level. If so, he should heed Eliot's warning that "criticism is too important to be left to the fellows who write for the newspapers," since in this opera, where everything is significant, the return to tonality at the climax begs an explanation.

When the strings sustain a C-major triad while Wozzeck gives Marie money, the commonplace chord, Mr. Perle says, represents Wozzeck's "sanity" and "ordinariness." But the emphasis is clearly on money, Wozzeck's words "we poor," immediately before, being those of the principal leitmotif of the opera. Whether or not Berg's intention was to associate C major with the evils of capitalism, he manages to make the chord sound sinister, at least for one listener. But this, too, is surely by design, namely, to turn aural perspectives inside out: the C-major triad in an "atonal" context—not introduced by tonal functions—becomes the *least* common of chords. Mr. Perle warns his readers not to be misled, especially those with "a tonally oriented ear." But which opera audience in the Western world has developed any other kind?

To "review" Mr. Perle's analysis of the opera's musical language, the most valuable portion of his study, would be to enter into technicalities requiring definitions that the author himself does not provide. He writes that "simultaneous voices moving by semitonal inflection are often symmetrically related to each other." "Semitonal inflection" is simply a long way of saying chromatic. "Symmetrically related," on the evidence, means "in contrary motion." The difficulty is that three examples are given, and since two of these are in diagram form, the reader is obliged to turn to the score to understand the quoted statement. There, in example one, he finds that the upper voice moves "by semitonal inflection" only if the major seconds, the minor third, and the several fourths between the chromatic steppingstones are not counted.

Mr. Perle believes that his book "should in large part be accessible to the general reader as well as to the specialist." To this one can only say that it would be much more readily accessible if the reader were not thwarted by so many verbal obstacles. In statements like the following, even the most inured specialist must heed the Captain's *"langsam, hübsch langsam"*:

Where it has seemed desirable to indicate exactly at which point in a given bar a cited passage begins or ends, this will be shown by durational symbols giving the portions of the initial and concluding bars comprised in the citation.

In other words, certain passages referred to in the score are identified by the time-values of their first and last notes.

A handicap even for specialist readers is that many of the music examples contain mistakes. Why, one wonders, does a publisher go to the expense of printing 186 examples in music type but fail to invest in an hour or two of editorial time to verify them?[3] Some of the errors are in rhythm,[4] but the main difficulty is that whereas the orchestra score leaves no doubt about accidentals, the book omits natural signs except where someone thought them to be necessary. In many places this is merely confusing, and in others no more than inconsistent—naturals are used in a chord in Example 86, but not in the same chord in Example 150—but the absence of the natural is definitely wrong in "the climactic bar of the final section" (Example 126, where the A flat that obtains from the start of the measure must be canceled on the second quarter), in Example 42 (before the last A), in Example 153b (before the last E), and in Example 23x (before the B in the double appoggiatura).[5]

3. It is also the fault of the publisher that music is misidentified (Example 2, for instance, shows the end of Op. 2, no. 3), that some of the signs are wrong (Example 149 needs an equal sign, not a dash, in the second measure), and that the footnotes between pages 131 and 148 (and again later) are found above the music examples.
4. Viz., Example 75, where the first chord in the treble clef should have the duration of an eighth; Example 136, where the bass part in measure 2 contains one quarter too many; and Example 163, measure 3, where the first two notes of the new part should be dotted quarters.
5. Some of the German in the book is wrong, too. Thus "better a knife" is rendered *"Leiber [sic] ein Messer"* (p. 114), and "I smell, I smell blood" becomes *"Ich reich [sic], ich reich Blut"* (p. 84).

Mr. Perle concludes that "Berg was the most forward-looking composer of our century, in the sense that he had progressed further than anyone else in the direction of that reformulation of postdiatonic compositional procedures that had motivated Schoenberg's discovery of the twelve-tone system in the first place." Formulation, surely, not *re*formulation. But no matter. Mr. Perle's analysis persuades us that Berg *was* the most innovative composer of his time, whichever direction proves to be the forward-looking one. Some of us would add that he was also the most prodigally gifted, with rare "natural" melodic powers and originality in form. When Mr. Perle warns against just such "premature generalizations," we disregard him only to say that if we meet such high standards of scholarship again in this decade, it will be in his sequel volume on Berg's and modern opera's most famous *femme fatale*.

Shadow and Substance

Gide's *"Victor Hugo, hélas"* expresses an attitude toward the French poet similar to the one that many musicians have about Richard Strauss. Yet the omnipresence of his operas on European and American stages is a phenomenon of the last decade as conspicuous as the failure of virtually any music by the far more influential and revered Arnold Schoenberg to enter the repertory. Almost all of Strauss's operas have been successfully revived, while in current criticial opinion, *Die Frau ohne Schatten* has taken its place beside, if not above, *Salome, Elektra,* and *Der Rosenkavalier. The New Grove* quotes Strauss's estimate of *Die Frau* as "Hofmannsthal's finest achievement," adding, "some think that it is also Strauss's," and the recent Mondadori volume *L'opera: repertorio della lirica dall' 1597,* generally balanced in its criticism, ranks this opera with *Tristan* and *Don Giovanni.* Moreover, such views are neither cultist nor elitist, as the Welsh National Opera's 1981 sold-out tour of *Die Frau* in Britain showed.

After a three-year interval, *Die Frau* was performed in October 1981 by the Met as a vehicle for Birgit Nilsson—a peculiar reason for its revival, since her role, the Dyer's Wife, is not the "lead" and does not make unique vocal demands. The Met's compliance with the prima donna's choice confirms once again the dominating influence of star performers over any consideration of the works themselves. It also indicates that the opera owes some of its astonishing popularity to the spectacular singing required of the three female characters—more to that, to be sure, than to the labyrinthine libretto, the dramatis personae of symbols rather than human beings, and the disastrous final scene; for if *Die Frau* occasionally rises above the three earlier Strauss operas, it also sinks far below them at the end, even below Salome's dance.

Well known as *Die Frau* has become, a critical discussion is not yet possible without some kind of summary of the story, even one, such as the following, that omits several episodes and even characters. Thus the reader must know that the action takes place in the geographically unrecognizable South Eastern Islands, and that these are nominally ruled by a human emperor but remotely controlled by Keikobad, the invisible commanding divinity of the Spirit World. A year before the story begins, the Emperor, hunting, was about to spear a gazelle when it turned into a beautiful woman (Keikobad's daughter), who then became empress and was installed in isolation in the Blue Palace. During her transformation, she both lost the talisman that gave her the power of metamorphosis and acquired a treacherous guardian nurse from the Spirit World.

When the curtain opens, the Nurse is hiding in the dark on the palace roof, awaiting the twelfth monthly visit (a symbol of the menstrual cycle?) of Keikobad's messenger. "Does the Empress cast a shadow?" (Is she pregnant?), he asks, and when the Nurse answers in the negative, he warns her that if after three more days the Empress is still *"ohne Schatten,"* she must return to her father in the Spirit World, and the Emperor will be turned to stone. Since the Nurse dislikes the world of humans, and is pleased with the prospect of the Emperor's petrifaction, she resolves not to tell this to the Empress. The Emperor enters and informs the Nurse that he will be away for three days to look for his Red Falcon, which has disappeared. The Nurse then goes to the chamber of the sleeping Empress, where the Falcon flies in and reveals the secret of the Emperor's impending fate. Determined to save him, the Empress obliges the Nurse to help her find a shadow. As the new day breaks, they set out on this quest.

This opening scene moves rapidly and could scarcely be more compact. The characterizations are also quickly drawn: the mendacious Nurse, the doting but shallow Emperor—his idea of a gift for his wife is a carcass from his hunt—the mysterious Empress herself, whom Strauss portrays with exotic, birdlike figurations. The music that evokes the contrast between daylight and the darkness of the Empress's world is some of the most effective, atmospherically, that Strauss ever wrote; nor are the loose ends in the libretto particularly disturbing: the Nurse's unexplained remark that the Empress's partisanship toward humankind is inherited from her mother, and the improbability that, a year after being wounded by the Emperor, the Falcon still weeps and its wing still bleeds.

The next scene takes place in the hut of Barak, the Dyer, to which the Empress and Nurse come disguised as servants. The Dyer's Wife, the woman *with* a shadow, though still childless,[1] desires only material things, including a young lover. The Nurse, conjuring a vision of a life of luxury, is able to persuade the Wife to exchange her shadow for it, but as a condition of the pact the Wife must stay apart from her husband for three days. The Nurse and Empress leave, and the moaning voices of the Dyer's Unborn Children cry out from a fire, "*Mutter, Mutter, lass uns nach Hause!*" The Wife is frightened, but recovers and hides from her spouse.

This synopsis does not mention the Dyer's three malformed brothers, but, arguably, they are superfluous characters, along with the anthropomorphic Falcon, whose heavily plaintive and unvarying music, moreover, soon becomes monotonous. Nor does the synopsis indicate the extent to

---

1. Since the Wife wants to be fruitful and has failed, the shadow must mean more than the capacity to conceive, but Hofmannsthal does not resolve the inconsistency. Later, of course, the shadow has a larger, moral significance.

which Act I is dominated by the Nurse, who has some 490 lines in the opera (in Eric Crozier's translation for singing,[2] which does not advise the reader about cuts and which misattributes some of the lines of the three brothers), as compared with 382 for the Empress: in the second scene of Act I the Empress is a near-silent observer.

The act as a whole is on a high musical level, with some delicate orchestral effects, above all in the evocation of the shadow partly through the use of a basset horn, and of unaccompanied flutes and harp at the Wife's line "We have no mirror," and of larger-scale sparkling combinations after the Nurse's "Let me arrange your diadem." The identification of Barak and "neoclassic" melodic and harmonic procedures is both established and overdone, as in the orchestral tone poem that "expresses" his goodness but contributes nothing dramatically and makes the character more ethereal than Hofmannsthal can have intended. Finally, the Watchmen's sixteenth-century-style chorale is incongruous in the South Eastern Islands setting—except that, from the beginning, the musical landscape is clearly identified as Mitteleuropa, the dramatic one as "Transylvania." As for the women's voices laughing in dotted rhythms ("Ha, ha-ha"), this, fortunately, is part of the background.

In Act II, Scene 1, the Empress and Nurse return, and the latter conjures an apparition of the promised lover for the Dyer's discontented Wife, making him vanish as Barak enters, followed by Beggar Children, whom he feeds. Barak's goodness so moves the Empress that she decides to become human. In Scene 2, in a forest by the falcon house, the Emperor discovers that his wife has become involved with humans; in consequence, his marriage must end. He asks the Falcon to lead him to a remote cave on a distant cliff.

In Scene 3 the disguised Empress helps the Dyer, and in Scene 4 she is disturbed by dreams of him and of the Em-

2. *The Woman without a Shadow*, English version of the libretto, published by the Welsh National Opera, 1980.

peror entering a tomblike cavern, after which she realizes that the fates of both men are in her hands. In the final scene of the act, the Dyer's Wife confesses to her husband that she has deceived him, as well as renounced her shadow and with it their unborn children. The light of a fire reveals that she is indeed without shadow, whereupon the Dyer is about to kill her—with a sword that obligingly flies into his hand through the intervention of the Nurse—but the Empress intervenes and refuses to take the shadow. Earthquakes and floods carry everything and everybody away.

The quality of the music in Act II is not consistent, but that of the Empress is sometimes spellbinding, especially at the end of the scene with Barak (*"Ich, mein Gebieter, deine Dienerin!"*), and the interlude that follows is one of the strongest passages in the opera. In the same scene, the Wife's $\frac{6}{8}$ music at *"Denn es ist nicht von heute"* could have come from *Der Rosenkavalier* (which could be said of other sections as well).

In the final act, the Dyer and his Wife, imprisoned in separate caverns, have grown wiser and wish to be reunited, but the Nurse misleads them in their search for each other. Scene 2 takes place in Keikobad's palace, where the Empress awaits her father's judgment for having shown compassion to human beings. The thought of what has happened to the Emperor obsesses her, but the Nurse tells her about a spring of water that can restore him—at the price of her own life. (The Nurse is finally banished to the hated society of mankind.)

In the next scene, the Empress enters a temple in the interior of the mountain, where her husband has become a stone statue. Though still *"ohne Schatten,"* she pleads with the invisible Keikobad to let her live in the world of humans. In response, a fountain of gold water appears; she is told that she will acquire a shadow after drinking of it. Fearing that this would be the Wife's, she refuses, and the fountain disappears. She then asks Keikobad to reveal himself, but a curtain parts exposing, instead, the statue of the Emperor.

The fountain reappears, and she is told that to drink of it will restore him to life. Hearing the voices of the Dyer and his Wife, she still refuses, and the fountain again ceases to flow. But a light now shows the Empress with a shadow, and the Emperor alive, and the opera ends with a quartet of the reunited couples, joined by a chorus of Unborn Children greeting their future parents.

The score of the first part of Act III is remarkably new, from the curious Debussyan prelude to the change-of-scene music (beginning at 40) that might have come from *Wozzeck*. But if Hofmannsthal's inspiration for this act was *The Magic Flute*, with its trials by ordeal and exploiting of socially contrasted couples, Strauss's was *Parsifal*, as well as, at the Empress's "*Mein Vater*," Brünnhilde. The dénouement, unfortunately, is as devoid of musical ideas as it is deafeningly loud.

The weaknesses of the libretto of *Die Frau* are not in its edifying concepts, but in its ill-conceived story, poor dramatic structure, and unconvincing characters. Hofmannsthal relied too strongly on the conventional trappings of fairy-tale models: the clichés of time (three days, a twelvemonth); place (a Tolkien never-never land, with a suggestion of the Enchanted Island of *The Tempest*); the intervention of superior powers, prodigies of nature, magic, disguises, and transformations; and the ultimate triumph of the Moral Principle. These, after all, are the marks of the genre, but so are disconnected adventures; and partly because of this, and the suspension of logic, the drama fails.

Furthermore, though the characters, like the tale, are archetypal—royalty and beggars, the simple and good human being (the Dyer), and the thoroughly evil spirit (the Nurse) —what they represent is not made sufficiently clear, and their behavior is inconsistent. Thus, when the Dyer threatens to kill his wife, his much-touted goodness becomes questionable, homicidal intentions not usually being a sign of virtue. His Wife, moreover, is even less believable, not because she is so easily corrupted, but because she lacks dimension. As for the

Emperor, the Nurse's description of him as "lovesick, and a hunter, but otherwise nothing" says it all, except that his punishment seems disproportionately severe, since he was unaware of the forces with which he accidentally became entangled. And the Nurse, with the opera's largest role, is a stereotype, a witch in whom no development takes place.

Who is Keikobad, and what is the moral basis of his Spirit World? He is a god, of course, since he presides over a system of predestination and at the same time allows his daughter to perform the acts of free will that provide the dramatic action. But why is his music so portentous, and why does the motif of this unseen being dominate the opera as that of the unseen Agamemnon does *Elektra?* Even if the libretto fails to convey Hofmannsthal's conclusions, he must have answered these questions for himself, and in reality he did believe in the preexistence of those Unborn Children who so remind us of today's clients of Right-to-Life groups.

That the Empress is the opera's only compelling character is due in large measure to her mysterious origins as the daughter of Keikobad, and to the strange concept of her physical makeup, a transparent (i.e., crystal) body. Yet it is through her selflessness, as she becomes conscious of the suffering of others, that the opera achieves its moral power. And it is through her, too, that the shadow's ultimate meaning, as distinguished from its first meaning of mere fertility, becomes clear: the willingness to lose one's life for another is the way to save it.

In the first important monograph on *Die Frau*,[3] Sherrill Pantle states his conviction that apart from "a belated recognition of artistic worth," the reason for the current fascination with the opera is that it "stands before the audiences of the last quarter of the twentieth century as the incarnation of a lost innocence and the realization of a lost hope." But do audiences really see the opera in that way, desirable as this

3. *"Die Frau ohne Schatten" by Hugo von Hofmannsthal and Richard Strauss: An Analysis of Text, Music, and Their Relationship,* by Sherrill Hahn Pantle (Frankfurt, 1978).

may be? And is its appeal not primarily musical? The author's estimate of Strauss's art is extremely restricted: "The pathological and the extraordinary had definitely shown itself [sic] to be [his] particular métier," Pantle writes, to which one can only answer that nostalgia is as much the composer's forte as the macabre, and that his musical characterizations of "whole" and "healthy" people are no less successful. Who in modern opera can be compared to the Marschallin as a portrayal of a "mature" individual?

But Pantle's book does not shed as much light on the music as it does on the drama, and such devices as his chart associating keys and moods in some of Strauss's tone poems are not very useful: F major may correspond to Strauss's "serene and carefree" feelings,[4] but the same can be said of countless other composers—though in the first place, one doubts that opera audiences recognize tonalities in such music, or are aware, even in much simpler operas, when an aria has been transposed. It must also be said that Pantle's chapter on the nature of opera contains meaningless statements—"music expresses feelings by presenting them to us in their logical contours"—that further complicate the study of a work already overendowed with perplexities. Opera combines two arts in opposition, the author says, owing to the antithesis between music as a suspension of clock-time and drama as a form "concerned with the *Future* or with the consequences of acts performed in the *Now*." But surely music has dramatic structures of its own that are "concerned with" the future of relationships formed in the "now."

What Pantle does provide is an invaluable guide to Hofmannsthal's language, its syntactic features, meter, vocabulary, and the nuances in German on which the purely verbal symbolism of the opera depends. And, secondarily, Pántle

4. In Strauss's mind, the correspondence between emotional states and tonalities and harmonies was absolute. He actually wrote in the margins of books of poems that he was reading "E flat," or "C-sharp minor," or whatever. See the essay "Richard Strauss's Pre-sketch Planning for *Ariadne auf Naxos*" in the July 1981 *Musical Quarterly*.

discovers the identities of many more of Hofmannsthal's sources. Those already known were *The Arabian Nights, The Magic Flute*, Schiller's adaptation of Gozzi's *Turandot* (in which both the Dyer and Keikobad appear—the latter, also mentioned in *Omar Khayyam*, having been an actual Seljuk monarch), and *Faust* (Hofmannsthal himself having noted the similarities between the Nurse and Mephistopheles). To this list, Pantle adds Chamisso's 1814 play about the selling of a shadow; Goethe's "seducing of Tyche," who resembles Hofmannsthal's Youth; and a number of Biblical correspondences, most convincingly between some of the Empress's lines and those of John of Patmos' vision of the Last Judgment. But Pantle sees the Dyer as a Christ figure, through the parallel of illumination following acceptance of death.

Unfortunately, the book's quotations are not translated, and though Nietzsche is available in English, this is not true of Hofmannsthal's notebooks and of the *Erzählung*, the quasi-parallel narrative version of the libretto. (Only Chapter 4 has been translated, in the Bollingen volume of selected prose introduced by Hermann Broch.) This novella contains psychological motivations necessarily absent in the dramatized form, as well as more background material and variants that offer different, sometimes helpful, perspectives.

Rudolf Hartmann, who staged *Die Frau* for Strauss himself, does not regard the opera's flaws as insurmountable, nor does he agree that bypass surgery is the remedy for the main problem in Act III, which is that no dramatic conflict remains to be resolved, the Empress already having refused the shadow of the Dyer's Wife at the end of Act II.[5] But then, Hartmann tends to disregard the opera's symbolism and moral lessons in order to focus on its theatrical requirements. For example, he warns that the shadowless Empress must be positioned next to pillars and props whose shadows absorb

---

5. *Richard Strauss: The Staging of His Operas and Ballets*, by Rudolf Hartmann (New York, 1981).

her own, since to keep her in darkness simply to avoid her real-life shadow is to diminish her primary place in the opera. He also points out that the realism of every aspect of the Dyer's world should be heightened to contrast it with fairy-land.

Hartmann believes, too, that the opera's Orientalism ought to be emphasized, and he suggests that the singers in Act III imitate the stylized gestures of people in Persian and Indian miniatures. Certainly the most stunning sets for *Die Frau* illustrated in Hartmann's book are very like enlarged miniatures. Emil Preetorius's design for the palace scene looks like a copy of an actual print, while, in another tableau, the falcon house might have been taken from a Chinese scroll. As for Alfred Roller's *maquettes* for the premiere (Vienna, 1919), these are not only Oriental, but also erotic, an essential quality in establishing the distinction between procreative and purely sexual love that is one of the opera's principal subjects.

The Metropolitan Opera's 1966 production of *Die Frau ohne Schatten*, revived in 1978, was designed to show off the mechanical resources of the company's new stage. These, at any rate, were the stars of the performance, the scenery rising into the firmament, sinking into the depths, turning around and inside out; the characters appearing and disappearing in bursts of smoke and light; the push-button geysers and flames. But the glitter and dazzle only pointed up the threadbare quality of the acting, of the principals lurching toward each other, arms outstretched, halting, backing up, starting again, then temporizing until the music permitted them to embrace or collapse. Another consequence of the theatrical fireworks was that the moral theme was lost. Next time around the audiences should do some homework, of the kind indicated in Pantle's book. They might then be able to follow Hofmannsthal's themes in Strauss's music.

La Grande Mademoiselle

Why does Nadia Boulanger merit a full-length, popular-style biography[1] when she was neither a composer of significance nor, after her youth, a virtuoso performer? The reasons for her continuing interest to both musicians and lay persons are her pre-eminence as a teacher and her place as the first female pioneer in the propagation of modern music. In the present period of women's liberation, she has won a high place in the pantheon.

Mlle Boulanger's fame is due first of all to her own phenomenal musicianship, to which there is much testimony. One witness, the late musicologist Arthur Mendel, wrote of her sight-reading at the piano of a modern string quartet: "For reliability of ear and a quick and accurate mind, she leaves [Vincent d'Indy] far behind." Her reputation as a pedagogue derives from such of her students as Marc Blitzstein, Elliott Carter, Aaron Copland, Roy Harris, Walter Piston, and Virgil Thomson, as well as from the thousands who sat at her feet at the American School of Music at Fontainebleau, the Ecole Normale, the Paris Conservatory, Wellesley College, Radcliffe, the Longy School, and privately. Nor were aspiring composers her only pupils: hardly

1. *Nadia Boulanger: A Life in Music*, by Léonie Rosenstiel (New York, 1982).

less impressive is the roster of instrumentalists and singers whom she instructed. The assimilation of her concepts and tastes in most of her pupils is so great as to have branded them members of the so-called Boulangerie.

Her teaching goals were unimpeachable: the development of self-knowledge, technical expertise, memory training, and a sense of quality. As an educator she believed in the early awakening of musical abilities—for example, in distinguishing tonalities. Like Schoenberg and Hindemith, she insisted on a general knowledge of music with thorough grounding in classical harmony and counterpoint before permitting departures from tradition. More than these two nonpianists, she sought to develop rapid reading and transposition at the keyboard, while cultivating a discriminating ear. The uniqueness of her approach was in requiring her students to declare and justify their preferences; she had no sympathy with anyone unable to do this, contending that a mistaken opinion is better than none. Although she worked unstintingly with her pupils, she also candidly discouraged the unpromising ones.

The essence of her teaching was in the analysis of classics and student work for methods, aims, and achievements, as well as for technical details. Mlle Boulanger's belief that "music depends on line, not on chord, for its meaning" may help to account for her primary interest in the contemporary, which she discussed in terms of extensions of tonality and harmony, innovations in rhythm and timbre, and new characteristics of "diction." She thought that "form," in the new music, had changed less than these other elements, though one wonders how any of them can be circumscribed. All of this seems to imply the exclusion of atonality, yet this was not always true. Stravinsky's Octet (1923) apparently had a decisive effect on her, and her Rice Institute lecture (1925) reveals that by this date her commitment to him as the composer of the age had become total. Obviously, Nadia Boulanger's significance is not as a teacher of academic musical language—those Americans did not migrate to Paris to learn textbook modulation—but as the high priestess of modern music *à la* Stravinsky.

Parallel to this, if less consequential, were her efforts in promoting the performance and appreciation of "old" music, though she was not a trained musicologist and was obliged to depend on her innate, but not always reliable, sense of style. Nevertheless, her performances of Schütz and other masters of the Renaissance and Baroque won many audiences to this music, and it is no exaggeration to say that her recordings of Monteverdi sparked the revival that continues to this day. In her music-history courses at the Ecole Normale, she taught stylistic principles instead of focusing on individual composers, and in this, too, she was ahead of her time. Scholars were outraged by her orchestrations of seventeenth-century masterpieces, to which she also added parts composed by herself. Fortunately, that which offends musicologists (except for the existence of their colleagues) often leads to progress.

Nadia Boulanger was born in Montmartre in September 1887, the oldest child of Ernest Boulanger, seventy-two, and Rosa (Raïssa) Ivanovna Myschetsky, thirty-one. The effect of this vast age difference on Nadia should not be minimized; it must have given rise to embarrassments and complications, in and out of the family, which are reflected in Nadia's personality. To mention only one difficulty, a father of a great-grandfather's age was surely too old to communicate emotionally with his child.

Though descended from "simple shopkeepers . . . members of the lowest acceptable stratum of bourgeois Parisian society," Ernest Boulanger was a professor of singing and violin at the Paris Conservatory—his wife was one of his students—a winner of the Prix de Rome, a successful minor composer, and a friend of Massenet, Ambroise Thomas, Saint-Saëns, and Gounod, who visited the Boulanger home and with whom Ernest was on *tu-toi* terms. Less is known of his St. Petersburg–born wife, who, unlike Ernest, had already been married, and who claimed descent from Russian aristocracy.

Raïssa must be held responsible for Nadia's class-consciousness and her lifelong boast that her mother was a princess. Raïssa, a strict taskmistress and disciplinarian whose pattern Nadia seems to have emulated, dominated the household until her death in 1935.

Nadia's father tutored her in piano and solfeggio until she was old enough, at age nine, to be admitted to the Conservatory. The outstanding event of the next seven years was her acceptance in the composition class of Gabriel Fauré, beginning her close association with him, to the point where he trusted her to substitute for him at the organ of La Madeleine. Believing that Nadia possessed a composer's talent, Fauré was disappointed when she forsook this pursuit. At sixteen, after graduating and winning all of the first prizes, she became the protégée of the fifty-two-year-old Raoul Pugno, pianist and composer, with whom she gave concerts, and whom she assisted for the remaining decade of his life. He helped her to enter the professional world, where she encountered formidable opposition in long-established traditions against women. Pugno lived in Montmartre but spent his summers in Gargenville, where the Boulangers followed him. They did not return to Montmartre, however, but moved instead to 36, rue Ballu, Nadia's home for the remainder of her life.

When her father died, Nadia, age twelve, was obliged to contribute to the support of her mother and six-year-old sister, Lili, who soon became the central figure in Nadia's life. Lili's musical endowments had manifested themselves in infancy, through her remarkable ear, and she soon outshone Nadia in every way, "learning in months what had taken her older sister years to master." Lili's gift for composition, unlike Nadia's, was immediately acclaimed, and she was the first woman to win the Prix de Rome, for which Nadia had competed unsuccessfully year after year. The sisters were inseparable, and the press treated them as a family phenomenon, but their temperaments were wholly dissimilar, Nadia being haughty, aggressive, and masculine, Lili charming, passive, and feminine. A more important contrast was that Nadia had a robust constitution, living to age ninety-two, whereas the frail and sickly Lili died at twenty-five after years of semi-invalidism. (Recent research seems to indicate that physical weakness is frequently found in the children of aged fathers: a still younger Boulanger child died in infancy.)

No rivalry between the sisters was ever apparent, and Nadia quickly adopted a protective attitude toward her sibling. The story of Lili's life in music, and of the perpetuation of her name by Nadia, is the subject of another book by the same author.[2] Nevertheless, the relationship must be examined here from Nadia's standpoint, since her *raison d'être* became the promotion of the legend of Lili's genius. Nadia reminded the world of the tragedy, observing it on each anniversary of her sister's death, and establishing the Lili Boulanger Fund. This was supported by concerts and publicized by the awarding of composition prizes in her name for music supposedly judged by Stravinsky but in truth merely rubber-stamped following Nadia's decisions. The question remains: Is the received picture of Nadia's feelings about Lili the true one? Wouldn't the older sister naturally have resented the very existence of the younger and have envied her successes? What assumptions can rightly be made from the remarks of observers about Nadia's frequent absences from the bedside of her dying sister? In keeping Lili's name alive, Nadia was also helping her own, though the motive may not have been conscious, and who would accuse Nadia of self-interest, instead of praising her undying devotion? Yet the extent of her torchbearing is slightly suspect. Lili's immortality was as much a part of Nadia's career as teaching and spreading the gospel according to Stravinsky.

Léonie Rosenstiel supplies some but not all of the keys to Nadia Boulanger's complex character. As with most people,

2. *The Life and Works of Lili Boulanger* (East Brunswick, N.J., 1978).

each of her positive qualities is matched by a negative one. Moreover, readers with personal experience will draw widely differing conclusions. The present reviewer, who knew Nadia as an acquaintance, not as a student, retains impressions that are sometimes at variance with the book and are admittedly influenced by Stravinsky, whose letters to Nadia in the later years do not conceal his disapproval of her less admirable traits.

One of these is snobbery. She was disingenuous even about her father's side, implying that she was related to General Georges Boulanger. Moreover, she courted the rich and titled. Her morning *musicales* were attended by prominent figures from the banking world and by potentates, both deposed (Queen Marie-José of Italy) and still reigning (Pierre de Polignac of Monaco). True, the Princess Edmond de Polignac and her niece, the Countess Jean (née Lanvin), were musicians, which made Nadia's appointment as *maître de chapelle* to the court on the Grimaldi gambling rock practically inevitable. In America Nadia tended to stay with the Blisses at Dumbarton Oaks, the Forbses at Gerry's Landing, and the Sachses at Santa Barbara. During the Camelot era, Nadia's friends wangled a White House luncheon invitation for her, French culture presumably providing the meeting ground.

Not surprisingly, Nadia placed great store by academic and other honors, avidly collecting degrees, prizes, scrolls, and medals. When by 1932 she had not been awarded the Légion d'honneur, she campaigned until she received it. Ms. Rosenstiel observes that Nadia's "inner ambition clashed with her outward humility," an insight that may conflict with the one-hundred-percent piety of this devout Roman Catholic, as does her tolerance of sexual relationships of a kind forbidden by the church. Nadia's faith is not in question, but in proselytizing and in actually converting non-Catholics she exceeded her role as a music teacher. Her pupils included nuns, monks, and priests, and she regularly went to convents on retreats.

Ms. Rosenstiel quotes from a letter sent from the Fontainebleau School in 1948 to a board member in the United States, but she does not deal frankly with the contents:

Last summer there was an over-large proportion of first-generation American Jews. . . . We are not adverse [*sic*] to Jews and negroes in a limited proportion, for they are often talented, but let this proportion be kept within bounds.

The sender's name is not supplied, or any more of the background than that "some members [of the French faculty were] unhappy about the ethnic and racial composition of their classes." Thus Nadia is absolved—until, three paragraphs later, we read that she "administered the Conservatoire like a total autocrat," and is therefore unlikely to have been unaware of the contents of the letter. Ms. Rosenstiel also writes that, "given a choice between a Jew and a Catholic of equal but unspectacular talent, Nadia would opt to teach the latter." Nadia's failure to program Copland's *Vitebsk* in Paris is attributed to a wave of anti-Semitism, oddly described here as a "fashionable international prejudice of the era"—as if anti-Semitism were not far deeper than fashion, and as if any "era" since C.E., A.D., or even before (if the Bible is to be believed) were free of this prejudice.

Nadia was tyrannical with her students, and the most vulnerable brought out the despot in her. She developed a severe manner from the very beginning of her teaching career, sometimes reducing her female pupils to tears and even pulling their hair, thus instilling fear along with respect, a combination that she sought throughout her life. She was possessive of her charges to a psychologically dangerous degree, and they worshipped her as a guru, except for the few who rebelled and departed. Though Nadia regarded Annette Dieudonné and Marcelle de Manziarly as among her "best friends," these two seemed more like slaves, at least to the present reviewer. Nadia was quick to take offense at supposed slights and was notoriously vindictive, as in the case of Ravel, who failed to answer a letter, and in that of Bartók, who did answer but too tersely to satisfy her. Both composers were stricken from her orbit.

Nadia's famous thoughtfulness in remembering important dates in her friends' lives, especially of family deaths, is also open to another interpretation than that of kindness. The condolences to Stravinsky on the anniversaries of the deaths of his first wife and daughter, for instance, seemed both morbid and intrusively moralistic (reminding the recipient of his duty to mourn).

Ms. Rosenstiel is at her best when describing the sexist bias of French institutions and social observances of the time, and Nadia's struggle to overcome the obstacles they presented. Unmarried Frenchwomen were officially declared old maids on their twenty-fifth birthdays, and on Saint Catherine's Day were entitled to parade through Paris wearing high, starched lace headdresses. Nadia's decision to participate in this primitive ritual may have been her way of announcing her espousal of music rather than of man. Less quaint discrimination was practiced in the universities, where some courses, even in music, were sexually segregated if not actually closed to women. Female music teachers received only half the salary of males. When Nadia first conducted symphony orchestras, she was treated rudely simply because of her sex. Even so, after participating in concerts in 1921 for the Union des Femmes Professeurs et Compositeurs de Musique and for the Ligue Française pour les Droits des Femmes, she took no part in feminist movements, actually declaring that women were too unsophisticated to have been given the franchise. Asked if a man could conduct *Petrushka* better than a woman, she replied affirmatively, yet she thought that women were quicker than men to perceive talent in others.

Those who read this book for enlightenment on the subject of Mlle Boulanger's sex life will find out little more than what was already obvious: that she was a very mannish woman, and that her students included disproportionately large numbers of both male and female homosexuals. The scraps of gossip about her alleged affairs with men prove nothing. An attraction to Camille Mauclair is touched upon, but the poet, out of loyalty to his mistress (rather than to his wife), did not reciprocate. A student remembered having overheard Alfred Cortot exclaim, "Look, Nadia, I love my wife!" But is this evidence of an involvement with Nadia?

Although sexual typecasting by appearance and mannerisms is hazardous, no one could deny that Nadia cultivated a masculine image. Her early adoption of tenebrous man-tailored clothes may be ascribed to a need for protective coloration, the young teacher's need to appear older and serious. At one time, she sported a monocle and fell into "the habit of locking her thumbs in the vest pockets of her somber suits." Ms. Rosenstiel believes that Nadia's Catholicism would have made "overt lesbianism . . . unlikely, even if she had felt any such inclinations," but to speculate on the covert is unwise, since survivors may yet come forward. Once, in class, Nadia blurted out that she was "just as much a woman as anyone [*sic*] else"—a *cri de coeur*, perhaps, but one that would scarcely certify her as hetero-, homo-, or even AC-DC.

The book's account of the relationship between Nadia and Stravinsky is far from adequate, since her championship of him and his public recognition of it are her main claims to a niche in the history of modern music.[3] Yet the book does not even mention their last reunions (in Paris, in November

3. Nadia Boulanger must be credited with certain improvements in the *Symphony of Psalms*. First, she convinced Stravinsky to redistribute the syllables of "Al-le-lui-a" (as he had written it) to "Al-le-lu . . . i-a." Second, by drawing Stravinsky's attention to the very slow tempo of his recording at 20 in the third movement, she seems to have influenced him to change the metronome at 22 to a half-note equals 37, and to add the word "Largo." Two of her other corrections should be followed in performance: at one measure before 13 in the first movement, the contraltos should sing B (not C) on the first note; and in the third measure of 28 in the last movement, the C's should have sharps. They are found in the original sketches; Stravinsky inserted the sharps in his score on October 1, 1931, then deleted them, perhaps because his first recording inadvertently omitted them. In other scores marked by him, the sharps are restored.

1968) or any encounter after 1956, and that one only in connection with a curious story. After the premiere of the *Canticum Sacrum* that year, Nadia is said to have remarked to her class that "this serial music does not work." But since her conclusions about the piece expressed to others contradict this, the reader deserves to be told who heard her say it. Ms. Rosenstiel thinks that Nadia may have felt some animus toward Stravinsky when, on the death of Paul Dukas in 1935, she did not inherit his chair as professor of composition at the Ecole Normale until Stravinsky was named her co-professor. She may have rankled when *Le Monde Musical* reported: "Further enhanced by the assistance of one of the greatest geniuses of our epoch, there is no doubt that Mlle Nadia Boulanger's composition class will soon be one of the most famous in the world." Yet Nadia herself had begged Stravinsky to "supervise" her classes, and a Geiger counter could not discover any trace of resentment in her correspondence with the composer concerning the matter, or, indeed, any other feeling than jubilation over what she clearly understood was a stupendous coup. (His letters are much less enthusiastic.)

The account of Stravinsky and Valéry at Nadia's Gargenville home in September 1939 is also misleading. Ms. Rosenstiel says that Valéry regarded Stravinsky's Norton lectures as "nothing less than philosophical plagiarism" and suspected Nadia of having helped him to write them. But the helping hand was that of Roland-Manuel, a messianic Jew whose philosophy was at the opposite extreme from that of the agnostic author of *Monsieur Teste*. (Nadia was in America, March to June, when the lectures were composed.) Valéry refers to the matter in a notebook, as well as in a letter to Gide: "Stravinsky read us his future *Cours de Poétique* (he too!) *Musicale*, which contains analogies with mine—something very curious." The allusion is to the emphasis on the artist as maker, a subject on which Valéry was then lecturing at the Collège de France, but also one very close to Stravinsky's mind since his friendship with C.-F. Ramuz a quarter of a century earlier.

Still another episode involving Stravinsky is told from a distorting angle, one worth correcting because it casts new light on Nadia. This is Ms. Rosenstiel's account of the way in which Nadia secured the commission for him to compose the *Dumbarton Oaks* Concerto—accurately told here except for the omission of the composer's annoyance with her for failing to press for his payments. The publisher of the piece, a friend of hers, advised Stravinsky to secure a contractual prerogative to conduct the premieres in the major American cities, lest "Nadia grab them for herself." Whatever the truth, Stravinsky and Nadia were at their closest in the year that she spent near him in California during World War II.

The major defect of *Nadia Boulanger: A Life in Music* is the lack of documentation and the failure to identify sources. Even direct quotes are unattributed, despite the nearly three hundred individuals and half as many more libraries and newspaper files named in the acknowledgments. Another shortcoming is that where Nadia or one of her pupils has overlooked an event, it does not appear in this record, which may explain why neither the Paris festival of May 1952 nor the 1964 Berlin trip is mentioned, though the former much impressed her. Still more surprising is the absence of a bibliography of Nadia's writings, a discography of her recordings, and an index to her Edition Boulanger transcriptions of Monteverdi.

Yet these lapses must be excused in gratitude for the very moving description of the later, tragic years when, well aware that all she stood for was being ridiculed by pupils of Messiaen, she continued, with indomitable courage, to teach the highest ideals of her art.

Virgil Thomson

From the autumn of 1940 to the end of World War II, Virgil Thomson was the man of the hour in American music criticism. With his cosmopolitan standards, open-mindedness toward the new, and skill as a writer, he almost single-handedly swept away the provincialism and managerial conservatism that had been in power from the beginning of the century. The quickness of his wit and his intelligence were extraordinary; his critical ability was unrivaled. Other attributes included a thorough musical training (by no means to be taken for granted in writers on the subject), a composer's insight into the art of composition, and a long apprenticeship in that vortex of the previous two decades, Paris. But his style, lucid and easy, original and engaging, as is reaffirmed in this latest collection of his criticism,[1] was his principal asset. Virgil Thomson's place in American letters is assured.

Installed at the *New York Herald Tribune*, Mr. Thomson proceeded to question the policies of America's mightiest musical institutions; to attack the Boss Tweeds of the operatic, symphonic, and concert-management organizations; to challenge the concept of repertory and the stereotyped program; to adjust the ratings of composers (notoriously of

1. *A Virgil Thomson Reader* (Boston, 1981).

Sibelius, who never thereafter regained his 1939 Dun and Bradstreet); and to dissolve the nimbuses of the most worshipped conductors (while taking sides with other conductors against their boards of directors). More important than any of these reforms was Mr. Thomson's championship of American music, which, he told his readers, should be regarded as part of our national wealth.

Best of all, Mr. Thomson was a practical man who proposed specific measures to implement his revolution. He said that new music, American, European, or any other kind, must be presented in carefully planned surroundings:

> A new work may not be the most important piece on the program; but unless it is the determining item in the choice of the whole program, it will always sound like second-rate music, because it is pretty certain to be placed in unfair glamour competition with the classics of repertory.

Unfortunately, too little attention has been paid to this advice, and today, more than ever, the new piece, especially in subscription concerts, is the throwaway.

Even though "the musical scene," as Mr. Thomson titled a collection of his writings, appears to be in ever greater disarray, neither his ideals nor his nostrums can be held responsible, though some of these may seem a bit wayward. Thus, Erik Satie may well be this century's only considerable composer with a new aesthetic. But surely musical substance, in which Satie's work is exceedingly thin, is more important than aestheticism, and his fun-and-games legacy has dubious value.

That Mr. Thomson is a Francophile must be taken into account when one is reading him on the music of Milhaud and the virtues of Gallic performers. But a soupçon of exaggeration *was* needed, given the overwhelmingly German-oriented academic atmosphere in which the Parisian-bred critic had to function. The favoring of Monteux and the deflating of

Schnabel must have jeopardized Mr. Thomson's position at first, but his philosophy was a safety valve: "The history of music . . . is the history of its composition, not of its performance," he wrote, and he continued to focus on the work rather than on the way it was played—with the notable exception of a 1954, somewhat out-of-character essay on Casals.

Surprisingly, perhaps, in the light of Mr. Thomson's primary involvement with new music, and the larger space allotted to the "seasonal offering that seems little likely to survive the frost," his most acute observations are of the Masters —and this though he seems reluctant to discuss the familiar: only in passing does he refer to Chopin as "quite possibly the very greatest" composer of his century. In a book remarkably free of received opinions, his freshest views are of the great untouchables, and one imagines the storm that the following must have blown up in the Department of Musical Monuments:

> [The choral writing in the *Missa Solemnis*] is too loud and too high too much of the time. . . . The scoring lacks color, as does the harmony, which is limited almost entirely to its architectural function. . . . There seems to be no satisfactory way of making this work sound less like a tempest over the Atlantic and more like a piece of music comparable in intrinsic interest to any of the same composer's symphonies.

The essay "Mozart's Leftism" should be read first by those not particularly interested in starting with autobiographical material and examples of early music criticism:

> *Don Giovanni* is the most humane and tolerant piece about sacred and profane love that anybody has ever written. . . . It is the world's greatest opera and the world's greatest parody of opera. It is a moral entertainment so movingly human that the morality gets lost before the play is scarcely started. . . . It is the work of a Christian man who knew all about the new doctrinaire ideas and respected them . . .

and who belonged to a humanitarian secret society. . . .
His life was the most unspeakable slavery; he wrote as a
free man. He was not a liberal; he was liberated.

Mr. Thomson is no less perceptive about Verdi, whose
Requiem is "gaudy, surprising, sumptuous, melodramatic,
and grand" and to whom "one is more often tempted . . . to
take off one's hat to his triumphs of pure musical theater
than one is to bare one's head before any revelations of the
subtleties of human sentiment or the depths of the human
heart." Some years later, Mr. Thomson concluded that Verdi
is "just possibly an equal" to Wagner, while, of course,
"Mozart remains a greater composer" than either.

As for Wagner, Mr. Thomson's position was original, indeed, at the furthest remove from any that most of today's
critics would take, or dare to take:

> What continues to fascinate this writer is not Wagner's
> music but Wagner the man. A scoundrel and a charmer he
> must have been such as one rarely meets. Perfidious in
> friendship, ungrateful in love, irresponsible in politics,
> utterly without principle in his professional life . . . he was
> everything the bourgeois . . . longed to worship in the
> artist. . . . His wit was incisive and cruel; his polemical
> writing was . . . aimed usually below the belt. . . . His in-
> tellectual courage and . . . plain guts . . . are nonetheless
> breathtaking. . . .
>
> The music remains . . . and it is available at virtually
> every opera house in the world. . . . But what your reviewer
> would like most of all is to have known the superb and fan-
> tastic Wagner himself.

Mr. Thomson is at his best in defining the reviewer's job,
and his relations with composers and performers. The
editorial-style articles on this misunderstood aspect of musical
life show much good sense and fairness, as when he writes of
himself (in the third person):

When another composer's music is unfavorably reviewed,
. . . he knows that . . . the reviewer has done his best. But
when his own . . . receives such a review he tries to convince
himself . . . that the reviewer is ignorant, stupid, and very
probably in the pay of some enemy.

Mr. Thomson admits:

The artist can perfectly well do without criticism. . . . The
composing fool thinks the press is out to get him, does not
realize that he is merely grist for its mill. . . . The reviewing fool thinks he can make his fame by praising successful
performers and dead composers. . . .

Reviewing performances of familiar music takes up the
largest part of a critic's week. It is also the easiest part. Reviewing new pieces is the hardest and the most important,
for that is where criticism touches history.

In another piece, Mr. Thomson reminds the reader:

Dead music is very beautiful sometimes and always pretty
noble, even when it has been painted up and presented by
the undertakers who play or conduct it with such solemnity
at our concerts. Live music is never quite that beautiful.

Mr. Thomson's code for reviewers requires that they never
lower the artist's dignity, and he points out that it is not their
right "to grant or withhold degrees." Above all, "the poorest
performance does not justify a poorly written review."
    Mr. Thomson's own reviews are consistently perhaps the
best written in any of the arts during the decade when he was
such a force in American cultural life. What might have
seemed an affectation in someone else—such as the frequent
opener, "Myself I think . . ."—is in his case simple candor and
directness. So is his language, well seasoned with the vernacu-

lar: the rendition of a piece by Liszt was "the berries"; other performances were "peppy" and "swell"; and a pianist "sassed" the critics. He makes telling effect with a cliché (the loudness of Monteux's horns "is bright, not heavy; it is a flash of light rather than a ton of bricks") and disarms his readers with asides ("I got to thinking," and "Well, all that is all that"). True, he does overwork the epithets "first-class" and "the boys"—"the Philharmonic boys," "the electronic boys," "the Harvard boys," "the taste boys," and so on—but this is nit-picking.

The later reviews lack the urgency of the red-hot stuff written for the *Trib*, no doubt because Mr. Thomson was no longer at the center. His analyses after the first years are not always illuminating, as when he writes that four of Schoenberg's Five Pieces for Orchestra are composed "almost wholly of phrases consecrated by Vienna to waltz usage," and that atonality is "the consistent employment of contradicting chromatics." Others have attributed this falling-off to a change of influences from Paris to Vienna, though the latter, meaning the Schoenberg school, arguably began its worldwide ascendancy in the former, in Messiaen's classes toward the end of World War II.

Mr. Thomson has managed to keep abreast of today's far more diversified American scene, and to report on it as open-mindedly as ever. But then, his catholicity encompasses nearly all music, indigenous, improvised, and composed, except for the products "of synthesizers and computers because in thirty years no striking repertory has been developed." No one can like everything, however, and the reader suspects that Mr. Thomson's evident interest in, say, the personality and pursuits of John Cage would seem to preclude a similar concern with the music of Milton Babbitt. (Mr. Thomson declares in one article that "there is no abstract music," but three pages later says of a Babbitt quartet that "at its least concentrated it goes a bit abstract.") Furthermore, the music of a composer-critic inevitably reveals something of his own tastes.

Sometimes Mr. Thomson's most offhand remarks come close to a truth but fail to develop his point, as when he writes that the "twelve-tone row . . . is merely a rule of thumb to make atonal writing easy," and that "an interesting complexity cannot be faked." Here the first statement requires elaboration, while the worthwhile premise of the second is not proved by his subjective example: "The complexity of Xenakis's music is real. . . . It would not sound so handsome otherwise. . . ."

Recently Mr. Thomson's brand of criticism has been supplanted by an altogether different and, to this reviewer, much less attractive and vital one, that of mandarin musicology, the writings for each other of academics who want the public to believe that it is musical scholarship that matters, not living music. Whereas Mr. Thomson kept us informed about events in the marketplace, told us what composers were doing, and predicted shifts in the wind, his successors (present company included) merely review books about historical forms and figures.

A Virgil Thomson Reader includes generous selections from his 1966 autobiography and from his 1971 summary of American music since 1910. These have not been discussed here for the reasons that Mr. Thomson's importance as a critic is so much greater than as a memoirist and chronicler, and because both volumes are in print and deserve to be read in their entirety, the former especially on his experience in film music. One of the highlights of the present book is the article "Hollywood's Best":

> Wherever Copland has provided landscape music, action music, or a general atmosphere of drama he has worked impeccably. Wherever he has essayed to interpret the personal and private feelings of Miss Loy, he has . . . stopped the action, killed the story, exactly as Miss Loy herself has done at those moments. His music at such times goes static and introspective, becomes, for dramatic purposes, futile.

In any case, samples of the Thomson autobiographical manner occur in the *Reader* in such gems as "I have never been psychoanalyzed, so I have no guilt."

Mr. Thomson's *Herald Tribune* reviews have survived the test of forty years and now belong to the small library of permanent music criticism. The following, for example, from 1942, is as pertinent today as it was on the day it was written:

> Orchestral conducting [has changed] from a matter of culture and of its personal projection into something more like engineering. Young conductors don't bother much anymore to feel music or to make their musicians feel it. . . . Poetry . . . [is] left for the last, to be put in as with an eyedropper or laid on like icing, if there is time.

But the book is full of quotables, making it difficult for the reviewer to choose the best, as between a reference to "a fifteen-minute [orchestral] footnote" in *Die Walküre* and some advice to song composers to "work closer to poetry," since "a good melody is not just a new suit. It must be a new skin, inseparable."

Congratulations and long life to Virgil Thomson on his eighty-fifth!

Testaments
from Shostakovich
and Prokofiev

A' bears the third part of the world, man . . .

Antony and Cleopatra

And art made tongue-tied by authority . . .

Sonnet 66

The following comments on *Testimony*,[1] Solomon Volkov's presentation of some of Dmitri Shostakovich's opinions, confessions, and recollections, were provoked by three events occurring within one week in November 1979: the refusal of the Soviet embassy in Bern to allow a microfilm of the 1917 manuscript of Stravinsky's *Les Noces* to be sent from a Swiss library to a musician in the USSR for a concert that was to have taken place in Moscow on December 6; the publication in the November 14 issue of the Moscow weekly *Literaturnaya gazeta* of a letter signed by six friends and pupils of Shostakovich denouncing Volkov's text as a forgery; and, at

1. *Testimony: The Memoirs of Dmitri Shostakovich*, as related to and edited by Solomon Volkov, translated by Antonina W. Bouis (New York, 1979).

long last, the appearance of an informed criticism of the book, Simon Karlinsky's in *The Nation*, November 24. Professor Karlinsky has also pinpointed other shortcomings of *Testimony*, but the main one is that first-person "memoirs" written by a second person must inevitably result in confusing obliquity.

The first of these provocations, the senseless banning of a musical score, merely serves as a reminder that the Stalin-period establishment still reigns over Soviet musical life. The second, the letter in the *Gazeta*, might seem to require no answer, since the reasons stated therein for condemning the book prove that the signatories have not even seen it; nor are they, or anyone else in the USSR, likely to be allowed to read so powerful an indictment of Soviet cultural tyranny. But the letter must be protested, if only for its argument that although the 1948 campaign against Shostakovich's "formalism" was "unjustified," he "courageously put up with the unfounded charge and in his music again and again showed his greatness. [Moreover], in 1958, the Communist Party's Central Committee formally removed the accusation." In other words, the official censure, the second of three, this one lasting a mere ten years, could not have been of any great consequence to Shostakovich, since he managed to stay alive and even to work! The question of possible damage to him is immaterial, therefore, and these brutal and humiliating assaults can hardly be blamed for the state of mind of a man who says:

> I'm certain that everyone is staring at me, that they're all whispering and watching me behind my back, and that they're all waiting for me to fall, or at least to trip. . . . I'm drawn to people . . . yet if I were to become invisible, I'd be happier. I think that this is a recent problem. Once upon a time I derived pleasure from appearing in public. . . . [Now] I'm afraid to go out. I'm terrified to be seen. I feel fragile, breakable.

Solomon Volkov's Shostakovich is the most humanly likable
of composers. And he is endowed with an insightful mind,
which is by no means self-evident from his music:

> Someone called up [the *Komsomolskaya pravda*] once and
> wanted to know why that day's paper didn't have a poem by
> Mayakovsky. "He's on vacation," they explained. "All right,
> but who's replacing him?" . . . The psychology is that every
> creative figure must have a replacement.

Volkov's Shostakovich has an appealing wit, too, and this was
not even suspected from his music, in which the playful passages are often the most painful:

> Zhdanov announced: "The Central Committee of Bolshe-
> viks demands beauty and refinement from music . . . ,"
> [but] our music was crude and vulgar, and listening to it
> undoubtedly destroyed the psychological and physical bal-
> ance of a man, for example a man like Zhdanov.

> Lenin in his "political will" said that Stalin had only one
> fault—rudeness. . . . Everything else was in good shape.

> Stalin could stand neither [*Hamlet* nor *Macbeth*]. Why? It
> seems fairly obvious. A criminal ruler—what could attract
> [Stalin] in that theme? . . . Pangs of conscience and guilt
> and all that. *What* guilty conscience?

Some of the drollest parts of the book are in Shostakovich's
account of plagiarism among Soviet composers. For example,
he felt certain that if he had died before his Fourth Symphony had been played, it would have appeared as the Second Symphony of Tikhon Khrennikov, head of the Composer's Union.

As a victim of a political and social system, Shostakovich
cannot be compared to any artist of the past, for he was subject not only to the judgments and decrees of his inferiors,
professional and otherwise, but also to their interference with

the content of his music. His position was far worse than that of Mozart, whom the archbishop could kick with impunity, but whose string quartets and symphonies were not "corrected" for their "ideology." Since much of *Testimony* is concerned with the effects of state control of the arts on a creative individual, readers must constantly remind themselves that Shostakovich was the first artist of world reputation who spent his entire life on Animal Farm. Political wisdom and artistic achievement do not generally go together, however, and Shostakovich's case is no exception. Understandably, he lacks a historical sense, as when he contends that art cannot flourish in tyrannies. This is true of some modern brands, but not generally, since many "enlightened" Renaissance princes, versed in Platonic ideas of freedom and justice, surrounded by buildings, sculpture, and paintings that express man's highest concepts, nevertheless ruled despotically and with uncontested power of life and death over their subjects. Shostakovich's social philosophy is moral rather than political. He believes that art should represent a people and cannot represent a nation, which is simply an arbitrary political unit. A national art is a contradiction in terms.

The authenticity of *Testimony* has been challenged. Proof of Volkov's veracity, however, surely lies in the very absence of endorsements by Rostropovich and other defectors in a position to confirm or deny episodes in the book, but who may still fear reprisals. The genuineness of Volkov's overall presentation will ultimately be shown by the inimitable character of his hero, whose voice, in *Testimony*, is that of a natural writer. If this is not Shostakovich speaking, then Volkov will soon have to produce other books. His preface, introduction, and notes are the work of a different person, noticeable in the main text, perhaps, in certain axe-grinding passages. But then, the continuous narrative of this book could hardly have been stitched together out of verbatim quotations from Shostakovich.

Professor Karlinsky reasons that Volkov's "musicological

expertise and his well-documented closeness to Shostakovich"
should give us confidence that Volkov "actually wrote down
what Shostakovich told him." Karlinsky then cites two important sections that Shostakovich had already published in
earlier books, which Volkov fails to acknowledge. And concerning Volkov's "musicological expertise," the less said the
better, at least on the evidence of the present book. He claims
that a piece by Shostakovich "harshly depicts the execution of
defenseless people with naturalistic authenticity," but does
not explain *how* the music conveys so explicit a depiction.
("Do you see yonder cloud that's almost in shape of a camel?
. . . Methinks it is like a weasel. . . . Very like a whale.")

Volkov's "closeness" to Shostakovich, moreover, is not
really "well documented." His widow, Irina, has testified that
the two men saw each other "no more than three or four
times." Other observers assert that, in the last years, meetings
were frequent, which is still no guarantee of "closeness."
Mme Shostakovich is also nonplussed by the possibility that
Volkov gathered material of book length from her husband.
But much of the book's substance was obviously obtained
indirectly and at several removes—just as were many of
Shostakovich's own stories, such as the one about Prokofiev's obnoxious behavior in a class of Rimsky-Korsakov.
Undoubtedly the book owes much to Boris Tischenko,
Shostakovich's favorite pupil, who introduced Volkov to the
master, who signed the *Gazeta* letter, and who was probably
less-than-politely interrogated.

Unfortunately, Volkov is careless about factual matters.
The chronology meanders, and he rarely gives precise dates.
More seriously, he fails to note the discrepancies between
Shostakovich's and other people's versions of events, as Soviet
biographers will be quick to point out. But the book as a
whole is inadequately annotated, while those footnotes that
Volkov does provide are not free from mistakes. Worst of
all, his *parti pris* is too apparent. If only for his own protection, he should have mentioned examples of Shostakovich's

music criticism in which his views obviously *do* conform to those of the party line, such as the May 31, 1964, article in *Pravda* calling "dodecaphonic and serial music . . . one of the great evils of twentieth-century art."

Volkov should also have tried to explain some of the text's many mysterious absences. At one place, Shostakovich alludes to Mme Furtseva (the Minister of Culture), or so Volkov identifies the reference. But since she played a role of major importance in the composer's life, he must have had some feelings, as well as inside information, about her fall from power and Roman-style wrist-slashing death—announced in *Pravda*, with no details, on the same day as the obituary for David Oistrakh.

And in the summer of 1976, in New York, when Volkov called on Vera Stravinsky, after publishers had requested her to read the manuscript, why did he not ask her to verify the story of the Moscow meeting between Stravinsky and the musicologist Boris Yarustovsky? According to Shostakovich, "Stravinsky offered his walking stick instead of his hand to one of these hypocrites [Yarustovsky], who was forced to shake it, proving that he was the real lackey." But this is a gross misinterpretation. Stravinsky, extending his cane for help in climbing some stairs, was quite unaware that one of his Soviet biographers was on the other end of it. The composer often made this gesture—for example, in stepping out of an automobile—but never insultingly. The truth is that he did not recognize Yarustovsky—and, incidentally, did not read his book, simply acknowledging its receipt on a calling card dated January 16, 1965.

Shostakovich "treats Solzhenitsyn with scorn because of his messianism and supposed religious fanaticism," Professor Karlinsky writes, and it is true that Shostakovich disdained the religious beliefs of almost everyone. But it seems to me that the particular grievance here is the inflating of Solzhenitsyn to an—in the composer's words—"overwhelming genius." Professor Karlinsky is also troubled by Shostakovich's

incomprehensible reference to Glazunov as "a great musician." What was meant, I think, is that Glazunov had a freak-
ishly keen ear, a phenomenal memory, and exceptional skill
in improvisation—all gifts of the virtuoso, perhaps more
rarely of the composer. Shostakovich does not rank Glazunov's
music as more than second-rate, admitting, at one place, that
his symphonies are boring. Nevertheless, Shostakovich's portrait of Glazunov is the high point of *Testimony*, a character
study that goes directly to the man's unique and interesting
qualities without overlooking or minimizing his weaknesses.

Shostakovich's best anecdote involves Maria Yudina, a brilliant pianist, a scandalously outspoken "dissident," and the
composer's school friend, of whom he says that "for her, the
ocean was only knee-deep." It seems that Stalin heard her
broadcast performance of a Mozart piano concerto and asked
for her recording of it. Since none existed, one was made in a
single day, a record in two senses. Stalin sent 20,000 rubles to
her, and she responded in a letter, which said something like
the following:

> I thank you Iosif Vissarionovich. . . . I will pray for you
> day and night and ask the Lord to forgive your sins. . . . I
> gave the money to the church. . . .

Nothing happened to Yudina, and it is reported that her
Mozart was on a turntable in Stalin's dacha when he was
found dead. (More than anyone else, this valiant old lady was
responsible for Stravinsky's 1962 visit to the USSR. In March
of that year, undecided about the trip, he wrote to a friend:
"But if I do not go, I shall hurt many people for whom my
presence there is not just a wish but vital—especially Yudina.")

Volkov has not been well served by his translator. The
book contains wildly incorrect meanings, and it is largely
written in American slang. Thus Shostakovich refers to a
Hamlet "screwing [Ophelia]. And she, pregnant, got drunk
and drowned herself"; mentions someone whose "popularity

peaked"; uses such expressions as "come off it," "phony," "con man," and "brouhaha"—all of which, needless to say, clash with our conception of the composer's dignity. The Russian and American languages are equally rich in slang, but slang is always local, temporary, untranslatable. A more formal, even if stilted, vocabulary would have been preferable.

Was Shostakovich a great composer? Not by any criteria of innovation in the language and style of music, or by virtue of extraordinary powers of invention. But the question that readers really want to ask is whether Shostakovich was *potentially* a great composer, stifled by a political system. The First Symphony, written when he was nineteen (1926), seemed to hold some such promise, as did, retrospectively, the transcendent final pages of the Fourth Symphony (1936), the opus that had to be withheld for twenty-five years.

The answer, of course, is that the history of what did happen is sufficiently difficult to understand, let alone adding the history of what might have been. The music that Shostakovich wrote does not exhibit a wide range of emotions. It depends on simple contrasts of the lyrical and the dramatic, the elegiac and the grotesque, the solemn and the "impudent." In some of the early postwar works, such as the Eighth Quartet and the Adagio of the Ninth, an intensity of feeling and concentration are evident, but not a strong shaping hand. The ideas are worked to death, the forms, with their clichés of crescendo and climax, tend to sprawl, and the substance is thin, maddeningly so, for instance, in the dialogue between bassoon and bass voice in the fourth movement of "Babi Yar." Finally, the music lacks rhythmic invention—the repetition of snare-drum patterns is excruciating—and the harmonic palette, though not closed to experiment, is conventional. Novelty occurs only in sonority and instrumentation, and the best of this may be in the first movement of the First Symphony.

. . .

If Shostakovich's memoirs are a document of importance in modern Russian history, those of Prokofiev[2] are a contribution of comparable value to Russian literature. Prokofiev's autobiography of his early years is by far the best that I know of by any composer, and the book unexpectedly changes the stature of the man. Some parallels between the two composers may be worth noting: both were students of Glazunov (Prokofiev not privately, but in a class), prodigies who never surpassed their spectacular beginnings, and victims of exploitation and control by the autocratic system. Above all, the musical styles of both contain numerous resemblances; but this is a subject in itself. As for opposites, Prokofiev very unwisely believed that "politics do not concern me."[3] The chief difference, however, is that the personality of Shostakovich was heretofore completely closed, that of Prokofiev wide open—for which reason the discovery of so engaging a narrator in this book is such a surprise.

Prokofiev by Prokofiev has not received due attention, no doubt for the reason that the story breaks off in 1909, at exactly the point when the career of the mature composer begins. He is a prose writer of astonishing skill, whose picture of his boyhood and education in a Ukrainian village, and in the two great cities, can stand comparison to Vladimir Nabokov's *Speak, Memory*. It is regrettable that Prokofiev did not continue his chronicle to include his experiences during the Revolution and in the Diaghilev years, as well as to explain his disillusionment with the West and the return to Russia—where the book was written, just before and after World War II.

Music is at the center of *Prokofiev by Prokofiev*, which is not the case with *Testimony*, and quite literally, in numerous examples in music type that offer valuable lessons about the development of the fledgling composer. Prokofiev's domi-

2. *Prokofiev by Prokofiev: A Composer's Memoir,* edited by David H. Appel, translated by Guy Daniels (New York, 1979).
3. *Sergei Prokofiev: A Soviet Tragedy,* by Victor Seroff (New York, 1979), p. 167.

neering and ambitious mother evidently preserved every scrap that the child wrote, and the book contains many amusing excerpts from his attempts to evoke scenes and moods in operas that he began even before his tenth year. His mother did not regard his talents as those of a "genius," and she deliberated at length before allowing him to risk a career as a composer, meanwhile providing the best teachers for him. One of these, Reinhold Glière, came from Moscow in the summers to give the boy lessons in composition and to live with the upper-middle-class, liberal, and intellectual Prokofievs.

Sergei's mother oversaw Glière's methods in order to continue with them during the winters. With the intelligence of observation displayed on every page of this book, Prokofiev says that "her attitude towards Glière's teaching was respectful, critical—and a bit jealous." The resourcefulness of her own teaching is shown by her requirement that her son transpose the simpler pieces that he played into several keys, then name the one in which it "sounded best"—which usually elicited the answer: "The key in which it had been written." Also at an early age, Prokofiev acquired the unsympathetic habit of grading everything that he played or heard. The *Egmont* Overture received a C-minus.

Parents of musical children should read these memoirs, if only because Prokofiev makes the points that many teachers overlook. For instance, he conceives a theme, devises a simple harmonic accompaniment for it, but does not know how to fit the music into a meter. Then, after choosing one, he is uncertain about the beat on which the music should begin, or where to place the emphasis. (Prokofiev was always troubled by this problem, and his opera *Love for Three Oranges* contains a dozen instances of set pieces that end "wrongly," on the weak part of the bar.) Another valuable lesson is offered in Prokofiev's description of his reluctance to fulfill assignments from Arensky's famous textbook. After a rule had been explained, the pupil was required to invent an example employing it. He found this difficult to do, simply because the result was "of no use to anyone." Wanting to write operas with marches, storms, and complicated situations, he felt that he was "being held back."

Prokofiev can bring his governesses and teachers to life in a few phrases, or even in a single one, as in this comment on the widow of the composer Serov: "She sang her own compositions in a low tenor." And here is a picture vivified by a few memorable details:

> Before class I liked to go down to the cloakroom, which had a window looking out on the square, and watch as the figure of Rimsky-Korsakov, on his way to the Conservatory, emerged from Glinka Street at the end of the square. When the weather began to get cold, he would wear a raccoon coat—very short and not at all right for his tall figure—belted in tightly, and his beard would stick out over the high, turned-up collar of the coat. . . .
>
> When he was correcting work he would first write the note and then put a sharp or flat in front of it. (I was used to writing the sharp or flat first, then the note.)

In a sentence or two, Prokofiev relates and disposes of incidents that would lead to pages of self-analysis from anyone else: "Until I was three I was kept in a little dress—a reminder of my dead sisters." When the infant was taken near the altar in the church, a forbidden area for girls, his mother whispered to Father Andrei, " 'A boy, a boy . . .' " And there the matter is dropped.

He tells us that in his teens he was

> generally secretive in matters close to the heart, and . . . I waged my whole struggle for religion internally, letting no one know about it and not discussing the subject with anyone. . . . At home we never talked about religion, so that gradually the question faded away and ceased to be of importance. When my father died—I was nineteen at the time—my attitude towards his death was atheistic. And

the same thing was true when, at the age of twenty-two, I lost a close friend who had written me a note saying "Farewell" before his death. I was especially grief-stricken by the "Farewell" as coming from a human consciousness which had departed once and for all time.

One of our received notions about Prokofiev is that his intellectual versatility may be in part responsible for a lack of depth in his music. He could have been outstanding as a chess player, mathematician, physicist, engineer, or anything else requiring brains and control. (He used to write amusing letters—according to Stravinsky—leaving out all vowels, and at age thirteen he invented an alphabet that looks like Hittite.) But whether he might have become a greater composer is not worth the speculation. One may regret that he abandoned the radical style of the first movement of the Second Symphony, some pages of which suggest the Varèse of *Arcana*. But when the public rejected this piece, Prokofiev's response was to give the audience what it wanted. Did the cocksure, head-of-the-class, always superior person lack conviction in his art? More certainly, Prokofiev realized that a composition by a compatriot ten years older—who was still unknown while the teen-ager was being viewed as something of a new Mozart—outstripped anything that he could do: *Le Sacre du printemps.*

From the Vedas to Wagner
(and Beyond)

SHORT REVIEWS

Anyone interested in Brahmanic religious philosophy and
Vedic verse meters, as well as in ancient music, should read
Wayne Howard's *Sāmavedic Chant*.[1] Another, incidental,
subject of Mr. Howard's book is that of international drug
culture, for Sāmavedic chanting, in its ritualistic form, takes
place uniquely during sacrificial ceremonies in which liba-
tions of the juice of the soma plant are offered to the deities.

In the 1960s, Western audiences became more aware of
Indian music, thanks in large measure to such virtuoso sitar-
ists as Ravi Shankar, who influenced the Beatles and jazz
figures like John Coltrane, and in small measure to the discovery of a parallel in the strictness of note order between
some ragas and the twelve-tone series. Instrumental improvisation is easier to appreciate, however, than a species of
chanting that cannot be exported even from one jungle village to another. Furthermore, correspondence exists between
ragas and Western music, both functionally, in the seasons

1. New Haven, 1977.

and times of day at which a piece is performed (the church's canonical hours), and in structure and content: one raga scale is identical with a Western mode, and ragas are harmonic in that the solo instrument forms two-note chords with the accompanying drone part (tala).

None of this is to suggest that a true comprehension of this infinitely subtle art form is imminent in the West, but merely to say that, compared with Sāmavedic chant, the raga is as close to us as Brahms. Yet in spite of the remoteness of thirty centuries, a vestige of the power of this venerable singing, and of the presence of the past—the Kauthuma notational numerals are believed to relate to the cries of animals—can be felt by wholly uninstructed listeners.

Some readers may wonder why Mr. Howard has devoted more than a third of his book to transcriptions, since the chants have come down to us by oral tradition. The Rgveda, for instance, the oldest of the Vedic collections, containing over ten thousand verses in more than ten thousand hymns, has been preserved practically unchanged for more than three thousand years—written texts are about nine hundred years old—a scarcely believable phenomenon to the Hebrew, Protestant, and Moslem who lives by his Book. The answer is that the music can be studied only through transcriptions, even though these are transposed (to facilitate legibility) and merely approximate even in relative pitch, and convey nothing of the qualities of sound. In Mr. Howard's book the transcriptions are in a far-from-calligraphic, not to say shaky, hand, and the notation of rhythmic values is unnecessarily dense: since long notes are rare, they could have been represented by halves, instead of quarters, thereby reducing the beams from four, the most common kind, to three.

At whatever the increase in the price of this already expensive book, audiovisual cassettes should have been packaged with it, especially since the Vedic priests employ hand and finger positions (mudra) while intoning the ritual chants (stotras). One hopes that Mr. Howard's tape recordings will soon be made available commercially. Besides enlightening us, they will encourage support for the study of the chants (and of Dravidian languages)—at the University of Mysore, to name only one center concerned with the continuation of this oldest of still-living musical arts.

A suggestion: read the glossary as an introduction, though at first only a few terms, such as "matras" (temporal units) and "parrans" (the division of the chant, each sung in one breath), need be remembered.

Wagner's "Rienzi"[2] reveals more of the genesis of a Wagner opera than any other book on the composer in English—except that the quotations from his writings, and a twenty-two-page draft of the libretto, have been left in German. Briefly, Mr. Deathridge demonstrates that, in *Rienzi* at least, Wagner thought of himself as a dramatist first, a musician second, extensively rewriting the text but leaving no written evidence that he felt greater confidence in his musical than in his literary gifts. It is surprising that only two musical notations, one of them for *Rienzi,* are found in the prose drafts for all of his operas.

Wagner and *Rienzi* is a subject of general historical interest, since the opera supposedly inspired the young Hitler's worship of the composer. Hitler acquired the eight-hundred–page original manuscript, and it was apparently with him when he died, no trace of it having been found. That Cola Rienzi, the prototypical fascist, attracted both the composer and the dictator is not astonishing, but Der Führer's fondness for the opera demolishes any claims for his musical discrimination. *Rienzi* is banal, inflated, and poverty-stricken in the quality of its musical ideas. To turn from Mr. Deathridge's absorbing reconstruction of the dramatic plan of the

2. *Wagner's "Rienzi": A Reappraisal Based on a Study of Sketches and Drafts,* by John Deathridge (New York, 1978).

full work to the opera itself will disappoint even the least optimistic expectations.

On the day following the first performance (in 1842) of the seemingly endless score, Wagner marked a number of cuts. But its success with the audience had been so great that the principal singers protested, and *Rienzi* remained intact but unpublished, the composer soon disassociating himself from it. After his death, Cosima Wagner, with the help of her Bayreuth protégé Julius Kniese, tried to revise the work according to the master's later philosophy of musical theatre, omitting, in the process, everything thought not to be absolutely essential to the action, including entire choruses, repetitions of words, and even musical ornaments. The first published score (1898–99) was falsely advertised as "based on" the original, but this had not been made available, and *Rienzi* as Wagner conceived it disappeared in the *"Götterdämmerung"* as Hitler staged it.

The cast in the East German recording (Angel) is stunning, hence the stilted vocal style and the extended passages in extremely high registers are less of a torture to the ears than they might have been. Mercifully, the performance is abundantly cut.

Derek Watson's *Bruckner*[3] contains fair appraisals (i.e., in agreement with the present reviewer's) of the strengths and weaknesses of Bruckner's music, as well as clear identifications of the composer's stylistic fingerprints: the unisons, octave leaps, homemade chorale tunes; the attraction to the mediant; the preference for brass instruments (Wagner called him "the trumpet"), both single and massed. But the modern aspect of Bruckner's rhythmic constructions, such as the simultaneous threes and twos, fours and threes, in the Adagio of the Fifth Symphony, is overlooked. These antici-

3. London, 1975.

pate the Webern of *Das Augenlicht*, as do the coupling of themes with their inversions, and the exploiting of silences.

The biographical chapters are less satisfactory. Bruckner's "complexes" and intermittent insanity demand a Freudian "life," or one by specialists in numeromania (the compulsive counting of everything, even the leaves on a tree); in hopeless infatuations with teen-age girls (Olga the waitress, Ida the chambermaid, and the Lolita to whom the unsuitably old bachelor daily brought flowers); and in the obsession, whether necrophilous or archaeological, with cadavers, skulls, mortal remains.

That Couperin's *L'Apothéose de Lully* and Richard Strauss's Lully arrangements in *Le Bourgeois Gentilhomme* are better known than any music by Lully in its original form indicates the present neglect of the "founder of French opera." Except for the 1880 Leipzig edition of the complete *tragédies lyriques*, found in only a few libraries, and a handful of volumes reprinted from Henry Prunières's *Oeuvres complètes* (Paris, 1930–39), which is not a performing edition, Lully's music is virtually unavailable. Moreover, of the pieces that have been recorded, none of the performances shows an understanding of proper rhythmic execution and of the realization of *agréments*.

These musicological standards are not improved in two new releases, one of *Plaude, Laetere Gallia* (Nonesuch), the motet for the baptism of the dauphin, the other of the *Te Deum* (Erato), yet they manage to suggest something of Lully's stature. The most affecting music is in the *Te Deum*, in the solo quartet "Te ergo," with its suspensions and falling thirds, and in duets briefly reminiscent of Monteverdi. The choral and instrumental tutti—or "*tous*," as Lully wrote, disdaining his native tongue—are Handelian in pomp, if not in majesty.

The Lully bibliography in English is slender indeed, and two recent volumes, *Jean-Baptiste Lully* and *Jean-Baptiste de*

Lully and His Tragédies Lyriques,[4] particularly the latter, should attract more than the standard two-to-three-thousand readership for such publications. R. H. Scott devotes as much space to the composer's pederasty as to his music, and, by a generous selection of the ribald rhymes he inspired, contributes to the history of buggery as well as to that of opera:

> *Un jour l'Amour dit a sa mère*
> *Pourquoi ne suis-je pas vetu?*
> *Si Baptiste me voit tout nu*
> *C'en est fait de mon derrière.*

In lieu of a discussion of the music, or even of the eight *comédies-ballets* that Lully wrote with Molière, Mr. Scott repeats anecdotes, some of them surely apocryphal, about the composer's quarrels with the likes of Boileau and La Fontaine. Even the *Te Deum* is not presented as an example of the *stile concertato,* but used merely to retell the story of Lully's death (March 22, 1687), for though he danced in his ballets, sometimes with the Sun King as a partner, corybantic conducting was not yet in fashion, and, while keeping time during a performance of the *Te Deum* by tapping the floor with a stick, Lully accidentally struck his foot and died from the injury.

Joyce Newman's book is thorough and well documented, and her analyses of forms and styles in the libretti as well as the music of the thirteen *tragédies lyriques* contain observations of substance, most of them pioneering. Ms. Newman has transcribed nearly seventy pages of music.

"There is nothing I long for more intensely . . . than to be taken for a better sort of Tchaikovsky," Arnold Schoenberg wrote in 1947, "or . . . that people should know my tunes and

4. *Jean-Baptiste Lully: The Founder of French Opera,* by R. H. Scott (New York, 1977); *Jean-Baptiste de Lully and His Tragédies Lyriques* by Joyce Newman (Ann Arbor, Mich., 1979).

whistle them." This condescension would be shocking if these ambitions were not so totally unreal: Schoenberg is not likely to be taken for *any* sort of Tchaikovsky, and no "tune" by the founder of serial composition shows the slightest promise of entering the repertory of whistlers. Yet it is the overplayed Russian, rather than the neglected Viennese, who is in need of just appreciation.

Tchaikovsky is the only composer of the late nineteenth century to have contributed enduring works in every branch of his art—opera and ballet, symphony and concerto, chamber and piano music, vocal music both sacred and secular. Admittedly the distance between his best and his worst is immense, but the worst does not count, except that in his case it is the chief obstacle, together with the popularity, to a fair appraisal of his music. Thus the famous movement in the first quartet obscures its other, more accomplished ones, the crashing-cymbal finales drown out the instrumental genius, and the repetitive and bombastic symphonic developments tend to conceal the great miniaturist of the ballets.

Mr. Warrack's survey of the man and his music[5] offers some reappraisals, including a higher place for the *Manfred* Symphony. He is a fair-minded critic who tries to defend Nikolai Rubinstein's rejection of the B-flat minor Piano Concerto by the academic criteria of the time, and because of supposed weaknesses in form and construction. The reader is not persuaded. Rubinstein, one of the founders of the Moscow Conservatory, where Tchaikovsky taught, should have been able to perceive the originality, and that it outweighed the faults.

Mr. Warrack adopts another perplexing critical attitude, regretting that "Tchaikovsky's inspiration was Delibes, whom . . . he preferred to Wagner as a composer." Without Delibes, however, *Swan Lake* and *The Sleeping Beauty* might not have been written, whereas a Wagnerian Tchaikovsky is too horrible to contemplate. Perhaps for the reason

5. *Tchaikovsky*, by John Warrack (New York, 1973).

that Tchaikovsky was not a harmonic innovator, Mr. Warrack offers no examples in music type—David Brown's book[6] contains nearly one hundred of them—but his verbal descriptions of themes might better have been omitted as well, especially the anthropopathic kind:

> . . . a single melodic phrase that attempts to heave itself up painfully and on its second statement is forced to collapse back onto the original note . . .

Mr. Warrack believes that too little is known about "Tchaikovsky's psychology" and the "causes of homosexuality" to attribute his "subsequent disposition to any definite origin," though this was surely a result, at least in part, of his mother's dominating affection, her tragic death, and the child's untransferable love for her. In any event, all editions of Tchaikovsky's letters are still expurgated, since Soviet scholars both acknowledge his homosexuality and ignore it, regarding such subjects as his identification with Tatiana and his artistic exhibitionism and self-pity as suitable only for the bourgeois non-science of psychopathology.

The book's photographs of the composer in his male entourage reveal more than the text, which does not consider that his patron Mme von Meck may have broken with Tchaikovsky because stories of his profligacy had reached her ears. Tchaikovsky's affairs with youths in Florence, Tiflis, and elsewhere were not well-kept secrets, and even in St. Petersburg and Moscow scandals involving blackmail must have been known. It was following an encounter with a woman who demanded money because of his relationship with her son that Tchaikovsky drank the fatal glass of unboiled water.

The first installment of David Brown's three-volume study contains the most thorough discussion in English of the first

6. *Tchaikovsky: The Early Years, 1840–1874*, by David Brown (New York, 1979).

two symphonies, the early operas, *Romeo and Juliet,* and much other, especially little-known, music. Concerning the B-flat minor Concerto, Mr. Brown ably refutes Rubinstein's argument as presented by Mr. Warrack on the so-called shortcomings of the piece. Mr. Brown also gives an excellent account of Tchaikovsky's years as a civil servant, apprentice composer, and music critic, as well as a study of the influence of Balakirev.

Pierre Boulez's *Conversations with Célestin Deliège*[7] can be read by the general musical public without undue mental exertion. Boulez's writings are tortuous, but his talk, even though he has now devoted himself "to a complex computer language LISP,"[8] is straightforward, and, in this volume, at least, he expounds his views lucidly. Nor can these be overlooked, since he is still the foremost conductor of new music and its most widely known spokesman. In fact his writings now outnumber his compositions, which could imply that he has more to say about music than in it. The reader of this new book is stymied not by conceptual complexities or convoluted language, but by the preposterousness of the pontifications.

Boulez summarizes his musical philosophy in an autobiographical framework. True, his appraisals of his various roles may not always tally with those made by other musicians, yet when attempting to reconcile his peak-of-officialdom present with his apache past, he surveys his career with candor. He claims to have become a conductor because the new music needed one, which is true. "[I would] find it difficult to recall how I conducted in 1955," he continues, disarmingly, but "I have always had a good ear, so that I was aware of mistakes and would put them right." A half-hour with his 1955 recording of *Le Marteau sans maître* would help him to recall how

7. Foreword by Robert Wangermée (London, 1976).
8. *New York Times,* December 7, 1980.

he conducted then, as well as reveal to him the countless mistakes that he failed to correct, most evidently in the vocal part, where scarcely a note in the recorded performance corresponds to the written pitch.

Boulez's musical philosophy is the same as thirty years ago, except that Berg and Webern have exchanged places in the pantheon. Otherwise, Boulez still comprehends "progress" and "advance"—words that appear on almost every page—in terms of technical "innovation," of "expanding possibilities" and of "pushing" existing ones "to their extremes." He believes that "instrument manufacture can progress, and musical invention is bound up with it." (To assume that he means "*may* be bound up with" would be charitable but mistaken, since every speculation, opinion, and judgment in the book is delivered no less dogmatically.) How, then, does he explain the impoverishment of invention in organ music since J. S. Bach and the simultaneous progress in organ manufacture? Coincidentally, Boulez himself is a living example of an improved instrument—his keen ear and extraordinary ability to decipher the most complex scores—whose inventiveness has not kept pace with the advance in technique that he personifies.

Boulez believes that music history should be stricken from the curriculum of would-be composers, and his book is evidence that he has had little exposure to the subject himself. He writes that Beethoven's use of the Lydian mode was

> based on very vague ideas, since he did not possess the documents on medieval music that we now have. He must certainly have read a treatise on the subject, but there is no reference to any particular kind.

Documents on medieval music? Treatises on the Lydian mode? The church modes are still in use and must have been as familiar to the young Beethoven as they are to anyone today who has had a semester of traditional harmony.

Amazing, too, is the statement:

The piano is not particularly interesting in that its sonority does not vary at all; it is precisely because it is such a homogeneous and standard instrument that it is the classical one.

In the first place, the sonority of the piano changed greatly from Mozart's day to Chopin's, and, in the second, the piano is the standard—and the household—instrument not because of its sonority but because it is polyphonic, the only instrument on which the whole repertory can be played.

"History as it is made by great composers," Boulez declares, "is not a history of conservation but of destruction." Perhaps he means simply that to create something new is to destroy something old. But the great composers have also preserved, if not always in immediately recognizable ways. In a critique of "the exclusive concentration of many modern French poets endeavoring to explore the frontiers," T. S. Eliot warned:

> Emotions themselves . . . can never be merely preserved, but must always be rediscovered; and it is as much this endless battle to regain civilization, in the midst of continuous outer and inner change . . . as the struggle to conquer the absolutely new, that is the occupation of the poet.

But then, the word "emotion" is not in the Boulez vocabulary and dogma: "It is essential that musical materials should . . . advance in parallel with the evolution of the intellect." Some of Boulez's notions about history are alarming:

> Strong, expanding civilizations have no memory: they reject, they forget the past. They feel strong enough to be destructive because they know they can replace what has been destroyed. . . . I once pointed out . . . that our Western civilization would need Red Guards to get rid of a good number of statues. . . . The French Revolution decapitated

statues in churches; one may regret this now, but it was proof of a civilization on the march.

"On the March"? "Red Guards"? "Strong, expanding civilizations"? Which ones does he have in mind—Attila's? Whatever the answer, the most prominent locution in this book is "violence," which Boulez believes to be "a kind of dialectic of existence that makes it possible to progress."

For the rest, the reader will soon realize, but perhaps should be advised from the start, that in such exchanges as the following neither Boulez nor his adulatory interviewer is pulling the other's leg:

DELIÈGE: . . . this proliferation of works from a single "global" work is obviously the path that links you most directly with Mallarmé, and perhaps also with Proust; yet doesn't it also link Proust, Mallarmé, and yourself with Wagner?

BOULEZ: Without any doubt.

Paul Griffiths, music critic for the London *Times*, is well qualified to write a monograph on Pierre Boulez,[9] but what would be a formidable assignment in two hundred pages is an impossible one in only sixty-four, many of which are filled with music examples, not all of them correctly transcribed. Thus a measure of subdivided silence appears as follows:

"This notation has no meaning for performer or listener," the author writes—or for anyone else, he might have added—but "it does turn out to be necessary to the deduction of the

9. *Boulez*, by Paul Griffiths (New York, 1979).

rhythmic structure at this point." (As shown, the rests exceed $\frac{4}{4}$.)

The technical terminology also presents obstacles. Thus a vocal line is given, one that is restricted in "pitch repertory" and in which "each note is fixed in register" (is this unusual?). The author then observes that

> Harmonic limitation of this kind . . . is common in *Pli selon pli*, and is largely responsible for Boulez's success in translating so exactly Mallarmé's sense of useless activity.

Though many listeners will grant that the music successfully translates a "sense of useless activity," few will grasp the role of "harmonic limitation" in this achievement—especially since the music example is not a vertical combination but a single horizontal line. Moreover, Boulez himself employs the term "harmony" in its conventional sense:

> What worried me increasingly in my early works . . . was the absence of control over vertical structure. Harmonic encounters took place more or less by accident.

Those who still regard harmony as one of music's primary dimensions might possibly read this admission as self-damaging.

Discussing the Sonatina for flute and piano, Mr. Griffiths helpfully identifies a "privileged motif," but then muddles his point by writing that Example 3 "displays an emphatic recall of the Ex. 2 flute part in minor ninths." But the flute does not play any minor ninths in either example. Et cetera, et cetera.

Now that the Lifar draft score of *Sacre du printemps* has come to light, Professor Forte's guide to the chord structure of the piece[10] may be in need of updating. Before revisions are begun, however, his tables of the score's harmonic vocabulary should be rechecked. In the simplest category—that of chords with only four different pitches—three out of nine music examples, one of them the familiar final chord, do not match the description in Table I.

Professor Forte regards the *Sacre* as essentially "atonal," earlier analysts as essentially tonal. Boulez, for one, assumed an underlying tonic, dominant, and subdominant structure, and referred to chords in terms of triads with "appoggiaturas." Undoubtedly much of the harmony of the *Sacre* does have a triadic character in spite of extraneous pitches. But the Boulez approach was limited; it could not explain the more complex constructions and the logic of their relations. For these reasons Professor Forte's system, with its larger scope, supersedes those analyses based on the principles of classical harmony. The chapter on the *Introduction to Part Two* and the one on the *Danse sacrale* are particularly valuable.

The title of Xenia Yurievna Stravinskaya's book about her uncle, *I. F. Stravinskom i ego blizkikh,*[11] is best translated as *I. F. Stravinsky and His Intimates*—rather than "family"— since the word *blizkikh,* an adjective used as a noun, means "those close to." Yet this rendering fits neither the people featured in the book nor the author, who saw her uncle on only two occasions, both when he was in his eighties. The title, moreover, leads us to expect some information about Stravinsky's university friends. Instead of filling this gap, the book provides a portrait of the composer as Russian patriot, untainted by irony—one of his chief characteristics. The account of Stravinsky's visit to Moscow and Leningrad in 1962

10. *The Harmonic Organization of "The Rite of Spring,"* by Allen Forte (New Haven, 1978).
11. Moscow, 1978.

does not mention his meeting with Nikita Khrushchev, since in Soviet history books no one by that name ever existed.

The photographs include one of Stravinsky with Shostakovich's boss, Tikhon Khrennikov, who cannot be described by any stretch of the word as being among Stravinsky's *blizkii*. If a Red Russian composer had to be shown together with *the* White one, Shostakovich should have been chosen, for though Stravinsky called the Eleventh Symphony "aesthetically and technically primitive" (letter to Pierre Suvchinsky, June 11, 1959), he had a far lower opinion of Khrennikov, dismissing his Violin Concerto as "unbelievable rubbish" (ibid.).

Interest in the book is confined to the letters home written by the author's sister, Tanya, during a sojourn of a year and a half in France (beginning in March 1925), most of which was spent with the Stravinsky family in Nice. Here we learn that "Uncle Igor lives in the best part of town, in a villa tucked back deep in a splendid garden. I was struck by the quantity of flowers. All of the rooms are decorated with multicolored anemones, beautiful carnations, and pansies. . . . The apartment is enormous, consisting of two floors joined by a staircase indoors." But Tanya's letters must have been censored, too, since she does not mention the altar, the icons, and the fervid religious life in the Stravinsky home.

Stravinsky specialists will learn a few facts from the book, among them the reason that the signature of A. E. Napravnik (1866–1938) appears as witness on Stravinsky's contracts with publishers at the time. This son of the pianist and conductor, Stravinsky's neighbor in St. Petersburg, was employed by the composer in Nice as a music teacher for his children. When Napravnik senior appealed to Tchaikovsky to advise and look after Napravnik junior, Peter Ilych answered that the boy was "dull-witted." Nevertheless, since he had been on familiar terms with Tchaikovsky, Napravnik's conversation would have interested Stravinsky.

In the summer of 1970, Xenia Yurievna came to Evian to see the Stravinskys and attempt to obtain the agreement of the composer's wife that, at his death, he would be interred with his Leningrad *blizkii*. In the meantime, Stravinsky had written to Suvchinsky:

> So the Zhdanovian prohibition of Shostakovich has started up again. . . . [This is] because Yevtushenko's words [*Babi Yar*] are anti anti-Semitic. Alexander the Third was a socialist in comparison. [January 19, 1963]

For whatever reasons, a photograph of Yevtushenko with Stravinsky was scissored out of a book, *Bravo Stravinsky,* which the composer had sent to his niece. By chance, seeing an unmutilated copy of it during her French visit, she pored over this picture, but did not otherwise react to the blatant example of censorship.

Josquin's Ars Perfecta

With the publication of E. E. Lowinsky's *Josquin des Prez*[1] and the release of excellent recorded performances,[2] the stature of Josquin (c.1440–1521) as the first universal composer can now be recognized by the general audience. That his contemporaries were aware of his greatness is attested to by the large numbers of manuscript copies of his works found in libraries from Czechoslovakia to Portugal, Uppsala to Palermo, and by the preponderance of his works in the first volumes of music ever printed (seventeen of his masses alone in three books: Venice, 1502, 1504, 1514). His popularity even survived the Schism, for he was a favorite composer of both Martin Luther and His Catholic Majesty, the Emperor Charles V.

In a much-quoted dialogue published in 1567, Johannes Ockeghem's "rediscovery of music" is equated with Donatello's of sculpture, while

Josquin, Ockeghem's pupil, may be said to have been in music . . . as our Michelangelo was in architecture, paint-

1. *Josquin des Prez: Proceedings of the International Festival Conference, Lincoln Center, June 21–25, 1971*, edited by Edward E. Lowinsky in collaboration with Bonnie J. Blackburn (New York, 1977).
2. *Josquin des Prez: Missa La Sol Fa Re Mi and Motets, Chansons, and Instrumental Music*, Munich Capella Antiqua, Philips 6775 005.

ing, sculpture . . . : both one and the other have opened the eyes of all those who delight in those arts or are to delight in them in the future.[3]

The prediction continues to be fulfilled, for the reason, Professor Lowinsky writes, that

Josquin's chief significance in the history of music lies in his . . . evolution from a great contrapuntist to the first composer to put all of his musical gifts into the service of expressing human affections.

Hardly less remarkable than Josquin's fame in his own age is the persistence of his reputation throughout the second half of the eighteenth century, when so many earlier composers, as well as such recent ones as J. S. Bach, suffered almost total eclipse. One essay in the new book examines, for the first time, the substantial body of Josquin transcriptions by Dr. Burney, the pioneer musicologist (and father of Fanny). Yet before Helmuth Osthoff's two-volume monograph,[4] and prior to Lowinsky's symposium and a few recordings, only those people capable of hearing music from reading scores were able to understand why Josquin, like Lasso, Monteverdi, and Schütz, is one of the giants of the art before Bach.

Josquin's compositions are better known than the facts of his life, for though recent research has opened up new probabilities, it has not greatly expanded the exiguous number of established facts. In 1956 it was discovered that Josquin had been employed in the choir of the Duomo in Milan at an earlier period than had been assumed, and, as a result, his birthdate had to be revised backward by at least a decade. Since this revelation, Professor Lowinsky and others, exploring the vast Archivio di Stato in Milan and the

---

3. *Ragionamenti accademici*, by Cosimo Bartoli (Venice). Bartoli translated many of Alberti's Latin writings, including *De re aedificatoria*, into Italian.
4. *Josquin Desprez* (Tutzing, 1962 and 1965).

Archivio Segreto Vaticano, have found data changing Josquin's picture from that of an unknown and underpaid singer to one of a composer and musician whose talents were recognized and remunerated by benefices and sinecures.

In the biography as reconstructed by Lowinsky, Ascanio Sforza, Josquin's patron, emerges as a central figure, and one whose musical discernment no longer need be questioned. Seeking clues to Josquin's career in the study of Ascanio's, especially after he became cardinal, Lowinsky contributes an absorbing history of the politics surrounding the papacy at the end of the fifteenth century. His deduction that Josquin remained with Ascanio during his term in exile, and later, now appears to be the only plausible explanation of the composer's unknown years (1479–86). Yet so far as direct information is concerned, the period remains a blank.

The date of only one composition, the *Deploration de Johannes Ockeghem* (1497), can be fixed with certainty,[5] and while publication provides a *terminus ante quem*, Josquin constantly revised his manuscripts and delayed submitting them to the printer—according to the contemporary theorist Glareanus. Another of Professor Lowinsky's reasonably certain attributions is that *Fama, malum* was composed in 1489 for the wedding of Duke Gian Galeazzo Sforza in Milan. Leonardo da Vinci planned the nuptial festivities, which included a scenic representation of Mercury flying from heaven and introducing Fama. A chronicler noted that this spectacle was accompanied by the singing of a *"carmen Latinum,"* which would fit Josquin's—and Virgil's—Fama, but the only evidence for a Leonardo-Josquin collaboration is circumstantial: Josquin was probably with Ascanio and definitely not in Rome.

The failure to establish a chronology for the composer is due not only to the difficulty in tying his compositions to

5. Lowinsky's arguments that the *Duke Hercules Mass* was written in 1457, and *Absalon fili mi* in 1497, are persuasive but lacking in documentation. The *De profundis* was probably composed in 1515, for the funeral of Louis XII, but music for such occasions was sometimes adapted from earlier work.

historical events but also to that of interpreting his stylistic development. No theory can be proposed for Josquin comparable to Charles Hamm's famous study suggesting that changes in Dufay's mensural practice provide a basis for dating his masses.[6] Some scholars have decided that Josquin's later music is less angular than the earlier, that it is characterized by less frequent rhythmic change and syncopation, by fewer cambiata figures (the resolution of a dissonance by leap rather than by step, as required by the rules of counterpoint), by more elaborate canonic techniques, and by more explicit relationships between words and music, with individual words inspiring musical symbols or configurations. For Professor Lowinsky, the later style is further distinguished by "bold modulation," though this is untrue of many other composers, notably Orlando di Lasso, who wrote the *Penitential Psalms* and the *Sibyllae* while in his twenties, and who became less chromatically venturesome with age.

Yet in Josquin's case, such analyses of style are tendentious, inadequate to support a proposition that, for example, his music became simpler as he grew older, or, the opposite, that it became more complex: a "late" motet proven to be an early one would destroy the whole chronological edifice. Even such general and accepted criteria of an artist's maturity as deepening powers of expression and increasing technical mastery do not apply in all cases, and especially not in that of a composer from a remote historical period.

On Josquin's life after his connection with Ascanio, Professor Lowinsky's contributors present more puzzles than they solve. Lewis Lockwood's essay on the composer in Ferrara ponders the questions of whether the "Josquino" in the service of Cardinal Ippolito d'Este, 1516–17, could be Josquin des Prez, but decides in the negative, without giving any reason, even that of the composer's old age. Yet in exactly those years, the music of Josquin des Prez enjoyed a vogue in Ferrara. What, one wonders, are the odds that

6. *A Chronology of the Works of Guillaume Dufay* (Princeton, N.J., 1964).

two contemporaneous musicians bearing the same uncommon foreign name were in one of the few places where Josquin des Prez certainly lived?

The mystery surrounding Josquin's employment and whereabouts during the final period of his life is even greater, since by this time his music was esteemed throughout Europe. Lowinsky believes that after Blois in 1501, Ferrara in 1503, and Condé-sur-l'Escaut in 1504, the composer spent the next seventeen years "in a quiet Netherlandish town." Perhaps, but is it likely that the greatest musician of his time lived in proximity to Marguerite of Austria's court at Malines without having been a part of it, particularly since she was a renowned musician, still celebrated for her chanson books,[7] which contain pieces by Josquin? "There is no evidence of any contact with Marguerite,"[8] Herbert Kellman reminds us, suggesting, instead, that as Josquin was incontestably "a composer of Louis XII," the French connection will prove the more rewarding subject for investigation.

If Josquin's personal associations with the Hapsburgs were "minor," as Kellman concludes, the same was not true of the music, at least posthumously. In a 1598 inventory of Philip II's chapel choir books, Josquin is more extensively represented than any other composer, and in Hapsburg Spain long before that date a large portion of his works, including masses, was intabulated for vihuela. As a ward of Marguerite, Charles V may have heard music by Josquin and surely did hear it after becoming emperor, since his court composer, Nicolas Gombert, was Josquin's pupil. When Charles entered Cambrai in 1540, the choice of Josquin's *Praeter rerum*

---

7. *The Chanson Albums of Marguerite of Austria*, by Martin Picker (Berkeley, Calif., 1965).

8. Joshua Rifkin conjectures that *Absalon* was composed for Marguerite, and he states categorically that Josquin "maintained a close contact with [her] court." Lowinsky's conclusion that this crucial opus was intended for Pope Alexander IV after the murder of his son, Juan Borgia, is more convincing, and surely the text is more appropriate for a grieving father than for Marguerite. Rifkin's essay is published in the liner notes of Nonesuch Records H-71261.

seriem for the celebrations must have been the monarch's own, at least indirectly. His love of music was genuine, his musicianship apparently of a high quality. He played a portative organ on his travels, and the reports of his last years, in the Hieronymite monastery at Yuste,[9] describe him listening to Flemish polyphony sung by fifteen or so of the order's best musicians transferred there for this purpose;[10] moreover, Charles is known, on occasion, to have corrected their wrong notes and faulty intonation himself. It is awesome to imagine Josquin's music being sung in the wilderness of Estremadura, supervised by the ex-ruler of the Holy Roman Empire.

Josquin des Prez consists of thirty-three studies of the man and his work. Some of these are for the specialist, but many of the others will interest general readers, as, for example, Arthur Mendel's explanation of the uses of the computer in analyzing Josquin's music to determine "the percentage of full triads in harmonic textures" and the relative frequency of "profiled motives and symmetrical phrase structures." As Mendel observes, the machine cannot provide statistics about the presence of "ecstatic fervor" or of "gentle piety and unworldliness"; yet he does not dismiss this type of subjective statement as entirely worthless, since it may provoke either corroboration or disagreement from other listeners. But won't the black-and-white "criticism" of the computer inevitably challenge the purplish variety?

The discography will also be useful to general readers, though out-of-date and statistically discouraging: eight recordings have been made of one mass, but none at all of twelve others, and while a single motet appears in fourteen complete and twelve incomplete versions, more than sixty

9. See Sterling's *The Cloister Life of Charles V* (1852) and R. M. Stevenson's *Spanish Cathedral Music in the Golden Age* (Berkeley, Calif., 1961), pp. 176–7.
10. Did the emperor pick the singers himself? After all, Charles VIII of France, invading Italy in 1494, personally auditioned wind-instrument players for service in Florence.

have never been recorded. The compiler of this information, Nanie Bridgman, expresses the hope that "some enterprising person will undertake an edition of Josquin's *Opera omnia* in sound." But surely the spurious must be separated from the authentic, and solutions found for numerous and perplexing performance problems before a "complete recording" would be desirable.

Ms. Bridgman comments on vocal malpractices, citing the famous statement by Franchinus Gafurius,[11] who had known Josquin personally and was his successor in Milan:

> Avoid a wide, ringing vibrato, since these notes do not maintain true pitch, and, because of their continuous wobble, cannot form a balanced concord with other voices.

The disregarding of this advice ruins most performances even today, especially those in the three records boxed with Professor Lowinsky's book, and which he considers to be invaluable. Though a well-intentioned product of the conference's "workshops," these renditions are of such poor quality as to add more fuel to the argument that musicologists and musicians are different species. Ms. Bridgman further warns against introducing dynamics and fluctuations of tempo; yet simply because Josquin did not write "più piano" and "poco vivace" is hardly proof that he never inflected his music with these means. In the Philips recording of *Planxit autem David*, the phrase *"in morte quoque"* is softer than the previous one, and at a reference to swiftness, the movement quickens slightly, naturally, and, for this reviewer, judiciously.

The book's most peculiar essay, its subject wholly tangential, is Maria Louisa Gatti Perer's "Art and Architecture in Lombardy in the Time of Josquin des Prez." Why only Lombardy, the reader may wonder, since Josquin also lived in

---

11. Gafurius's *Practica Musicae* (1496) is available in an English translation by Irwin Young (Madison, Wis., 1969).

Rome, Ferrara—where the Schifanoia frescoes might contain links with his Fortuna (in classical mythology, Venus turns the wheel)—and Condé-sur-l'Escaut, where he would not have been far from Hieronymus Bosch? "In what kind of artistic environment did Josquin spend his most impressionable years?" Ms. Perer asks, but clearly these were his childhood ones in the Low Countries, rather than those of the *oltremontano* in Milan. Moreover, in his native Flanders, or northern France, the apprentice musician might have watched the making of tapestries and the endless combining of the three vegetable dyes, which at least is analogous to the weaving of voices in polyphony and the infinite juxtaposing of the same few harmonic colors.

Instead Ms. Perer imagines Josquin spending "long hours . . . meditating on . . . the truth and reality [of the art in the Portinari Chapel]," standing before the *Game of Tarot*[12] in the Palazzo Borromeo, and observing the construction of the Duomo, in the midst of scaffoldings, building yards, tool sheds, piles of stone. She takes the composer to Castiglione Olona in order to relate his music to Masolino's linear perspective, following Alberti's theory of proportion and the correspondence of the parts in music and architecture in a mathematically structured universe. Obviously Josquin might have been affected by such experiences of the visual arts, but the only irrefutable deduction from his work is that he was profoundly impressed by his experience of the verbal ones, for Josquinus Pratensis was the first composer to treat the text as of primary importance, not only in meaning, but also in the rhythms and sounds of words.

For those who believe that the findings of musicology should be made functional, the most edifying section of *Josquin des Prez* is the forum on problems of interpretation, and this though the subjects change abruptly, the discussions

12. A small reproduction of this picture, sometimes attributed to Pisanello, is included in *Josquin des Prez*. For a color photograph of it, see Italo Calvino's *Tarots: The Visconti Pack in Bergamo and New York*, translated by William Weaver (New York, 1976).

are inconclusive, and the participants cavil at and contradict each other. Professor Lowinsky stands above the mêlée, by virtue of his talents as a moderator, his vision as a ground-breaker,[13] and his expertise in such matters as musica ficta and text underlay; his qualifications to direct the conference, and to edit its proceedings, are never more apparent than in these open meetings.

The questions touch on such pertinent subjects as instrumental doubling in the vocal music,[14] ornamentation, and whether, in a conflict between a natural and a flat, the literalness of a Gregorian chant should be sacrificed to consonance; the chants, Lowinsky reminds the assembly, are found in many variations, and in any case should not be thought of as inviolable. Casuistry intrudes with the posing of the non-problem that if a work by Dufay were given together with a group of motets by Josquin, should Dufay's double leading tones at cadences be kept, or should his music be Josquin-ized? One of the performing musicians sensibly answers that Dufay's style should be observed in his piece, Josquin's in his, whereupon a musicologist irrelevantly remarks that the Dufay "sounds very pleasing with the leading tone in the superius only."

Absalon fili mi inevitably enters any discussion of Josquin, for this motet, opening the door to the whole of harmonic space, changed the history of music. Yet the conferees only cover the same old ground: *Absalon* was probably not in-

13. Lowinsky's *Secret Chromatic Art in the Netherlands Motet* (New York, 1946) seemed to promise a musicological "thriller" when it first appeared, and the text does contain references to "smuggled modulations," "diatonic camouflages," and "hidden contrapuntal devices." His thesis is that chromaticism, which the Inquisition and the Council of Trent considered subversive, went underground, thereby necessitating the application of musica ficta in performance. *Secret Chromatic Art* established Lowinsky as music's iconographer, its Panofsky or its Gombrich, yet the book failed to win unanimous acceptance (see Robert Wangermée's *Flemish Music and Society in the Fifteenth and Sixteenth Centuries*, translated by R. E. Wolf, New York, 1968), and the 1969 Josquin supplement included Lowinsky's decoded version of *Fortuna d'un gran tempo* only as an insert alternate. The standard criticism of *Secret Chromatic Art* is that its music examples are inadequate—too few and these

tended for the church (though laments were used liturgically on the Saturday before the seventh Sunday in Pentecost) and undoubtedly should be performed in the low range of the British Museum manuscript (the oldest and most reliable version) rather than in one of the ninth-higher German printed ones (Augsburg, 1540; Nuremberg, 1559), which, Dr. Kirsch notwithstanding, are different. "The German version comes out clearer," Ludwig Finscher says, and Lowinsky replies that lucidity was not Josquin's main purpose. That transparency need not be lost in the somber colors of the low voices is proved in a new recording[15] at the notated pitch, in spite of an otherwise wretched performance, coarse in tone and dragging and unsteady in rhythm.

The musicologists neglect to say that *Absalon* was composed not to demonstrate that the world of tonal harmony is round and circumnavigable by modulation through successive dominants, but to satisfy an expressive purpose; and if the circle of falling fifths parallels the descent into hell, then the jolting of strange and unexpected keys may also have been intended to represent the turmoil in David's soul. The vividness of the music is unprecedented: the wailing on "*ultra*"; the anguish in the deceptive cadence on "*plorans*"; the bitterness of the cry "*Absalon!*" in the only place where all four voices utter it together (made still more harsh by a sesquitertia rhythm in one part); and, most astonishing of all, the seventh chord on "*non*" (for this construction is not a

---

from minor composers—and that the evidence from ecclesiastical history of the need for these clandestine musical practices is insufficient. Lowinsky's later writings, espec'ally in his edition of the Medici Codex of 1518, contribute more than anyone else's to the knowledge of cinquecento chromaticism.

14. The performance by the Hamburg Monteverdi Choir of six of Josquin's Marian Motets (Archiv 2533 110) is a powerful argument against using instruments, and the conductor's claim that "the *a cappella* tradition was cultivated in the Sistine Chapel only" is untrue as well as insufficient reason not to do the same elsewhere. His *colla-parte* orchestration, which employs pommers, dulcians, and, so it seems, bazookas, overweighs the music and impedes the flow. Furthermore, the voices meander in pitch even more disastrously with instruments than without them, perhaps because the accompaniment increases the difficulty for the singers of tuning to each other. At one place in *Missus*

mere passing dissonance but a harmonic pivot). The direct appeal of *Absalon* to us, and its independence from its contexts—though these must be understood if one is to appreciate Josquin's achievement—result from his musical imagery, just as Dante's similes (of the "old tailor peering at the eye of his needle," for example) leave behind the world of *De monarchia* and leap over six and a half centuries.

Planxit autem David is the only one of Josquin's truly great works to have been recorded that can be recommended without significant reservations.[16] A dramatic narrative in four parts, like Schütz's *"Es ging ein Sämann aus . . . ,"* Josquin's motet resembles a litany, in that questionlike, unresolved (first-inversion) cadences are followed by pauses and by responses in the F Ionian tonic. The dialogue concept is extended to the alternating of major and minor (into which the ancient modes have been assimilated), parallel and contrary motion, wide-interval and stepwise progression, and harmonic and linear textures—this last also constituting a kind of peristalsis of retarded, then of forward movement. Other marks of Josquin's style are manifest, too, such as paired imitation and the distribution of the thematic material in all four voices.

Planxit autem David is unique in its dramatic silences and dissonances. The harmonic clashes are not associated with single words—an exception is *"super vos"* at the beginning of Part Two—but express the mood of the entire piece, and

---

est Gabriel, when the upper two lines are alone for only a few measures, the pitch sags to the extent that the re-entry of the bass instrument seems to be in another key.

15. Nonesuch Records (see note 8, above). Rifkin writes that "the words *'sed descendam in infernum plorans . . .'* call forth one of Josquin's most remarkable harmonic inventions leading through the series of fifths to the previously unheard of tonal realm of B-flat minor." Actually, the music enters the realm of B-flat minor before, and the piece does not end in this tonality, since the third of the triad is omitted.

16. *Qui velatus,* on the same side of this Philips recording, is no less superbly sung, and the purity of sound, especially at *"Qui jacusti mortuus,"* is unforgettable.

the listener cannot fail to hear the parallel seconds and parallel sevenths, and the two instances of three dissonances in succession.

Josquin exploits the sounds of words in this great composition, obtaining an expressive staccato in *"sic"* and *"ego,"* *"coccino"* and *"incircumsisorum"* by setting the plosives to detached notes. The crossing voices on *"in excelsis"* imitate weeping, and when the daughters of Israel are bidden to mourn for *"Sa-ul,"* the second syllable positively ululates. Meanings of words are symbolized by such devices as an octave leap upward at *"valde,"* and by a duet when David's brotherly feeling for Jonathan is recalled.

"Israel" and *"filae Israel"* are identified with a three-note dotted figure and with triple meter, the perfectum; this is rhetorical, and the feminine connotations of the triplum, introduced at the mention of anointing, are the same as in the music of the Flower Maidens in *Parsifal*. The changes in meter are extraordinarily subtle. For example, when the second switch to three is partly obscured by a hemiola, the resulting accent on the weak part of the beat suggests a dance.

These and other inventions should not be discussed in isolation, but the two most affecting must at least be mentioned. These are the suspended fifth's eventual subsidence on the third at the end of a movement, and the introduction of the Good Friday lamentation tone, especially in the superius at the climax of the motet, the ending of Part Three; the chant has no significance for today's secular audience, of course, but Josquin's contemporaries would have recognized the melody and been stunned by its meaning.

Scire gaudere est.

Light on Lasso

Of the great composers in the second half of the sixteenth century, Orlando di Lasso had the widest range. His personality was also the most complex, so far as this is possible to determine about anyone who lived before the advent of the fully documented modern biography as exemplified in the work of Alfred Einstein,[1] one of the first scholars to establish a connection between a man's life and his compositions. Comparing Lasso's setting of a Petrarch sonnet with that of another composer,[2] the great musicologist deduced that since Lasso's version contains only two-thirds as many measures, he must have been "impatient."

Born in the Walloon city of Mons, Lasso lived in Italy, Antwerp, and Bavaria. The most cosmopolitan musician of

1. *The Italian Madrigal*, Vol. 2, translated by Alexander H. Krappe, Roger Sessions, et al. (Princeton, N.J., 1949).
2. Adrian Willaert (c.1490–1562). The liner notes accompanying the Nonesuch recording (71345) of five of his four-voice motets assert that Willaert "dominated the musical life of his adopted Italy from almost the moment of his arrival until his death." But how can it be said that Willaert dominated *anything* during the period immediately before he moved to Venice, since even his whereabouts in these years have only just become known? And can it be true that his influence in Rome in the 1550s exceeded that of Palestrina? As for the contents of the album, the sampling of a single genre may

his age, he was also the most versatile, a master of every form. Lasso is best known today for his sacred cycles—Psalms, Lamentations, Passions, Magnificats, Litanies, Fratres motets (the salutations of Paul's Epistles)—but his secular Italian madrigals and many of his French and German part-songs have retained their popularity. Wolfgang Boetticher goes so far as to describe the canzonetta *La non vol esser più mai,* written during the final, austerely contrapuntal period, as an experiment in monody, though the polyphonic voice-leading makes the classification debatable.

Lasso's multifariousness might suggest a divided personality, but the evidence shows that he grew progressively melancholic, a development not attributable to the external circumstances of his life. In fact, few composers have enjoyed so much fame at so early an age, or been so fortunate in finding such appreciative, generous, and powerful patrons. Two of Lasso's seven children became successful musicians in their own right. After collaborating with their father, then— like the sons of Bach—diverging from him to follow a new mode, they continued to revere him and to preserve his musical legacy. In 1594, at the end of a prosperous, seemingly healthy, and comparatively long life, Lasso died, honored throughout Europe.

The British musicologist Jeremy Noble introduces a recording of three Lasso motets and numbers I and IV of the *Septem psalmi poenitentiales:*

Two things distinguish Lassus among the great composers of the high Renaissance: his extraordinary creativity (his list of individual compositions comes to something like 2,000) and his equally extraordinary diversity.

---

be the best way to introduce a major but still little-known composer, yet a variety of pieces, including the chromatic quartet *Quid non ebrietas,* and a sprinkling of instrumental compositions—the character of the medium makes a difference—might have stimulated greater interest.

But are quantity and diversity of any consequence apart from the consistent quality of the achievement in each category?[3] Indeed, the number and different types of his compositions are scarcely believable, and although the secular music is less important than the sacred, he is a supreme artist in both domains. While, for example, Josquin's motets are generally regarded as superior to his masses, the same, if true of Lasso, is by no means so obvious. But then, only a few scholars, Boetticher pre-eminently, are qualified to pass judgment on the more than one thousand motets, to say nothing of the other music.

Lasso was drawn to the subject of death and to tragic figures, like the Prodigal Son, Rachel, and Dido. One of his earliest works is *The Lessons of Job*, an unusually morbid theme to inspire a privileged young man. Among the poems of his favored Petrarch, Lasso preferred the sonnets for Laura the deceased to those for Laura the living. No doubt modern psychiatry would have an explanation for the fervor of Lasso's religious devotion and the concomitant licentiousness and carnality of his imagination, for this representative composer of the Counter Reformation conformed his polyphonic art to the dogma of the Council of Trent, while also writing blasphemous and bawdy Rabelaisian songs and indulging a worldly taste for Villon, Clément Marot, Du Bellay, and Ronsard. He was producing *villanelle, moresche,* and *canzoni* at the same time as he was dedicating masses to pontiffs and archbishops.

Lasso has been shamefully neglected in the English-speaking countries, and it is to be hoped that a British or American publisher will issue a translation of Horst Leuchtmann's life of the composer,[4] the most comprehensive mono-

---

3. Noble is adrift on Lasso's style, writing that he "avoids the illustrative strokes that would become commonplace in the next generation, such as sharp dissonances for '*amara.*'" In truth, Lasso frequently employs illustrative dissonances on such words, one of the sharpest occurring at "*in haec lacrimarum valle*" in the eight-voice *Salve Regina mater*.

4. *Orlando di Lasso*, 2 vols. (Wiesbaden, 1966 and 1977).

graph to date on any cinquecento musician. The bibliography, extending from 1566 to 1975, lists only one contribution in English, the entry in *Grove's Dictionary*. Most of the studies are in German and French, with a few Latin articles from the early years and an increasing number in Italian. Leuchtmann's documentation is exhaustive, but his book will interest readers other than scholars pursuing technical details. In the composer's youth the story is an exciting one, and all of it, then and later, takes place in the highest courts of church and state on both sides of the Alps. Lasso's correspondence alone is worth the price of the two volumes, and despite the mandated obsequiousness of the form of his addresses to noblemen, he is clearly on unusually familiar terms with them. Lasso was not only a composer of genius but also polyglot, literary, and socially cultivated, the least parochial of men.

Leuchtmann sets forth the life in calendar form first, beginning with the birth, sometime between 1530 and December 1532, and ending with the dates of the most significant posthumous publications of the music. He then substantiates and verifies this abbreviated information with countless shreds of historical evidence, some of it derived from woodcuts and epitaphs, as well as from printed documents. Other sections include all known references to the composer, genealogical tables, a chart of contemporary historical and artistic events, pictures of patrons (Samuel Quickelberg, Ferdinand de Gonzaga, the Bavarian dukes), specimens of the handwriting, photographs of Lasso's coat of arms and seal (he had been knighted in 1570 by Maximilian II), and even an early print of his house in Munich. All of the portraits of him, including the three-quarter relief on his tomb, are reproduced, and all agree on the wide-set, large, and intelligent eyes, thin nose, pointed face with dimpled chin, and oversized ears often found in composers.

Leuchtmann supplies new facts in the life of the exceptional child singer Roland de Lassus (*de là-dessus*), whose name was Italianized when, after abductions by rival choirmasters in his own country, he was whisked into the service of the Gonzagas, first in Mantua, then in Palermo (November 1545) and Milan. After these adventures, he worked under a different aegis in Naples from 1549 to 1551, then went to Rome, as a guest of the Archbishop of Florence, becoming *maestro di cappella* at San Giovanni Laterano. After more than a year and a half at this post, he returned (1554) to Mons, because of the fatal illnesses of his parents. After two years in Antwerp, where he became well known as a result of the printing of his music there, he moved to Munich (1556), entering the service of Duke Albrecht V of Bavaria. Lasso married (1558) the daughter of a maid of honor to the duchess, then, in 1559, went to Augsburg. In the same year, his twelfth and thirteenth chanson books were published in Paris. In 1562, he accompanied his patron to Prague and Frankfurt for the coronation of Maximilian II as Holy Roman Emperor. In this and the following year, collections of motets and madrigals were published in Venice and Rome. Almost annually thereafter, books of secular music appeared in Paris, and of sacred in Venice, where one containing five masses was advertised for its *"suavissimis modulationibus."*

Historians could learn something of the power structure of mid-sixteenth-century Central Europe by noting Lasso's dedications to the monied, the mitred, and the crowned—a book of six-voice motets to Jacob Fugger, another of three-voice ones to the three sons of Albrecht, and a volume of masses to Pope Gregory XIII, who responded with the Order of the Golden Spur. Lasso traveled to Italy, Verona, and Loreto as well as Venice, where, in 1558, ten masses were published. On May 8, 1594, he dedicated his last volume of motets to the Archbishop of Augsburg, and, on May 24, his final work, the *Lagrime di San Pietro*, to Pope Clement VIII. Lasso died on June 14. Ten years later, his two composer sons published a *Magnum opus musicum Orlandi de Lasso*, containing over six hundred motets. This became the cornerstone of the first modern edition of his works (1894–1953, twenty-one volumes), though Boetticher, using both paleographic and stylistic criteria, has recently shown that some of the contents of this collection are not authentic Orlando but compositions by his sons, and possibly by others.

Linguists, as well as music lovers, should acquire Leucht-mann's biography, if only for the second volume, which con-tains fifty-seven of the composer's letters from a seven-year period beginning in 1572. Most of these are written in a pan-European language of Italian, French, German, and bad Latin, with dialect words and expressions jumbled together in the same sentences and paragraphs. All except nine of the letters are addressed to Albrecht's successor, Duke Wil-helm V, who seems to have been entertained by Lasso's *Finnegans Wake*–like punning; scholars able to read the letters agree that the author was witty as well as verbally gifted. That Lasso did not normally converse in this lingua franca is shown by his purely Italian, French, and German letters to other correspondents. Leuchtmann provides modern German translations, and copious etymological and other notes. A single letter by a composer of Lasso's time being a rarity, this sizable collection is unique as literature.

Only a few years ago, in a chapter on Lasso in a survey of Renaissance music, Howard M. Brown rightly observed that the composer's

> mastery and the range of his capabilities were so great that his music is still only half understood. There are . . . almost no completely satisfactory recordings of any of his works. . . . It is no easy task to bring subtlety . . . within the typically dense mass of counterpoint.[5]

In truth, Lasso's music is much less than "half" understood, since no more than small bits of it are even known, the first *Gesamtausgabe* having reached only the twenty-third of sixty projected volumes, while, to judge from the rate of publica-tion of the new one, an optimistic date for the appearance of

5. *Music in the Renaissance* (Englewood Cliffs, N.J., 1976).

the actual complete works would be well into the next millennium.

But a promising event in Lasso affairs can now be reported: the release of two recordings[6] that capture the sound, character, and spirit of his music. These discs feature the fifth and seventh sets of the *Psalmi Davidis poenitentiales,* as well as the Venetian-style Mass *Bell'amfitrit'altera*—a mass on "the beautiful Amphitrite"!—and a group of the greatest eight-voice motets, exemplifying not only the virtuosity and perfection of technique attained toward the end of the polyphonic period, but also the threatening decline into grandiloquence.

The recordings were made at Merton College Chapel, Oxford, whose acoustics suit the period and style of the music, which is sung *a cappella,* immaculately on pitch, and with translucent tone. The results in, for example, the cadences on *"meditaber"* and *"descendentibus in lacum"* in the seventh Psalm series are rapturously beautiful. Moreover, the conductor paces and phrases the music intelligently, achieves balance, and successfully paints the chiaroscuro so essential to Lasso's style, spectacularly at the dazzling *"Dominus dei coelo"* and the dark *"In terram aspexit,"* in Psalm series V.

Whoever hears the Oxford performances will want to listen to the other Psalm cycles, but, incredibly, only the first and fourth are recorded, and these far from satisfactorily.[7] For one thing, the instrumental doublings overemphasize particular lines, thicken textures in music generally low in range, and drag the tempo. The use of instruments is historically justified, but here they distort Lasso's architecture of changing vocal combinations and shifting weights. In the *Miserere mei Deus* cycle, he intersperses the five-voice pieces with a duet and two trios, while concluding the whole with a

---

6. *Missa Bell'amfitrit'altera* and Penitential Psalm VII, Argo ZRG-735; Motets and Penitential Psalm V, Argo ZRG-795. Christ Church Cathedral Choir, Oxford, conducted by Simon Preston.

7. *Penitential Psalms I and IV, Motets,* Archiv 2533 290, Pro Cantione Antiqua, London, with Hamburg Wind Ensemble, conducted by Bruno Turner.

sextet; but the instruments reduce the effectiveness of these contrasts. Also, the conductor displays little affinity for the music and no knowledge of its requirements; in one place, in the key of E flat, with alternating A naturals and A flats, he settles on the natural, thus creating a sustained diminished chord on, of all words, *"Filio"*!

Admirers of the Psalm cycles will also wish to hear the *Prophetiae Sibyllarum* and the *Sacrae lectiones novum ex propheta Job*.[8] But the recorded performance of the *Prophetiae* is catastrophic, densely chromatic music being unbearable with less than perfect intonation. *Job* is disappointing, in this case the music itself as well as the presentation. The composition is not only early but also immature, and the performance, punching each note, emphasizes the rhythmic monotony. The piece is unrelievedly scored for four voices, whereas Lasso, the great colorist, is more comfortable with five and six, and excels with eight, ten, and twelve, and the many subgroupings that these numbers afford him. Furthermore, *Job* is written in the *misura breve*, and when this switches momentarily to ternary meter, the transitions are graceless. The syncopations are bumpy as well, and, at this stage of Lasso's development, his music is not equal to such lines as

I should have been as though I had not been; I should have been carried from the womb to the grave.

The Psalm cycles are made up of short pieces complete in themselves but subtly related. Suspense is created by such surprises as ending on the dominant minor, or in a remote key, as in the seventh cycle, where one movement begins in B flat and concludes in C; suddenly dropping a whole-tone in the bass, and from a B-flat triad to an A-flat triad; ignoring the metrical accent; and placing the cadence on the weakest

8. Nonesuch 71053 and Telefunken 641274, Prague Madrigalists, conducted by Miroslav Venhoda.

beat. But Lasso's principal means for avoiding uniformity is varying the vocal combinations.

If obliged to choose only one recorded work by Lasso, the reader will not be able to pass over the eight-voice motet *Salve Regina mater*. A close second choice would be *Omnes, Omnes, de Saba Venient,* with its jubilant antiphonal "allelujas," but the twisting chromatics of the *Salve Regina* are even more alluring, and the different registers of its two choirs provide a richer palette. At times, Lasso switches from one chorus to the other on every word, which both dramatizes the text and heightens the sense of movement. The two vocal groups often overlap by a single, scarcely perceptible line, which further emphasizes their separation and juxtaposition. And, finally, at *"O clemens pia,"* the large tessituras enable Lasso to employ canonic imitation in ascending sequence of each choir as a whole. Such moments surely inspired Mathurin Regnier's lines (1567):

> *To Josquin the palm, for he was the first,*
> *To Willaert, the myrtle, to Cipriano, the laurel;*
> *To Orlando all three, the master is he.*

Evviva Vivaldi!

A CONSUMER'S REPORT FOR
THE TERCENTENARY

In a hospital delivery room the obstetrician
could not move the baby until [Dr.] Clements
played Vivaldi. The baby then danced free
and was born normally.

London *Sunday Times*
December 11, 1977

In recent years the music of Antonio Vivaldi (March 4,
1678–July 1741) has inundated concert programs and FM
stations, outnumbered listings of Handel in record cata-
logues, and so vastly expanded the repertory of chamber
orchestras that new ensembles have been formed to play it.
This ubiquity contrasts with the two centuries of eclipse[1]
following the death of the "red-headed priest."[2] Though a
comparatively large portion of his music was published during his lifetime and remained accessible in libraries, the

1. Saverio Bettenelli's history of Italian music, published forty years after
Vivaldi's death, does not even mention him, and the date of his birth was
unknown until 1963.
2. Vivaldi's father, a respected violinist, is listed as "Rossi" in the account
books of the Ducal Palace in Venice. That the composer's two youngest
brothers also had red hair is known from a less reputable source: both had
police records.

Venetian's name did not arouse curiosity until the nineteenth-century Bach revival and the unearthing of a "Concerto del Sig^{re} Ant. Vivaldi accomodato per l'Organo . . . del
Sig^{re} Giovanni Sebastiano Bach" and of twelve other concertos *"elaborati"* by Bach. Even this endorsement did not
lead to reprintings of Vivaldi's music or to its presentation
before a wide audience.

The principal event in the annals of Vivaldi's posthumous
works is the Turin National Library's acquisitions in 1927
and 1930 of the manuscripts of some three hundred compositions whose existence had not been suspected, a discovery as
momentous for lovers of Baroque music as that of the Dead
Sea Scrolls for students of religion. The story of this retrieval
must be reviewed, if only to understand the difficulties for
anyone wishing to explore Vivaldi's instrumental music beyond the popular concerto cycles, *L'estro armonico, La
stravaganza, Il cimento,* and *La cetra.*

In 1926 the Fathers of the Collegio San Carlo in Piedmont
asked Luigi Torri of the Turin Library to appraise a large
number of "old volumes" and advise about their sale. Torri
consulted Turin University's Dr. Alberto Gentili, who found
that they contained a prodigious number of autograph
Vivaldi manuscripts of vocal works sacred and secular that he
was not known to have composed, as well as of operas and
instrumental pieces. The discovery was kept secret until, on
February 15, 1927, a sponsor, Roberto Foa, purchased the
music for the library.

Meanwhile, Gentili had noticed that the scores were hap-
hazardly bound and that in some cases the last pages were
missing, indicating that the collection could be part of a still
larger one. He learned from the Collegio that the volumes
had been the bequest of the widow of Marcello Durazzo of
Genoa, and that the original owner had been Count Giacomo
Durazzo (1717–94), Gluck's patron and a one-time Austrian
ambassador to Venice. The count's heirs had effected the
division, and Marcello's nephew still possessed the complementary half.

How the ambassador acquired the music is not known. One theory suggests that he bought it directly from Vivaldi, another that it came from the Ospedale della Pietà in Venice,[3] the convent, foundling home, and conservatory[4] on the Riva degli Schiavone where the composer had been a teacher and *"maestro de' concerti"* for almost four decades. But is an institution of the church a likely repository for opera scores and other secular music? And since Vivaldi died in Vienna in obscurity and poverty when Durazzo's career had hardly begun, where could the transaction have taken place? It is improbable that the semi-invalid composer—he had only a few months to live—would have transported the equivalent of twenty-seven bulky volumes from Venice to Vienna, and that if he had received even a small sum for the manuscripts, he would have had a poor man's funeral, "with a small peal of the bells."

Count Durazzo's twentieth-century descendant proved to be more demanding than the Fathers of San Carlo, and less discreet: Gentili's negotiations were threatened by competitive offers from dealers. Luckily, a second Maecenas, Filippo Giordano, came to the rescue, and the Italian government, which had confiscatory powers over art treasures, forced the issue. In October 1930 the Durazzo collection, constituting the largest part of Vivaldi's total work, was reunited in the Turin Library.

Publication has been dilatory even by Italian standards. The general audience's recognition of Vivaldi—some cognoscenti have not yet reached this point—was interrupted by

3. The tercentenary of Vivaldi's birth, in September 1978, was commemorated there by a concert that also inaugurated the newly restored church of S. Maria della Pietà.

4. Venice had four of these musical orphanages, and their orchestras and choruses of teen-age women were renowned throughout Europe. The most famous descriptions of them are by J.-J. Rousseau, Charles de Brosses, and Dr. Burney. As further testimony to the eclipse of Vivaldi in the 170 years following his death, Vernon Lee's history of music at the Pietà, in *Studies of the Eighteenth Century in Italy*, written about 1900, does not even name him, but provides full biographies of Porpora, Jommelli, Marcello, et al.

World War II, following a "Settimana Vivaldiana" in Siena in September 1939.[5] In the 1940s, Antonio Fanna, with the collaboration of the Edizioni Ricordi and of G. F. Malipiero as artistic director, founded the Istituto Italiano Antonio Vivaldi in the composer's native city, and in 1947 the music began to appear. The composer's phenomenal popularity since that time is due in considerable measure to the long-playing record and the continuing ascendancy of this medium of the gigantic repertory over that of the comparatively meager live-concert program. By 1975, orchestra scores were available for most of the instrumental works, but for only a few choral pieces and none of the operas. These Malipiero editions, however, are little more than transcriptions, often careless, with some rudimentary editing—the addition of parenthetical dynamics, articulations, bowings, realizations of figured basses, and footnotes showing notational problems in manuscripts. In view of the musicological muddle concerning performance practices in Vivaldi's time, the absence of commentaries on interpretation from the 1940s and 1950s is surely fortunate.

Marc Pincherle's 1913 Sorbonne thesis and later monograph[6] on Vivaldi established the French musicologist as the leading authority on the subject, and his analyses of the music's stylistic features and elucidations of late-seventeenth- and early-eighteenth-century instrumental forms have remained the basis of all studies of the composer. But Pincherle's *Inventaire thématique*, numbering each concerto, sinfonia, and sonata, accompanied by his initial ("P"), has not been universally adopted; and, in fact, each subsequent Vivaldian—except Olga Rudge, the violinist and friend of Ezra Pound, who published the first thematic index of the

5. See *Ezra Pound and Music*, edited by R. Murray Schafer (New York, 1977), for the poet's account of this festival as well as the history of his involvement with the Vivaldi revival.

6. *Antonio Vivaldi et la musique instrumentale*, 2 vols. (Paris, 1948). Pincherle published a shorter book in 1955, translated into English by Christopher Hatch as *Vivaldi: Genius of the Baroque* (New York, 1962).

Turin manuscripts[7]—has introduced his own system, with unfortunate results.[8] The volume of essays by six younger French writers,[9] evidently inspired by the devotion and superior standards of the pioneer Pincherle, can be recommended, if only for its handsome illustrations.

Michael Talbot's *Vivaldi*,[10] concise but comprehensive, and sound in its musical analyses, might have become the standard popular English-language "life and works" if the subject had been any other composer. But Vivaldi is still being discovered, and unknown works, such as the trio-sonata recently come to light in Dresden, are certain to appear. Though Peter Ryom's *Les Manuscrits de Vivaldi*,[11] a monument to library, leg, and mental work, describes hundreds of autograph scores, sometimes with the aid of ultraviolet screening, the reader is far from convinced that the last aria, sinfonia, and opera fragment has been found, and that the problems of attribution, authenticity, and self-borrowing or *contrafacta* can soon be solved.

Vivaldi the man emerges in Talbot's pages in a fuller dimension than in other biographies, partly because of his perceptive reinterpretations of writings by such contemporaries as Goldoni, De Brosses, and Benedetto Marcello. Whereas only a few years ago the dates of the composer's birth and death were matters of conjecture, these, and much more, have been established from recent research, primarily in Venice and Vienna.

The feature of Talbot's survey of the "Red Priest's" music is that the vocal works, scarcely mentioned in earlier monographs, receive almost as much space as the instrumental. Vivaldi's contemporaries admired his concertos more than his operas, and the posthumous neglect of the latter was predict-

7. Siena, 1942.
8. See "The Vivaldi Numbers Game" at the conclusion of this article.
9. *Vivaldi*, by Roland de Candé, Jean-Pierre Demoulin, Norbert Jonard, Marcel Marnat, Carl de Nys, and Claude Samuel (Paris, 1975).
10. London, 1978.
11. Copenhagen, 1977.

able. Moreover, unsure of himself in his first stage works, he sometimes gave the most important melodic lines to the orchestra, and to some extent his development as an opera composer can be measured in the increasing independence of his vocal style from his instrumental one. Apart from these considerations, the reader is not left with a compelling desire to learn the operas. Of the sixteen out of forty-five that survive complete, all suffer from dramatic diffuseness and a lack of structural variety in the individual numbers. Talbot believes that one factor contributing to the superiority of Vivaldi's sacred over his secular music is that the liturgical texts do not permit excessive use of the da capo form. In any event, the staging of the operas today may pose insuperable obstacles.

The book also includes a brief history of the effect of the shift in music publishing early in the eighteenth century from Venice to Amsterdam and the North, precise descriptions of instruments (earlier writers failed not only to identify the *salmo* as a chalumeau, for instance, but even to distinguish recorders and transverse flutes), and some judicious comments on Bach's transcriptions of Vivaldi. Although these last enriched the music contrapuntally, "a streak of pedantry sometimes made [Bach] gild the lily," besides which he added or subtracted measures "to produce a symmetry more characteristic of his own music than of Vivaldi's." An example in music type shows Bach missing the point of a sequence in the finale of Concerto RV 580.

Some of Talbot's statements are peculiar. Thus, while establishing the dates of the Mantuan period, he writes that "if Vicenzo [*sic*] di Gonzaga had lost Monteverdi to Venice . . . the recruitment of Caldara [to Mantua] . . . showed that the pull could as well come from the other direction." But a more unequal exchange would be difficult to imagine. And Talbot characterizes the finale of Concerto RV 159 as "frankly experimental," a "collage . . . of two thematically self-contained movements—one of a three-part *concertino* . . . the

other for a four-part *ripieno* . . . [a] crazy quilt of a form." A
"crazy quilt"? In fact, the music, all in one tempo, is a simple
dialogue between a solo trio and a full string group taking
regular turns. So far from being "experimental," the piece
is an expression of the Venetian tradition of antiphony.

Reviewing a London concert by a Swiss chamber orchestra,
Stanley Sadie of *The Times* remarked unfavorably on the decision of the group to be heard in an all-Vivaldi program
rather than in

> first-rate music like Bach or Mozart. Moreover, by electing
> to play mainly slight, major-key works (Vivaldi is almost
> always at his best in the minor), they [*sic*] may not have
> given themselves much of a chance. . . . Mr. Tylor played
> a mandolin concerto.

The mandolin concerto. And if the ensemble had performed
Vivaldi-Bach, would the music have been first- or second-
rate? Mr. Sadie must possess an enviable familiarity with this
immense body of music if he can generalize about it in terms
of key. But does the quality between major and minor really
fluctuate this predictably? Approximately 350 of 480 concertos counted by Pincherle are in major keys, and two out of
three slow movements are in the minor. Yet major and minor
are often less important in characterizing a concerto as a
whole than they are internally, where they are a principal
element of that contrast which is the essence of Vivaldi in
slow tempos as well as fast. The delectable "crazy-quilt" last
movement of the Concerto for Strings, mentioned above,
contrasts a concertante ensemble playing in A minor and a
ripieni orchestra playing in A major. The quality of the
music is evenly sustained, and this and countless other examples attest that the value judgment is more complex than
Mr. Sadie's statement has allowed.

That Vivaldi lacks the depth, dimensions, intensity, and much else besides of Bach and Mozart, and must be rated far below them, scarcely needs to be said. Like them, however, he is wholly alive: we do not listen to him "historically"; and he shares with them a strength of personality, if almost purely physical in his case, his music being more of the body than of the soul. In a Beethoven scherzo, the choreographic impulse is satisfied in the music alone. A Vivaldi finale, in comparison, is an actual dance, difficult to listen to standing still. Other considerations aside, how much poorer our musical life would be if it were restricted to Bach and Mozart, and if the second-rate masterpieces of Vivaldi were ostracized.

The anomaly of Vivaldi the composer-priest is that he apparently lacked a religious vocation and, so the evidence suggests, took the tonsure for material reasons. He was required to compose a minimum of two masses a year and two motets a month, in addition to music for vesper services, funerals, and other official church occasions. Yet only one complete mass by this most prolific composer has been found, and though his "Gloria," "Magnificat," "Domine," and other sacred pieces have become popular, in forty years of ecclesiastical service he produced a far greater quantity of secular than of sacred music, and, of works imbued with religious profundity, perhaps none. Several of the concertos are named for saints' days and church festivals, but the spirit of the allegros in these pieces is more *"da camera"* than *"da chiesa,"* the ariosos are more operatic, and the vivacity is suited more to the carnivals of Venice than to its Lenten pieties. Vivaldi's one distinct "religious" mood is a lugubriousness, most powerfully conveyed in the "Santo Sepolcro" Concerto, music whose harmonic construction might easily be misattributed to Charles Ives; yet even here the feeling is more theatrical than penitential.

In a 1737 letter to a patron, Count Bentivoglio, Vivaldi revealed:

An ailment has burdened me since birth. When I had barely been ordained a priest I said mass for a year or a little more. Then I discontinued saying it, having on three occasions had to leave the altar . . . because of this ailment. For this reason I nearly always stay at home, and when I go out it is only in a gondola or a coach. . . . I can no longer walk on account of this chest ailment, or tightness in the chest. . . . Knowing of my ailment, no nobleman invites me to his house.

This disability is usually thought to have been asthma, since the other complaints that fit the description, such as angina or a congenital heart condition, would have killed so active a man at an earlier age. But if he were too short of breath to walk, or to say mass, how was he able to lead such a strenuous life in music, playing the violin during lengthy concerts, conducting his operas and supervising productions of them, traveling frequently and extensively? The conclusion seems inevitable that he resorted to poor health to avoid the routine duties of a priest, and to devote himself to music. If this hypothesis were true, he would undoubtedly have developed an aversion to saying mass, and the asthmatic seizures would have had a psychological component. Indeed, the whole charade, with the simulated inability to walk and the necessary acting out of the affliction for others, even to the self-exclusion from the homes of the nobility, sounds like a case history from Georg Groddeck. This would also explain the discrepancy between the apparently invalid and neurotic composer and the health and high spirits of his music. Vivaldi had to save his energies for his art.

Vivaldi is a more resourceful composer than he is held to be by those whose received opinion of him was formed during the 1950s by Luigi Dallapiccola and others. Thus the music is said to be harmonic and not at all contrapuntal, though the development of themes—and even the repetitions of them, in chaconnes—is not infrequently canonic and fugal.

Thus, too, the *bon mot* that Vivaldi did not compose six hundred concertos but a single one six hundred times is quickly refuted simply by exploring beyond the dozen or so of the best known. In fact, each is unique, if only by virtue of an unexpected change of key, phrase extension, or instrumental novelty. Obviously the creation of so many pieces depends on formulas, but the freedom of construction is far greater than is generally believed, and the chord progressions, enharmonic modulations, and dissonances (Pincherle compares one passage to *Petrushka*) are often startling, as are the distributions of large ternary rhythms within meters of four, the overriding of bar lines and their accentuation, and the use of syncopation. Vivaldi experimented with the principle of thematic unity, with constructing melodies on single pitches, and, at another extreme, with extending ritornellos almost indefinitely. He follows prescriptions, to be sure, and sometimes slavishly, but no less often he obeys the original instincts of his genius. In a few instances he concluded pieces in a different key from the one in which he began, not out of capriciousness, some of his critics have said, but from "forgetfulness" attributable to the high speed at which he composed. Is it not more reasonable to assume that, like Bach (in the fughetta *"Was furcht'st du, Feind Herodes, sehr"*), Vivaldi deliberately ignored the rule?

Vivaldi was inspired by programmatic ideas, and his imagination was freed by them to the extent that he could transcend his historical period and its conventions to create music similar in feeling to Mozart's (in the middle movement of the bassoon concerto, T 28), Schumann's (the Largo of the Opus 11 C-minor Concerto), and even Tchaikovsky's (the Andante of the "Favorito" Concerto). But interest in Vivaldi the harbinger of nineteenth-century lyricism is overshadowed by an obsession with his place in musical morphology, the influence of his concertos on the development of the classical sonata, the symphony, and the "new" virtuoso solo concerto.

Vivaldi's sentiment was more modern still. The "Dormienti ubriachi" ("Intoxicated Slumberers") movement from

L'autunno anticipates Debussy. The formal outlines are blurred, and even the boundaries between harmony, melody, rhythm, texture, and color (muted strings), these elements merging to create an effect of unreality and improvisation. Whether the result was recognized at the time as music, the composer was probably excused because of his title; but this and his other verbal tags, such as those in *L'inverno* purporting to depict a "horrible wind," or sliding on ice, are irrelevant: very different ones for the same music would make its imitations of other events, actions, and situations seem no less apt. What matters concerning Vivaldi's evocative intentions is that they provoked some of his most astonishing music.

Vivaldi scholars devote a large part of their space to his use of instruments, solo and in ensembles. He is so preponderantly a composer for violin and the other strings, however—only one concerto in four employs winds—that these discussions seem superfluous. The pieces for *"molti stromenti"* are disappointing, especially those with horns, which restrict his harmonic and melodic range to fanfare patterns (see *Per la solennità di S. Lorenzo*, but the Concerto T 248 for viola d'amore, oboes, bassoon, and horns is an exception). In the Concerto T 318, the sonorities of flutes and salmos, violins in *"tromba marina,"* mandolins, lutes, and theorbos are exotic, but the music is dull. The double-orchestra concertos,[12] too, are interesting chiefly as examples of the continuing antiphonal tradition of San Marco. In short, Vivaldi's importance in the development of the orchestra is in having helped to establish its independence by creating such a substantial literature for purely instrumental ensembles. By contributing to a shift away from the predominance of vocal music, he elevated the orchestra from the role of mere accompanist and in some degree formed the path toward the sovereignty that Beethoven achieved for the symphony.

Great composers create the character of the instruments

12. The manuscript of the concerto for two orchestras and scordatura violin, T 136, was destroyed in the bombing of Dresden, but Ezra Pound had procured a photocopy, now in the Chigiana in Siena.

they use, but Vivaldi did little in figuration and qualities of tone to differentiate his oboe solos (for instance) from those that he wrote for violin. A comparison of the obbligato parts for these instruments in Bach's *Aus der Tiefe* demonstrates this, for the cantata exploits the sustained notes of the double-reed and gives it a dominating role never entrusted to it by Vivaldi. As for his thirty-nine bassoon concertos, it is hardly fair to reproach him because they display none of the characteristics that later composers have associated with the instrument, yet the solo parts are not specially designed for the woodwind as distinguished from the cello. Also, the one good movement in the horn concertos does not use the horn at all but is a cello solo, one that might have come from a nineteenth-century French ballet score. Vivaldi is more successful *imitating* wind-instrument music with strings, as in the hunting horns in the solo violin part in *L'autunno*.

The exceptions are the brilliant *concerti a cinque*, which mix violin and winds, the concerto for flautino, T 105, whose $\frac{12}{8}$ movement reveals the potential pathos of the instrument, and the concerto for two mandolins. That this last has become one of Vivaldi's most popular pieces is largely owing to the sound of the instrument, its sparkle in the allegros, tenderness in the serenade, resonant lower notes (and facility in playing wide intervals); tremolo, Eliot's "pleasant whining of a mandolin," is not indicated but was surely used. The finale is a breathtaking acrobatic display, with the most spectacular somersaults saved for the very end.

Oddly, Vivaldi's vast corpus of concertos does not include a single one for cembalo. Possibly he did not like the instrument, or the organ, for that matter, since the treble parts in his two organ concertos are violinistic. In any case, he substitutes string arpeggios and pizzicati for keyboard elaboration (viz. the concerto for three violins, T 88, and the concerto for flute, violin, and bassoon, T 144), and certainly the cembalo, or continuo, is absent from a surprising number of slow movements, as well as during long stretches of fast ones. C. P. E. Bach censured him for his heretical practice, but

Vivaldi obtained striking effects of contrast and relief with it, as did J. S. Bach, in the interlude for unaccompanied flutes and gambas between the fugal expositions in *"Und der du Vorbild grosser Frauen."* Vivaldi favored accompaniments in the alto register by a single, unharmonized line, a suspension of the conventional bass that might be counted as another similarity with *Petrushka*. Finally, his neglect of the keyboard is as comprehensible as François Couperin's or Domenico Scarlatti's neglect of the violin.

For the most part, Vivaldi on records is still played "as written," while the few attempts to observe semblances of Baroque style are rarely successful. The conflicting instructions of musicologists can scarcely be blamed, since musicians do not read musicologists, yet the obliviousness of the world's most eminent conductors to even the most elementary interpretative necessities of this music is something of a phenomenon. Karajan, for instance, performs *Le stagioni* much as he does *Verklaerte Nacht*, with great refinement of tone, perfect graduation of dynamics, the smoothest articulation—which is virtuosity of a kind, but not Vivaldi's.

No doubt Karajan would answer that since the string instruments in his orchestra are modern, the revival of a style of two and a half centuries ago is unjustified, that such devices as *bariolage* and *brisure* are different with curved bows. This is true; but the character of the music is entirely altered by such essentials as the lengths of notes, which, when too long, can transform dances into songs.

Many star instrumentalists are equally unenlightened, perhaps the worst offender being the flutist Jean-Pierre Rampal, who, to begin with, simply plays everything at the fastest possible speed in order to exhibit his technique and without regard for the music. Unlike him, Heinz Holliger, the oboist, embellishes the music intelligently, but often fails to recognize Lombardian rhythmic figures and hence does not play their first two notes fast enough. George Malcolm, harpsichordist, and Julian Bream, lutanist, are exceptions, ornamenting the music expertly, and, what is more, delineating the diagrammatic version of a line before embroidering it. Vivaldi was obviously fond of the lute, as he was of the mandolin, and it could be used as a continuo instrument in many of the slow movements.

No statement about the performance of Baroque music has engendered so much debate as that of Vivaldi's friend J. J. Quantz to the effect that "notes of equal value are more pleasing when played unequally." Rather than digress on this subject, the present writer invites the reader, and all lovers of Vivaldi, Bach, and Handel, to listen to a performance that uses "*notes inégales*" in a spontaneous and convincing way. Frans Brüggen's recording of Handel's Sonata in C for recorder and cembalo[13] does this in the Gavotte, though the ornamentation, articulation, phrasing, and *messa di voce* (the natural crescendo and decrescendo on long notes) in all of his playing is no less accomplished. Hearing this, the listener will surely recognize for himself that the Baroque performance of Baroque music is incomparably the most expressive kind.

THE VIVALDI NUMBERS GAME

Marc Pincherle's thematic inventory of Vivaldi's instrumental works was published in 1948. In 1947, in Rome, Mario Rinaldo had already brought out a "*catalogo tematico*," in which each work is identified by his "MR" number. The Malipiero scores were marked "Tomo,"[14] 1 through 535, though Ricordi, who published them, listed the music in the sequence of the company's general catalogue ("PR," for "Partiture Ricordi"). In 1968, Fanna's Institute issued still another thematic index ("F") of the "complete" orchestral

13. ABC Classics ABCL 67005/3.
14. The present article, which is intended for musicians as well as general readers, identifies the concertos by their sobriquets, and, where none exists, by Tomo and opus.

works, dividing them into sixteen categories according to instrumentation: concertos for strings, *"complessi vari,"* etc. This attempt to introduce some order was laudable but limited, since it provided no subdivision beyond an inadequate grouping by key. Thus the entries occur in the sequence C major, C minor, D major, D minor, and so on up the scale to B minor. Vivaldi having written thirty-three violin concertos in D major, however, the classification should have been broken down a step further. Fanna's appendices supply the corresponding numbers between "F" and "P," and between "Tomo" and "PR," but no concordance for all four, and "MR" is excluded altogether.

The Fanna catalogue gives the sources, in fifteen European libraries, of the manuscripts used for the thematic incipits of all of the movements of 401 instrumental works that Vivaldi did not publish, but omits fragmentary and unfinished pieces, and those of uncertain attribution, helpful as these might have been in providing clues to the authorship of other music. Nor does Fanna describe the differences between one manuscript version and another, beyond such vague statements as "The orchestra in the Naples mss. requires fewer instruments"; "This manuscript contains an additional Adagio"; "The second movement is different in this version." But what *are* the changes in instrumentation in the Naples copy? And why, in a so-called complete edition, was this extra Adagio not included? In what ways do the two versions of that second movement differ? Moreover, since approximately a hundred works exist in two or more versions, these should have been cross-indexed, and the movements that Vivaldi adapted from operas noted.

While Fanna's guide was being prepared for the press, Peter Ryom, working in Poland and Scandinavia, found fourteen previously unknown instrumental works (as well as eighteen copies of known ones).[15] Not surprisingly, he com-

---

15. Ryom's total discoveries have increased since then.

piled his own catalogue, assigning a number from 1 to 768 (and the abbreviation "RV," Ryom Verzeichnis)[16] to each composition, whether single movement or full-length opera. His earliest findings are included at the end of the Fanna volume, thereby exposing a weakness in the systems of both: that newly discovered works can be assimilated only as addenda and not in their proper order.

Still another complication is that Vivaldi himself numbered the collections of concertos that he chose for publication, 129 works in all, and, since these include the best known, record companies and concert organizations have preferred to use the composer's opus numbers and programmatic titles. Mario Rinaldo attempted to follow Vivaldi's example in this, but could not do so for the reason that "opus" implies chronology, which could only rarely be ascertained from dedications, notices of special performances at the Ospedale, production data about operas (such as the three given in Rome in 1723–24), the composer's correspondence, and the sudden output of a quantity of music for a particular instrument traceable to the visit of a performer, such as that in 1726 of the flutist—and most informative writer on music of his time—J. J. Quantz.

The confusion in numbering is disastrous. To illustrate, anyone wishing to find the score for a new recording of RV 114 would somehow have to learn—Ryom, as the latest arrival, is the least widely known—that this concerto is F XI 44, P 27, PR 1168, and Tomo 493, this last being the number on the only edition of the music currently available. The Schwann catalogue has generally adopted P, less frequently F, but many albums are still labeled according to the defunct MR, or with nothing at all. A record collector who decides to purchase a new release of "Ten Vivaldi Concertos" should consider himself fortunate if this package contains even one piece that he does not already own. Moreover, the

16. *Verzeichnis der Werke Antonio Vivaldi*, by Peter Ryom (Leipzig, 1974).

information he needs is seldom obtainable from the record jacket. So, too, the concert-goer who wishes to follow the score of one of those D-major violin concertos must take a small suitcase of them—unless the preliminary advertisements for the program include two or three catalogue numbers.

In Search of Mozart

Wolfgang Hildesheimer's *Mozart*[1] aims to debunk the myths propagated by earlier biographers and to establish what is definitely known, or can be safely conjectured, about the man. Popular legends are demolished along with some of the conclusions of such eminent Mozartians as Abert, Paumgartner, and Einstein. Re-examining the sources, Hildesheimer attempts to separate the grains of truth or likelihood from the inventions ("mostly for personal reasons") of the witnesses. Not many of his arguments are plausible, but the novelty of the presentation makes the book readable.

Hildesheimer jumps from the music to the life, and from one aspect of the subject to another, often disregarding chronology. Thus an analysis of Mozart's melodramatic style in a late money-begging letter to one of his Masonic brethren is placed near the beginning of the book, because it illustrates a feature of the composer's personality. Brief, detached sections replace chapter divisions, thereby allowing for digressions, most of them ending with unresolved questions. These techniques, not surprising from a novelist and author of the fictional biography *Marbot*—Hildesheimer is not a musicologist—sustain suspense. The best things in *Mozart* are the

1. Translated by Marion Faber (New York, 1982).

uncovering of clues and motives, and the imaginative gap-filling in both the narrative and the testimony of observers. Understandably, the book has been a best-seller, albeit a much overpraised one.

The author is familiar with the music, but many of his "insights" are unreliable and his judgments dead wrong. Anyone who could write that Mozart's compositions of the Salzburg and Italian years do not "step beyond the conventions of the various genres" has not listened carefully. And while Hildesheimer recognizes such precocious marvels from the early years as the Piano Concerto K. 271 (he might have added the middle movement of the A-major Violin Concerto, which Mozart himself thought too recherché), he does not seem to see that the emotional intensity in these pieces is as great as in almost any of the late music.

Approaching *The Magic Flute* with a da Ponte–oriented prejudice against the libretto, Hildesheimer writes, incredibly: "The importance of *The Magic Flute* in Mozart's oeuvre has always been overestimated." In fact, this opera, one of mankind's supreme achievements, has been largely *under*estimated. Moreover, the music cannot be fully appreciated apart from its theodicy—perfect love overcoming fear, light and the forces of good driving out darkness and evil. Sarastro, only a "cardboard cut-out figure" to Hildesheimer, inspired the noblest music for any character in all opera, endowing this "cut-out" with a godlike nature.

The author's philosophizing is an encumbrance. What can be the point of telling us that "music is replaceable when it expresses something that need not be expressed exclusively in music"? And what is meant by the attempted distinction, "In Mozart's music he is not the bearer of a will (like Beethoven) but rather the will itself, unaware of the imperative it is obeying"? Then, too, who can agree that "our pleasure consists in identifying with the creator, in feeling after him what he might or 'must' have felt during the creative act"? Obviously, what happens is that we respond to the intended effect, and the degree of our awareness of the means by which it was produced varies from individual to individual. But who could possibly follow Mozart's creative acts, let alone know what he "felt"? Still another assertion, "In the end we always experience Mozart's music . . . as the catharsis resulting from one man's sublimation of his personal crisis," requires Mozart to have suffered crises during most of his waking hours. In fact, the independence of Mozart's muse from the events of his life can be demonstrated by the futility of trying to match his compositions with the biographical facts. Similarly, in the play of mistaken identities in *Così fan tutte*, it is impossible to tell the difference between the genuine emotions of the Neapolitan suitors and the fake ones of the "Albanians," since Mozart touches equal depths of feeling for both.

Hildesheimer's psychologizing also mystifies. He writes that "until late (too late) in Mozart's life, he did not know who he was," and that, unlike Beethoven, Mozart did not have a "metaphysical aura" (whatever that may be). But surely both composers were conscious of their identities at relatively early ages. Mozart could hardly have been unaware that his powers were superior to those of other musicians. The author might better have contrasted Beethoven's *music* with Mozart's, pointing out, for instance, the active listening required by the former, versus the passive listening often suitable for the latter.

Turning to Mozart the man, I find myself in agreement with most of what the book says he *was not*, but not with what it claims he *was*. The author has a tendency to state as fact what is no more than speculation—the fault that he condemns in his predecessors. Thus he says that Mozart was in love with Nancy Storace, the first Susanna in *Figaro*, though this is not supported by evidence. It may be, too, that "the composition itself was usually complete long before Mozart wrote it down," but this is not proved by Hildesheimer's point that the manuscripts are rarely marred by corrections. And the statement that Mozart's masses "are infused not with belief but with the will to portray it" is also impossible to verify. The absence of documentation concerning Mozart's attitude toward the church in the period after his service with Archbishop Colloredo in Salzburg does not confirm anything about the composer's beliefs, whereas his berating of Voltaire as "godless" surely does.

Hildesheimer is mistaken in stating that "the *Zeitgeist* spoke to Mozart without touching his consciousness." Actually, both the career and the works challenge the abuse of power, in the spirit of the French Revolution. Moreover, Mozart was the first free-lance composer, the first to rebel against a feudal system of patronage. If *The Abduction from the Seraglio* implicitly criticizes tyrannies, *Figaro* is a full-scale frontal attack on them. Some of the ideals of the Revolution are embodied in *The Magic Flute*, as Jean Starobinski remarks in his *1789: The Emblems of Reason*. In *Don Giovanni*, "victory goes to the old order, the outraged father. . . . [In *The Magic Flute*] the dawn that breaks at the end and drives away Monostatos and the Queen of the Night is solar Good. . . . It is absolutely basic to *The Magic Flute* that all should end in a new age, a glorified beginning." In another passage, Starobinski refers to the "eschatological promise" with which the opera concludes.

Hildesheimer believes that the relationship between father and son deteriorated into a conflict of wills. But surely differences of personality were as much to blame and became increasingly difficult to reconcile. Wolfgang was extroverted, at least in comparison with Leopold, who had an interest in the development of science, was widely read, and was a considerable pedagogue. Whatever Leopold's gifts—and his Trumpet Concerto is the work of a skilled, if minor, composer—he did not perceive his son's stature until Joseph Haydn informed him of it.

On the question of the paternity of Mozart's last child, Hildesheimer provides a new twist: Süssmayr, Mozart's pupil, might have been an informant on Constanze rather than her lover, since she "was angry" with him at the end, whereas Mozart entrusted him with the completion of the *Requiem*. But if Süssmayr were the father, would she have advertised the fact by giving his Christian names, Franz Xaver, to the boy? Hildesheimer is not an apologist for Constanze. She was not a musician, he says. Yet she was immediately attracted to Bach fugues, more so, apparently, than Mozart himself ("I am no great lover of difficulties"); and how could anyone sight-read an aria in the C-minor Mass, as she did, and not be a proficient musician?

One of the author's theses is that Mozart's fortunes declined after *Figaro*, when "an unconscious drive" came to the surface and tempted him "to stop living according to the rules imposed on him from the outside." By 1790, "Vienna had temporarily abandoned Mozart; it seemed to be waiting until this unpleasant and ultimately asocial character . . . had transformed himself by his death into a great man. . . ." *Figaro* is the turning point in Mozart's life, certainly, but not so much because of its reception as because he had to have known that in this work of unprecedented scope he had discovered a musicodramatic world. Surely this realization compensated for the loss of his performing career, as did the sense, even if unshared, of his achievements in *Don Giovanni* and *Così fan tutte*.

That Mozart became more isolated toward the end, and correspondingly more inward and pessimistic, is the accepted view, but it fails to take into account *The Magic Flute*. In Starobinski's words, the opera's dénouement involves "a shift of power . . . that marks the advent of universal happiness." Surely this sentiment corresponded to Mozart's own; still, the conclusion of the opera is also "the Parousia, the end of the world."

If it is true that Mozart was "unpleasant," wouldn't this have been an inevitable consequence of his greatness, which was a natural irritant to those who envied it? He was definitely no diplomatist, sycophant, or flatterer and was probably outspoken in his criticism of other musicians. He also seems to have been unable to restrain himself from demonstrating his superiority—as when, after someone had played a composition, he would go to the keyboard and improvise a better one—in a playful spirit and not intending to offend, though this was not likely to have been appreciated. It is hardly surprising that Mozart's widow reported he had been slandered at the end; also, her brother-in-law described him as a "victim of envy and intrigues."

Admirers of *Amadeus* who consult *Mozart* for the facts about the composer's fecal humor will learn that this was common to the Mozart family, including the composer's mother. Whether or not toilet functions were more openly discussed in Mozart's time, his lifelong anality is abnormal. Stefan Zweig, who owned originals of nine of the twenty-one-year-old Mozart's letters to his female cousin, the "Bäsle," thought that they threw light on his erotic nature, which "has elements of infantilism and coprophilia" (from a 1931 letter to Freud). But Hildesheimer regards the two predispositions as entirely separate. Whether real or fantasy, Mozart's expressions of his desires toward the susceptible young woman are clearly erotic; furthermore, the same phrases occur in a later letter to his wife (in which Mozart reminds us of Leopold Bloom).

Perhaps the next biography of Mozart will contain an estimate of how much of his life was spent *writing* music—for he *composed* it in his head while he bowled (and no doubt during other activities as well). Some of the difficulties of such a project are admittedly insuperable, since Mozart was capable of composing the second movement of a piece while writing out the first, and since manuscripts are still being discovered (most recently of an early symphony, in A minor, in Odensee, Denmark, and of a revised version of *Exultate, jubilate*, in the collection of St. Jacob's Church in Wasserburg, Bavaria). Still, the computer could provide parameters for the writing time of the complete works, aided by beta-radiography, which can help to date the manuscripts by revealing their watermarks. (Using this method, Alan Tyson has recently shown that Mozart labored during a period of two years to complete the quartets dedicated to Haydn.)

Meanwhile, Hildesheimer's book enables us to piece together a sufficient number of details to form a portrait of Mozart the man. We can visualize him rehearsing an orchestra (and speaking to the players in a soft tenor), gambling, bowling, playing billiards (a green baize table was among his effects), riding horseback (a doctor had ordered this), and executing a balestra (à la Don Giovanni). We believe Clementi, who said that Mozart "dressed elegantly," and Tieck, who noted that the composer was "small, quick," had "weak eyes" (but not that they were crossed, as in the Hagenauer-Barducci portrait), and was "an unimpressive figure." (That the eyes protruded and the nose was large are confirmed by other observers.) It can even be understood that one of the hardest-working men who ever lived considered himself lazy, since his father so often scolded him for his indolence. What is not comprehensible is how any mere human being could have composed Mozart's music.

Diaghilev

GENIE OF THE BALLETS RUSSES

Our fascination with Serge Diaghilev, founder of the Ballets Russes, seems to grow with our increasing knowledge of his unattractive qualities. He was autocratic, jealous, snobbish, vindictive, casual about financial and contractual obligations, ruthless in the treatment of colleagues who failed to remain à la mode. Richard Buckle's comprehensive biography[1] depicts these traits no less forthrightly than it does the impresario's genius as a catalyst and arbiter in the arts of the theatre. Yet a poll of the ballet world would probably show that sympathies are more often with Diaghilev than with his critics and adversaries, even when he was clearly in the wrong. Great personal seductiveness would seem to account for this popularity, the moral being to beware of charm—though evidently few can do so when it is exerted on the scale of a Diaghilev.

Buckle—also the author of *Nijinsky*[2]—perpetuates the Diaghilev myth, in the sense that much of the biography was derived from oral history. (What other kind could be ex-

1. *Diaghilev* (New York, 1979).
2. New York, 1971.

pected where sexual proclivities and practices, and even physiological details, are concerned?) And though in such matters fact and fiction are difficult to separate, concocted tales can point to true characteristics. Buckle is especially adept at evoking the sexual scene of Diaghilev's kingdom (or principality), partly by introducing such observations as "Frohman was extremely good-looking . . . and it was not long before Diaghilev [in Karsavina's words] 'had his eye on him.' "

In Diaghilev's case, both sex per se and sexual politics are of the essence. He was, after all, the first openly accepted homosexual among public figures of the era, and in this respect his career contrasted sharply with, for instance, that of Tchaikovsky, Wilde, and the closeted literati of Bloomsbury. In addition, whatever Diaghilev's motives in "exhibiting" Nijinsky in a sexually explicit act in *L'Après-midi d'un faune*—and the broadening of public taste scarcely seems to have been one of them—this ballet marked a turning point in contemporary mores. Ironically, too, in view of Diaghilev's cynicism about sex, he and his worshippers elevated a homosexual affair, in the tragic relationship with Nijinsky, into one of the twentieth century's great love myths. But how many readers are aware that Diaghilev's sexual conduct was the principal reason that his Ballets Russes never appeared in Russia, and that he remains a non-person there, even today?

Our knowledge of the Ballets Russes is vastly enlarged by Buckle, who brings documentation to light from unsuspected sources and tracks elusive information to its hiding places. He is particularly learned in the genealogies of the "well born" and the wealthy who surrounded Diaghilev, more so, perhaps, than many American readers will require. Buckle also writes in a personal manner, stepping out of his book in brief asides, and sometimes tweaking noses, as, for example, in footnote 91 of Chapter 14, which reads: "I have mislaid my source."

Though *Diaghilev* is compendious, it has gaps that could have been closed by reference to Russian primary sources—as distinguished from the memoirs of dancers, régisseurs, balletomanes, and aesthetes. To name only three important lacunae, nothing is established concerning Diaghilev's St. Petersburg trip in October 1912; concrete information is not supplied about the rapprochement with Michel Fokine, following the greatest crisis in Diaghilev's life, the break with Nijinsky; and Diaghilev's most valuable statement of his philosophy of dance is omitted.

For the first, the *Petersburg Gazette,* in an interview with Stravinsky, October 10, 1912, indicates that the premiere of *Le Sacre du printemps* was planned in the Russian capital at that time. Among other references to this work, which was to make the Ballets Russes the medium of the modern movement, the composer said: "*Spring* will be performed in Paris in Gabriel Astruc's new theatre on the Champs-Elysées." But the most remarkable comment in this article reveals Stravinsky's outspoken preference for Nijinsky's sister to dance the role of "The Chosen One": "Nijinskaya is extremely talented, a fascinating ballerina, fully the equal of her brother, and when she and her brother dance together, all others pale by comparison."

As for the reconciliation with Fokine, Buckle offers no more than speculation about the agreement, which, he says, "must have been reached before December 27, 1913." Returning to St. Petersburg from Moscow, December 9, 1913, Diaghilev held a press conference giving full details of the contract. The following excerpt is from the next day's report in the *Petersburg Gazette:*

"I have settled nearly everything now and can give you my program," Sergei Pavlovich said. "I have signed a contract for two seasons with M. M. Fokine and his wife. . . . M. M. Fokine will choreograph seven ballets and dance the leading parts, performing most of Nijinsky's roles. . . . As in previous years, there will be several new works on the program. First among them is Richard Strauss's ballet *The Legend of Joseph.* . . . We will also do *Scheherazade,* with

Chaliapin as the Shah [sic], *Antar*, by N. A. Rimsky-Korsakov, a ballet by his son-in-law, Steinberg, based on Ovid, and a new ballet by I. F. Stravinsky [*Les Noces*], which, as yet, does not have a title. . . . All of these new productions will be choreographed by M. M. Fokine."

In regard to Buckle's third major oversight, that of Diaghilev's declaration of his artistic philosophy, it is not surprising that he chose to formulate it in his native language and for his fellow émigrés. It must also be said that a French or English periodical is unlikely to have published the article, since he refers so abusively to Ida Rubinstein, ridiculing her appearance ("her bent figure and hopelessly crooked knees") and not veiling his anti-Semitism ("our Biblical Ida"). The piece, which appeared in a December 1928 issue of the Paris newspaper *Vozrozhdenie*, is long, but one passage, still valid and pertinent today, should be quoted:

Classicism is an antiquated university for modern choreography, yet ballerinas and ballet masters must graduate with degrees in classicism—just as Picasso had to have a precise knowledge of human muscular anatomy, and Stravinsky had to learn how to avoid parallel fifths. For the development of theatrical art, however, it is not enough to become a professor, and the attitude of the choreographer who supports dress-coat classicism befits the Society for the Protection of Ancient Monuments (whose members should not be giving advice to modern architects). In choreography, the foundation of our plastic and dynamic structures must be that of the classical style, yet be flexible enough to admit new forms. The classical style is a means, not an end.

Buckle has also overlooked a number of other valuable sources. First, Soviet monographs of some of Diaghilev's painters and composers, whose once-banned work is now being "rehabilitated" in the motherland, could supply answers to a number of questions. For instance, Buckle fails to establish Diaghilev's whereabouts after the London season of July 1911 and makes no mention of the wartime sojourn in Viareggio with Massine, yet a memo in Stravinsky's letter copybook indicates that the impresario went to Carlsbad in the first instance, and correspondence between Gerald Tyrwhitt and Stravinsky reveals the facts of the Italian experience in the second. The collection of Boris Kochno is acknowledged as the principal source of the biography, but Buckle has not always chosen the most relevant material. His account of the origins of the quarrel between Léon Bakst and Diaghilev that ended in the permanent rupture of their relationship does not cite the crucial document, the painter's letter to the impresario of April 26, 1922. Bakst had been promised the assignment of designing the sets and costumes for *Mavra*, the Stravinsky-Pushkin-Kochno *opéra bouffe*, but Michel Larionov connived to procure the commission for his brother-in-law, Léopold Survage. Mistakenly deducing that Stravinsky was behind the intrigue, Bakst reminds Diaghilev that his commitment was made in front of witnesses and demands 10,000 francs, suggesting that this sum be subtracted from the honorarium of the "Yankel Shtravinsky." ("Yankel" is a reference to the Shylock—roughly speaking—in *Taras Bulba*.)

The 1979 Diaghilev exhibition at the Bibliothèque Nationale, Paris, unearthed still another, and extremely important, source: the letters of Ernest Ansermet during his years as chief conductor of the Ballets Russes, which is to say during World War I and extended periods thereafter. Ansermet is a uniquely qualified observer, a man of keen intelligence, who also understood Diaghilev: "His continuing power is explained because, in spite of everything, he is the only impresario who does interesting things, and one is always obliged to return to him." Ansermet had the further advantage of not being part of Diaghilev's entourage; Diaghilev did not like him, in fact, as this snippet from an Ansermet letter, sent to Stravinsky from New York, illustrates:

> Diaghilev has not let my slightest mistake pass unremarked, and I have not conducted many ballets without having him pursue me with criticisms. Nevertheless, his exaggerated and unjust attitude is for the best; thanks to his perpetual criticisms, he maintains control. . . . Nijinsky is here. If he had come with a conciliatory attitude, everything would have been smoothed over, but he has been unfeelingly callous ever since his arrival. His first encounter with Diaghilev and Massine was tragic. [April 7, 1916]

Ansermet relished the sarcastic side of Diaghilev's wit, and the letters quote many examples. When the conductor was planning a concert of Stravinsky's chamber music, in London, July 1920, Diaghilev advised him to "add thirty pounds to your expenses and bring Igor here; if he comes, you will certainly succeed, but that is the one indispensable condition." Ansermet, too, clearly enjoyed Diaghilev's implication that Stravinsky could readily be bought for thirty pieces of silver.

Can Buckle's book be described as a portrait of Diaghilev? Yes, but in the sense of one of Cocteau's faceless heads: the form is clearly delineated, the person is instantly recognized, and even the hairs are in order, but the eyes, ears, nose, and mouth are replaced by a blank. Perhaps Diaghilev's picture frame cannot be filled in for the reason that he did not leave tangible works of the kind created by other artists. Certainly Buckle can draw exact portraits when that is his goal, such as the one of Alexandre Benois, achieved by pinpointing his chief limitation: "He had rather a literal mind." But nothing quite so concise can be said about the fascinatingly complex personality of Serge Diaghilev.

. . .

Synopses of Diaghilev's ballets and accounts of their performance are frequently in contradiction, like the details of his life. Charles Spencer, in *The World of Serge Diaghilev*,[3] writes that "Ida Rubinstein and *Cleopatra* were the greatest hits" of the 1909 season, but John Percival, in *The World of Diaghilev*,[4] does not mention Mme Rubinstein in connection with this ballet. Even in minor matters, agreement is remarkably rare. A photograph of Diaghilev, Nijinsky, and Bakst in Venice, dated c.1912 by Spencer, 1911 by Buckle, 1910 (and "on a railroad bridge") in the Bibliothèque Nationale catalogue, is credited in most other publications to 1909. But, more importantly, none of these books attempts to supply what is most needed—a complete, twenty-year list of all of Diaghilev's programs.

To compare the Spencer and Percival digests, anniversary-inspired, slightly updated reprints, it must be said that the illustrations in the former are superior, twenty-one of them in color, and many of the others, especially of posters and programs, not overly familiar. Moreover, the Spencer book contains a short essay by Martin Battersby that touches on the not yet fully explored subject of "Diaghilev's Influence on Fashion and Decoration." But Philip Dyer's three introductory chapters are badly written (Benois was "a young man already besotted with the theatre") and worse conceived ("Moral attitudes no longer create false perspectives as much as they once did"). Still, the study provides a measure of the difference between Diaghilev's day and ours, when, turning to the roster of Ballets Russes artists, Pavlova, Picasso, et al. (and *ad nauseam*), Dyer notes that not only did Diaghilev bring these people together, but also "these often disparate elements were made to cohere." Individuals, in the past, could not be referred to as "elements."

Percival discusses choreographers, designers, composers,

---

3. Chicago, 1974.
4. New York, 1971.

and productions in separate chapters. As might be expected, this results in some duplication. Furthermore, in evaluating the legacy of the Ballets Russes, he states that sixteen works are "still being given today in substantially the same form as when created for Diaghilev." But most of the ballets named are not among the company's masterpieces, and many are quite faded. Though Percival considers *Apollo* the greatest of all Diaghilev's ballets, his assessment of George Balanchine does not show any perception of the man's true stature. "Neither Anton Dolin nor Serge Lifar can be said to have achieved as much as de Valois or Balanchine," Percival writes. But can the first three, as choreographers, even be mentioned together with the fourth? Many of Buckle's readers will be disappointed that he did not devote a chapter to Balanchine, but this may be attributed to the lukewarm British attitude toward Balanchine's stripped-down concentration on musical choreography, so remote from Diaghilev's emphasis on decoration and glamorized solo dancers. The Balanchine offshoot, nonetheless, is the one that has dominated ballet in our era.

Keeping Up with Mr. B.

Among those who regularly review the arts in America today, Arlene Croce is without peer. The present collection[1] of eighty-three pieces originally published in *The New Yorker*, January 1977 to August 1981, and here slightly amended, includes at least one essay of enduring value, "News from the Muses" (on *Apollo*), and forty or fifty of exceptional interest. Ms. Croce's criticism is distinguished by penetration and understanding of the subject, a large and novel scope of reference, and a creative imagination. Never "superior," she does not display her erudition, though she has plenty of it, and to spare. An exception to Yeats's "the best lack all conviction," she possesses a justified confidence in her own vision, powers of analysis, and judgments. She refers to someone as an "in-touch" person, and is one herself, which helps to account for her lively and enjoyable blend of the literary and the vernacular: plotzed, shlockier, glitzy, laid-back, ticklability, sleaze (as a noun), jocular-jock, and—surely with no *double entendre*—crotch-happy.

Dance, in its heyday, is America's most exportable artistic commodity, the one in which we have the most favorable balance of trade. No dance company in the world can hold a

---

1. *Going to the Dance* (New York, 1982).

spotlight to our best, nor can any country rival the fecundity, variety, and abundance of our dancing ensembles. Britain may have the edge in sending us plays, Russia certainly has it in defecting performers, and the Far East is at least a match in breeding musical prodigies. But in the dance we are far ahead, the demand for it increases, and critical standards become ever higher. This phenomenon has given birth in Arlene Croce to a spokesperson well able to take its measure in every manifestation: ballet, modern and postmodern, experimental, tap, acrobatic, mime, ballroom, figure skating, not to mention "the pitiless verve of contemporary Broadway." Ms. Croce is a born theatre critic, one who could easily move into the drama and movie reviewers' chairs, as well as manage a column on the graphic arts, to judge from the way that she tweaks Rouben Ter-Arutunian for the most aureate of his set designs. And while not a musician, she reveals a sensitivity to music that must unsettle those equally untutored critics who have not for this reason been deterred from writing about it.

Only a decade ago, ballet reviewing was entrusted to the music departments of the press, but the expansion of the dance world has required specialization. What, then, are the tasks of its particular criticism? A symposium on the subject of writing about the dance, held at PEN headquarters in New York, December 6, 1978, elicited the following view from the choreographer Carolyn Brown:

> I don't believe the written word can recreate the experience of seeing *any* dancing. Should it try, is the question? It seems to me that writing has to do something else.

But the written word cannot convey the experience of any of the arts except the verbal. That none of the panelists, of whom Ms. Croce was one, proposed "something else" is hardly surprising. After all, the dance critic, unlike his colleague in music, lacks such tangible tools as recordings and printed scores, and even when the ballet repertory has been videotaped, the result cannot be similarly definitive. Individual dance performances differ more radically than musical ones do, thanks in part to music's more highly developed notation. Even the most self-indulgent conductor cannot totally override Beethoven, and the differences between renditions of the Brahms concerto by two equally capable violinists will be less significant than those between Mikhail Baryshnikov and Peter Martins in a narrative role. The dance critic, it follows, must be sensitive to the most subtle differences effected by casting. Arlene Croce herself remarks this and more:

> Since ballets have no existence apart from performance, it's inevitable that, like dancers, they change over the years.
>
> Dances are perishable goods. . . .
>
> Dance is a present-tense art form with no precise way of recalling or predicting itself.

Dance action, if not the experience of the dance, can be pictorialized verbally, and in this lies much of the critic's effectiveness. The vividness is generally proportionate to the lapse of time between reading the review and attending the performance (though the ballet that Ms. Croce most clearly revived in my memory is *Calcium Light Night*, which I last saw at the New York City Ballet four years ago). In my case, the effect of words is usually limited to reminding me of positions and poses with specific performers executing them. But descriptions of movements in succession fail to form trajectories: I can see stills, but continuous movement only with rare exceptions. Thus some of the images in the following excerpt take shape in my mind, but I cannot link them:

> There is a brisk fugue for the corps, flanked by two solos for the male star. In the first, we recognize an elaboration and mobilization of the simple preparatory stretch-and-

point exercise with port de bras that had occurred at the outset of the theme. The dancer swings from side to side and then from front to back in low vaults through space. A flurry of pirouettes decelerates in a seamless return to the "theme" gesture.

This passage has been torn from its far more technical context, and since I am not familiar with the ballet under discussion, the words do not make a picture for me (as the figured bass "A♭I, IV, $_0$V^7, I–IV^7, I" would probably not suggest the first phrase of one of Bach's best-known chorales to anyone except a professional musician). Incidentally, I doubt that choreography can represent much more of fugues than the exposition of their subjects, though parallels for stretti and other devices might be realized by color and lighting.

Although Arlene Croce's book will mean more to those who already know the dances it discusses, it can be read with pleasure by anyone interested in the art, or if not that, in a good writer with a first-rate mind. Understandably, a volume of reprinted reviews, some of them updated reports of the same work, and including such vital statistics as the names of the orchestra conductors, is not for reading straight through. Nonetheless, the dross is minimal.

Most of the essays are cast in a format that begins with an apothegmatic pronouncement, some good ("Book musicals are dying, revues are dead"), others less so ("In choreography, if you can't be a genius, then you must be ingenious"). The arguments depend on comparisons, hence the frequency of "sounds like" (a Morton Feldman score sounds like "someone playing slow organ chords at night in a basement two houses away"), "looks like" ("[Heather] Watts, in her crimson unitard sheared off at calf and bustline, looks like a thermometer"), and "as" ("[Cynthia] Gregory was as severe as the edge of a knife"). Some of these metaphors are dazzling, but not the one that tells us a certain dancer "gave us moments of illumination as wide and blank as fate." We wish the sentence had stopped sooner: the theory that fate is "wide and blank" (hardly my conception of it) takes us off on a tangent.

Occasionally, too, Ms. Croce strains for paronomastic effects that might better have been avoided, such as "double and triple canons cannonading between piano and orchestra," and, writing of the Théâtre du Silence's production of Merce Cunningham's *Summerspace*, "the French are temperamentally nonmercist (*non, merci*)." But then, I don't care for the echoic, even "Le Monocle de Mon Oncle."

Croce's best epigrams, maxims, precepts, and distinctions seem to form themselves:

> Having pursued a mixed objective, he comes away with mixed results. . . .

> One must try to distinguish history from the wistful preservation of a legend. . . .

> Slow is a dancer's idea of serious, but the danger is that her accent will smear, her line turn ropy.

("Accent" and "line" subtly invoke a parallel with verse, in which, generally, the pace retards with the intensification of thought.)

> Style [is] a system of preferences. . . .

> [Baryshnikov's] Orpheus is a romantic hero, a protagonist. Balanchine's is a disinterested artist. . . .

> Ritualistic repetition [in postmodernism] . . . sentimentalizes the process of repetition by attributing to it more power than it possesses.

> Dance impetus that comes from nothing more than mood isn't interesting enough to sustain a whole ballet. . . .

> Obscenity of every description is one of the two great driving forces behind the ballet; the other is the belief in forgiveness and salvation.

Croce's wit can be devastating:

> Every time I see the Béjart dancers, they've lost more muscle tone and added more makeup.

> What happens next in one of [Grigorovich's] ballets is generally what happened a minute ago.

> As a choreographer, in the innocence and shamelessness of his ideas, [Valery Panov is] under the divine protection of bad taste.

> At peak moments in a performance [the benefit audience] will begin perusing its program to see why it came.

I find myself not only concurring with most of Arlene Croce's judgments but also discovering that we are attracted to the same women, the "coldly enticing" Diana Adams; Suzanne Farrell, who is "sexually very potent on the stage"; Twyla Tharp, who has "beautiful, sexy legs"; Merrill Ashley, who has "lovely" and "voluptuous" ones; and Patricia McBride, who, in *Voices of Spring*, "looks lusciously round and rosy." (Yummy!) The description of a Zobeide, "legs braced in deep fondu, body arched backward in a swoon of anticipation," is positively venal (but doesn't "fondu" refer to only one leg?). Croce can pull a leg, too (a "pure danseurnoble type [dances, at times,] as if he had all that and more to uphold"), while offering valuable comments on the relationship of sex, dance, and dancers. Thus, so I believe, she correctly perceives that Prokofiev's *Romeo and Juliet* "may be the only ballet in standard repertory that homosexuals can identify with emotionally without distortion." Obviously this depends on the staging—the way the San Francisco Ballet costumes "the boys . . . in tights and codpieces"—but to Croce's several additional reasons, one might add that the heterosexuality in Shakespeare's play is on the puppy-love level anyway.

The *New Yorker* critic supports Vera Krasovskaya, Nijinsky's biographer, in her interpretation that his role as Petrushka was a sublimation of his real-life humiliation by Diaghilev. Going further, Croce sees Nijinsky's choreographic creations as a sexual autobiography, progressing from the "self-induced" orgasm of *Faune,* to the "consciously manipulated" one of *Jeux,* and the "communal seizure" of *Sacre.* But her conclusion that "Diaghilev's personality as we know it is more Noël Coward suave than John Barrymore unctuous" makes one wonder whether "unctuous" could ever have applied to Diaghilev. Not as he appears in Stravinsky's archives,[2] where the most frequent descriptions of his character are "liar," "cheat," "false friend," and "insanely jealous."

I agree—and think Stravinsky also would have—with Arlene Croce's verdict that Paul Taylor's *Sacre* is the ultimate post-Nijinsky staging. If it serves no other purpose, Taylor's should protect the piece from ravages of the Béjart type for at least a generation. True, it is the four-hand piano version that evokes the silent-movie atmosphere for this hilarious drama of living bas-reliefs: Taylor's high jinks are inconceivable with the mammoth orchestra. Nevertheless, the music retains some of its apocalyptic power in any form, and it is a measure of Taylor's imagination that he understood that bloody murder had to be committed, even *à la* Bonnie and Clyde. My only doubt is of Croce's statement that Taylor heard the music as that of "automatons chugging to their doom in a deterministic universe." Mightn't he simply have seen the comedy in the belly of the tragedy?

2. This material unfortunately does not contain the intimate memoirs of Nijinsky that Stravinsky began to write in 1957—until Doubleday prematurely showed the first paragraphs to his widow, Romola. Under threat of lawsuit, the composer abandoned what would have been a profound testament of friendship for the dancer, and something of the opposite for the impresario, with whose name Stravinsky's is permanently linked, as are their bones in a Venetian cemetery. Having been Adolph Bolm's neighbor in California for three years, and never finding him or Stravinsky reluctant to discuss Diaghilev and Nijinsky, I can only regret that the popular use of the tape recorder came so much later.

Croce's intuitive sense of the relationship between music and choreography is almost always helpful, even when translated into visual terms:

> Having frozen his dancers to shivering tremolos, he does not unfreeze them when the music melts into droplets of pizzicati.

She correctly deduces that in *Apollo* Stravinsky may not have intended the lute as a stage prop, since he did not include "its sound in his orchestration." She notices that when choreography responds wrongly to music, we are "getting a statement about [the choreographer's] uncertainty as an artist." Though she may be right in her assertion that "most people identify a song's meaning through its lyric, not through its music," her example seems mistaken: "Irving Berlin's 'Blue Skies' . . . is a 'happy' song, even though its music is a dirge." A *dirge?* She is more certainly on target when writing that "the pounding disco beat is of no use to a choreographer," and that the disintegration of the beat in present-day "pop" is a real obstacle:

> Pop used to be made for dancing. Since it became a troubadour's art form . . . harmony has become more important. Dancers are looking for a releasing rhythm or a good tune, and the music just keeps on changing chords.

Not that many chords, either. Of a David Tudor score for a Merce Cunningham event, she asks,

> . . . how can you watch a dance with V-2 rockets whistling overhead? . . . Some of the dissociated-sound scores that Cunningham uses are more interfering and dictatorial than planned settings would be.

Other Croce comments on music deserve mention, but first the lack of one: she never refers to the disruptive timing of so much New York City Ballet applause, revealing the audience's insensitivity to music. Musician-readers might wonder why she calls the viola the "testiest of string instruments"; Balanchine's *Symphonie concertante,* one of his greatest masterpieces, is partly a work of homage to the beauties of the only feminine-gender string instrument in the modern orchestra. Yet her best remarks more than atone for a questionable few. Satie's *Relâche* "is a relic, not a classic," she writes, and "Verdi's *La Traviata* . . . lavishes great music on a story that should have waited for Puccini."

Ms. Croce devotes space to the use of words in dance pieces, writing of Gertrude Stein's text for *A Wedding Bouquet:*

Language so majestically impartial has power in the theatre—maybe only in the theatre.

Nothing is said, however, about the independence of verbal rhythms, a large ingredient in Stein's hypnotic language in this ballet. In an offering by Cage and Cunningham "they kept the words and dancing on separate planes, and the result was that Cage distracted us every time he opened his mouth." The problem is that "either the dancing reports what the words are already saying or it strays so far from the verbal meaning that I can't guess what connects the two."

George Balanchine is, of course, the hero in Arlene Croce's chronicle. She hangs on his words as well as his deeds, reporting on a conversation with the artist in his later years: "It's disappointing to get stainless steel when you've been expecting old gold." As for the young Mr. B.'s daredevil Michelangelesque creation-gesture in *Apollo:* "Only geniuses are really young at twenty-four; the rest of us are just childish." For this reader, her most absorbing discussions are of the choreographer's revisions and changes in his classics throughout the years—in the Mozart *Divertimento No. 15,* for example, music that now seems to me incomplete without the choreography. When Balanchine reworks traditional ballets, the audience demands that he express a "contemporary point of view." She remarks apropos of his *Harlequinade:*

The steps may not be Petipa's but their quality of expression is. And is Balanchine's at the same time. For a comparison, see his *Swan Lake*, in which both the surface and the depths of an old ballet have been organically reconceived.

In her assessment of the City Ballet's 1981 Tchaikovsky Festival, Croce is forced to distinguish House of Balanchine from Balanchine, comparatively little of real value by the master having emerged. Her shrewdest comment on the occasion pertains to the dependence of the music as choreographic material on the visual arts, for "Tchaikovsky cannot be expressed in absolutist, abstract terms." Because of this, perhaps, her article focuses on the personality of the composer, and her remarks on him are based on Constant Lambert's rather shopworn distinction between the side that "is crying for the moon" and the one that is "content to gaze at its beauty." But can it be said, *tout simple*, that Tchaikovsky "really was sacrificed on the altar of social hypocrisy" without suggesting that more profound inner causes were also responsible for his suicide?

Finally, let me say of Arlene Croce as she says of a dancer:

We recognize the analytical powers of an artist [who is aware of] the most delicate emotional distinctions in movement and makes us see them, too. . . .

She loves the dance, and in her patient, close attention to it conveys this love to us. What she writes about the art will affect our thinking for a long time to come.

Too Little Waugh

Evelyn Waugh's variety as a critic could have been far better displayed if this first anthology of his reviews, articles, prefaces[1] had been more comprehensive. The editor's comments, betraying reservations about present-day interest in some of the unselected material, could hardly have been worse timed, since we are apparently on the verge of a Waugh boom. Thanks to such developments as the Arab occupation of Britain, Waugh's views not only seem much less rabidly reactionary now, but are even being embraced by the liberals he once attacked. Unlike his diaries, which *he* did not choose to publish, his journalism is never dull, and the writing is a continual delight. For marksmanship and elegance, as well as economy of language, no one currently reviewing books even approaches the standard of the best in this much-too-slender volume.

The earliest pieces in *A Little Order* are the most surprising, especially some remarkably accomplished paragraphs on cubism, written when he was fourteen. Reaching twenty-one (1924), Waugh recommends a new war, suggesting, among possible provocations, the invasion of (Eighteenth Amend-

1. *Evelyn Waugh: A Little Order, Selections from His Journalism*, edited by Donat Gallagher (London, 1977).

ment) America "in the cause of alcohol." A few years later, calling attention to the existence of a "younger generation," he observes, "I do not know why that should be so, because, of course, people are born and grow up daily, and not in decades." By the late 1920s he is increasingly epigrammatic: "The arts offer the only career in which commercial failure is not necessarily discreditable." By this date, too, he is fabricating dialogue that might have been used in *Vile Bodies*, as, for example, in this exchange at the time of a fad in *romans à clef:* " 'Have you read so-and-so's new novel?' 'No. Who's in it?' "

The choice of articles and reviews by Waugh, the Roman Catholic convert, must be faulted. The *Open Letter to H. E. the Cardinal Archbishop of Westminster* should have been reprinted, partly because the published text is so rare,[2] mainly because of Waugh's reply to critics of his description, in *Black Mischief*, of the character Prudence being eaten at a cannibal feast:

> It cannot matter whether she was roasted, grilled, braised, or pickled, cut into sandwiches or devoured hot on toast as a savoury; the fact is that the wretched girl was cooked and eaten, and that is obviously and admittedly a disagreeable end.

The book lacks a specimen of Waugh's war reporting, of which "Commando Raid on Bardia"[3] must be among the finest of its kind; nor does it include any of the travel pieces, not the Spitzbergen expedition, or the trip to Goa, or even "Honeymoon Travel" (an article that refutes the statement in Christopher Sykes's biography that Waugh does not allude in any of his work to the 1946 visit to Spain). Missing, too, are such specialties as the reviews of handbooks on etiquette ("The Amenities in America") and of *Who's Who* ("Why is

2. London, 1933.
3. *Life*, November 17, 1941.

Sir Ranulph Twisleton-Wykeham-Fiennes listed under F and
Adm. the Hon. Sir R. A. R. Plunkett-Ernle-Drax under P?").
On the other hand, the writer at his most querulous is more
than amply represented in the reply to J. B. Priestley's critique of *The Ordeal of Gilbert Pinfold,* and in the patho-
logically vindictive description of an encounter with two
would-be interviewers. The latter article might at least have
been offset by the inclusion of the impersonal and entertaining skit on "today's interviewing technique."[4]

The novelist is admittedly less brilliant when bestowing an
accolade, in the sense of "a light blow with the flat of the
sword," than when using the weapon as a skewer. But the
book's most outrageous piece, the review of Stephen Spender's
World within World, animadverts upon the editor for having
chosen to include an assault on only one living writer; Mr.
Gallagher would have been kinder to offer, as well, such
massacres as those of Truman Capote[5] and Cecil Beaton,[6]
which also would have put Waugh in a different perspective.
Furthermore, these additions would have enhanced the contents, since Waugh is at his best when inveighing against
abuses of syntax and fumbling prose. Still another solution
would have been to place the two pieces on Cyril Connolly
immediately after the one on Spender, beginning with, as
Waugh calls it, "The *Horizon* Blue-Print of Chaos." One of
Connolly's precepts for social reform was that "light and heat
[should be] supplied free, like air and water." But, as Waugh
notes, "air is not 'supplied,' and water is rarely 'free.' " Incidentally, his analysis of Connolly's failure to achieve "his
avowed object of writing a durable book" seems extraordinarily perceptive today:

What makes a writer, as distinguished from a . . . cultured
man who can write, . . . is a breadth of vision which enables
him to conceive and complete a structure. Critics, insofar

4. *Vogue,* July 1948.
5. *Spectator,* March 20, 1954.
6. *Spectator,* July 21, 1961.

as they are critics only, lack this, Mr. Connolly very evidently. . . .

On the evidence of *A Little Order*, Waugh was at his peak as an essayist in 1944, in his demolition of Harold Laski's Stalin-worshipping *Faith, Reason, and Civilization*, an article that will be read with rather more approval today than it was at the time. Waugh's indignation is not yet ill-tempered, his language is without fat and the alliterative indulgences that sometimes mar the later reviews ("Scobie arrogates to himself the prerogatives of Providence"), and the writing is dated only by its excellence. This last cannot be said of Laski, of whom Waugh remarks:

> Had we not the Professor's assurance that his book is "essentially an essay, nothing more," we might take it for something much less. . . . Diffuse, repetitive, and contradictory, . . . the argument so far as I can claim to have followed it through the hairpin bends and blind alleys in which it abounds . . . is that the "values" of the past are dead; they are not to be found in art because Mr. T. S. Eliot is not understood by manual labourers and James Joyce is understood by nobody. "Values" can only be found now in Soviet Russia; the battle of Stalingrad proves it. . . .

Waugh's historical examples quickly dispose of the argument that "heroic military defense" is "conclusive evidence that the defenders have superior 'values' to the attackers." He turns to Laski's analogy between Christianity and Marxism:

> The latest imposture [Marxism] is more grossly impudent than its predecessor, Christianity, for the latter said, "ye will be happy hereafter," and cannot be proved wrong (until Professor Laski's scholars get to work), while the former says, "My dear comrades, you may not realize it, but you *are* happy at this moment."

Many readers will enjoy *A Little Order* primarily for the particulars of its criticisms of fiction—rather than its literary judgments, which may be attributable either to teasing ("The best American writer, of course, is Erle Stanley Gardner") or to friendship ("[Ronald Knox's] *Enthusiasm* is the greatest work of literary art of this century"). Defending Angus Wilson's *Hemlock and After* from critics who had condemned one of the book's characters (Mrs. Curry, the procuress) as unbelievable, Waugh says:

> I was able, at a pinch, to accept her . . . it would not be surprising to learn that she had in fact been drawn quite accurately from life. This is often the case with the least plausible characters in fiction and when it happens it marks an artistic failure on the part of the writer.

But surely Waugh's distinction that the character is credible, but not her methods, is splitting hairs. He goes on to answer the critics' further objection that the odiousness of the characters places them beyond interest:

> There is a superfluity of . . . wicked [people], but there is almost an equal number of people who under other eyes than Mr. Wilson's might be quite likable. Mr. Wilson is unique in his detestation of all of his creatures. . . .

The reason for this, Waugh speculates, might be a preoccupation with class that could detract from Wilson's artistry. The observation is shrewd, even prophetic, for of late Wilson has seemed to be more sociologist than novelist.

And Waugh's own class obsessions? Certainly they do not damage *A Handful of Dust* or "Mr. Loveday's Little Outing," the best products of his imaginative world. This, we once thought, was too thickly populated by charlatans and cads, too sparsely by decent victim-types, while the inexorable rule of chance seemed exaggerated. Today, however,

whether we regard Fate as a script written long ago and waiting to be enacted, or simply as hindsight, the end no longer
seems preposterous—to use one of Waugh's favorite words.

Touched off by a single typographical error in a book that
he reviews, Waugh fusses about "imperfect proofreading."
But *A Little Order* is strewn with such slips as "I know what
I lilke," "A Sèvres vase," "[the comedian] Mr. Charles
Chaplain," "the world seemed full of exicting new books,"
"We do not except them to grow any older." More distracting still, the editor assigns each piece to a category: "Myself,"
"Aesthete," "Man of Letters," "Conservative," "Catholic."
But even if Waugh's opinions warranted this kind of separation, these writings do not fit the compartments. Thus about
half of his notice of Peter Quennell's *Hogarth* is omitted for
the peculiar reason that "it is unrelated to narrative painting"
—as if anyone would read a book review because of an interest in that subject rather than in Waugh on no matter
what.

Thus, too, Waugh's discussion of *The Heart of the Matter*
is not found in the sections under "Aesthete" and "Man of
Letters," but under "Catholic," and this though he disclaims
competence in the theological questions raised by the novel,
and though his most valuable observations concern Greene's
style and cinematographic storytelling technique; even the
remarks on the Péguy epigraph to the book are centered less
on doctrinal validity than on the use of words. One suspects
that *A Little Order* does not include the review of *The Quiet
American* simply because it could not be classified under
"Catholic."

The editor is obtrusive in other ways, too, but is not on
hand when needed.[7] He introduces his five categories unnecessarily and not always literately, referring to the novelist

7. In a memorial for Alfred Duggan, Waugh mentions that the novel *Count
Bohemond* will appear posthumously, but a footnote should have informed
the reader that this book was published in 1964, and with a preface by
Waugh, a better-written tribute than the radio talk included in *A Little
Order*.

as "far too daemonic" (can one be acceptably daemonic?) and "apt [*sic*] . . . to rewrite," a habit evidently not shared by the editor, who admires "the discipline and strength of purpose which enables [Waugh] to defy the temper of the times and his natural inclinations. . . ." But can anyone be certain that Waugh was not following, rather than defying, his natural inclinations?

Scholars' English

A PECULIAR LANGUAGE

The accelerating decline of correct English usage is no less apparent in the higher literary journalism than in cue-card prose, to say nothing of the verbalizing on television without these aids. Watergate revealed the extent to which the speech of American congressmen and other government officials had become inflated, hyperbolic, stereotypical, and cliché ridden; but this might have been expected. When professors of English and of philosophy at the universities of Cambridge and Oxford can publish sheer nonsense, the language is in a parlous state. The examples cited here were selected both because of current interest in the subject matter and because the authors are featured contributors to two standard-setting publications, each of which is read on both sides of the Atlantic. Equally bad writing abounds in most academic periodicals.

Christopher Ricks's review of Helen Gardner's *The Composition of "Four Quartets"*[1] should establish him as the Spiro

1. *Times Literary Supplement*, September 15, 1978.

Agnew of literary criticism, thanks to such gems as "learned lumber," "insouciant uncertainty," "pricked by Faber's percipience," "piece of Old Possum's pussy-footwork," "to twinkle at Eliot's trouble with his teeth," and "fiery flickering musk." (What on earth, or elsewhere, is a "fiery flickering musk"?)

In addition to his alliterative obsessions, Mr. Ricks displays an inordinate fondness for the prefix "un-," offering such attractive specimens as "un-kowtowing," "unlingering," and "undidactic." The sentence in which this last appears might better have been devised by this Cambridge professor of English as a model of practices to be avoided by his students:

> As with a great deal of poetry, in part Eliot's achievement is to incorporate immediately an undidactic and tacit assistance as to how we should hear his poetry, and one crucial thing about the final text is the way, at once tactful and unignorable, by which the opening lines 1, 3, and 5 now all end in *-ing*.

"As to how"? (Does he mean "as to the manner in which"?) But the professor often writes even below the level that this sentence suggests; in the same article he fails more than once to make his verbs and subjects agree, overlooks redundancies ("a memory which had been lying dormant in his mind"—where else?), and indulges in the most embarrassing platitudes ("The imagination moves in a mysterious way").

Besides "un-" words, Mr. Ricks favors nonexistent ones, like "significational," and obscure forms, such as "inaugurative" (defined in the *OED* as plain "inaugural"). He also employs words eccentrically, as when noting that if Dame Helen had not resisted the temptation to comment on the changes in all of Eliot's drafts, her work "would have made for gigantism [and] arbitrariness. . . ." But in many dictionaries, the first meaning of "gigantism" is that of the pathological condition (acromegaly). And is it not reasonable to assume that the more complete a comment, the *less* arbitrary?

Still more peculiar is a Ricks reference to 1927 as Eliot's "crucial year of accession to England." Was Eliot a pretender to the throne, then, perhaps crowned in secret? (After all, the Missouri-born bard, who believed that Richard III was the last rightful English monarch, wore a white rose on the anniversary of Bosworth.) Or does the phrase merely signify that in 1927 Eliot became a British subject? Whatever the answer, the Ricks method relies on the avoidance of the most common meanings of words, the circumvention of clear communication, and the pursuit of small points beyond the endurance of the laity. All three features are exemplified in his claim that Eliot's "waning dusk" image is "hauntingly felicitous" and "at the heart of perhaps the most intractable of all Eliot's wrestlings with words." (No matter that this combination of words is not Eliot's but John Hayward's, as is the choice of "laceration"—in preference to Eliot's "rending pain"—in "the laceration of laughter at what ceases to amuse.") Yet to most non-German readers, "waning dusk" is initially confusing, evening rather than dawn coming to mind first. Professor Ricks devotes thirty lines to a discussion of the inspired locution.

Professor Ricks's more recent criticism, appearing on the front page of a *New York Times Book Review*,[2] shows no improvement. In the first few lines alone, we read of "subtle, supple talents," of "vivid versions," of "Pyrrha . . . seen in all her marine predatoriness as piranha"; we meet "gigantism" again; we struggle with a sentence beginning: "The poems' self-respect is at one with their unenvious respect for other poets. . . ." May the reader ask how poems can respect "other poets"?

The *New York Review of Books*[3] soon followed the *Times Literary Supplement* with a review of *The Composition of "Four Quartets,"* this one by Irvin Ehrenpreis, who begins with the remark that in 1914, Eliot

2. December 2, 1979.
3. December 8, 1979.

. . . wrote to a friend about the unpleasantness of meeting sexual opportunities in the street and feeling his own refinement rise up to obstruct them.

Surely the poet's "refinement" could not have obstructed "opportunities" external to him, but merely his response to them. And, if only for the reason that Eliot was not Henry Miller, the reviewer should have quoted the puritanical poet's exact words.

Professor Ehrenpreis goes on to remark that "the theme of suffering leads us to the shape of *Four Quartets* because it recalls Beethoven's development." No. Beethoven's development cannot be characterized by the word "suffering." Insofar as such things are comparable, he may have suffered more at the time of the Second Symphony, when he realized that his deafness was incurable, than he did while composing the "Ode to Joy" and the "Dankgesang." Many emotions, including exultation, are deepened in Beethoven's later music. Furthermore, the parallel that Professor Ehrenpreis draws between Eliot's "the sea has many voices" and Beethoven's apportioning himself "among the voices of his instruments" is misleading: the "voices" of the composer are not necessarily identified with one instrument or another.

In a subsequent *New York Review* essay, "Jane Austen and Heroism,"[4] Professor Ehrenpreis "floats" the subject ("But living in a milieu in which overstatements of zeal were suspect, it [?] was natural for her to look askance . . ."), mixes metaphors ("Other touches, barely audible, evoke a frame . . ."), and perplexes the reader with inappropriate imagery: in *Emma*, he writes, "Mr. Woodhouse reposes at the peak of the social pyramid, as Miss Bates stands at the bottom. . . ." The peak of a pyramid is not the right place on which to repose. The reader would feel more comfortable imagining Mr. Woodhouse standing there, in *retiré* position, leaving Miss Bates to repose at the bottom.

4. February 8, 1979.

Stuart Hampshire's *Two Theories of Morality* (first published in the *Times Literary Supplement*) may contain an illuminating comparison between Aristotle's and Spinoza's philosophies of ethics, but Professor Hampshire's syntax presents major obstacles to understanding his distinctions. Much of the time he does not say what he means:

> Will a preferable outcome [,?] on the whole, flow from preserving the freedom of the individual in these circumstances than [or?] from protecting the individuals [?] against death and misfortune? A murderous disposition is dreaded not because of the act of murder which is threatened, but because of the unhappiness and suffering that are the threatened consequences of the murder.

What this actually says is that the fate of the victim is of no importance, and that if no one else is around to suffer, then murder, in itself, is nothing to be alarmed about.

The Oxford philosopher writes, further, that

> recognition of perceived objects as being of a certain size is the obvious case of belief or knowledge which is usually intuition, as is also recognition of persons and reidentification of many other types of individuals.

But how can "recognition" be a "case" of anything, and since when are "belief" and "intuition" equatable with "knowledge"? A belief can be acquired intuitively, but the same is not true of many kinds of knowledge—that of the history of China, for instance. Moreover, what are the referents of the phrase "as is also"? And, apart from "persons," what *are* "other types of individuals"? Ghosts? Martians?

Hardly a paragraph is free of similar examples of muddled thinking and writing:

. . . the moral intuition which I share with many other men less incompletely than my other theory does. Secondly [there has not been a "firstly"], the theory can find a place within the framework, and it can therefore explain, other conflicting theoretical frameworks which cannot in their turn find a place in it.

Some readers may succeed in puzzling out the punctuation and the pronouns, but who can solve the mystery of how a person and an abstract idea can share *anything*, let alone "less incompletely"?

Professor Hampshire writes that

the theory of prima facie duties and obligations can . . . explain most agonizing moral dilemmas . . . as well as calm decisions. . . .

Yet a decision in itself cannot be "calmed," although those who make it may be affected.

Incredibly, the professor does not contest the view that

an unphilosophical man of experience, who is of good character, usually reasons correctly on practical matters.

This implies that men of thoroughly bad character are not able to reason correctly on practical matters, which is surely not the case, while saints, from all that is reputed about them, are notably impractical.

The reader wonders what Professor Hampshire can possibly mean by the remark:

Every worthwhile game, craft, or art has its theory, which stands in opposition to its practice.

If, on the one hand, the practice comes first, and if the theory derives from it—which is often the case in art—theory cannot be in opposition to practice. On the other hand, if practice derives from theory and the two *are* in opposition, then the statement is backward and should read: "Practice stands in opposition to theory." But is it not true that some games, crafts, or arts are practiced in perfect conformity with their theories, such as those arts governed by rules of religions? And by what criteria is a game, craft, or art considered "worthwhile"?

Astonishingly, the professor says that

> clearing one's mind of confusions and superstitious fears will always involve getting rid of the idea of oneself as an original cause and as a sovereign will and as an island in nature.

But does anyone, even an Oxonian, think of himself as an "original cause"?

Almost as surprisingly, Professor Hampshire includes "honesty and the will to please" in his list of "conflicting virtues." Certainly "the will to please" may be essential equipment for a politician, but does it deserve to be rated as a virtue? "The will to please" is obviously something very different from consideration for others, since the former, tending to lead to corruption, could easily become a dangerous quality, while the latter is always a good one. Yet the professor actually attempts to illustrate the will-to-please "virtue" through an example:

> A man wants to be fair in making a particular award; but he also wants to avoid suffering, and he knows that he cannot . . . do both these things, because the man who deserves to lose will suffer greatly and the one who will win will not be greatly pleased, nor would he suffer much if he lost.

Here, after being led to imagine that the potential sufferer is the bestower of the award, the reader is confounded on reflecting that anyone who is indifferent to winning and losing

poses psychological—or spiritual (is he transcendent?)—
questions, not ethical ones.

Professor Hampshire's *New York Review* essay, "The Illusion of Sociobiology,"[5] further demonstrates that he cannot
mean what he says:

> [Among] the most elementary facts about us [is] the fact
> that we are born with the physical equipment that makes
> it possible for us to think and talk to others about our activities and movements tomorrow.

"*Tomorrow*"? Surely some essential words have been
omitted? Does the professor mean: " . . . talk to others about
our activities and movements *that may take place* tomorrow"?

But the confusion that this essay displays is so serious that
to quote more than one further example from it might have
a deleterious effect on the reader:

> Yesterday's . . . scientific speculations soon acquire a fusty
> look. Having been born in the excitement of today's discoveries, they are then extrapolated into a golden scientific
> future, which turns out to be quite different.

How in heaven's name can yesterday's speculations have been
born today, and *from what* will that "golden scientific future" be "quite different"?

5. October 12, 1978.

Some Rediscovered
Philosophy Criticism
by T. S. Eliot

Apart from his 1916 doctoral dissertation, *Meinong's Gegendstandstheorie Considered in Relation to Bradley's Theory of Knowledge*, widely reviewed at the time of its belated publication,[1] Eliot's writings on philosophy are little known. This dereliction is the more remarkable in that he taught philosophy at Harvard for three years; his principal philosophical publications are contemporary with his first mature poems; he reveals more of himself in this category of his criticism than in any other, as when he questions the wisdom of aligning his views with Christian dogma:

> A spirit such as mine is too inclined to measure everything according to the rules of a dogmatic conception, and tends to become more and more rigid and formal;[2]

1. As *Knowledge and Experience in the Philosophy of F. H. Bradley* (1964).
2. *Nouvelle Revue Française*, April 1, 1925.

and his teachers included Russell, Royce, Santayana, William James, Bergson, and Irving Babbitt.[3]

The ten newly identified Eliot reviews of philosophical books and essays, dating from 1917 and 1918, should stimulate interest in his other writings on philosophy, though these short pieces are also valuable in themselves and because they reveal a hitherto unknown link with Russell. Apparently on Russell's recommendation, Philip Jourdain, his pupil and the English editor of the *Monist* (Chicago), proposed to invite Eliot to review "all books on philosophy and science [not of] a formal character." The exhumed writings[4] date from Eliot's "Russell period," which began in 1915 at Merton College, where the poet spent most of his time on the *Principia* ("It gave me a sense of pleasure and power, manipulating those curious little figures"), and moved on to a "Dear Bertie," "Dear Tom" stage, during which Eliot adopted the view that "the truths of mathematics are not true absolutely, but are true and proper for the human mind." In 1920, asked whether his essay "The Perfect Critic" was philosophy or criticism, Eliot fell back on Russell's argument in the *Principia* (Chapter 2, on "The Theory of Types and the Cretan Liar") that "the statement of Epimenides does not fall within its own scope, therefore no contradiction emerges."

Eliot continued to admire Russell's intellect, which "would have reached the first rank even in the thirteenth century,"[5] and his prose. Reviewing *Mysticism and Logic and Other Essays*, the poet remarked that while

no philosopher can be judged entirely on his prose, a good deal of light can be thrown on a philosopher by holding

---

3. Irving Babbitt and Paul Elmer More seemed like "the two wisest men that I have known," Eliot wrote (*Princeton Alumni Weekly*, February 1937), but neither sage will be discussed here, for the reasons that Eliot's essay on Babbitt is still in print ("The Humanism of Irving Babbitt," in *Selected Essays*, 1932), and that More, though one of Eliot's exemplars, did not become one of his teachers: "More, a St. Louisan, . . . had known my family, and if he had remained there for a few years longer, he would have

his work up to the standards of literature. For literary
standards help us perceive just those moments when a
writer is scrupulously and sincerely attending to his vision. . . . The point is, where is Mr. Russell's insight, his
peculiar vision, to be found? For where that is, there will
the style be; and where the style does not convince, the
vision will be lacking. . . . His style . . . neither increases
nor dissimulates the difficulty of the subject. The liberation of English philosophy from German influence[6] will
have been the work, not of Mill (who is an amateur), but
of Mr. Russell; he is a philosopher who has invented a new
point of view; and a new point of view is style.[7]

It was Russell who first identified Eliot as the author of this
unsigned piece, and who recognized himself as the satyr in
"Mr. Apollinax":

I heard the beat of centaur's hoofs over the hard turf
As his dry and passionate talk devoured the afternoon.

The rest of the story is well known. In the 1920s, Eliot decided that Russell had

never been really convinced that philosophy was possible
at all—the mathematician in him [being] impatient of the

---

taught me Greek as he had taught my brother." Eliot was indifferent to
More's writings when the two men first met—at the Harvard home of Babbitt—
and Eliot recalled that it was not until the publication of the later volumes
of *The Greek Tradition* that "I came to find an auxiliary to my own progress
of thought, which no English theologian at the time could have given
me. . . . " (Ibid.) One of Eliot's most precise statements of a philosophical
position of his own is found in his first article on More: "The fundamental
beliefs of an intellectual conservatism, that man requires an ascesis, a *formula*
to be imposed upon him from above; that society must develop out of itself a
class of leaders who shall discipline it; distrust of the premises of the future,
and conviction that the future . . . must be built upon the wisdom of the
past—this is what we find in all of Mr. More's writings." (*New Statesman*,
June 24, 1916) In later years, Eliot emphasized the limitations rather than
the achievements of the author of *The Demon of the Absolute:* "More is at
times narrow, as in his treatment of the mysticism of St. John of the Cross,
. . . and at times downright heterodox, as in his treatment of the Doctrine of

philosopher. Hence his history presents the curious spectacle of a very powerful mind . . . at war with itself . . . destroying not so much other men's systems (though Russell has laid flat a good many) as his own.[8]

Shortly after publishing this, Eliot struck back at Russell's dictum that science is the nineteenth century's "only claim to distinction,"[9] and the war of "the two cultures" had begun. The best of the newfound *Monist* pieces relate to Eliot's poetry and beliefs. His presentation of Sorel, for example, closely resembles views put forth in *For Lancelot Andrewes*:

The reaction against romanticism which is one of the most interesting phenomena of our time . . . [the hatred] of middle-class democracy . . . the skepticism . . . which has developed the craving for belief . . . Sorel longs for a narrow, intolerant, creative society with sharp divisions. He longs for the pessimistic, classical view. . . . It is not surprising that Sorel has become a Royalist. . . .

And not surprising that Eliot was to become one, too. Another review, of Harris's *The Ascent of Olympus*, a history of the thunder-god from phytomorph (the oak tree, which is the kind most often struck by lightning) to anthropomorph (the deities Dionysus and Apollo), points to *The Waste Land*, though Eliot was already familiar with the thunder

---

the Eucharist. . . . More had an inadequate conception of the divine nature of the Church as the Living Body of Christ. . . ." ("An Anglican Platonist," *Times Literary Supplement*, October 30, 1937)
4. The ten review articles contributed to the *Monist* in 1917 and 1918 were discovered by Alan Cohn and Elizabeth Eames. See *The Papers of the Bibliographical Society of America* 70, no. 3 (1977): 420–24.
5. *Criterion*, January 1926. Cf. "The Renaissance Platonists [were] inferior philosophers to the scholastics of the thirteenth century[,] scientific thinking [having] displaced philosophic thinking." (*Times Literary Supplement*, December 6, 1926)
6. "Russell and Bradley, between them, have nearly laid metaphysics in the grave." (*New Statesman*, December 29, 1917)
7. *Nation*, March 23, 1918. In this article, Eliot refers to the *Principia* with-

fable (Datta, Dayadhvam, Damyata), perhaps in Sanskrit first (the Brihadaranyaka-Upanishad), or in German (Deussen's *Sechzig Upanishads des Vedas*), if not in English (*Hindu Law and Custom as to Gifts*, by C. R. Lanman, who was Eliot's Sanskrit professor).

In another of the *Monist* reviews, of a book of Jainist texts, Eliot questions the differences between the precepts of *ahimsa* (nonviolence to living beings) in Jainism and in Buddhism, and between the dualism of the former and that of early Sankhya. But the most aggressive of these ten articles is aimed at Durkheim, whose "group consciousness" Eliot did not believe to be "capable of articulate expression," and whose theory of the genesis of knowledge "has doubtful philosophical implications. . . . Durkheim leaves epistemology . . . precisely where it was before." Jourdain's requirement that Eliot sign his pieces with his cognominal initial in Greek (*eta*) undoubtedly helped to hide them these sixty-five years.[10]

Eliot's references to his former teachers are always respectful and sometimes affectionate. He recalled that his unpublished 1913 paper "The Interpretation of Primitive Ritual"[11] was intended for the eye of "that extraordinary philosopher, Josiah Royce,"[12] . . . "my old master, now mostly forgotten but a great philosopher in his day. . . ."[13] Eliot had attended Royce's seminar on comparative methodology—was it here

---

out mentioning Whitehead. In a later essay (*Bookman*, February 1930), Eliot acknowledges Whitehead as "one of the greatest . . . exponents of formal logic." The statement is a prelude, however, to an attack on Whitehead's "summoning of Shelley and Wordsworth to prove something in connection with a philosophy of nature . . . [While] poetry provides intellectual sanction for feeling, and aesthetic sanction for thought, . . . [it] cannot prove that anything is true."

8. *Vanity Fair*, February 1924.

9. *Criterion*, April 1924.

10. Eliot described his Greek as "inadequate to the appreciation of Pindar's Odes," but E. R. Dodds (*The Greeks and the Irrational*) testified that, in a seminar on Plotinus' *Enneads*, the young poet's command of the language was equal to that of the best scholars. Eliot deprecated his knowledge of languages—"I began with a public school knowledge of Latin, a traveler's

that Royce described Hegel's phenomenology as a *"Bildungs-roman"?*—and Royce graded Eliot's thesis on Bradley "the work of an expert." As for Santayana, Eliot recalled his "slightly amused gaze," and his "tender reverence and admirable restraint" toward Hegel, whose Idealist philosophy, that "colossal and grotesque achievement,"[14] constituted "the orthodox doctrine of the American universities, [where] it had begun to turn manifestly mouldy."[15] Since Eliot, in the preface to his *Dante,* acknowledged a debt to Santayana's study of Goethe for the apt classification "a philosophical poet"—although regretting "Goethe's philosophy [as] that which the nineteenth century took up with . . . Love, Nature, God, Man, Science, Progress"[16]—the failure to credit Santayana as the originator of the phrase "objective correlative" is difficult to explain.

So, too, the tone of Eliot's review of William James's lectures on immortality reveals a fondness for the man, however remote his pragmatism:

He had great curiosity, and a curiously charming willingness to believe anything that seemed preposterous to the ordinary scientific mind. He hated oppression in any form. . . . James is characteristically democratic, genially drawing a picture of a future life which includes animals and savages. . . . [He] has an exceptional quality of always

smattering of Italian" (Preface to *Dante,* 1929)—but admitted to enjoying Lallans, even though "I read [it] with difficulty." (Letter to Hugh MacDiarmid)
11. Substantial excerpts from "The Interpretation of Primitive Ritual" have recently appeared in Piero Gray's *T. S. Eliot's Intellectual and Poetic Development: 1909 to 1922* (Atlantic Highlands, N.J., 1982).
12. Introduction to *Savonarola* (1926).
13. *Listener,* March 23, 1932.
14. *Nation and Athenaeum,* January 12, 1929. Earlier, Eliot had written that "Hegel's *Philosophy of Art* adds very little to our enjoyment or understanding of art, though it fills a gap in Hegel's philosophy." (*Athenaeum,* August 6, 1920)
15. Introduction to *Leisure: The Basis of Culture,* by Josef Pieper (1952).
16. *New English Weekly,* June 6, 1935.

leaving his reader with the feeling that the world is full of possibilities. . . .[17]

Eliot's deepest philosophical involvement was with Bergson, especially with his shortcomings, for the creative world-will did not "provide an answer to the question of whether reality might be found in the object or in the consciousness."[18] Bergson's use of science sometimes concealed "the incoherence of a multiplicity of points of view," and his exciting promise of immortality was "a somewhat meretricious captivation."[19] But while Eliot condemned Bergson's time doctrine for inherent "*fatalism* which is wholly destructive,"[20] Bergson, in the following passage, says much the same thing as the end of the first part of *Burnt Norton:*

> Time, as we ordinarily envisage it, is a division of reality into existent and non-existent parts. From the reality which now is, is excluded the reality which will be. Duration knows no such distinction. The past exists in the present which contains the future. The concrete and ever-present instance of duration is life, for each of us living individuals in his own time.

Looking back, Eliot felt that

> to have truly understood the Bergsonian fervor, one must have gone, regularly, every week to the Collège de France, and the hall, full to bursting, where he gave his courses. (It was necessary to arrive an hour and a quarter ahead of time. . . .)[21]

From a still greater distance, the poet continued to express a "longing for the appearance of a philosopher whose writings,

17. *New Statesman*, September 8, 1917.
18. Unpublished paper on Bergson, Houghton Library, Harvard.
19. *Criterion*, October 1927.
20. *Vanity Fair*, February 1924.
21. *What France Means to You* (1944).

lectures, and personality will arouse the imagination as Bergson aroused it forty years ago."[22]

From the same retrospective, Eliot wrote:

Though I was unconscious of it, the reason for my dissatisfaction with philosophy as a profession I now believe to lie in the divorce of philosophy from theology.[23]

Even his earliest philosophical reviews are preoccupied with theology, and his attraction to Leibniz may be attributed to the monadist's "strong devotion to theology." Leibniz "had the mind of a doctor of the church," Eliot wrote, and a power of intellect in which he is "the equal of Aristotle or Plato, though for all the curious fables of *Timaeus* or the *Physics*, [Plato and the Stagirite] were more secure, better balanced, and less superstitious."[24] Nevertheless, Leibniz's theory of mind and matter, of body and soul, "is in some ways the subtlest that has ever been devised. Matter [for him] is an arrested moment of mind, 'mind without memory,' "[25] or what Bergson called mind "running down."[26]

Eliot's notes on his reading in the Harvard years show that his main interests were mysticism and the psychology of religious experience. At the time of his conversion to Anglo-Catholicism (1928) and his espousal of "classicism in literature" and "royalism in politics,"[27] he excluded mysticism as a nostrum for the present: "Mysticism nowadays" is simply

22. Introduction to Pieper, op. cit.
23. Ibid.
24. *Monist*, January 1916.
25. Ibid.
26. Unpublished paper on Bergson, op. cit.
27. Eliot's royalism can best be studied in his analysis (*New English Weekly*, February 27, 1937) of the legal issues on the abdication of Edward VIII. That Eliot published his views on the affair is surprising and may in some way be connected with his friendship with *Mr*. Simpson. Eliot challenged the role of the press ("seldom edifying . . . whether righteous and sanctimonious or demagogic") and the usefulness of public opinion ("When we cannot trust our own feelings [which might vary several times a day], why should we put faith in the collective feeling?") and he concluded with the warning: "Those

a "warm fog."[28] He elaborates on this in reviewing a volume of Hügel's letters, after confessing that he has not read *The Mystical Element in Religion*, partly because the style is so difficult—"[Hügel's] feelings were exact [but] his ideas were often vague"—partly because he was

> neither a great philosopher, nor a theologian. . . . Mysticism is not the issue of our time. We demand of religion some kind of intellectual satisfaction. . . . True mysticism is so rare and unessential and false mysticism so common and dangerous that one cannot oppose it too firmly.[29]

Whereas "true mysticism is a gift of grace," the false kind produces "pathological ecstatics."[30] Yet the doctrine of John of the Cross ("perhaps the greatest psychologist of all European mystics"[31]), the denial of self in the love of God, was to be the foundation of Eliot's Faith in the years immediately before World War II, a period during which he also accepted the *Dhammapada*, recognizing that the belief in karma and reincarnation "was so deep in the mentality [of Buddha's followers] as to be a category of their thought. . . . His teaching assumes its truth."[32]

In later life, Eliot wrote that what remained to him of his Harvard studies was "the style of three philosophers: Plato's Greek, Spinoza's Latin,[33] and Bradley's English"—this last with reservations:

---

who saw in Edward a more democratic conception of the monarchy are enjoying the vision of an idealised past and preparing the way for a certainly not democratic future. . . . 'When that the poor have cried, Caesar hath wept.' "
28. *Listener*, April 2, 1930.
29. *Dial*, February 1928.
30. *Listener*, March 12, 1930.
31. *Listener*, April 2, 1930.
32. *Revelation* (1937).
33. Eliot considered the beginning of the Third Book of the *Ethics* "especially brilliant" (*Athenaeum*, April 4, 1919), but he supported Leibniz's refutation of Spinoza's theory of the relation of mind and body ("With Spinoza the reason does not possess ideas, it is an idea"). The switch of focus from

even in the austerity of [his] dry and boney prose one recognizes here and there a feverish flush which is wholly alien to the tradition of Hobbes, Berkeley and Locke.[34]

As he had established in the early article on Russell, Eliot first evaluated most philosophers by the quality of their writing. He cites Dewey's "ungrammatical" thinking[35] as symbolic of the "dark labyrinths of the American philosophical mind," and condemns Péguy because

> his style . . . is not a style to think in; it is too emphatic, too insistent. His sentences, a dozen pages long, convey an emotion, but thought is submerged. It is a style with a refrain which compels one to lock step. . . .[36]

Péguy has a "sensibility for the emotional value of words, completely unrestrained by either logic or common sense."[37] He was handicapped in coming from a Paris "surfeited with criticism [and with] radical and reactionary movements which were largely movements for the sake of moving." *Plus ça change, plus c'est la même chose.*

Nietzsche is the exception to this rule of clear writing. His

> philosophy evaporates when detached from its literary qualities. . . . Such scholars always have a peculiar influence

---

Spinoza's philosophy to his personality provoked the remark, "A study of Spinoza worship from Goethe, Renan, and Arnold on one side, and Rousseau on another would show a considerable influence affecting liberal theology." (*Times Literary Supplement,* April 20, 1927) Yet Eliot himself had romanticized Spinoza, as in the following daydream about Shakespeare: "In the middle of a rowdy seventeenth-century playhouse pit, the thought of Shakespeare, the feeling and the shuddering personal experience of Shakespeare, moved solitary and unspoiled; solitary and free as the thought of Spinoza in his study. . . ." (*Athenaeum,* May 14, 1920)

34. Eliot to Aldington, October 8, 1923: "If I can write English prose . . . it is due to two causes: an intensive study of two years of the prose of Bradley, and an inherited disposition to rhetoric [which] gives my prose, I am aware, a rather rheumatic pomposity. . . ." But Eliot had a blind spot where Bradley

over the large semi-philosophical public, who are spared
the austere effort of criticism required either by metaphysics or literature.[38]

Confusion of thought, emotion, and vision is what we find
in *Also sprach Zarathustra*.[39]

Since Wagner's on-and-off disciple did not have a theory of
knowledge, let alone a "consistent moral policy," Eliot seems
to have been drawn to Nietzsche only because of his "pessimistic views [on] the future of art." Yet *The Birth of Tragedy* exerted an influence on *The Waste Land*, and not simply
in the line *"Oed' und leer das Meer,"* which is as likely to
have attracted Eliot in Nietzsche's book as in the *Tristan*
score.

Except in the thesis on Bradley, Eliot's own style in his
philosophical writings is admirably lucid and grammatically
smoother than in much of his other prose. To some extent
this may be the result of the tutoring (1916) of Harold
Joachim, to whom Eliot acknowledged a "debt for instruction in the writing of English. . . . He taught me to avoid
metaphor and taught me the importance of punctuation."[40]

Eliot's philosophical reviews are enlivened by prickly remarks:

Professor Parker has come by philosophy to conclusions
which most thinking people have absorbed from the atmosphere.[41]

---

was concerned, and the passage from *The Principles of Logic* that Eliot
praises (*For Lancelot Andrewes*, 1928) contains more than one embarrassing
locution (viz., "an unearthly ballet of bloodless categories").

35. *Times Literary Supplement*, September 2, 1926.

36. *New Statesman*, October 7, 1916.

37. *Cambridge Review*, December 12, 1928.

38. *International Journal of Ethics*, April 1916.

39. *The Sacred Wood* (1920).

40. *Times* (London), August 6, 1938. Eliot never mastered punctuation, however, and though he writes that "correct language is civilisation" (*Listener*,
April 9, 1930), his own language is often careless: "The modern world suffers

Professor MacKenzie is over-modest. . . . If he would re-write his book in a kind of arrogant contemptuousness for other philosophers, affirming his conclusions without defending them, this would be an excellent essay.[42]

by epigrams:

Every significant philosopher is a man who has had one insight, or two or three, which no one before him had had; one new insight which excuses a hundred new errors.[43]

and by a vividness that makes even the "bald millionaire, *maestro di color che sanno*," seem to be our contemporary:

In reading Aristotle . . . we are in touch with a mind that has regarded the world quite freshly and independently; when we read him carefully, we discover the world again with him, and find him, halting, stumbling, too intent upon the truth, at any moment, to be always consistent: sometimes at a dead stop in the face of insuperable difficulties.[44]

But Eliot's greatest skill is in differentiating:

For the Greek, the human was the typically human, individual differences were not of scientific interest; for the modern philosopher, individual differences were of absorbing importance.[45]

---

from two great disasters," he wrote, "the decay of the study of Latin and Greek and the dissolution of the monasteries. These defects can be supplied." ("The Modern Dilemma," published in *Christian Register* [Boston], October 19, 1933) *"Supplied"*? Surely he means "countered." See Robert Graves and Alan Hodge's dissection (in *The Reader over Your Shoulder*) of the first three paragraphs of Eliot's essay on Massinger.
41. *New Statesman*, July 13, 1918.
42. Ibid.
43. Ibid.
44. *New Statesman*, December 29, 1917.
45. *Monist*, October 1916.

Eliot is most conspicuously in error in overestimating the importance of Bradley; in misrepresenting Hobbes (who falls short of Eliot's ideal of "impersonality and detachment" and is guilty of cynicism, or what is now called egoistic psychology); and in relying on an out-of-date anthropology—though this was also true of the books that he reviews, such as Wundt's *Elements of Folk Psychology*, with its animistic totemism, the "diremption of primitive soul ideas into . . . moving forms . . . a bird, a snake, or a lizard."[46] Yet some of Eliot's own anthropological speculations should be reprinted:

It is possible to assert that primitive man acted in a certain way and then found a reason for it. An unoccupied person finding a drum may be seized with a desire to beat it; but unless he is an imbecile he will be unable to continue beating it . . . without finding a reason for so doing. The reason may be the long continued drought. The next generation or the next civilisation will find a more plausible reason for beating a drum. Shakespeare and Racine—or rather the developments which led up to them—each found his own reason. The reasons may be divided into tragedy and comedy. We still have similar reasons, but we have lost the drum.[47]

In gamuts that extend from Maimonides to Moore, Heraclitus to Husserl (from whom Eliot borrowed the line, in his "Triumphal March," "The natural wakeful life of our Ego is a perceiving"), and Pantanjali to Frobenius ("The *Schicksalskunde* is an example of modern mind in its most unpleasant form"[48]), distortions naturally occur. But within the bounds of general reading, Eliot scores a high proportion of "right judgments," remote though many of them are from those prevailing at the time when he published. Thus

46. *Monist*, January 1918.
47. *Nation and Athenaeum*, October 6, 1926.
48. *New English Weekly*, June 14, 1934.

Diderot was a mere "echo of a name" in 1917, when Eliot wrote:

The Diderot problem is that he did not write a master-piece. The *Letter on the Blind* and the *Letter on the Deaf and Dumb* are, . . . as an exposition of sensationalism, in-ferior to Condillac's systematic treatise. [Yet] wherever the intellect of the century stirred, Diderot dropped a grain into the ferment; he provided leading ideas which force the scientist to look in certain directions, which force the artist to develop certain forms. . . . Whosoever wishes to understand how the nineteenth century sprang from the eighteenth must read Diderot as well as Rousseau.[49]

In distinguishing between the century of Newton, which, un-like that of Bruno, could "achieve a synthesis," Eliot re-marks:

The [sixteenth-century] mind which epitomizes all or nearly all that is best in these forgotten speculations, so far as one mind can do it, is the mind of Montaigne [, who] is so much himself [but] also representative of some perma-nent attitude of the human spirit.[50]

Aesthetics was the one branch of philosophy that Eliot delib-erately avoided—for the reason that

abstract studies which turn upon the practice of one's art are dangerous. Aesthetics may make us conscious of what operates better unconsciously. . . . The great characters of drama and prose fiction may themselves provide material for study to psychologists, but out of the psychologists'

49. *New Statesman*, March 17, 1917. As for the author of *Candide*, Eliot was fond of quoting Baudelaire's *"Je m'ennuie en France, où tout le monde ressemble à Voltaire."*
50. *Athenaeum*, October 10, 1919.

abstractions no character can be put together. The dramatist must study, not psychology, but human beings. . . .[51]

After his conversion to Anglo-Catholicism, Eliot repudi-
ated all "one-man philosophies," even that of the *Summa,*[52]
since

> the whole truth of Christianity [does not] depend upon the
> validity of the philosophy of St. Thomas Aquinas—[an]
> impression which, I suspect, some of his main apologists
> have sometimes given.[53]

To Eliot's mind, Maritain, the "lyricist of Thomism," was
not "an original thinker . . . [but] a propagator [who] stim-
ulates the intellect without always satisfying it [and who]
persuades us before we have reasoned."[54]

Eliot reserved his greatest eloquence for opposing all
"world view projections of the personalities of their authors":

> Was [Blake] a great philosopher? No, he did not know
> enough. He made a universe; and very few people can do
> that. But the fact that the gift is rare does not make it nec-
> essarily valuable. It is not any one man's business to make
> a universe; and what any one man can make in this way is
> not, in the end, so good or so useful as the ordinary Uni-
> verse which we all make together.[55]

51. *New English Weekly,* June 14, 1934.
52. Eliot read the *Summa* in French, in the Sertillanges translation.
53. *Listener,* April 6, 1932.
54. *Times Literary Supplement,* March 8, 1928.
55. *Nation and Athenaeum,* September 7, 1927.

On T. S. Eliot's Criticism
of Prose Fiction

There was, you must remember, a well-known
character in fiction named Uncle Tom.[1]

Late in life, T. S. Eliot reaffirmed "the general aversion to
prose fiction which I share with Paul Valéry," and declared
that

with the exception of one article and two prefaces, and a
very few pieces of literary journalism which remain uncol-
lected, I have never attempted criticism of prose fiction; it
follows that I have no special competence to criticize criticism of prose fiction.[2]

Nevertheless, Eliot's writings in this category are far more
valuable, both in themselves and for the light they cast on his
poetry, as well as more voluminous, than the statement suggests. His range is astonishing, from Sir Philip Sidney, who
"wrote one of the dullest novels in the language,"[3] to Flan-

---

1. Letter to H. Sherek, February 6, 1953, in *The T. S. Eliot Collection of
the University of Texas at Austin*, compiled by Alexander Sackton (1975).
2. Foreword to *Katherine Mansfield and Other Literary Studies*, by J. Middleton Murry (1959).
3. *Athenaeum*, April 4, 1919.

nery O'Connor ("My nerves are just not strong enough"[4]); from Thomas Nashe ("a very great writer indeed [whose] *Unfortunate Traveller* is the first really interesting English novel"[5]) to O. Henry ("still unappreciated and unknown [in England]"[6]); and from Marivaux (whose "novels, *Marianne* and *Le Paysan parvenu*, deserve more attention [than his plays]"[7]) to Anatole France, who exploited "a taste for scepticism without having submitted himself to its merciless rigors."[8] Furthermore, the originality of Eliot's views ("Hans Christian Andersen [is a] frightening writer, not suitable for children"[9]) is as remarkable as his power of making distinctions (Joyce "did not compose a novel through direct interest in, and sympathy with, other human beings, but by enlarging his own consciousness so as to include them"[10]) and his ability to define ("The essential of tradition is . . . in getting as much as possible of the whole weight of the history of the language behind [the] word. . . . Joyce has not only the tradition but [also] the awareness of it"[11]). Finally, Eliot's soundness of judgment compares favorably with many of his contemporaneous pronouncements about fellow poets.[12]

Few English novels are "really well-written,"[13] Eliot

4. Letter to Russell Kirk, February 20, 1957.

5. *Listener*, July 19, 1929.

6. *New Statesman*, July 29, 1916.

7. *Arts and Letters*, spring 1919.

8. *Time and Tide*, January 5, 1935. In 1944, recalling his life in Paris c.1910, Eliot wrote, "*On avait toujours une chance d'apercevoir Anatole France, le long des quais. . . .*" (*What France Means to You*, 1944)

9. *Yorkshire Post*, August 29, 1961.

10. *Listener*, October 14, 1943.

11. *The Three Provincialities* (1928).

12. Viz.: "There are poems by Mr. Herbert Read and Mr. Aldington which endure." (*Dial*, March 1921) "Mr. Frost's . . . verse is uninteresting, and what is uninteresting is unreadable, and what is unreadable is not read." (*Dial*, May 1922) "Mr. Yeats has too little of the power [of creative will] to vindicate himself of the charge of idle dreaming." (*Athenaeum*, April 4, 1919)

13. *Egoist*, April 1918. In discussing English prose styles, Eliot does not mention novelists, assuming as axiomatic that poets write the best prose, the poet having "a power over the word" that the prose writer lacks. (*Spectator*,

thought, and he rated the best of them well below those of Stendhal, whose mind was "an instrument continually tempering and purifying emotion."[14] The authoress of *Amos Barton* "is a more serious writer than Dickens," Eliot noted—Rosamund Vincy, in *Middlemarch*, frightened Eliot more than Goneril and Regan, the daughters of King Lear—"and the author of *La Chartreuse de Parme* is more serious than either."[15]

Yet Eliot's strongest affinities are with Dickens, a "visual writer"[16] primarily, who "knew best what America looked like," though Whitman knew "what it felt like."[17] The identification of *The Waste Land*'s canceled subtitle, "He do the Police in different voices" (from *Our Mutual Friend*), of the cat who "will do / As he do do" (an "echo" of the "solid and eternal Podsnap"[18]), and the recent discovery that the author of *Four Quartets* considered prefacing the poem with an observation by Mr. Roker (*The Pickwick Papers*),[19] give new relevance to Eliot's well-known aperçu that Dickens's figures belong to poetry like figures of Dante or Shakespeare, in that a single phrase, either by or about them, may be enough to set them wholly before us.[20] Eliot's early criticism

---

February 23, 1934) Among contemporaries, "The author of 'The Shropshire Lad' . . . is one of the finest prose writers," Eliot declared, and "Mr. Pound can write good prose when he forgets to write badly." (Eliot's parody of Pound at his worst is too little known: "Now, sir, I am going to set round the chimbly and have a chaw terbacker with Miss Meadows and the gals; and then I am going away for a 4tnight where that old Rabbit can't reach me with his letters nor even with his post cards." [*New English Weekly*, June 14, 1934]) Otherwise, the "finest prose style of the nineteenth century is Cardinal Newman's." Macaulay was "a literary demagogue," and Pater's prose is "restricted by its limited emotional range." Joyce "puts an end to the tradition of Walter Pater" (though *Anna Livia Plurabelle* has recently been characterized as "Pater without punctuation"). Eliot goes on: "*Ulysses* bears the unique literary distinction . . . of having no style at all [in the sense that] it has none of the marks by which 'style' may be distinguished." (*Dial*, July 1923) In the *Athenaeum*, May 2, 1919, Eliot wrote: "It is not . . . periods and traditions but individual men who write great prose."
14. *Athenaeum*, July 4, 1929.
15. *Dial*, December 1920. Whatever Eliot means by "serious," the word is one of the most often repeated in his criticism. Thus he observes that Valéry is

contains many references to Dickens: the practice of doubling parts in sixteenth-century plays "affected the plots of
the Nicholas Nicklebys of the time";[21] "Little Em'ly is not
nearly so moving to me as the chancery prisoner in *Pickwick*";[22] Henry James's Mr. Striker (*Roderick Hudson*) is
"too suggestive of Martin Chuzzlewit";[23] and Henry Adams
"remains little Paul Dombey asking questions."[24]

Eliot's taste for detective fiction helps to account for his
comparatively extensive writings on Wilkie Collins. In fact,
the poet continued to review detective fiction—twenty-six
books in the first half of 1927 alone—during a period when he
devoted only one essay to a major novelist, D. H. Lawrence,
and this less as literary than as religious and philosophical
criticism.[25]

The poet's interest in Paul Bourget's *Lazarine* (and in
Bourget's *Essais de psychologie contemporaine*) may be explained by a subconscious fascination with a plot in which, in
fortuitous and undiscoverable circumstances, the hero shoots
his estranged wife—the theme of uxoricide that emerged later
in *The Family Reunion*.[26] Otherwise, *Lazarine* is dull, since

---

not concerned with the question of relating a poem to the rest of life "in such
a way that the reader will undergo not merely an experience, but a serious
experience"; that his "seriousness" resides not simply "in the value of the
materials out of which the poem is made"; and that "no agreement shall
ever be reached about the extent to which the seriousness is in the subject,"
although "the seriousness of Valéry's finest poems is self-evident" and some
of them are "very serious poems indeed." (Introduction to Valéry's *The Art
of Poetry*, 1958)

16. *Vanity Fair*, July 1923. Three years later, Eliot remarked that "the majority of readers of novels have their taste impaired by an indulgence in visual
detail." (*Times Literary Supplement*, August 29, 1926)

17. *Nation and Athenaeum*, December 18, 1926.

18. *Dial*, April 1921.

19. Helen Gardner, *The Composition of "Four Quartets"* (New York, 1978).

20. *Times Literary Supplement*, August 4, 1927.

21. *Times Literary Supplement*, December 8, 1927.

22. Preface to Charles Louis Philippe's *Bubu of Montparnasse* (1932).

23. *Little Review*, August 1918.

24. *Athenaeum*, May 23, 1919. Nevertheless, the line in "Gerontion," "In de-

Bourget fails to make us understand "particular feelings at particular moments." His novels derive from the "talent of analysis in company with the talent of curiosity,"[27] but in *Lazarine*, the sense of curiosity has evaporated, and only analysis remains. "With such anatomists as Racine and Stendhal, life has an interest to which analysis is never adequate; there is always something unexplained."[28]

Eliot is less attracted to mystery stories per se than to the detectives in them, and to the pitting of wits against those of an Arsène Lupin,[29] to whom the poet once promised to devote a full study. The rules that Eliot adduced for writers of detective fiction are that the sleuth must not be so highly intelligent that we are unable to keep pace with his inferences; that love interest holds up a story; and that the characters need not be fully drawn, the most satisfactory kind being just real enough to make the story work. Also to be avoided are dependence on disguises; bizarre characters and motives; elaborate stage properties; involved mechanical business; the occult (including ghosts); and scientific discoveries. As for

---

praved May, dogwood and chestnut, flowering judas," is indebted to the beginning of Chapter 18 of *The Education of Henry Adams.*

25. Eliot's views on Lawrence as a novelist, on his *"romans splendides et extrêmement mal écrits,"* are found in the *Nouvelle Revue Française*, May 1, 1927.

26. Eliot's fascination with murder warrants analysis. "A man murders his mistress," he wrote in 1917. "The important part is that for the man the act is eternal, and that for the brief space he has to live, he is already dead. . . . He has crossed the frontier. Something is done which cannot be undone . . . a possibility which none of us realize [*sic*] until we face it ourselves. . . . The medieval world, insisting on the eternity of punishment, expressed something near the truth." (*Little Review*, May 1917)

27. Cf. "Passionate curiosity in individual man . . . together with a complete detachment from all theory, all faith, all moral judgement, go to make the peculiar talent of Sainte-Beuve." (*New Statesman*, June 24, 1916) "What is permanent and good in Romanticism is a curiosity—a curiosity which recognizes that any life, if accurately and profoundly penetrated, is interesting and always strange." (*Athenaeum*, May 2, 1919)

28. *New Statesman*, August 27, 1917.

29. "I like detective stories but especially the adventures of Arsène Lupin,"

the last, Eliot attributes H. G. Wells's "triumphs" in science
fiction partly to his scrupulous observances of the limits of
the genre.[30]

Turning to Sherlock Holmes,[31] and exposing some of his
inconsistencies and illogicalities, Eliot describes him as a
mere "formula and not even a very good detective." He has
no "rich humanity," moreover, no "knowledge of the human
heart," and none of "the reality in any great character in
Dickens or Thackeray or George Eliot. . . ." Even so, "every
critic of the Novel who has a theory about the reality of
characters . . . would do well to consider why Holmes . . . is
just as real to us as Falstaff or the Wellers."[32]

Exasperatingly, Eliot reveals neither his own theory about
this nor, in another article,[33] the nature of his doubts about
The Turn of the Screw, though he refers to "that transfinite
world with which Henry James was in such close inter-
course."[34] But surely the reality of Holmes, attested to by
the tourists who still ask directions to Baker Street, is created
by the vividness of some of the other characters, especially

Eliot wrote in the *Harvard College Class of 1910, Seventh Report*, June 1935.
In the 1960 *Report*, he said that he had come to prefer Inspector Maigret, a
change of taste that had occurred at least a decade earlier: "I never read
contemporary fiction—with one exception: the works of Simenon concerned
with Inspector Maigret, of which I may mention the most recent, *L'Amie de
Madame Maigret*." (*Sunday Times*, December 24, 1950)

30. *Criterion*, June 1927. A year later, Eliot wrote: "Wells has positive self-
contained gifts for one or two types of imaginative fiction which are peculiarly his own. . . . His imagination depends upon facts. When he uses the
facts for imaginative purposes he is superb, when he uses his imagination to
expound facts, he is deplorable." (*Cambridge Review*, June 6, 1928) A dozen
years later, Eliot placed Wells "among the loudspeaker voices of our time,"
but went on to say that "some of his short stories, such as 'The Country of
the Blind,' and certain scenes from his romances, such as the description of
survival on the moon in *The First Men in the Moon*, are quite unforgettable."
(*New English Weekly*, February 8, 1940) In an interview in the *Yorkshire
Post*, August 29, 1961, Eliot said: "Wells had marvelous imagination. . . .
The Time Machine is a fearful, though a wonderfully imaginative piece. It
is a great story. . . . There is much that I respect about Wells. He seems to
me a tragic figure. . . . Shaw seems complacent. I don't think Wells was, in
his later years. . . . Wells, I think, had more imagination, and I think that
'The Country of the Blind' is one of the greatest short stories ever written."

Dr. Watson and Professor Moriarty, and of the London gas-lights, hansom cabs, and fore-and-aft caps.[35] Curiously, Eliot never acknowledged that he borrowed the word "grimpen" in *East Coker* from *The Hound of the Baskervilles*, and some dialogue in *Murder in the Cathedral* from *The Musgrave Ritual*.[36]

In the aforementioned Lawrence essay, a review of J. Middleton Murry's "mother-complex" biography, *Son of Woman*, Eliot challenges the thesis that Lawrence cannot be judged as a pure artist because he did not think of himself as one and because "he had an axe to grind." Eliot's response is that if Lawrence was not trying to make works of art, he should have been: "The less artist, the less prophet; Isaiah[37] succeeded in being both." Moreover,

> to be a pure artist is by no means incompatible with having "an axe to grind." Virgil and Dante had plenty of axes on the grindstone; Dickens and George Eliot are often at their best when they are grinding axes. . . . Unless there was grinding of axes, there would be very little to write about. . . . The false prophet kills the true artist.[38]

---

31. "At the mention of the name [Sherlock Holmes, Eliot] lit up like a torch: 'I flatter myself that I know the names of . . . even the smallest characters,' [he said]." (Lawrence Durrell, *Atlantic Monthly*, May 1948)

32. *Criterion*, June 1927.

33. *Little Review*, August 1918.

34. *Dial*, August 1922.

35. Eliot believed that in *Dr. Jekyll and Mr. Hyde*, "the literary craftsman is too obviously the manipulator of the scene." (Introduction to *All Hallows' Eve*, by Charles Williams, 1948). But Eliot complimented Chesterton on the observation that "though this story is nominally set in London, it is really taking place in Edinburgh!" (*Nation and Athenaeum*, December 31, 1927) Eliot was an admirer of Charles Williams's "series of remarkable novels with a supernatural element which began with *War in Heaven* in 1930." (*Times* [London], May 17, 1945)

36. Doyle: "Whose was it?"—"His who is gone."—"Who shall have it?"—"He who will come."—"What was the month?"
   Eliot: "Whose was it?"—"His who is gone."—"Who shall have it?"—"He who will come."—"What shall be the month?"
Nor did Eliot ever acknowledge his debt in *Burnt Norton* to Lawrence's pref-

The last statement may apply to D. H. Lawrence, but not in general, as Richard Wagner's life and work illustrate.

Eliot's assessment of Lawrence is more fair than the received impression of it, but the ill-tempered and badly timed attack on E. M. Forster's obituary tribute to Lawrence—"the greatest imaginative novelist of our time"[39]—redounded on Eliot to the extent that he suppressed his letter, or, at least, did not permit its inclusion in Gallup's bibliography. Here are some of Eliot's comments on Lawrence:

> The most objectionable feature of *Lady Chatterley's Lover* is surely the view of the male as merely an instrument for the purposes of the female.[40]

> He still theorizes . . . when he should merely see. But there is one scene in *Aaron's Rod* . . . in which one feels that the whole is governed by a creator who is purely creator, with the terrifying disinterestedness of the true creator.[41]

> In *Aaron's Rod* is found the profoundest research into human nature . . . by any writer of our generation.[42]

---

ace to *New Poems* (1920) for such motifs and images as "Now, *now*, the bird is on the wing . . . ," "of before and after," "the quick," and "beginning and end."

37. "Only the greatest, the Hebrew Prophets, seem to be utterly caught and preserved by God, as mouth pieces; in ordinary human poets the human personal loss, the private grievance and bitterness and loneliness must be present. [But] we envisage . . . a Villon . . . holding nothing back in a passionate cry to God—and there is, in the end, no one else to cry to." (*Literature and the Modern World*, November 1935)

38. *Criterion*, July 1931.

39. *Nation and Athenaeum*, April 5, 1930. Exactly what is meant by "greatest imaginative novelist"? Eliot asks of Forster. But are these adjectives really in need of elaboration and dissection, and is it not likely that most of Eliot's and Forster's readers understood much the same thing by "novelist"?

40. *Revelation* (1937).

41. *Dial*, August 1922. "What gives Machiavelli's book its terrifying greatness is the fact that he does not seem to care." (*Twentieth Century Verse*, November/December 1937)

42. *Vanity Fair*, July 1923.

Not only are there magnificent descriptions . . . but there are marvelous passages . . . of dialogue and narrative in which Lawrence really gets out of himself and inside other people. . . . In one story, "Two Bluebirds,"[43] he states a situation which no one else has ever put. . . . He is a great tragic figure, a waste of great powers of understanding and tenderness.[44]

On the other side of the ledger are Lawrence's egotism, spiritual pride, and heresy, which Eliot assaults while pointing to his own Unitarian background, as if to fend off a charge of bigotry. Furthermore, Lawrence was "ignorant," a word that Eliot changed to "uneducated" in a later essay in which he elaborates on the novelist's search for "a religion of power and magic, of control rather than propitiation. . . . He was not an artist at all but a man with a sketchbook. . . . His poetry . . . is only notes for poems." Being "educated" means

having such an apprehension of the contours of the map of what has been written in the past as to see instinctively where everything belongs, and approximately where everything new is likely to belong; it means, furthermore, being able to allow for the books one has not read and the things one does not understand.[45]

A desirable condition, certainly, but how many attain it?

Religious questions do not enter into Eliot's earlier criticism of fiction, but to some extent they are anticipated by his

43. For the connection between Lawrence's story "The Shadow in the Rose Garden," which Eliot analyzed in *After Strange Gods*, and *Burnt Norton*, see Gardner, op. cit.

44. *Criterion*, July 1931.

45. *Revelation*. Cf. Paul Elmer More's belief in an "imagination in its power of grasping, in a single, firm vision, the long course of human history, and of distinguishing what is essential therein from what is ephemeral." Eliot singled out this statement in his review of More's *Aristocracy and Justice* (*New Statesman*, June 24, 1916). Also compare Eliot's remark, "By education, I do not mean erudition but a kind of mental and moral discipline." (*Nation and Athenaeum*, September 17, 1927)

expatriate prejudices, a vantage that provides the main interest in his remarks on American writers and is surely responsible for the unusual perspectives in his comparisons of French, Russian, and English novelists. In his view, the uniquely American qualities are a result of environment:

> That granite soil which produced the essential flavor of Hawthorne is just as inevitably the environment which stunted him. . . . Hawthorne, Poe, and Whitman are all pathetic creatures not because of the lack of intelligent literary society, this being much more certainly responsible for some of their merits. The originality of these men . . . was forced out by the starved environment.[46]

Comparing "Ulalume"[47] with "The Witch of Atlas," Eliot says that Poe's poem is "more creative" than Shelley's, just as *Leaves of Grass* is "more creative and original, at least in single lines," than Browning's "Dramatic Monologues" [*sic*]. A similar judgment is made in favor of *The Scarlet Letter* over *Adam Bede*. The handicap suffered by the Americans is that "their world was thin, and, worst of all, . . . secondhand . . . a shadow."

If some Americans were less than pleased by these homilies and their accompanying gibes at Boston society, many a former fellow countryman must have been properly indignant on being told that "the essays of Emerson are already an encumbrance," and that Hawthorne "gets New England, as James gets a larger part of America [, but] none of their respective contemporaries get [*sic*] anything above a village or two, or a jungle." One wonders, however, what can have been intended by the assertion that "Hawthorne grasped character through the relation of two or more persons to each other, [as] no one else except James has done." Apart from

---

46. *Little Review*, August 1918.
47. Elsewhere (*Nouvelle Revue Française*, March 1926), Eliot compares "Ulalume" to "Un coup de dés," in that both poems "replace philosophy with incantation."

monologue and pure narrative, what other means are there? Peculiarly American, at least in Hawthorne and James, is a concern for what the latter called "the deeper psychology":

Neither Dickens nor Thackeray, certainly, had the smallest notion of this; George Eliot had a kind of heavy intellect for it . . . but all her genuine feeling went into the visual realism of *Amos Barton*.[48]

And the poet pictures his namesake "walking in the garden and denying God as she affirmed the Moral Law with fuliginous solemnity."[49] A few years later, he wrote that *"George Eliot est un romancier philosophique, Dostoievsky un romancier psychologique, Henry James un romancier métaphysique,"*[50] but without expatiating on the distinctions.

Eliot's criticism of James a few years later reflects postwar changes in taste:

His technique has received the kind of praise usually accorded to some useless, ugly and ingenious piece of carving which has taken a long time.[51]

In the same essay, Eliot says that James was not concerned with the portrayal of character in the usual sense, and that critics have failed to understand that "character is only one of the ways in which it is possible to grasp at reality." He goes on to affirm that James is "more pertinent for the present age

48. *Little Review*, August 1918.
49. *Nation*, March 23, 1918. In the introduction to his mother's *Savonarola* (1926), Eliot says that unless *Romola* "gave a faithful presentation of Romola's time to George Eliot's contemporaries, it would have little to say to us about George Eliot's time." In *Experiment in Criticism* (1929), the poet noted, "We cannot write a purely literary criticism of George Eliot, unless it is admittedly a very imperfect criticism: for as the interests of the author were wide, so must be those of the critic."
50. *Nouvelle Revue Française*, March 1926.
51. *Vanity Fair*, February 1924.

than Dostoevsky," and "no less profound." The "profundity" of Meredith, for comparison, is "profound platitude."[52] By the late 1930s, James's popularity had declined to the extent that, in a draft of *The Family Reunion*, Eliot gives one of the characters the phrase "the jolly corner," then has him apologize for having alluded to "an author whom you have never heard of."

Among Eliot's elders, the fictionalists for whom he had the highest regard were Kipling,[53] Conrad, and Hardy. Eliot's writings on the first extend from 1909 to 1959, and the titles of two of his poems are indebted to Kipling ("The Love Song of J. Alfred Prufrock" to *The Love Song of Har Dyal*,[54] and *The Hollow Men* to *The Broken Men*[55]). In a 1909 college essay, "Defects of Kipling," Eliot rated *Without Benefit of Clergy* "perhaps the best thing which Kipling has done." Ten years later, he described *Plain Tales from the Hills* as "the one perfect picture of a society of English, narrow, snobbish, spiteful, ignorant, vulgar, set down absurdly in a continent of which they are unconscious,"[56] an opinion not reaffirmed in the introduction to his selection of Kipling's verse published during World War II.[57] Although a journalist and a "pompier,"[58] Kipling was also "the greatest master of the short story in English,"[59] whose "genius . . . lay in his

52. *Egoist*, October 1918. Nevertheless, the last line of Eliot's poem "Cousin Nancy"—"the army of unalterable law"—was borrowed from Meredith's sonnet "Lucifer in Starlight."
53. When Lord Birkenhead's biography of Kipling finally appeared (1978), it was revealed that Mrs. Bembridge, Kipling's daughter, had followed Eliot's advice against publishing the book.
54. *Kipling Journal*, March 1959.
55. In a letter to the *Times Literary Supplement*, January 10, 1935, Eliot said that *The Hollow Men* combines Kipling's title with that of William Morris's *The Hollow Land*.
56. *Athenaeum*, May 2, 1919.
57. Eliot's reply to Lionel Trilling's review of this anthology, "On Kipling's Anti-Semitism" (*Nation*, January 15, 1944), contains the astonishing remark, "I am not aware that Kipling cherished any particular anti-Semitic feelings."
58. *Nouvelle Revue Française*, May 1, 1927.
59. *Criterion*, October 1926. On the connection between Kipling's story "They" and *Burnt Norton*, see Gardner, op. cit.

powers of observation, description and intuition. That he was an intuitive and not an intellectual may account for his being underrated by intellectuals who are not intuitive."[60]

Eliot's first published criticism of any prose fiction was a review of a book on Hardy's Wessex novels.[61] The young reviewer remarked that the slaughter of Sue Bridehead's children in *Jude the Obscure* is "horror nearer to Cyril Tourneur than to Sophocles," a statement that suggests Sweeney/Agamemnon's cry, as well as the epigraph from Conrad in the first draft of *The Waste Land* ("The horror! The horror!") and the phrase from Tennyson—or did Eliot take it from Conrad's "Return"?—that remained in the poem ("handful of dust"). Many years later, Eliot wrote that

in a world without meaning[62] there can still be horror, but not tragedy, [for tragedy] belongs to a world in which right and wrong, and the soul and its destiny, are still the most important things.[63]

Later still, Eliot suspected that the locution "liquid siftings" in "Sweeney among the Nightingales" was "suggested by the rain dripping on the coffin of Fanny Robin in *Far from the Madding Crowd*."[64] At about this time, Hardy's philosophy, as expressed in his blank-verse poems,[65] struck Eliot as "uncongenial," and he condemned a scene in the novel as "deliberately faked."[66] Two years after the novelist's death, Eliot wrote:

60. *Kipling Journal*, March 1959.
61. *Manchester Guardian*, June 23, 1916.
62. "If I had thought that death was final, it would seem to me a far less serious matter than it does." (*Time and Tide*, January 12, 1935)
63. *Listener*, September 18, 1941.
64. *Sunday Times*, April 16, 1958.
65. In the *Granite Review* (Summer 1962), Eliot said that he was eighteen or nineteen when he read Hardy's novels, "but I did not know of him as a poet until years later."
66. *Saltire Review*, summer 1957.

The philosophy . . . of Thomas Hardy's novels seems to be based on the mechanism of science. I think it is a very bad philosophy indeed, and I think that Hardy's work would be better for a better philosophy, or none at all. . . . Has he not exploited determinism to extract his aesthetic values from the contemplation of a world in which values do not count?[67]

But at the time of Hardy's death, Eliot said that

if any man was ever worthy to be buried in the Abbey on grounds of literary greatness alone, it is the author of *The Dynasts, The Mayor of Casterbridge,* and *A Group of Noble Dames.*[68]

Eliot's critical comments on the fiction of his contemporaries is often remarkably acute, as when he says of Gide's writings: "They belong to a class of literature . . . in which the author is moved partly by the desire to justify himself. The greatest authors have never written for these reasons. . . ."[69] Eliot wrote clairvoyantly of Aldous Huxley: *"Son talent pour l'assimilation rapide de tout ce qui n'est pas essentiel et pour le don du chic, combiné avec le désir du sérieux, donne ce monstre redoubtable: une religiosité chic. C'est là ce que l'on doit craindre pour M. Huxley."*[70] Also, Eliot's characterization of the novels of Léon Blois as "violent and rhapsodical"[71] is apt, though the estimation of Bernanos's *Sous le soleil de Satan* as "a novel of great interest"[72] is not shared by at least one other reader.

67. *Bookman,* February 1930.
68. *Criterion,* March 1928. *The Mayor of Casterbridge* is Hardy's "finest novel as a whole," Eliot wrote in the *Saltire Review.*
69. *Revelation.*
70. *Nouvelle Revue Française,* May 1, 1927.
71. *Times Literary Supplement,* November 8, 1923.
72. *Times Literary Supplement,* August 19, 1926.

At another extreme are Eliot's unbalanced proclamations on Wyndham Lewis, "the most fascinating personality of our time," whose "Kreisler and Bertha" are "characters permanent for literature."[73] True, this judgment of *Tarr* was retracted in a letter to Henry Regnery, June 17, 1953, by which time the novel had come to seem "a not altogether satisfactory composite of satire and tragedy." In the 1950s, Eliot preferred *Rotting Hill*, "a good book," *Self Condemned*, "a novel of almost unbearable poignancy, greater than *Tarr* or *The Revenge of Love*,"[74] and *Monstre Gai*, "a development in humanity" over *The Childermass:* "I can only *suspect* that Mr. Lewis is the most distinguished living novelist."[75]

Eliot's encomium for Virginia Woolf in the *Nouvelle Revue Française* contrasts oddly with his clumsily written obituary for her, which begins with the disclaimer, "I have never been able to interest myself in criticizing contemporary writers"— not Joyce? not Lewis? not Pound?—and ends by saying no more of her novels than that "the future will arrive at a permanent estimate of their place."[76] As for Gertrude Stein, though Eliot had told her in 1925, "I am immensely interested in everything you write," he was soon predicting that *The Making of Americans* will "remain unread . . . Miss Stein's . . . work is not improving, it is not amusing, it is not interesting, it is not good for one's mind. . . ."[77]

He was no less harsh on her "school," averring that "a society which has [patronized] such novelists as Mr. Thornton Wilder [and] Mr. Hemingway . . . is decidedly decadent." On the other hand, *The Great Gatsby* seemed to be "the first step that American fiction has taken since Henry James,"[78] while Djuna Barnes's *Nightwood* was "so good a

73. *Egoist*, September 1918.
74. *Hudson Review*, Summer 1957.
75. *Hudson Review*, Winter 1955.
76. *Horizon*, May 1941.
77. *Nation and Athenaeum*, January 29, 1927.
78. Letter to F. Scott Fitzgerald, published in *The Crack-Up* (1945).

novel that only sensibilities trained on poetry can wholly appreciate it."[79]

Among the Russians, Eliot's kinship was with Turgenev, both in artistic philosophy—that "austere art of omission" which in the end may prove "most satisfying to the civilized mind"—and as the exemplar of the writer living abroad:

> Turgenev's grasp of the uniformity of human nature [and his] interest in its variations made him cosmopolitan and made him a critic. He did not acquire those two qualities in Paris, he brought them with him.[80]

Turgenev's form par excellence is the *conte*, not the novel, for he

> could not get lost in a character,[81] could not become possessed by the illusion that any particular creation was, for the time being, the center of the universe. His detail, therefore, is not that of the exaggeration of the trivial in an abnormally stimulated consciousness, but really a way of setting the balance right. Hence the importance of the frequent interruptions of external nature, and interruptions always come to correct the seriousness of life with the seriousness of art.[82]

With Dostoevsky, too, and in contrast to Balzac, the

> most successful, most imaginative flights are projections, continuations of the actual, the observed. . . . [Dostoevsky's] point of departure . . . is a human brain in a human environment.[83]

79. *Criterion*, April 1937.
80. "Dostoevsky is none the less universal for having stopped in Russia." (*American Literature and the American Language*, 1953)
81. But is this true of *A House of Gentlefolk?*
82. *Egoist*, December 1917.
83. *Athenaeum*, May 30, 1919. In the *Monist*, October 1916, Eliot emphasized that "the self is a construction in space and time. . . ."

Yet,

> so much of Dostoevsky's effort is due to apparent pure receptivity, lack of conscious selection, to the irrelevancies which merely happen and contribute imperceptibly to a total impression.[84]

Furthermore, Dostoevsky had

> the gift, a sign of genius in itself, for utilizing his weakness; so that epilepsy and hysteria cease to be the defects of an individual and become the entrance to a genuine and personal universe. I do not suppose that Dostoevsky's struggles were fundamentally alien to Flaubert's.[85]

Eliot warns, however, that Dostoevsky is a dangerous model, since the "method is only permissible if you see things the way that Dostoevsky saw them."[86] In later life, Eliot recalled that he had first read *Crime and Punishment, The Idiot,* and *The Brothers Karamazov* in French translation, in 1911, having been urged to do so by Alain-Fournier.

Perhaps the essence of Eliot's views about the art of fiction is in his article "Beyle and Balzac."[87] Here he challenges Victor Hugo's[88] formula of the "union of imagination with observation," arguing that "the greatest artists do not bring these two together," that in Balzac the combination produced little more than an "aura":

> Balzac, relying upon atmosphere, is capable of evading an issue. The greatest novelists dispense with atmosphere. Beyle and Flaubert strip the world[89] and they were men of

84. *Egoist,* September 1918.
85. *Egoist,* December 1917.
86. *Dial,* August 1922.
87. *Athenaeum,* May 30, 1919.
88. Hugo "had no gift whatever for thinking." (*Cambridge Review,* June 6, 1928)
89. In *Time and Tide,* January 19, 1935, Eliot quotes Remy de Gourmont's

far more than common intensity of feeling, of passion. It is
this intensity . . . and consequent discontent with the inevitable inadequacy of actual living to the passionate
capacity which drove them to art. . . .

This is the familiar "impersonality" creed of the most personal and autobiographical of modern poets, and the reader
is not surprised to be told in the same article that

a great part of the superiority of Beyle and Flaubert to
Balzac is the exposure, the dissociation of human feelings.[90]

"*La Vie est un dépouillement*" (*Le Problème du style*), and comments: "To
be free we must be stripped, like the sea-god Glaucus. . . ." And "[Marivaux's]
world is a very stripped world; there is no moral earnestness, and no sentimentality. It does not deny the emotions; it analyses them." (*Arts and Letters*,
Spring 1919)
90. In a review of Charles Whibley's *Literary Studies*, Eliot states that, in
addition to the standard tools of the critic, comparison and analysis, the artist
must have "the dissociative faculty." (*Athenaeum*, December 12, 1919) William
Empson wrote: "The view of T. S. Eliot that you are meant to regard Jon-
son's and Dickens's eccentrics not with love but with icy contempt, is completely upside down." (*William Empson and the Philosophy of Literary
Criticism*, by Christopher Norris [Atlantic Highlands, N.J., 1978]) The "dissociation of feeling" and the feeling of contempt are hardly the same, of course,
yet Eliot *did* find in Hawthorne "the true coldness, the hard coldness of the
genuine artist."

Stravinsky

A CENTENARY VIEW

The following remarks are more personal than they might have been had I not made so many "stand-in" conducting appearances for Stravinsky in the year of his centenary, and not also begun to go through my mementos, most of which had been stored away in the decade since his death. Looking through these again, I was engulfed by a wave of affection, surprising in view of the estrangement I had felt of late as a result of annotating his 1930s correspondence, in which he sometimes scarcely resembles the man I knew. Seeing the memorabilia, however, I was transported back to the events and emotions of our first years together.

Of course I did not save everything. No one could have been thinking constantly of Stravinsky's immortality while living with him—sharing three meals a day, spending most evenings together, and traveling all over the planet in automobiles, trains, ships, and airplanes. But in perusing the contents of these old packing cases, I was more poignantly touched by his mortality than at any time since April 6, 1971. Here were those neatly typed letters—some with drawings: a heart in red ink, a California desertscape in spring—and the calligraphically addressed postcards sent during later separations. (He kept *my* cards, too, even pasting some of them in a music sketchbook—not for their contents, but as exhibits of engineering skill in cramming two hundred words into a three-by-four-inch space!) Here, too, were those sheets of my questions with his answers, later destined for books; on one page that I had asked him to return urgently, he wrote: "You cannot complain."

I was particularly moved to find again the manuscript copies that he made for me of a canon by Mozart, three pieces by Lasso, and Gesualdo's *Io pur sospiro*, all given to me on special occasions, as well as scores of his own music, always with original dedications: on the first page of the *Monumentum*, for instance, he wrote: "To Bob, who forced me to do it and I did it, with love, IStr"—a statement that might have been inscribed on *The Flood* and the *Requiem Canticles* as well, and that could serve as an *apologia pro vita mea*. The boxes also contained lists of passages in scores to be rehearsed; scraps of paper with messages, passed across the aisles of airplanes or from adjoining seats in concert halls; and menus, paper napkins, backs of envelopes on which he had jotted down bits of music. What disturbed me enough to make me stop this nostalgic rummaging was the sight of my baggage tags filled out by him in July 1951 before we left California for Venice and the premiere of *The Rake's Progress*—these and packets of pills that he had given me for pre-concert nerves. To reiterate, my deepest feelings for Stravinsky have returned and have inevitably influenced these observations about him.

Our present view of Stravinsky is almost exactly the opposite of what it was when I met him in 1948. In the 1940s, it often seemed that rather than pursuing an inner-directed course, Stravinsky was allowing himself to be led by circumstances, composing music that diverged widely in subject and form from what was thought to be his proper genus. The man who during the late 1920s and early 1930s had been inspired by the Psalmists, Homer (*Perséphone*), Sophocles

(*Oedipus Rex*), Virgil (*Duo concertant*), and Petrarch (*Dialogue between Joy and Reason*) was now writing a cabaret vocalise (the 1940 Tango[1]), reharmonizing our sprawling national anthem, fulfilling commissions for the big bands of Paul Whiteman and Woody Herman, providing a polka for pachyderms, and composing music for the cinema (none of it used for that purpose, but converted into concert pieces, in the *Ode, Norwegian Moods, Scherzo à la russe*, Sonata for Two Pianos). Stravinsky was also writing for the symphony orchestras of Chicago, Boston, and New York; for Balanchine's ballet; and for the church (though not the one to which he belonged). But it is the extravagant variety of these other works that bewildered even his most faithful followers.

Only now do we see how these diverse creations both fit together and integrate with Stravinsky's earlier and later music. Thus a passage in the 1965 Variations (measure 103) might have come from a sketch for the *Ebony Concerto* of twenty years earlier, the two-note dirge-rhythm in the Interlude of the *Requiem Canticles* had already appeared in the *Symphonies of Wind Instruments*, while the "Te Deum" in *The Flood* (1962) recalls *Les Noces*, the flute-and-piano figures at the beginning and end of the storm, *Petrushka*. *The Flood*, moreover, is best described by the subtitle "to be read, played, and danced" introduced in 1918 for *Histoire du soldat*. These random examples—they can be multiplied a hundredfold—help to demonstrate that continuing threads as well as new departures, evident in Stravinsky's music of all periods, are the secret of its unity.

A change came about in the 1950s; Stravinsky was finally conceded to have found a path—or vehicle—when he jumped on the twelve-tone bandwagon. Few people accepted this new

---

1. "The music of my little Tango was composed in 1940 with a view to cabaret performances. The publisher was supposed to have commissioned the words from a 'song writer' with whom he never reached an agreement. For this reason my Tango remained in a provisional form (a kind of piano reduction) until last year, when I decided to make a special instrumentation." (Letter to Hans Rosbaud, July 13, 1954)

music as the real Stravinsky, and even fewer liked it, but by 1956, with the *Canticum sacrum,* his use of series was clearly no mere experiment but here to stay. At this point I must emphasize that Stravinsky's *modus vivendi* in the first half of the 1950s differed in almost every respect from that of the monumentalized master of today—though, paradoxically, even if he had died in June 1913 (or any time thereafter), he would have ranked, with Schoenberg, as one of the century's two great composers. In the early 1950s his music was comparatively rarely performed and only sparsely represented on records, while his new pieces of whatever kind met with open hostility. If the popular audience was aware of him at all, it was as the composer—probably dead—of *Firebird*. Having been with him through this period of trial, watching him struggle to support his family—which he had to do by conducting, not composing—yet steadily advancing from the Septet (1952–53) to *In Memoriam Dylan Thomas* (1954), the *Canticum,* and *Agon* (1957), I believe that this last was the turning point in Stravinsky's later life and art.

Ironically, *Agon*'s success came about through Balanchine's smash-hit ballet, and not through concert performances of the score. Today, according to publishers' figures, the piece in either form is one of Stravinsky's most popular, and no one seems to notice a Webern influence, though this was a principal objection at the first audition. Today, we recognize Stravinsky's characteristic gestures, temperament, and energy on every page of the score. Most of it was written during a period of recovery from a near-fatal stroke, and the first performance took place on the composer's seventy-fifth birthday. Nevertheless, the music, from beginning to end, especially in its fleetness, is that of a young man. The rhythms (changing meters, syncopations, jazz patterns), the sonorities (new but inimitably Stravinskyan), the harmonic structure and canonic games, contrasts (of speed, dynamics, and everything else), and the shapes of individual dances and of the work as a whole link *Agon* to *Histoire du soldat*—to name only one predecessor: I am thinking of the parallel function between the castanet part in "Bransle gay" and the string-bass part in the "Marche du soldat."

As could be expected, the audience at the concert premiere grasped none of this, while today the piece is regarded as a comfortable classic. With *Agon*, other composers began to fellow-travel with Stravinsky in his idiosyncratic use of tone rows, for it is true that he did not keep abreast of developments in academic serial theory, simply borrowing what he required in order to write masterpieces.

Stravinsky's eightieth-birthday year was marked by another turning point, the return of the native to Russia, for the first time since 1914. That deep-freeze in which his music had been stored since the early days of Stalin began to thaw. It did not matter that while Stravinsky was being welcomed by Khrushchev in the Kremlin, the fifty-one-volume Soviet Encyclopedia (1958 edition) did not even contain the composer's name, or make any difference that he was not permitted to play his post-*Agon* music—which by then included Movements and *The Flood*—since audiences were not prepared for it anyway. But now, belatedly recognizing their greatest son in the arts of this century, the Russians are performing not only *The Rake's Progress* (in their own language) but also the *Requiem Canticles*, and are publishing more studies of his music than any other country in the world.

I am often asked what Stravinsky believed to be his place in the history of music, in the sense that Schoenberg viewed himself as the bridge into atonality and saw his twelve-tone row as ensuring the supremacy of German music for another hundred years. In relation to Stravinsky the question is more complex, first because his notion of what constituted music history was so very much larger than Schoenberg's, extending not only backward to Machaut and earlier (music that Schoenberg regarded as of no more than antiquarian interest) but also outward to Oriental and ethnic art. Stravinsky maintained that the motets of Josquin should be heard at least as frequently as Brahms lieder, Monteverdi madrigals rather more often than anything by Dvořák. But Stravinsky's affinities, technical and aesthetic, *are* closer to the composers of the Renaissance than to those of the late nineteenth century, although in old age his catholicity expanded to include that period as well: finally, he gave up referring to himself as Wagner's Antichrist and even learned to appreciate Mahler's Ninth Symphony.

Whatever Stravinsky thought of Schoenberg before 1950, after that date the Russian-American regarded the Austro-American not as the embodiment of an antithesis but as a great colleague from whom he could and did learn. (It is important to remember that Stravinsky was always a student, never a teacher, and that, of the great composers, he had the most perpetually acquisitive mind, the keenest antennae.) If Stravinsky is the center of excitement in twentieth-century music—try to imagine it without him!—this is not only by virtue of his innovations and all the other qualities of his music, including its power of personality, but also because he captured more of the whole contemporary world, American as well as European, than did his counterpart. When I speak of synthesis, therefore, I am referring not to any merger with the school of Schoenberg but rather to the assimilation of a vast range of elements filling the sound waves of the last seventy-five years, from Ukrainian folk music to Broadway variety shows, ragtime to Kabuki. I realize that I have not answered the question, but I cannot, and when I once asked it of Stravinsky himself, he replied, curtly: "That is for history to decide."

Nevertheless, Stravinsky clearly saw his place in his *own* time. In Munich, February 1, 1933, he told an interviewer:

Audiences want the familiar, that to which they are accustomed. . . . People feel confident in putting the great masters of the past against a musician of today, against a "cultural Bolshevik," as I am called. Perhaps in twenty-five years, my works, which will then have become familiar, will be held up as examples of *real* music to younger composers.

A week later, when a reporter in Milan addressed him as "the recognized leader of modern music," he responded, "Perhaps, but there are *good* and *bad* modern musicians. I am Stravinsky and that is enough." Although some would attribute this remark to conceit, I would not, believing it to be the honest statement of a man with rare self-knowledge. Stravinsky knew the value of what he was doing and was simply asserting that his music would endure. The retort was also a way of refusing the crown and scepter of a school or movement. To these characteristic rejoinders, one should be added from the rehearsal record in CBS's thirty-one-disc Stravinsky album, where he can be heard correcting a musician, then saying, "Excuse me, please, but I *like* my music."

Looking backward from the 1980s, we can also see that Stravinsky's music interacts more organically with architecture, choreography, painting, and poetry (in three languages) than does any other composer's. This is a subject for another essay, and little more can be said here than that he was at the hub of the arts, both bestowing and receiving inspiration thereby. It is well known that the five domes of St. Mark's suggested the five-movement form of the *Canticum sacrum*. But Palladian principles, such as surrounding a central axis with rooms of sequentially different sizes, also influenced Stravinsky, who was familiar with many of the great architect's villas, as well as with the Venetian churches. (The *Canticum* even has a portico.) Besides the *Canticum*, with its "Trinity of Virtues" as the centerpiece, the Cantata (the tenor Ricercar), *Agon* (the pas de deux), *Threni* (the middle section of the second part), and *Requiem Canticles* (Interlude) have axial movements. Fewer listener-viewers are aware that the orthogonal style of *Sacre* and the falcated one of *Apollo* determined the choreographic postures that Nijinsky and Balanchine created for these works. It should also be mentioned that at least one painter has testified that his cubism owed more to *Les Noces* than to Picasso.

Poetry and its relation to Stravinsky's music is a still larger subject, and, because both are formed with sounds, more closely connected. Some musicians—the composer Leon Kirchner is one—have even detected an intuited comprehension of Chomsky's deep-language structures in Stravinsky's use of words in parts of *The Rake's Progress;* but however that may be, Stravinsky did borrow technical concepts from verse patterns and poetic forms. The first examples to come to mind are of Pushkin and Boileau in *Apollo,* of Gide's alexandrines that the music of *Perséphone* sometimes duplicates, and of Auden's haiku. Moreover, the changing meters, unequal time intervals, and shifting accents in Stravinsky's music are devices comparable to the rhythmic innovations of the poets of the time, Americans as well as Russians, though no modern writer, including Pound, understood Stravinsky's techniques to the degree that he had understood theirs. Still another parallel could be mentioned between Stravinsky's pilferings from the past and Eliot's chrestomathy in *The Waste Land.*

What are some of the principal reasons for Stravinsky's pre-eminence? First, he continued to grow, as minor artists do not. *Abraham and Isaac* (1963), the masterpiece of his late years, is more concentrated music than he had ever written before, as "passionate" as *Oedipus Rex* and utterly new in sonority, rhythm, the treatment of the voice. As for the *Requiem Canticles* (1966), composed at the end of a sixty-five-year evolution, this is a no less astonishing epiphany from a man of eighty-four than that of *Firebird* from one of twenty-seven. The *Requiem* combines a new Stravinsky—in, for one example, the melodic intensity of the music for four solo flutes—with such of his older, though mutated, devices as the verse and response in the Lacrymosa, the ostinato with concertante upper parts in the Prelude, and the apotheosis of bells in the Postlude. When the *Requiem* was first given by the Los Angeles Philharmonic, Harris Goldsmith remarked that Stravinsky chose the minatory rather than the consolatory portions of the text.[2] In fact, I chose them, not Stravin-

2. *Performing Arts Magazine,* March 1970.

sky, as the libretto, excerpted from Verdi's *Requiem* and containing Stravinsky's markings drawn over but not fully deleting mine, reveals; but this does not change the observation, since I was guided by the conviction that he was becoming more defiant and less mellow with age—as well as by the realization that the octogenarian was naturally somewhat short-winded.

Another reason why Stravinsky is one of the dominating artists of his century is that he introduced a new medium, as did Haydn in his century and Wagner in his. True, Stravinsky composed, in Mozartian variety, operas, oratorios, cantatas, melodramas, symphonies, concertos, overtures, sonatas, incidental music, divertimentos, songs, string quartet pieces. Yet his epochal creations were ballets, or choreodramas, as he called them. It cannot be coincidental that he is also music's greatest revolutionary in rhythm, in which dimension, but not only, he irrevocably altered our lives.

Finally, Stravinsky was a great artist because he knew that depth of allusion can be attained only by using the past, and that creation depends as much on the old as on the new.

To turn to the forward view, what should be placed on the Stravinsky agenda for future generations of music lovers? First, his published music is in an unspeakable condition. The example that comes to mind is the 1919 *Firebird*, with its more than three hundred errors;[3] but this is not atypical, since every Stravinsky score has quantities of them. To some extent the Russian Revolution is to be blamed, having deprived the composer of copyright protection in much of the world and exposed his music to legalized piracy. Despite his American citizenship and the new U.S.-USSR copyright agreement, the abuse continues; in their original versions, all of his pre-1931 compositions are permanently in the public

3. On March 8, 1952, Stravinsky wrote to Willy Strecker of B. Schotts Söhne: "Last year in the Augusteo in Rome, the parts of the 1919 version were in such poor condition and so full of mistakes that [Paul] Kletzki, who happened to be there before my arrival, had the kindness to devote an entire rehearsal to correcting the parts."

domain in this country. Even so, a "complete works" must be begun, the variorum edition his publishers promised him (in November 1968, in Paris). A small body of compositions, including Stravinsky's arrangements of his own and other people's music, has never been published at all, while some pieces that were in print have long been unavailable, which explains the absence of an accurate catalogue, let alone a corrigenda.

The first step in correcting this situation would be a search for markings, traceable to him, in the scores of vocalists, instrumentalists, and such conductors as Monteux and Ansermet, Malko and Rosbaud, Desormière and Dorati, Goossens, Collaer, Molinari, and others whose names are less well known but whose libraries should be examined for the possible information. For example, Stravinsky rewrote some of *The Rake's Progress* harpsichord part for piano, in Santa Fe in July 1957. The pianist understandably kept the manuscript, which, for that reason, surely still exists and can be found. Detective scholars should embark on an all-out search.

Stravinsky's recordings are both a help and a hindrance to the improvement of performances of his music. Norman del Mar's book *Orchestral Variations*[4] demonstrates how the composer's recordings of *Apollo*, the Etudes for Orchestra, and *Danses concertantes* not only correct but also supplement the published scores. What Mr. del Mar overlooks are the obstacles that arise when Stravinsky's recordings of the same work contradict each other. For a time, Stravinsky believed that he could establish performance traditions through his recordings. But he did not tell us which tempo we are to follow for the final section of the *Symphony of Psalms*, whether that of the recording he made closest to the time of composition, the twice-as-fast version released in March 1949, the still-different tempo of the suppressed recording, made in Los Angeles in June 1961, or that of the one taped in Toronto in the spring of 1963, after he had had the

4. London, 1981.

most experience conducting the piece (*mutatis mutandis* concerning the advancement of technological influence and the dangerously enlarged co-conductor role of the recording supervisor).[5]

The aforementioned CBS album credits me as the conductor of ten or so pieces under the composer's "supervision," though in some cases the supervising was remote indeed.[6] Naturally I tried to carry out what I believed Stravinsky wanted, but who knows how different his performances might have been if he had broken ground with them and done all of the conducting himself (i.e., if I had not rehearsed them and inevitably suggested tempos and other questions of interpretation)? The facts are that when Stravinsky *wanted* to record, in the early 1950s, Columbia would not support his projects, and in the 1960s, when the money was offered him, he no longer believed in the recording process.[7]

The next item on the Stravinsky agenda should be the completion of the oral history. When London Weekend Television began its Stravinsky documentary, only three survivors with pre–World War I connections could be located, and since then two, Dame Marie Rambert and Michel Pavloff, the Diaghilev dancer, have died. Some seventy interviews were taped with people who had known the composer in

---

5. See fn. 3 on p. 65.

6. The notion that I might conduct recordings under Stravinsky's supervision was inadvertently suggested to him by David Oppenheim of Columbia Records, in a letter of August 25, 1954: "I am wondering whether you are planning to conduct at the recording sessions or whether Bob will do that. I have not the slightest reservation about the kind of job Bob would do. It occurs to me that in this series we are making absolutely authentic performances under the supervision of yourself." I had already conducted *Three Songs from Shakespeare* in a Los Angeles concert and was about to conduct *In Memoriam Dylan Thomas* in another one. Stravinsky, who had not had any performing experience with either piece, wanted me to record them but finally did it himself. In a letter to Columbia, October 27, 1966, Stravinsky protested against the pretense "that I conducted the Capriccio [recording]."

7. By contrast, in the 1940s Stravinsky's records were remarkably popular

various degrees of intimacy; but seventy is far below the actual number of those who might have contributed, and this quotient excludes some valuable witnesses, a Dominican Sister living in Wisconsin, for instance, and a violist living in California, both in their nineties, both *compos mentis*, and both directly involved with Stravinsky premieres.

To judge from the London videotapes, this now-popular method for producing history should be classified as a branch of autobiography, since the participants really only recount incidents in their own lives, regardless of the bearing on Stravinsky's. What struck me is that certain apocryphal stories revealed more significant truths about his character than some of the readily verifiable material. Thus Kyra Nijinsky, daughter of the dancer and an incontinent reminiscer, first saw Stravinsky when she was two, and only once or twice in later life. This does not prevent her from describing an encounter with him in Venice in September 1937, walking between his actual wife, Catherine, and his common-law wife, Vera, both of whom he introduced as if such public threesomes were the foundation of respectability. But in truth Catherine was in a tuberculosis sanitarium at the time, and though she and Vera were friends and did take walks together, it is highly doubtful that Stravinsky ever promenaded with both women at once.

Nonetheless, the anecdote is not without value, since it describes behavior that anyone who knew Stravinsky would

---

and accounted for a major part of his income. Between 1940 and 1944, more than 28,000 sets of the *Sacre* and 11,148 sets of the *Petrushka* Suite were sold, and, within six months of release (in January 1947), 25,000 albums of *Firebird*. But the most surprising figure is 7,237 copies of the Symphony in Three Movements sold within one month of its appearance (May 1947). In later years, however, Stravinsky became convinced that the danger of misrepresentation through bad performances was not offset by any "documentary" value, and he wrote to Columbia, February 27, 1967, asking the company not to release the *Requiem Canticles* recording: "The contralto and bass solos are faulty in intonation, and there are a number of wrong notes and other errors . . . an immature performance: you are quite right in opposing any recording of any new piece on its trial run. . . ."

agree is characteristic of him and of his logical, as opposed to psychological, mind. The concocted story was based on well-known true ones. In 1920, at the beginning of his affair with Chanel, he immediately told his wife, because, as he said, she was the person most concerned. A few months later, he again fell in love, this time with Vera Sudeikina. He again told his wife, and for the same indisputably logical reason. Soon after, he brought the two women together, insisting that since they were the people he most cared for, they really had to know each other.[8] The logic is still consistent, yet something seems to be wrong!

The last item on my Stravinsky agenda concerns publications, musicological, analytical, and—most difficult of all—biographical. Such technical works as Richard Taruskin's study of folk-music sources, and Allen Forte's of the harmonic structure of *Sacre*, set new and high standards. But a comprehensive biography is still far from being a possibility, for the reason that the crucial information about Stravinsky's formative years through the period of *Firebird* is lacking. We need a book similar to that of Bronislava Nijinska about her brother.[9] The diary of Stravinsky's father, which covers Igor's life until age twenty in great, especially financial, detail, provides some but not all of the essential clues, and the few Russian musicologists who have had access to the volume do not employ an even remotely psychoanalytical approach to the biographical material about the infant and the young child.

This, I submit, is central for a man who was extremely anal, exhibitionistic, narcissistic, hypochondriacal, compulsive, and deeply superstitious. He was also quarrelsome and

---

8. Some of Stravinsky's demands on Catherine seem inconsiderate in the extreme, as is revealed in a letter from her to him, December 29, 1934: "I gave Vera 6,300 francs yesterday, as you asked me to do. I asked her to come to the bank, and we sat in the car for a little while and talked. In a day or so, we will set a time for me to come and visit her."
9. *Early Memoirs*, translated and edited by Irina Nijinska and Jean Rawlinson (New York, 1981).

vindictive, which is stated not as moral judgment but merely as description of behavior. The probable cause of all this goes back to the cradle, and the deprivation of the mother. Indeed, the patterns of Stravinsky's Oedipal conflict can be seen both in family relations and in the choices of subjects (e.g., Orpheus, the punishment of Jocasta, the sacrifice of the virgin in *Sacre* and *Noces*). But we do not have the evidence: no observation of the infant Igor has so far surfaced, or, at least, been made available in the West. The combative relationship existing between the young boy and his parents extended throughout his life to others in authority, most prominently music teachers and orchestra conductors. He repeatedly said that he wrote *Le Sacre du printemps* in order "to send everyone" in his Russian past, tsar, family, instructors, "to hell"—in other words, all who failed to recognize his genius. The *Sacre*, after all, is music's masterpiece of iconoclasm.

Finally, who is qualified to write Stravinsky's biography? To the suggestion that I might be, let me answer with an analogy to the obstacles encountered by Flaubert's niece in describing the initial inaptitude of the future author of *Madame Bovary* in his attempt to master the alphabet and consequent backwardness in learning to read. First, her main source was Flaubert himself, and, second, she had to find an objective and unobtrusive way of presenting herself. My difficulty is of the same order, since I play a very large part in the narrative from which, to achieve perspective, I must detach myself. I was too close to Stravinsky to do this, and I do not yet understand the real relationship between us, personal, professional, psychological, cultural, not to mention the irrational, such as "karma"—or, for that matter, Hamlet's "there's a divinity that shapes our ends."

Why Stravinsky in my life, and why me in his? The question paralyzes me now more than it did while he was alive. After all, we came from the ends of the earth, had entirely different backgrounds, and were forty-two years apart in age —though this last was a factor only very near the end, for generation gaps did not exist with Stravinsky. (The poet Eugenio Montale, describing the dress rehearsal for *Threni* in Venice, September 24, 1958, wrote: "The frequent interruptions showed that the good preparatory work done by the young Craft in pulling it all together was thrown to the winds by the still younger Stravinsky. . . .") But in many ways we were also alike. A biochemist at MIT, the late Max Rinkel, one-time physician to us both and a man of uncommon insight, noted that our nervous systems and temperaments were virtually the same. We were similarly ironic, hypercritical, perfectionist (in our unequal ways), and intransigent, and our eupeptic-dyspeptic cycles usually coincided. Moreover, our taste in people, as well as in music, art, literature, and cuisine, was amazingly compatible.

Stravinsky's personality was overwhelming and dominating, of course, and I had to seek refuge from it in order to preserve my identity. Yet my personality—whose features, as I see them, were my certainty about musical values and my crippling Libran indecisiveness and procrastination in most other things—must actively have contributed to the relationship. It goes without saying that Stravinsky shared the first of these qualities but not the second (did anyone ever act so positively and immediately?), which probably promoted our friendship. As it flourished, Stravinsky discovered that I was more independent than he had first supposed, and markedly unlike his children and the numerous acolytes schooled by Nadia Boulanger. Yet I think that, after an initial shock, he welcomed this difference in me. No one before ever seems to have contradicted him, or questioned a patently foolish statement (of which he was as capable as anyone else). No doubt my bad manners were to blame when I talked back, as much as the feeling that disagreement should not always be swallowed. But we did adjust to each other.

What was the magnet that brought us together? Our letters immediately before and after we met reveal conscious and unconscious motives on both sides that helped to establish the basis of the twenty-three-year symbiosis. But Stravinsky's correspondence also exposes a prescience concerning me, at least to my hindsight, that goes far deeper. Was I looking for vicarious or reflected glory? I don't think so, and certainly I succeeded in avoiding it in the formative period to which I am referring, that of the private, even hermetic three years during which Stravinsky composed the *Rake* and began the Cantata, years interrupted only by rare forays for conducting engagements. The sole observer present then, when we stayed home together, and crossed the continent five times by automobile, and took innumerable other trips exploring the Western states, was Mrs. Stravinsky, and she alone understood our relationship. From the first, she believed that I, or someone like me, was essential to her husband if he was to remain in the midstream of new music. She sensed—as she had done in the early 1920s, when she introduced Arthur Lourié to Stravinsky—that he needed a musical confidant and sounding board, which is not to say that my role was comparable to that of Lourié, who had a family life of his own and was near to Stravinsky in age and cultural background. In any case, and as their correspondence shows, Lourié was never as close to Stravinsky as I was from the beginning.

When I met Stravinsky, in the spring of 1948, his fortunes were at low ebb. Most of his music was not in print, he was not recording, and concert organizations wanted him to conduct only *Firebird* and *Petrushka*. More important, he was becoming increasingly isolated from the developments that extended from Arnold Schoenberg and had attracted the young generation. Stravinsky was aware of this, despite the acclaim for *Orpheus*, his latest composition, and he wanted to understand this other, unfamiliar music, but did not know how to go about it. Perhaps the time has come for me to say, as I have not done before, that I provided the path and that I do not believe Stravinsky would ever have taken the direction that he did without me. The music that he would otherwise have written is difficult to imagine.

The 1948 meeting occurred at a propitious time and place —a crossroads—in other ways as well. Until then, the Stravinskys had lived largely in a world of non-English-speaking refugees, most of whom were returning to Europe. On the very day that we met, Stravinsky received the English libretto of his next work, which automatically made me useful to him. Interactions began to take place, and, inevitably, he was Americanized through the exposure—to the extent that this transmogrification can be said to have taken place. Finally, though it is scarcely believable today, Stravinsky in 1948 lacked performing champions of his music, and was himself its only specialist conductor. He saw me, at first and increasingly in later years, as an interpreter of his works.

Music historians are aware that understanding my role is their greatest obstacle, and I dread to contemplate their prurient hypotheses and tendentious projections concerning the nature of the glue that held us together. What I can say with certainty is that my friendship with Igor Stravinsky endured because of continuing exchange; because of an ever-increasing mutual dependency; and, above all, because of an affection that, though not always visible to others, was abiding and profound.

Encounter and
Metamorphosis

In the following article I attempt to describe the reverse side of my relationship with Stravinsky, the effect that he had on me, from the moment that I first heard his music to the impact of the face-to-face meetings. Though *my* biography is of minuscule importance, except where it intertwines with Stravinsky's, more of it must be told than can be found in parentheses and footnotes in writings about *him*. As a study in culture shock, my peculiarly American artistic and intellectual rags-to-riches story that could not happen but did may have an interest of its own.

Stravinsky's origins and mine could hardly be more disparate. Kingston, New York, at the time of my birth there, had been a prosperous Hudson River port since the seventeenth century. The pace of life that I knew was slow, the economy being based on farming, river trade, and small manufacturing. New York City, ninety miles away, was another world, to be visited only on special occasions for viewing such wonders as skyscrapers, Chinatown, elevated trains, double-decker buses, and the Bronx Zoo. In contrast, Kingston retained its colonial Dutch flavor in the many old stone houses surrounding the beautiful Reformed Church, whose spire is still the city's chief landmark, and one of whose congregation, in 1942, earned the admiration of Wallace Stevens for having begun a pamphlet with the phrase, "When Spinoza's logic went searching for God." The society in which I was reared, however, was pure Babbittville.

My paternal great-grandfather Craft, in appearance a Biblical patriarch, was a prodigious reader and a failed writer. My grandfather Craft established stores in the Far West for the Great Atlantic and Pacific Tea Company and barely escaped with his life during the San Francisco earthquake. My grandmother Craft's great-grandfather played in the Royal Philharmonic in Haydn's time, and his son emigrated to the United States, fought in the Civil War, and survived imprisonment at Andersonville. The paternal ancestors of my mother's father came to America with a grant from Queen Anne for what is now Coney Island, and on the maternal side he was descended from Huguenots-turned-Quaker. His mother had met General Lafayette. *My* maternal grandmother's ancestors were Huguenot, Dutch, and English farmers, original settlers of Ulster County, and my mother is a proud member of the D.A.R. and the Huguenot Society.

For their time and class, my parents were better educated than their peers, my father having attended Syracuse University and my mother a teachers' college. As a stock investor, my father was sufficiently prosperous to afford private schooling for his three children, a Cadillac and chauffeur, a live-in maid, a tennis court, family photographs by Bachrach—in other words, the trappings of the nouveau riche. (I did not realize my true social status until I went to boarding school, where my classmates included James Farley, Jr.—son of the Postmaster General—the Shattucks of Schrafft's, the Philadelphia Annenbergs, and the scions of South American diplomats and dictators: therein was born the lifelong sense of social inferiority that turned me inward.) In the Great Depression my father lost everything except our home and was forced to engage in various businesses, but his children were hardly aware of the straitened circumstances and remained sheltered from life's realities.

Both of my parents had musical talent and could play the piano, albeit their repertory did not extend much beyond popular songs and Anglican hymns. Nevertheless, as children we were taken to the Metropolitan Opera, the New York Philharmonic, and chamber-music concerts, as well as to local musical events. The most important factor in our early education, however, was my mother's dedication to schoolteaching. She read to us and made us study, taught us to speak grammatically (if in clichés), to respect all authority (beneath the picture of her in a middy in her high-school yearbook is the caption: "He who does not rule must obey"), to attend church, and, above all, to be punctual—the root, no doubt, of my "deadline" neurosis.

Our childhood home was a handsome fourteen-room Victorian residence whose secret passageways, dumbwaiter, tiled fireplaces, bay-window seats, and hideout attic-above-the-attic still haunt my dreams. By good fortune, most of the furnishings had been purchased along with the house from the estate of a widely traveled collector of Oriental art. As I became conscious of the mysterious treasures surrounding us—a carved Chinese dragon chair, Indian incense burners and cobra-shaped candelabra, Siamese teakwood objects, samurai swords, tooled brass and copper wares from Egypt, Persian rugs—I began to fantasize about them. Our most conspicuous European antiques were some faded French tapestries— distinctly not the fashion in a 1920s provincial American town. None of this exotica reflected the tastes of my parents, but it stimulated my imagination, desire to travel, passion for the visual arts, and future hobby of collecting Indian miniatures.

The most consequential part of the previous owner's legacy was a large library containing Shakespeare, Dickens, Scott, Byron, the Brontës, George Eliot, Ruskin, Hawthorne, the 1893 edition of Emily Dickinson's *Letters*, Cooper, Stevenson, Mark Twain, and Thackeray; I still remember *Van-*

ity Fair more vividly than any other novel. The history books and those about African explorers were particularly engrossing, as was the four-volume *World of Today* illustrated with color photographs. To these my parents added a dictionary, Compton's *Pictured Encyclopedia*, and *My Book House*, an anthology of fairy tales, myths, and fables. No music corner existed until I began to read biographies of composers and to collect scores, notably the Eulenburg pocket series. In the enjoyment of all of this, I had the guidance and companionship of a sister two years older whose dominant interests were also literature and music. Together, over the years, we replaced the Victorians with Everyman and the Modern Library.

Of inspiring teachers I remember only one, the organist and director of the choir at St. John's Episcopal Church, in which, at age six, I became boy soprano soloist. Here I learned Bach's Mass and Passions, and sacred classics by Mendelssohn, Gounod, and César Franck. This choirmaster convinced my parents that my musical gifts were worthy of training. Luckily they were able to follow his advice because of the proximity of Woodstock, where a colony of musicians from New York had summer homes. I not only attended concerts there, but also, between the ages of ten and thirteen, was enrolled in a nearby music camp whose faculty boasted Percy Grainger, Henry Cowell, the cellist Horace Britt, the concertmaster of the Metropolitan Opera Pierre Henrotte, and the flutist Georges Barrère. Not until years later did I learn that Barrère had been coached by Prokofiev in a performance of Stravinsky's *Pribaoutki* in New York in 1919. Had anyone told me this, I would have questioned Barrère about it, for by age twelve I already knew that my goal in life was to study with Stravinsky. As the first step in this direction, I approached the head of the camp, a former member of the Philadelphia Orchestra when Stokowski was introducing Stravinsky's music in America. My aspiration was ridiculous, I was told, and not for the expected reason—lack of preparation—but because Stravinsky's music was horrible noise!

Meanwhile, I had written songs and an elementary but overorchestrated tone poem. Eric Leidzen, composition teacher at the camp, sensibly informed my disappointed parents that these efforts showed no evidence of unusual talent. Nor did they betray any influence of the Cowell experiments, which fascinated me, let alone of the music I loved most, *Firebird*. At this stage and from then on I was spending all of my time studying scores and applying myself to exercises in harmony and counterpoint. My academic grades suffered accordingly, and in order to qualify for the Juilliard School, which I entered in 1941, I had to enlist the help of another Woodstock resident, a business acquaintance of my father, the historian and Columbia professor James T. Shotwell.

I should also mention the yeast that was entering upstate cultural life in the persons of German-Jewish refugees, whose cosmopolitanism contrasted sharply with the narrowly circumscribed world of the natives. One elderly Berliner's reminiscences about Salzburg and Bayreuth made me especially aware of my limitations as a small-town American. (Coincidentally, Woodstock was also the home of the painter Serge Sudeikin, ex-husband of Vera Stravinsky, but this I learned years later.)

Like other young musicians, I suffered one infatuation after another among the great composers: the Tchaikovsky mumps, then the Brahms measles, and the Wagner scarlet fever. (An exception: I discovered Beethoven's quartets at an early age, and my love for them has never diminished.) When I heard recordings of *Les Noces* and *Histoire du soldat*, I was more thrilled by this music than by even the greatest classics, and I realized that the moderns, Stravinsky above all, exerted the strongest appeal for me. The two decisive listening experiences in my adolescence occurred within the same year, the Sunday-afternoon New York Philharmonic broadcast (April 7, 1940) of Stravinsky conducting *Le Sacre du printemps*, which I followed in a Kalmus miniature score, and the recording of *Pierrot Lunaire,* made after Schoenberg's Town Hall performance (November 7, 1940). No score of *Pierrot* being available, I stole the one from the 58th Street Music Library.

I first glimpsed Stravinsky in the flesh in January 1946, when he led the New York Philharmonic in the premiere of his Symphony in Three Movements. He seemed very tall, and his sandy hair surprised me, since photographs showed it to be dark. He walked faster between the wings and podium than any conductor I had ever seen. (Until he underwent a prostate operation shortly after his seventy-first birthday, his movements were remarkably rapid, which contradicts the impression conveyed by his late-in-life television documentaries.) After the performance of the Symphony, I waited outside Carnegie Hall's stage door in the bitter January cold, but when Stravinsky finally emerged, I did not immediately recognize him beneath his high fur collar and with his head swathed in scarves and towels. His height, which seemed hardly more than half that of his closely protecting wife, misled me. I followed them at a respectful distance as they walked to the corner to a waiting car, which, as I learned years later, took them to their hotel, the Sherry Netherlands.

When I next saw Stravinsky, again in Carnegie Hall, on February 8, 1946, he was playing the piano, and Joseph Szigeti the violin, in *Duo concertant.* The composer's brisk, detached stage presence and businesslike reading of the music were utterly different from the emoting of most soloists. Unsmiling and aloof, he acknowledged the applause, his right hand above his heart and with a single deep bow—which I assumed to be Russian-style, Rachmaninov having done the same when I had seen him in a concert with Ormandy and the Philadelphia Orchestra in October 1941.

Juilliard had been a terrible disappointment to me, partly for the reason that Stravinsky's music was almost totally ignored there. The discussion that followed a classroom reading of the *Sacre,* played four-hands by pupils of Frederick Jacobi, was jejune, and the analysis of the Capriccio in one of Bernard Wagenaar's composition classes was confined to a superficial examination of the orchestration. Compositions by William Bergsma, Robert Ward, and William Schuman were played by the student orchestra, but why, I wondered, did it never attempt the *Symphonies of Wind Instruments* and *Pulcinella*? I tried to remedy this by organizing a chamber ensemble, which presented Stravinsky's Octet and, later, *Histoire du soldat* and the Concerto in E flat. I cut classes to give time to this, as well as to explore New York's art museums and galleries, and to earn money by playing trumpet in the Radio City touring orchestra. Here I lost all contact with Stravinsky's music except for a Philharmonic broadcast heard while our orchestra was on a three-week tour. I must also mention my lost year as a draftee in the U.S. Army, a period during which I heard no music above the level of "You Are My Sunshine," and only managed to survive by reading Stendhal and Proust.

I spent the summer of 1946 at Tanglewood, already familiar because I had hitchhiked to Boston Symphony concerts there since the inaugural years. I soon met a young musician, Claudio Spies, who was as fanatically devoted to Stravinsky as I was, who knew as much about his music, and who was my undisputed cultural superior. A refugee from Germany by way of Chile, Spies's multilinguality intimidated me, as this accomplishment has always done. Moreover, he knew the Stravinskys and had actually had lunch with them and Alexis Haieff a few months before. Another Stravinskyite at Tanglewood, Harold Shapero, was enough older to attract his own generation of followers, but all of us were insufferable prigs, snobbish in our tastes for Stravinsky as well as the music, such as Monteverdi, that he was known to admire. (After giving a concert in Madison, Wisconsin, in February 1982, I was told by the director of the orchestra that he recalled Spies and me, in that summer of 1946, pronouncing all non-Stravinsky-lovers "dunces.")

In January 1947 I was able to observe Stravinsky at close hand during rehearsals for Ballet Society's *Renard*, performed on the 13th at Hunter College Playhouse, and during rehearsals and a studio broadcast performance of *Perséphone* two days later. As Leon Barzin conducted *Renard*, Stravinsky, towel around neck, rushed down the aisle complaining in French about the tempo and shouting in Russian to Balanchine. The voice was a deep basso whose timbre and volume seemed incongruous issuing from such a small man. The composer spoke to the orchestra players and the singers in heavily accented English, and, going on stage, mimed movements for the dancers. The focus of attention at every instant, he interrupted frequently with a loud *"Non, Non,"* less often with *"Da, Da."* A music stand with a light had been installed for him a few rows from the orchestra pit, and I found a place directly behind him. He licked his thumb before turning the pages of his score and, each time that he looked up, exchanged his reading glasses for the spectacles on his forehead. He beat time and counted meters aloud. But it was his speed and energy as he bobbed up and down from his seat that distinguished him from everybody else.

Two years later I learned from him that he had not noticed me at either the *Renard* or the *Perséphone* rehearsal. During the latter I managed to squeeze myself into a group photograph with him and to watch him change his shirt and undershirt, at which time I caught a glimpse of his naked torso, and of the gold cross and cluster of religious medals suspended around his neck. After he had dried his back with a towel, like a shoe-shine boy's polishing, and had doused himself with *"4711,"* his wife handed him dry clothes, a flask, and a cigarette and holder. The *Perséphone* performance made me determined to see the as-yet-unpublished score, and the next day I went to Juilliard's dean, Mark Schubart, to ask him if he could arrange to borrow a manuscript copy for me to study. He very kindly did this, procuring the one that Stravinsky himself had used. (Is it ungrateful of me now to repeat

Stravinsky's remark at a later date when someone mentioned
Juilliard: "Oh, that's the place with the wrong Schubert, the
wrong Schumann, and the wrong Wagner!"?)

The year 1947 is the crucial one in my story. That summer
I had gone to Maine to study conducting with Pierre Monteux but dropped out when I realized that, whatever my apti-
tudes, I wanted to concentrate on certain music only, and not
on the pop masterpieces. Returning home, I was amazed to
find a letter from Stravinsky. Having written to him previously without a reply, I was so nervous that I waited hours
before opening it. Although this letter has long since been
published, the one from me that provoked it has not, and this
makes clear that Stravinsky was responding primarily to my
request to borrow the parts for the *Symphonies of Wind Instruments*. Strange as it seems now, apparently nobody else
took any interest in the piece, and, as he told me later, on the
very day that he received my letter he was going over a proof
score of the unpublished original version. The possibility of a
performance by my Chamber Arts Society evidently motivated him to rewrite the work.

Between that day in August and our meeting in Washington, D.C. (March 31, 1948), our letters became increasingly
friendly, and to a degree unparalleled in any of Stravinsky's
other relationships. Why did he offer to conduct the new
Symphonies for me, gratis, when he had been known to
spend as long as six years in litigation to collect a fee, and had
given only one charity concert (for war relief) in all of his
years in America? My letters to him contain no clue to this,
and they are certainly not impressive. I know that he received
favorable reports about my performances of his music in a
New York concert in the autumn of 1947, but this hardly
explains his generosity. He never told me why he did it, and
it remains a mystery.

Although my book *Chronicle of a Friendship* describes our
first meeting, from today's perspective I would see it very
differently. Now I ask myself how I found the courage to go
at all, and managed to brazen my way through it. One ex-

planation is that the presence of W. H. Auden helped to shield me, since he was speaking English and was almost as awkward and shy as I. Stravinsky must have noticed that although I was tongue-tied with him, I could talk freely with Auden, at least about literary matters. Undoubtedly this made me look better than I would have otherwise, given Stravinsky's enormous regard for the poet's intelligence.

The *Chronicle* does not show any awareness of *my* effect on Stravinsky, but at the time I could not tell. Furthermore, only after living with him did I learn that he could wear many masks, for initially I would not have guessed that he could be anything but straightforward and ingenuous; certainly on that day he was without equivocations. He was the most gracious man I had ever met, and I was reminded of Saint-Simon on the Roi Soleil: *"Jamais homme si naturellement poli."* I was immediately conscious of being an entirely new breed to him, quite unlike his Harvard pupils (in 1939–40) and the privileged young people that he had known while being entertained in wealthy American homes. From today's distance, the most striking thing about him was the intensity of his concentration. Unlike others, he did not switch from subject to subject but pursued each one to the extreme, demanding definite, not provisional, answers. "Do you know the best way to render *'se rendre compte'* in English?" he asked, and of course I did not, in spite of five years of school French. (Auden was equally nonplussed.) When our forthcoming Town Hall concert came under discussion, Stravinsky asked how many strings I would have and how much rehearsal time. Knowing that both were insufficient, I feared that he would cancel. His animal energy seemed to be on the verge of exploding, and he expressed his impatience with grunts, headshaking, and knee slapping. (I am not sure that I ever adjusted to this quality in Stravinsky the man, but I never ceased to admire the supreme patience of the artist, who could wait calmly for days until the right note in a chord came to him.)

After lunch I walked along the Potomac, elated but also

apprehensive about the fate of my concert. When I returned to the Stravinskys' hotel suite, I could see that whatever they had concluded about me, their curiosity had been aroused, and so, I felt, had their affection.

Of the culture shocks that took place during the next four and a half weeks in New York, the most painful was the luncheon to which I invited the Stravinskys and their friend Lisa Sokolov. I chose the wrong restaurant, the now-defunct Town and Country on Park Avenue, my mother having mistakenly believed that they might enjoy American cooking, and paying no heed to Saint Paul's advice to Timothy: "Drink no longer water, but use a little wine for thy stomach's sake." There was no wine list, but plenty of popovers, and the stiff and prim waiters disapproved of these loud, Russian-speaking autocrats. Although Mrs. Stravinsky tried to subdue her husband, he did not conceal his desire to leave and go to an Italian or French cafe, no matter how poor. My blunder embarrassed me, the more so because we had become the cynosure of the room. The Stravinskys forgot the incident an hour after it had happened, but it has stayed with me these thirty-six years. I was soon converted to their kind of cuisine but never became accustomed to their dining-out etiquette—hitting a glass with a fork to get a waiter's attention, complaining audibly about anything that did not please them—all so very unlike my own family's meek and easily intimidated restaurant manners.

Some of the events of the next three and a half months are related in published correspondence, but not our next two encounters, in Denver on July 20, and in the Stravinsky Hollywood home ten days later. Despite the warmth of the interim correspondence, and the reiterated invitations to make these trips, I felt upon arrival that I was not quite so important to them as I had seemed at their leave-taking in New York after our wonderful weeks together in the spring. They had left a message at their Denver hotel for me to meet

them at the home of the conductor Saul Caston, where Soulima Stravinsky had been practicing the Capriccio on the
piano with his father conducting him, in preparation for their
concert at Red Rocks. For lunch we went to a country club
as guests of a wealthy, well-bred American who had just returned from travels in Africa. Being politically and socially
left-wing, I considered our host to be the kind of effete dilet-
tante who should be overthrown, and Stravinsky dismayed
me by referring to him as the paragon of American gentility.
(*My* idea of a true American aristocrat was Stravinsky's good
friend Stark Young, an articulate and learned Southern gen-
tleman who was even permitted to call him "Mr. Igor"; it
seems ironic that I should have met this fellow countryman
through Stravinsky.)

Another culture shock occurred in the evening as the Stravinskys and I were window-shopping. Seeing some modern
American paintings, I voiced my preferences, unasked, and
was gently rebuked and told that I knew nothing about art.
This was true, not in the sense of book knowledge or even in
the amount of time spent looking at masterpieces, but in my
lack of expertise in discrimination. Stravinsky saw with his
eyes as he heard with his ears, and viewed any painting, or
scene in nature, as a composition. Sitting at a table he would
habitually rearrange the objects on it, placing them in relationships that enhanced their individual forms and resulted
in new designs. His own drawings of people, of Diaghilev,
Picasso, and Ramuz, for example, reveal his gifts of perception and for capturing the essential features. He could have
been a brilliant cartoonist.

The young Stravinsky *had* been a painter and had wanted
to study the art. As a guide, his criticisms cut directly to the
bone and were always illuminating—which I say because visits to exhibitions were to become an important part of our
life together. His tastes, from Coptic textiles to Piero della
Francesca, were catholic (with the exception that, when I
first met him, his admiration for Picasso and the school of
Paris left no room for Klee, Kandinsky, and Mondrian).

Visiting the temples of Kyoto, the Cairo museum, the Villa Papa Giulia, and the Scythian collection in the Hermitage with Stravinsky was one of the great privileges of my life.

In Denver, Stravinsky had talked about Mexico, not the pre-Columbian, but the Baroque, encouraging me to take a side-trip there en route to Hollywood. He urged me to go by train from Juarez to Mexico City in order to see the villages, but when I followed his advice, I experienced a new culture shock, less that of the usual tourist's reaction to the country than bewilderment at what Stravinsky had found most interesting. What had fascinated him, and no doubt reminded him of tsarist Russia, was the picturesque, the old people begging from the train passengers and the crippled children pointing to maimed limbs to indicate that they could not earn money. I was appalled, and even more so at Guadalupe, which he had placed at the top of my itinerary as an awesome holy site. I could hardly wait to leave Mexico, which I did on July 30. (Twelve years later, when I returned to Guadalupe with Stravinsky and saw him kneel next to praying peons, I realized that I had changed, at least to the extent of believing in his belief.)

My plane put down in Nogales and then in Los Angeles, and I arrived in time for dinner at the Stravinsky home, where I was overwhelmed with their Russian hospitality, unlike any I had ever known in America—another kind of cultural difference. Stravinsky showed me through his studio, familiar from photos, but still the *sanctum sanctorum* for me. I slept on the couch in his den, after my height had been recorded on its closet door, several inches below the tallest marks, for Charles Olson and Aldous Huxley. The next morning Stravinsky took me to the studio and played his recently completed *Mass*, as well as what he had composed of *The Rake's Progress*. He sang various parts, groaned while searching for notes, and looked very pleased afterward when I showed how deeply I was moved by the beauty of both works. Seeing creation from the inside this way was the peak experience of my musical life.

When I finally returned to New York, I had indeed undergone a metamorphosis. From being with Stravinsky at his rehearsals in Washington, New York, and Denver, I had learned more about music than in my entire life until then, and I knew that I had sat at the feet of a man whose horizons were broader and farther away than those of other men, one who, in Pascal's phrase, possessed "the greatness of wisdom visible to intellectual people only if it comes from God."

As for my own horizons, they had expanded far beyond my means, or so my friends and family quickly noticed and I myself realized. But my uprooting was forever.

Influence or Assistance?

Mikhail Druskin's *Igor Stravinsky: His Life, Works, and Views*, first published in the USSR in 1974 and now in England and the United States in a translation by Martin Cooper (Cambridge University Press), has provoked me to give a long-overdue account of the part I played in the composer's life, especially during the crisis in his development in the early 1950s, after which, until the mid-1960s, my main function was to rehearse and co-conduct his concerts and recording sessions.

Druskin's survey allots considerable space to the music of Stravinsky's final years, unexpectedly giving it a higher value than such accepted masterpieces of the 1930s as *Perséphone* and the Concerto per due pianoforti soli. The book's emphasis on aesthetics rather than biographical detail is also surprising, in view of the crippling limitations imposed in the Soviet Union on serial and all other "socially reactionary" music. Not surprisingly, the bibliography is small: the principal studies on the composer (especially the Boretz and Cone *Perspectives on Schoenberg and Stravinsky*) are still unavailable, or untranslated, there. Druskin met Stravinsky briefly—in Berlin, in 1931[1]—but there was no subsequent

---

1. F. V. Weber of the Russischer Musik Verlag wrote to Stravinsky from Berlin, April 8, 1931: "On Saturday, April 11, the pianist Druskin (remember, he

contact between them, and even the film documentaries, the best presentation of the man, seem not to have been shown in Russia.

Druskin's greatest handicap is his inability to transcend his Marxist orientation, surely a necessity in attempting to understand a composer for whom religious beliefs are at the core of both life and work. Forced to skirt the issue, albeit forgiving Stravinsky on the grounds of his being a victim of his capitalist environment, Druskin develops the notion that the composer was perpetually homesick for Russia, could not adjust to the United States, and compromised his art when he tried to do so. If this article were a book review, such misleading interpretations, as well as numerous factual mistakes, would require comment. But despite them, Druskin impresses the reader as a fair-minded critic who has thought deeply about Stravinsky.

This said, some of the book's premises are based on erroneous assumptions that must be corrected and that compel me to cite certain historical facts that Druskin strives conscientiously, but perforce blindly, to understand and explain. He writes:

> In the composer's own hallowed phrase, quoted by Craft, "[*The*] *Rake's Progress* was the end of a trend." After this there was an abrupt change in Stravinsky's [style]. He wrote first the *Cantata* . . . and then the *Septet*, in which he experimented for the first time with the use of a series. From now onwards his whole attitude to the New Viennese School was different. . . .
>
> What had in fact happened? Had Schoenberg's death had such a deep effect on him? Had he in fact wished to study dodecaphonic methods earlier and been embarrassed by the

---

was in your hotel in Berlin) is playing your Concerto in Königsberg on the radio." (Weber added: "Today I am sending you the pocket score of Schubert's Octet.") On February 1, 1932, Weber wrote again: "In January Druskin played your Concerto, and it was very successful, with both the public and the press. He played truly well and accurately, but the conductor was awful."

existence of a rival whose death alone could liberate him from this inhibition? There is no answer to a psychological question of this kind. . . .

The questions that Druskin raises *do* have answers, some of them matters of record, to which he simply had no access. It is true that Schoenberg's death affected Stravinsky, but hardly to the degree suggested here. The composer of *Sacre* had such a powerful ego that he could soon put any death behind him, even that of his beloved daughter, after whose passing he almost immediately resumed work on his Symphony in C.

It is true that Stravinsky and Schoenberg had been cast in opposition for four decades, their so-called feud being most publicized during the eleven years when they were neighbors in California. But they had not met in all this time, and had glimpsed each other infrequently. Although Stravinsky had always held his counterpart in the highest esteem, he could not have felt a deep personal loss when there had not been a personal association. Druskin's description of the reaction as "mourning" is inappropriate.

When I first entered Stravinsky's household, in 1948, he was curious about Schoenberg but hid this fact, and the name was never mentioned. Sol Babitz and Ingolf Dahl, who were among Stravinsky's closest musical associates at the time, did not tell him of their connection with the father of twelve-tone music. Babitz had played Schoenberg's Violin Concerto in Hollywood (May 25, 1941, Evenings on the Roof) and managed to conceal this from Stravinsky, and Dahl was no less secretive about conducting *Pierrot Lunaire*. Why, I wondered, did these two friends of Stravinsky, the first to whom he introduced me in California, whisper and tiptoe when I raised the subject of Schoenberg? It was not long before I discovered what everyone else knew: that the name had been *verboten* for years. This explained Samuel Dushkin's flustered and embarrassed manner when I ran into him in

April 1950 at a New York performance of *A Survivor from Warsaw:* he realized that, talking to Stravinsky, I would refer to the meeting. What still seems incredible, however, is that Stravinsky never learned that Erich Itor Kahn, who had worked with him on the piano reduction of *Jeu de cartes,* and who was Dushkin's accompanist, belonged to the Schoenberg school.

Visitors to the Stravinsky home, including Darius Milhaud, a friend of many years, also refrained from mentioning Schoenberg to Stravinsky, though I knew from Mrs. Schoenberg that Milhaud regularly called at their house when he was in Los Angeles. Even the far-from-surreptitious Otto Klemperer never pronounced the name "Schoenberg" to Stravinsky. One day when the eminent conductor came to lunch, I greeted him with, underarm, a score I was to conduct in an Evenings on the Roof concert. He grabbed the music, glanced at it, pointed to the first notes, counted aloud from one to twelve, and said to me in his stentorian voice: "Nowadays no one is doing anything else." Stravinsky overheard this but made no reference to the twelve-tone vogue. During the meal, he did not inquire about Schoenberg, probably assuming that Klemperer would be going to his house as well. When Klemperer had left, Stravinsky and I examined the score together, but its serial aspect did not interest him at all.

An incident told to me by Dahl indicates that Schoenberg's followers were as cautious as Stravinsky's in mentioning the "enemy" name. One day when David Diamond knocked at the Schoenberg door, Richard Hoffmann, a pupil and distant Viennese relative of Schoenberg, opened it and exclaimed: "Zomeone from ze ozzer camp." I did not find the story unusual, having heard many like it. I did wonder, however, if the cold war was being fueled by disciples, especially when Schoenberg defended Stravinsky against René Leibowitz's abuse and also received me so cordially, despite knowing which "camp" I was in. But then, Schoenberg realized that the motive for my visit was pure admiration, and some member of his family must have told him that Mrs. Stravinsky herself had driven me there and waited in the car.

Nonetheless, subordinates usually echo their masters, and in this case must have known that no love was lost between them. It is reasonable to assume that the rivals themselves were jealous of each other: Schoenberg of Stravinsky's popularity, Stravinsky of Schoenberg's mystique with the intellectual elite. I think that I alone was aware that neither composer knew anything about the other's music, having recognized that each of them had been unwilling to examine his own prejudice—Schoenberg's being that Stravinsky depended on formulas and a bag of tricks, Stravinsky's that Schoenberg was a slave to a rigid, abstract system.

When did Stravinsky begin to explore Schoenberg's music and methods? The question is important, since Mikhail Druskin hypothesizes that Schoenberg's death was the crucial factor in freeing Stravinsky to do so. To me, Druskin's Freudian interpretation of Stravinsky's *volte-face* as a case of "creative mourning . . . the ego's identification with the lost object" is mistaken, another of Freud's theories being the one that really applies: relief at the death of someone perceived as a threat.

Let me recall the events of the morning of July 14, 1951. After the secretary of the Evenings on the Roof concerts telephoned me with the news of Schoenberg's death during the night, Mrs. Stravinsky went to her husband's studio to inform him and came back saying that he was deeply shocked. Within a few minutes, he had sent a telegram of condolence to the widow. During lunch he hardly spoke, but he resumed his work in the afternoon. Later in the day, I heard indirectly that his message had been the first to be received, and that it was greatly appreciated. Later still, a member of the Schoenberg household told me about the memorial service, hinting that Stravinsky's attendance would be a welcome gesture. Though I think he wanted to go, he did not, his sense of irony probably intervening: the two men having avoided each other for so long, the survivor's attendance might seem insensitive.

On July 19, when the Stravinskys and I were having dinner at the house of Mrs. Mahler-Werfel, her sculptress daughter, Anna, unexpectedly stopped by on an errand. She had Schoenberg's death mask with her and offered to show it to Stravinsky. He expressed interest, but when he saw the image was visibly upset and must have been badly shaken. Here, a foot away, was the face of the man who had haunted his thoughts since 1912, but whom he had scarcely seen, and never, since that date, at close range. Schoenberg, after all, was the one composer who challenged Stravinsky's supremacy in twentieth-century music. Furthermore, the sculptress, who had taken the impression, told Stravinsky he was the first to see it. As a superstitious man and a believer in patterns of coincidence, he must have been struck with thoughts of his own mortality.

I have already said that Stravinsky could quickly turn his energies to new projects; he had just done so after the death of Koussevitzky, a friend since pre–World War I—though it must be admitted that in this instance what most unsettled Stravinsky was the harassment of reporters requesting statements. He was not asked for any tribute to Schoenberg, however, for which reason *I* wrote one (for the *Saturday Review*). Schoenberg's death receded rapidly in Stravinsky's mind as he prepared to leave for Europe two weeks later.

In September, in Venice, *The Rake's Progress* was regarded by most critics as the work of a master but also a throwback, the last flowering of a genre. After the premiere, conducting concerts in Italy and Germany, Stravinsky found that he and Schoenberg were everywhere categorized as the reactionary and the progressive. What was worse, Stravinsky was acutely aware that the new generation was not interested in the *Rake*. While in Cologne, he heard tapes of Schoenberg's Violin Concerto (played by Tibor Varga) and of the Darmstadt performance of "The Golden Calf" (from *Moses and Aaron*); he listened attentively to both, expressing no reaction. (In an interview in Seattle not long after, Stravinsky said that "the endless quality of atonality" was "repulsive" to him.) In contrast, a few days later, in Baden-Baden, when a recording of Webern's orchestra Variations was played for him, he asked to hear it three times in succession and showed more enthusiasm than I had ever seen from him about any contemporary music. In Rome, Stravinsky learned that even his future biographer Roman Vlad wrote twelve-tone music, and that Luigi Dallapiccola, a Schoenberg follower, had become Italy's most esteemed composer.

Back in the United States, Stravinsky was preoccupied with the Metropolitan Opera's plans to produce *The Rake's Progress* and with conducting for the New York City Ballet. Schoenberg and Webern were momentarily set aside. Then, on February 24, 1952, at the University of Southern California, I conducted a performance of Schoenberg's Septet-Suite (in a program with Webern's Quartet, Opus 22), with Stravinsky present at all the rehearsals as well as the concert. This event was the turning point in his later musical evolution.

On March 8,[2] he asked to go for a drive to Palmdale, at that time a small Mojave Desert town, where the Stravinskys liked to eat spareribs and drink Bordeaux from thermos bottles in a

2. On February 25, Stravinsky had played me his setting of "Tomorrow shall be my dancing day . . . ," scored for tenor, two flutes, and cello. I was deeply affected by the music, and told him so, but I also expressed concern that the flutes had to play for a long time without relief. By March 4, after having spent four days in bed with influenza (February 26–29), he had added two oboes to the score. On his return from concerts in Mexico (March 22–30), he reorchestrated "The Maidens Came" for the same ensemble. He played "Westron Wind" for me on April 5 and on the 8th told me that he intended to complete the Cantata with instrumental chorales as prelude, interludes, and postlude. Other entries from my diary during this period remind me that I was reading Heinrich Zimmer's *Philosophies of India* to

cowboy-style restaurant. On the way home he startled us, saying that he was afraid he could no longer compose and did not know what to do. For a moment he broke down and actually wept, whereupon Mrs. Stravinsky convinced him that these feelings and the musical problems, whatever they were, would pass. He referred obliquely to the powerful impression that the Schoenberg piece had made on him, and when he said that he wanted to learn more, I knew that the crisis was over; so far from being defeated, Stravinsky would emerge a new composer.

To divert him, I suggested that he undertake an orchestration of one of his pieces, advice he would have given someone else in the same situation. I said that the Concertino for String Quartet was a work that the younger generation much admired, and perhaps he could reinstrumentate it, employing winds from the Octet and Cantata, works that he had agreed to conduct in an autumn concert. The next day, he started work on the Concertino and completed the score on March 13. The first ricercar of the Cantata, a manuscript page of which, with the setting of the words "and through the glass window shines the sun," he gave to me, inscribing it—I believe in reference to the crisis—"To Bob whom I love."

In Paris, in May 1952, Stravinsky watched the same audience that had cheered Berg's *Wozzeck* hiss and boo Cocteau narrating *Oedipus Rex*—though the target was not only Cocteau but the piece itself and its aesthetics, as I think the composer understood. In the same month, in Brussels, Stravinsky heard discussions about Webern between me and Paul Collaer, as well as a tape of Webern's *Das Augenlicht*, which he bor-

---

Stravinsky and that this provoked him to state many of his own beliefs, for example, in "the physical Devil . . . The Devil wants us to believe he is only an idea, since this would make it easier for him." On April 6 Stravinsky came to the conclusion that "angels do not have to breathe." On the 9th, the manuscript of Auden's "Delia, A Masque of Night" arrived, and we read it together.

rowed. Collaer's comparisons of this music to that of the Flemish masters of the Renaissance held Stravinsky's attention—as did Ernst Krenek's talk on the same subject later.[3] Back in Hollywood, Stravinsky completed his Cantata and began the Septet, in which, for the first time, he used a series, and, in the last movement, suspended most references to the tonal system.

In the autumn of 1952, I conducted four Schoenberg memorial concerts at Evenings on the Roof; Stravinsky attended these, as well as the rehearsals and the subsequent recording sessions of the Septet-Suite. All of the music was new to him, and he was so taken with the Serenade[4] that he used a mandolin in *Agon* and a guitar in a new instrumentation of his Four Russian Songs. Yet the Septet-Suite, with its serial language, had the more profound influence on him, its Gigue movement directly inspiring the one in his own Septet. Writing to me on August 24, 1982, one of the players in those concerts of thirty years ago, Don Christlieb,[5] remembers "the musicians' awareness of the miraculous transformation in Stravinsky. We noticed that he could not resist looking at the scores you would lay on the table. We knew how involved he was becoming when we were rehearsing the Schoenberg Quintet. He sat on the couch with the score and after the second day said, 'It is the finest work ever written for this combination.'"

3. In an article on the best-selling pop song-writer Warren Zevon (*New York Times*, July 18, 1982), Robert Palmer wrote: "Mr. Zevon has been a composition student of Robert Craft and a frequent visitor at Igor Stravinsky's house. . . . Mr. Zevon has been writing classical music since his teenage years, when his composition class with Mr. Craft included poring over the latest Stockhausen and Berio scores *with the perpetually curious Stravinsky* [looking on]." (Italics added) I quote this because Zevon, who was thirteen at the time, has observed Stravinsky exactly as he was (and, unlike many other interviewees, has not falsely claimed a relationship), and because the adverb and adjective describe a characteristic of Stravinsky as a listener in conversations.

4. Stravinsky had attended a rehearsal of the Serenade on April 12, 1952, but the execution scarcely gave an idea of the piece.

5. Mr. Christlieb's memories of the two great Los Angeles composers should be preserved by oral historians. He wrote to me, November 25, 1982: "When

In April 1953, while Stravinsky was in Caracas for concerts, I arranged a meeting between Mrs. Stravinsky and Mrs. Schoenberg. This was made possible because of my acquaintance with Nuria, Schoenberg's attractive daughter, whom I had occasionally escorted to concerts, restaurants, and movies, and through whom I became a regular visitor to the Schoenberg house. While there, I learned a great deal from her mother, who knew her husband's music so well that in a matter of moments she could locate any passage in his sketchbooks; for example, when I showed her a sheet of manuscript for *Moses and Aaron* that I had acquired, she immediately found its place in the score. On one of my first visits, she gave me a paper on which Schoenberg had written: "Do not discourage people, friends. They will 'break' the Schbrg clique. Encourage Craft." (Schoenberg realized that the possessiveness of his "old guard" was against his best interests; the note was in response to a criticism of me from Fritz Stiedry.)

I asked Mrs. Stravinsky to invite Nuria and her mother to dinner. On April 12, when we greeted them at the door, Mrs. Schoenberg said, very movingly: "This should have happened years ago." She asked to see Stravinsky's studio, and looked at everything very carefully. During dinner, at the Knickerbocker Hotel, the talk centered on the personal and character

---

Schoenberg was invited to conduct his *Pelleas*, we combined three WPA orchestras, which included twelve horns, and gave a performance. You can imagine the instrumentalists of that time. Nevertheless, Schoenberg's face was love-in-communication such as I have only experienced once again— with Stravinsky. We broke for lunch, and Schoenberg sat with us at a great table in the Trinity Auditorium (near Ninth and Figueroa). During one of these lunches, Schoenberg asked me if it would be possible to perform the Beethoven Septet for his composition class. We did it, and I asked him if he would be interested in hearing a rehearsal of his Quintet, which we were preparing for a performance. This rehearsal took place in his home, where his daughter was asleep in a crib next to us. On a card table nearby was a manuscript. Schoenberg explained that he was preparing a string quintet version of the piece simply in the hope that he would be able to hear the music once again. . . . At that time Julius Toldi (you remember him, the violist in the Bing Crosby radio orchestra) was delivering weekly 'CARE' packages to Schoenberg because his yearly salary was $2600."

similarities—which proved to be more important than the differences—of the husbands. Mrs. Schoenberg had brought a gift for Stravinsky, a bottle of Schoenberg's favorite Knize toilet water, and was delighted to hear that it was also Stravinsky's brand. (On April 13, Mrs. Schoenberg wrote to Mrs. Stravinsky: "Thank you for taking the initiative and for the wonderful evening I and Nuria enjoyed in your company. Hope to see you again in my house. With *herzlichsten grussen*.")

In spite of the existence of some common ground between the two men, Mikhail Druskin's conclusion that Stravinsky was "attracted to Schoenberg's personality, his rock-like conviction, his inflexible will" is mistaken. To Stravinsky, the personality, as expressed in the music and in what he had read about Schoenberg, was not sympathetic. The real reason for Stravinsky's avowals of admiration later on was his indignation at the neglect and ill-treatment Schoenberg had suffered. Stravinsky was pleased to hear about the evening, and soon the three of us went to the Schoenbergs' for dinner.

Coming to Los Angeles in the summer of 1953 for a season at the Greek Theatre, George Balanchine got in touch with Mrs. Schoenberg because he wanted to choreograph one of her husband's pieces. She invited Balanchine to dinner (which he barbecued himself) on July 29. She also invited me, as a friend of his and because I could act as a bridge between the Russian and Austrian cultures and between the two arts— she being ignorant about ballet, he about Schoenberg's music. Stravinsky was not asked to come, and not only because he was in the hospital after a minor operation; Schoenberg's music was the focus of the meeting, and the presence of Stravinsky would have inhibited Balanchine. During the evening, I convinced both Balanchine and Mrs. Schoenberg that the best choice would be the *Begleitungsmusik*, Op. 34. Balanchine avoided telling Stravinsky about the episode, and when I did so it was evident that Stravinsky felt betrayed. Yet this latest evidence of the increasing interest in Schoenberg's music motivated Stravinsky to study such books as Jelinek's analyses of chordal construction in the Septet-Suite.

When Stravinsky declined Mrs. Schoenberg's invitation to hear a tape of *Moses and Aaron* in company with other people, relations cooled. He sent her a courteous note, but she later refused his request for a copy of an early letter from him to her husband. Several years passed before they met again, this time at a dinner in the Stravinsky home, for which occasion she gave him a facsimile of the *Jacobsleiter* score and a tape of the BBC performance. Perhaps Schoenberg's death did "liberate" Stravinsky, but not in Druskin's "psychological" sense. What really happened is that Schoenberg's music began to be performed only after his death—in those first few years, more of it by me, I am proud to say, than by anyone else. After that, the story switches from private to public annals. Upon hearing the *Canticum sacrum* and *Threni*, the poet Eugenio Montale wrote: "By adopting the twelve-tone system, Stravinsky took the most perilous step in his career."

Now to the remainder of Mikhail Druskin's thesis:

> People sometimes talk as though Craft were a kind of "tempter" in Stravinsky's life, the man who "converted" him to the serialist faith. This is manifest nonsense. When Craft first met Stravinsky, who was already a world famous composer, he was twenty-four years old. He was gradually to become the composer's indispensable assistant, his travelling-companion, a not unbiased witness and correspondent of Stravinsky's last years, a kind of Eckermann to his Goethe, though a much more enterprising and masterful personality than Eckermann. . . . But can anyone seriously suppose that a composer who all his conscious life had composed in accordance with an inner artistic law which he had deliberately imposed on himself, who was spon-

taneous and impulsive in his . . . aesthetic tastes—that such a man would be untrue to his own character and allow himself to be persuaded by a young man who had not as yet in any way proved himself as an artist? Assistance must not be confused with influence. Craft could help Stravinsky to become better acquainted with the works and the methods of the New Viennese School . . . but he could not, of course, direct or control the spiritual interests of a composer of genius.

Whether or not I was an artist at age twenty-four—or ever —is inconsequential. What matters is that Stravinsky valued my musicianship enough to write to Toscanini asking him to give me the opportunity to guest-conduct the Symphony in C with the NBC orchestra; that Schoenberg not only expressed his confidence in me in letters but encouraged me to direct his *Pierrot Lunaire* and Septet-Suite; that Schoenberg's pupil Eduard Steuermann, who had played the piano parts in the premieres of both works, would not have agreed to perform them under me if, during rehearsals, he had not found me capable of conducting them; and that Edgard Varèse chose me to record *Arcana,* in preference to Leonard Bernstein and the New York Philharmonic, who had already performed the piece several times (whereas my recording had to be made in three hours with a sight-reading orchestra). But how would Druskin know anything about all of this?

Surely it is a quality of youth to be strong in convictions, partly because of limited knowledge and experience. Another quality of twenty-four-year-olds, at least one of them, is outspokenness; I always revealed openly to Stravinsky my preferences in any music we discussed, including his. Having tried to compose before I met him, I regarded music with a composer's rather than a conductor's eye. He understood that I had nothing to say *in* music, but he must also have sensed that I had something useful to say to him *about* it. During our first sessions together at the piano, I began to realize that he trusted my judgment when he asked my opinion about doubling a note in a chord, choosing between alternative courses in a modulation, or the advisability of repeating a figure. I was dumbfounded. Here was the man I had worshipped since my twelfth year, the man who *had* to know more about every aspect of music than I could ever learn. Was it possible that in the very crucible of his creation he was really seeking *my* confirmation? Until this began to happen regularly, I suspected that he was simply testing me.

In fact, Stravinsky was seeking my opinion precisely because of my age, my lack of position, and my nonalignment with any academic or other organization. I was slow to understand this, and that my elders had axes of their own to grind: careers as composers, conductors, and performers. If I had been his near contemporary, as was Arthur Lourié, his amanuensis in the 1920s, Stravinsky would probably not have exposed himself in this way. Moreover, since his coevals knew less than he did, had less imagination, and came from the same European culture, they had no new perspective to offer. He quickly saw that a member of a much younger generation, and a native American at that, could react in fresh and possibly stimulating ways. What must be admitted is that Stravinsky *wanted* to be influenced.

As I grew older, I suffered from, to borrow Harold Bloom's phrase, if not his meaning, "the anxiety of influence," because I *had* "directed" and "controlled" Stravinsky —and who could want the responsibility of advising a great composer in any way related to his art? In the years immediately following his death, I was torn with doubts, wondering whether I had been right, not about repeating a phrase of music but in urging him to compose one piece rather than another; for, in truth, every Stravinsky opus, after and including *Three Songs from William Shakespeare* (1953), was undertaken as a result of discussions between us. The texts of *A Sermon, A Narrative and A Prayer* were entirely my choice, and in this case Stravinsky paid me for the work of selection. Stravinsky's publisher was alarmed when the critic Hans Keller submitted an article for its house review,[6] *"In Memoriam Dylan Thomas:* Stravinsky's Schoenbergian Technique." By this date Stravinsky was pleased to be described as a Schoenbergian, however, and annoyed with his publisher.[7]

Apart from subject matter, I sometimes went so far as to suggest forms that new pieces might take. A year or two after Stravinsky died, I looked through his manuscript sketchbook for *The Flood* and saw that in the center of it he had pasted several pages of my notes to him concerning the work, whereupon I impulsively tore them out. A few minutes later, I was distraught at what I had done, recognizing that he had wanted to give me credit for my contribution. My notes dealt with technical questions as well as musical symbolisms, mentioning, for one example, the music in the film sequence in *Lulu* as a model retrograde for the biblical storm scene in *The Flood.* I did not want my part in this to be known, but *he* did—and it *will* be, since the manuscript had already been preserved on microfilm, a fact I had forgotten.

A full account of what most readers would call my "influence" on Stravinsky is too extensive for this article. I can only repeat to Druskin that without me Stravinsky would not have taken the path he did after *The Rake's Progress.* Those music lovers preferring another opera (Auden's *Delia,* perhaps), more pas de deux, and some additional concertos will feel that they have been cheated; others, admirers of *Abraham and Isaac,* of the Variations and *Requiem Canticles,* will thank me.

I understand the wishes of the Druskins to believe that their hero always discovered, cogitated, and acted completely independently. But Druskin's assertion that Stravinsky was

---

6. *Tempo,* spring 1955.
7. Stravinsky even sent Keller the negative Boston reviews of the piece with a note:
  "Excellent idea to (ab)use* them in your book.
  * Better without the parentheses."

already "acquainted" in 1948 with "the works and the methods of the New Viennese School" is breathtaking in its ignorance not only of Stravinsky but of American musical life from 1948 to 1953. When I met Stravinsky, he did not know a single measure of music by Schoenberg, Berg, or Webern, had no copy in his library of any of their pieces, and did not understand the meaning of the word tone-row. Just before my arrival, Benjamin Bok, brother of Derek Bok of Harvard, an aspiring young musician, son of a close friend of both the Stravinskys and the Aldous Huxleys, had come for lessons in composition. As it happened, the young man was uniquely interested in twelve-tone technique, and after a single session did not return, telling his mother, who told me, that Stravinsky did not know the first thing about this music.

Not only Druskin but most people do not realize how little the "New Viennese School" was known before the past decade, and how infrequent were the opportunities to become acquainted with it. In Stravinsky's entire career of concert touring in Europe and the United States before 1951, he had heard performances of only *Pierrot Lunaire*[8] and the Chamber Symphony by Schoenberg, possibly of the early string quartet and violin pieces by Webern (at any rate, these were on programs with his own works), and of nothing at all by Berg; *Der Wein* shared a program with the Capriccio in Venice in 1934, but Stravinsky was present only when conducting his own work. In Venice three years later, he happened to hear a rehearsal of Schoenberg's Septet-Suite and told interviewers afterward that this was an experiment, not music.

In the recent survey "Stravinsky in Los Angeles,"[9] Lawrence Morton, a musicologist who in the mid-fifties and early

---

8. In 1924 the German critic Walter Tschuppik questioned Stravinsky closely as to which Schoenberg pieces he had heard, and the answer was, "Only *Pierrot Lunaire.*"

9. Los Angeles Philharmonic Association, 1982.

sixties knew Stravinsky better than anyone else outside of the household, devotes several paragraphs to my position, calling me the last of a breed of associates cultivated by the composer since the early 1920s. I differed from the others, Morton says, in remaining very much longer than my predecessors, in being younger, and in having the status of an adopted child. But the Stravinskys and I were more like companions than parents and son. This was particularly evident in our almost constant travels. Although it was *his* as much as *my* avidity for new experience, without me Stravinsky probably would not have gone to African game parks, Inca ruins, or on one of the first flights across the Pole.

Morton notes that one of the advantages of belonging to the Stravinsky ménage was the opportunity it gave me to mingle with the artistic and intellectual elite. But in truth, the Stravinskys were less interested in that society than I was, and the friendships with T. S. Eliot, Ortega y Gasset, Dylan Thomas, Alberto Giacometti, Christopher Isherwood, Gerald Heard, Isaiah Berlin, and many others began at my instigation and were often continued by me. (I have twenty-two letters and cards from Sir Isaiah covering a short period in the late 1950s to 1962, during which he and Stravinsky had exchanged only a few telegrams.) The Stravinskys had known the Huxleys before I appeared on the scene, but the period of their close friendship, during which they dined together two or three times a week, flourished thereafter.

Stravinsky never shed his Russian culture, of course, and in his exclusively refugee circle in Hollywood, 1940 to 1947, he was more French than American.[10] It was my ignorance of his other languages that forced on Stravinsky the Anglo-American dimension, which eventually became more important to him than any except the Russian. When I entered

10. In indexing Stravinsky's books in 1948, I was amazed at the preponderance of titles concerned with the Dominicans: *La Retraite aux hommes chez les dominicains*, for example, with a dedication by the author, André David (1944). There was also an eighteenth-century volume of the *Sermons* of Massillon, and René Bazin's life of the hermit Charles de Foucauld.

the home, the library contained only a handful of books in English, whereas in a few years there were thousands, on every subject. In fact, the Stravinskys soon sold their eighteenth-century Voltaire *Oeuvres complètes* to make room for Henry James, Thoreau, and Melville, as well as many British authors. Stravinsky was a rapid learner, and English soon became the language of his professional and literary life, though he continued to count money and baggage, and to converse with his wife, in Russian. Was his English sufficiently fluent to write books of "conversations" without me? The answer is no, for which reason I helped him, as must always have been obvious to those familiar with the idiosyncratic wording in his correspondence ("I would like to be through with the recording work that same day at lunch time, because I do not want to kill entirely myself"[11]). Druskin quotes from these books as if my part in them were exclusively that of the interrogator, but, though I no longer remember my exact contributions, certainly there were *some*, and without both of us the books would not exist.

Did I influence Stravinsky's politics? Yes, but only in two instances, and I failed to convert this monarchist to democracy. The man who had hated and feared the Bolsheviks since 1917 required a great deal of encouragement before deciding to return to his native land in 1962, particularly when his White Russian friends were opposing the trip. Finally, is it plausible that without some very strong influence he would have outgrown his inherited Russian religious prejudices and composed a cantata in Hebrew, traveling to Israel for its performance?

I am indebted to Mikhail Druskin for inspiring me to "pull back the curtain" in my relationship with Stravinsky. Some listeners will think I have pulled it back too far, and that I should not be my own advocate ("*Le moi est haïssable*"). I am well aware of the opinion that I "wormed" my way into Stravinsky's life, exploited him, put words into his

11. Letter to Columbia Records, December 1, 1953.

mouth, and basked in his fame. But if such brickbats are the price of twenty-three years with Igor Stravinsky, I am willing to pay it. Not a day has passed since his death in which I have not sorely missed the exciting originality of his mind, the weight and concentration of his intelligence, the infectiousness of his buoyant spirit, and the guidance and the joy of making and listening to music with him.

Conversations with
Stravinsky

> If God wills me to live a very long time, I will
> write many more things, because I still have
> many more things to say.[1]

Apart from program notes and "open" letters, the "conversations" books are the only published writings attributed to Stravinsky that are very largely by him.[2] Unlike the entirely ghosted *Poétique musicale* and *Chroniques de ma vie*, the pamphlet on Pushkin and the essay on Diaghilev, most of the "conversations"—for which many of the manuscript and typescript drafts survive—were in fact written or dictated by the composer.

Although six "conversations" books were published in America (1958–69) and only five in England (1958–72), the British edition is more complete.[3] The titles and most of the

---

1. Stravinsky in *La Liberté* (Paris), April 27, 1935, apropos of the publication of *Chroniques de ma vie*.
2. The article in *Montjoie!* on the *Sacre* is a special case (see *Stravinsky in Pictures and Documents*, by Vera Stravinsky and Robert Craft [New York, 1978], pp. 522–26), as is "Le Sacre d'automne," which Stravinsky wrote in collaboration with C.-A. Cingria.
3. One chapter, "Some Observations on V.D.," in the Knopf *Themes and Episodes*, was omitted from the British versions as too specifically American in interest.

contents of the first four are the same in both the Faber & Faber and Doubleday editions. Stravinsky signed the contracts for *Conversations with Igor Stravinsky* with Doubleday on March 31, 1958, and with Faber on April 29, 1958. Dr. Donald Mitchell edited all of the Faber books, the late Herbert Weinstock the third and fourth Doubleday volumes and the Alfred A. Knopf *Themes and Episodes* and *Retrospectives and Conclusions*—books five and six—published in 1966 and 1969, respectively.[4]

Only a fraction of the contents of books four, five, and six (in the American series) was devoted to my questions and Stravinsky's answers, the larger part consisting of excerpts from my diary. Faber consolidated books five and six into one volume entitled *Themes and Conclusions*. In order to include the interviews, reviews, letters, and program notes of the last years, the publication was delayed, for which reason this posthumous edition (1972) is the most thorough. By my own request, my diaries were excluded from *Themes and Conclusions;* as early as 1961, I had wanted to effect this separation, as my correspondence with Virginia Rice, Stravinsky's literary agent, reveals.[5] On May 17 of that year, answering her inquiry "When will I receive the chapter from Volume 4 about *Oedipus Rex?*," I wrote:

> The *Oedipus* section has grown so large that we will need two more weeks. . . . It is obvious that my "questions" are *ex post facto*, and, followed by such long answers, they look idiotic; yet they must be retained, if only as a device to switch the subject. . . . I do not want this business in dialogues to drag on, and I do not want it to conflict with my own book [on modern music]. [June 3, 1961]

4. Knopf had wanted to publish the first book but did not meet Stravinsky's financial terms.
5. In February 1976, shortly after Miss Rice's death, her executor, Judge Morris Lasker, released to me the files of her thirteen years of work for Stravinsky and myself.

Shortly after Stravinsky's death, when Knopf was preparing a selection of my diaries for publication,[6] I wrote to Weinstock (who had left Doubleday for Knopf) proposing that Knopf follow Faber's example, even though

> this might damage my own book and would raise the cry that Stravinsky had written my stuff or that I had written his, though surely the separation would draw a line between his mind, packed with absolutes, and my bagful of doubts. [September 9, 1971]

But *Retrospectives and Conclusions* was selling too well— "Herbert says that if this keeps up, they will go into a second printing," Miss Rice wrote to me, May 11, 1970—and my suggestion was rejected. Nevertheless, when the books began to be padded with my diaries, many readers assumed that Stravinsky was actually the author of my contributions, as I first realized at a dinner in New York in November 1963, when Luigi Barzini complimented Stravinsky on *his* description of his return to Russia the year before.

The subject matter of Faber's *Themes and Conclusions* stems in large part from Stravinsky's medical experiences (he was engrossed in the treatment of his polycythemia), from his reading (which was his chief diversion after 1966, when he stopped composing), and from the music he listened to and played: not many days, including those spent in hospitals, were without recorded "concerts," nor did he neglect his daily diet of Bach on the small muted piano that was installed in his bedroom in each residence. Many of Stravinsky's comments about scientific developments, people, television, and New York City in the vicinity of the Essex House can be traced to entries in the logbooks of his nurses. But since much of the language of the book is mine, Stravinsky's spontaneity may not be discovered. Compensation may be

6. *Stravinsky: Chronicle of a Friendship, 1948–1971* (1972).

found, however, in the acute irony that emerged as the composer lost tolerance both for the musical scene and for his tribulations at the hands of doctors.

The *Themes and Conclusions* interviews tend to follow a formula, the one noted in my reply to this letter from Miss Rice:

> I just had a phone call from Murray Fisher . . . about the delivery of the interview. . . . Murray implores you to mention all of his questions, and if Mr. Stravinsky does not want to answer some of them—as, for example, the question on rock 'n' roll—will he please say why. He can be as brusque as he wants to be, but it seems that the readers, and many of them are very young, will be eager to hear Mr. Stravinsky's reaction to popular music. . . .

I answered:

> I can do nothing about Fisher's questions . . . since they arouse no interest in Mr. Stravinsky. Moreover, they do not fit in with the mood of the piece. Perhaps this has become stereotyped: a "sardonic" first part, a "serious" middle, a "personal" ending. But the ending, Stravinsky's old-age view of his childhood, is the justification of the whole, and I do not want to destroy its effectiveness.

And, of course, these reminiscences will provide whatever lasting interest the books may have, regardless of the slips of memory and other inaccuracies exposed by subsequent studies (such as the annotated omnibus of the conversations published in the USSR in 1973). The "Conversations" capture some of Stravinsky's feelings about his past and the people in it, something that is far beyond the power of biography.

In April 1956, Deborah Ishlon of Columbia Records in New York wrote to Stravinsky asking him to read passages from his

books for a record of his voice. He answered, from Hollywood, on April 18:

> A few days ago . . . I read through the possible material
> which was a lecture I delivered at various American uni-
> versities and the *Poetics of Music*. My feeling is very
> strong that this material is inappropriate for recording.
> More than that I no longer would say the same things in
> the same way. . . . A further problem is that when I wrote
> these lectures over a generation ago I was entirely at the
> mercy of translators for my English style. I do not like read-
> ing myself in another person's style. And now for me to
> compose in English, which would be the only suitable
> thing to do, is too great a labor to undertake just at this
> time. . . .
> . . . I do not consider the project as definitely closed. I
> am indeed very interested in it and would like to do it at
> a later date when there is more time. It would certainly be
> of more interest to you to have a statement from me in my
> own style and from my present point of view. I will try to
> write this during the free time on our travels, and I can
> work on it with Bob Craft during our concert tours. . . .

In New York, in late June, at the start of a six-month tour,
Stravinsky consented to talk to Miss Ishlon. The tape-
recorded results had been destined for *Newsweek*, whose
music and dance editor, Emily Coleman, was a friend of Miss
Ishlon's. Stravinsky spoke at length, but only a fraction of his
comments were transcribed, and he did not allow these to be
published:

> To be a good listener you must acquire a musical cul-
> ture . . . you must be familiar with the history and develop-
> ment of music, you must listen. The person with the
> subscription ticket for concerts is not necessarily a musi-
> cally cultured person. He is musical only because the music
> is performed in front of him. To receive music you have to

open the ears and wait, not for Godot, but for the music; you must feel that it is something you *need*. . . . To listen is an effort, and just to hear is no merit. A duck hears also.

The larger the audience, the worse. I have never attached much importance to the collective mind and collective opinion. . . . Music never was for the masses. I am not against masses, but please do not confuse the value of music addressed from one ear to a million ears. . . . Do not make the mistake of merely multiplying.

No audiences are good anywhere, but . . . the best musical level is that of the Germans. They have a higher level of listeners because of their musical history and musical culture. . . . In the seventeenth and eighteenth centuries, the people who listened to music were much more learned; music was for them a language which they knew well. They knew not only by passive listening but by active playing. Everybody played—harpsichords, organs, flutes, violins. They had the habit of music played with their own hands. . . . Now we hear music by the gramophone. This gives maybe more people a connection with music, but the result is not the same because the passive is not the active. . . .

We think that very difficult works, like all the last works of Beethoven, are better understood now. No, people are simply more accustomed to them. It isn't that they understand better. . . . A composer thinks about the audience, but not primarily. If you think about audiences, you do not think about your work, but about a reaction. . . . If the audience is yourself that is quite different, but to be the audience yourself is difficult [for] it is difficult to multiply yourself.

Clearly, Stravinsky's conversational partner would have to be someone who was almost constantly in his company.

The next development occurred on December 3, 1956, in the Ritz Hotel, Paris, where I met with Pierre Suvchinsky, Pierre Boulez, and Gerard Worms of the Editions du Rocher (Monaco). Worms commissioned me to write a book, *Avec*

Stravinsky, and tried to persuade me to obtain a preface to it by its subject. When I mentioned the matter to Stravinsky, who had been visiting with Pavel Tchelitchev in another part of the hotel, he suggested instead that he contribute a dialogue touching on a variety of subjects. Much of the result, "Answers to Thirty-six Questions," was written during Boulez's visit to Los Angeles three months later, and under his influence.[7] He promised to translate the text into French and to check the French version of the remainder of the book (which was published in German as well). "Answers to Thirty-six Questions" appeared in several languages at the time of Stravinsky's seventy-fifth birthday (June 1957) and became the cornerstone of the "conversations." A televised "conversation" between Stravinsky and myself in NBC's "Wisdom Series," filmed at the same time, provided impetus to continue. The questions for the NBC chat came from Robert Graff, the director of the film. Here are some of them with Stravinsky's written answers from the first, rejected set:

Q: Where do musical ideas occur to you?
A: Well, sometimes in the bathroom.
Q: Do you write them down?
A: Sometimes.
Q: Does chance or accident play a role in musical ideas?
A: Of course.
Q: How do you know when a work is finished?
A: Because *I* finished it.

7. Stravinsky wrote to Deborah Ishlon, March 14, 1957: "May I ask you to note a change in the last frase [*sic*] of the questionnaire? Here is the new text: 'Webern is for me just before Music (as man can be "just before God") and I do not hesitate . . .' etc. till the end. I made this change because the French [*juste*] was not clear enough for the reader and the sentence is so important to understand. . . ." A letter to Boulez from Miss Ishlon, April 8, 1957, establishes that Stravinsky had entrusted her with the preliminary editing of his manuscript. On March 21, she telegraphed to Stravinsky: "Weinstock interested republishing *Chroniques* with questions [and] new updating chapter. . . ." Stravinsky answered the same day that no more "answers" would be forthcoming until he had finished *Agon.*

Q: Of all of your music . . . which [piece] do you like best?
A: All of them, when composing them.
Q: Do music critics perform a useful function?
A: They could if they were competent.
Q: How does a composer of serious music survive economically in our time?
A: The same as in any time, very badly.
Q: How would you define music?
A: An organization of tones.

Stravinsky, soon besieged with requests for more "interviews," realized that he had found a way of controlling their contents, and a gainful enterprise. His acumen in discerning what should be published is evident from the deletions, rephrasings, underlinings, marginal comments (*"ridicule,"* *"non"*) in his hand on the contract with Editions du Rochers for the "Thirty-six Questions" (superseding the agreement signed by myself and Edouard Dermit, Cocteau's adopted son, October 28, 1957).

By December, Stravinsky had completed additional sets of answers. On the 2nd of that month, Miss Ishlon wrote to him:

> I find each set even more interesting than the previous one and I especially admired your answer about the false "limitations" on music and the stagnation of one-time explorers. I have, in fact, placed this answer at the end of the manuscript. . . .

A "book of dialogues of mine," as Stravinsky described the "conversations" in a letter to T. S. Eliot, was quickly compiled and offered to Faber & Faber in January 1958. Two months later, after Doubleday had purchased the American rights, the question of the title and accreditation of authorship arose. On March 25, Stravinsky wrote to Doubleday's Ken McCormick:

Columbia wants to record me reading excerpts from the book [and] we can't have "Conversations with Igor Stravinsky by Igor Stravinsky" but really should call the book "Conversations with Igor Stravinsky by Robert Craft."

McCormick counterproposed "Afternoons with Igor Stravinsky," or "almost anything but 'Conversations,' since we already have another title with this word on our fall list." On April 18, he suggested "Dialogues with Igor Stravinsky, edited by Robert Craft," which "does away with the cumbersome repetition of your name and gives Mr. Craft proper credit." Stravinsky objected, giving his reason that "a dialogue must involve two people." But the word "edited" had been anathema to him ever since the Russian Revolution rendered him a stateless person, and his music publishers customarily appended "edited by . . ." to his works in an attempt to copyright them under a different name.

On June 6, Richard de la Mare of Faber & Faber wrote to me:

> Our suggestion is that the main title should be given as: *Conversations with Igor Stravinsky*, and that we should then put as a sort of sub-title *Igor Stravinsky and Robert Craft*, with a short rule, perhaps, between the two, but not, we think, "by."

Mr. de la Mare wrote in the same letter:

> I spoke to Mr. Eliot, who is now home again from America, about those queries you raise in the Satie letters, and his opinion was that the original words could be quoted without undue offense. His opinion was that to omit them and to insert dots would be a mistake, but he suggested that the words immediately preceding the offending words in those letters in the French originals should be substituted for the English translation.

Stravinsky wrote to McCormick that the book should appear at the time of "the first performance of a new work of mine, *Threni*" (on September 23, 1958); but since a letter dated June 10 directs the publisher to send the proofs to Venice, the impossibility of this conjunction must already have been recognized. On August 27, Stravinsky wrote to Miss Ishlon from Venice:

> As Bob has already gone to Hamburg and instructed me to open his mail, I answer you in his place about the photos. It seems to me ridiculous not to use photographs of the people discussed in the text . . . and silly to use photographs of Prokofiev, Gide, Cocteau, who do not figure in this book but only in the one we are now preparing.

As was the case with the 1935 *Chroniques*, the first installment of the "conversations" was too slender and failed to embrace any subject in sufficient depth, despite which the book received wide attention and favorable, if puzzled, notices. One source of controversy was Stravinsky's endorsement of the Schoenberg school and certain of its younger progeny. The response of William Schuman, for instance, betrayed his irritation with the apparent turnaround. When McCormick was soliciting blurbs for the second book, Stravinsky asked Doubleday to try to place it in the hands of general reviewers rather than music critics. "The second volume is even less specifically musical than the first," he wrote, and "the reactions of the New York music critics to my works are as automatic as the Russian veto at the U.N."

Stravinsky's outspokenness about his contemporaries and collaborators, particularly in the original text of *Memories and Commentaries*, led to the bowdlerizing of the autobiographical portions of this and later books. McCormick sent a copy of the composer's remarks about Nijinsky to the dancer's widow, provoking a letter from her San Francisco attorneys, Erskine, Erskine, and Tulley (July 28, 1959) withholding permission for the publication of any of her husband's correspondence with Stravinsky unless he deleted the comment "although it is true that Mr. Nijinsky's brother became insane . . ." and certain allusions to stories of intimacies with Diaghilev. Stravinsky complied, and his excisions, now irreparable, included valuable information about such matters as Nijinsky's hereditary syphilis, something about which few others would have known.[8] The composer wrote to McCormick, August 2:

> I regret Mrs. Nijinsky did not see the entire chapter of my book . . . for she would there see that the Nijinsky portion of it is, or so I think, very fair and very friendly. In fact, I had expected her to regard my discussion of Nijinsky here as something of a retribution for my remarks about him in my *Autobiography*—which she did not like. . . . I even hesitated to include Nijinsky's letter because of the damage it might do to Diaghilev. But it seemed to me such an extraordinary document, and so entirely favorable to Nijinsky's reputation, that I decided to publish it.

In retrospect, I regard the "conversations" as a monument to a million missed opportunities. But at the time that the books were written, Stravinsky resisted efforts to explore his past. Furthermore, he refused to open his archives even to verify matters of fact. *His* interest in the "conversations," unlike mine, was not to continue his autobiography, but to air his critical views, and the books provided an ideal rostrum from which he could express his musical opinions. It must also be said that he was not indifferent to the pecuniary potential: the correspondence concerning this aspect of the publications is nearly as long as the dialogues themselves.

8. On May 4, 1934, Stravinsky had received a letter from Romola Nijinsky asking him to conduct *Petrushka* in a charity gala, to take place at Covent Garden on July 3 to raise money for her husband. In the same letter, Mme Nijinsky says that she is requesting the composer's support because she knows he was "a friend and comrade of my poor husband." Evidently Stravinsky did not reply, which may in part explain the widow's reluctance to condone his statements about Nijinsky.

Asaf'yev and Stravinsky

It has taken a centenary to bring out an English-language edition of the one crucial book so far published about Igor Stravinsky. I refer to *Kniga o Stravinskom—A Book about Stravinsky*—by Igor Glebov, *nom de plume* of Boris Vladimirovich Asaf'yev.[1] This brilliant interpretation of Stravinsky's music and its meaning for the twentieth century appeared in Leningrad in 1929 and was virtually banned on publication. In 1977 the volume was reissued in the USSR, with the music examples corrected, and now Richard French has performed the great service of translating it.[2]

After conducting concerts in Russia in the spring of 1928, Ernest Ansermet wrote to Stravinsky:

> There is no place where you are more loved and better understood than in Leningrad, at least among an elite, and notably by a man who is very close to your ideas and your tastes as well as to your music. Boris Asaf'yev is a marvelous

---

1. 1884–1949. Asaf'yev is better known as one of the villains in the persecution of Shostakovich. See *Testimony: The Memoirs of Dmitri Shostakovich*, edited by Solomon Volkov (New York, 1980).
2. Ann Arbor, Mich., 1982.

human being, extremely sensitive and incredibly intelligent. Not only does he know you intellectually, but he also has an intuition of you. . . .[3]

This last statement does credit to Ansermet's own perspicacity, despite Stravinsky's curt answer: "You would think otherwise about Asaf'yev if you had been able to read him."[4]

A Book about Stravinsky is a classic of criticism, the peer of that great work on Leonardo da Vinci by Asaf'yev's younger fellow countryman, V. P. Zubov, which I mention because the strengths of both studies are in their insights rather than in their histories, and because both books continue to outlive more recent and exhaustive ones. The fifty-year delay in the appearance of the volume in this country is partly the fault of the composer himself. Asked for a blurb to promote a proposed English edition, he refused, explaining that any interest in Asaf'yev was misplaced. This attitude is understandable in a man who hated the communism and atheism of the new Russia that Asaf'yev represented and that he describes as having been preceded by "a millennium of credulous and naive faith." Philosophically the two men could hardly have been further apart: a Christian who believed in the divine nature of artistic inspiration versus a dialectical materialist who sought to explain artistic phenomena in terms of a constructivist social theory. Indeed, the party-line polemics with which the book commences make one wonder why it was

3. Letter of April 10, 1928, in which Ansermet also reports that the *Sacre* and *Symphonies of Wind Instruments* were remarkably well played and received in Leningrad. He adds that Stravinsky's brother and sister-in-law there desperately want to emigrate, and the conductor describes an incident when an icon, a gift entrusted to him by the composer's sister-in-law for his mother in France, was confiscated at the border. Ansermet was more successful in smuggling "*un ouvrage ancien,*" presumably a Stravinsky manuscript, between the pages of a score.

4. Stravinsky's library c.1924 contained a volume of Asaf'yev's essays on Russian composers, including Stravinsky.

placed on the Soviet index, except that Stravinsky himself, a White Russian reactionary in the official eye—in Asaf'yev's, one of the greatest composers who ever lived—was considered an unsuitable topic. Clearly, the subject of *Kniga o Stravinskom* began to read it with strong political and religious prejudices.

Stravinsky's animus against his disciple had other causes as well, perhaps dating back to the time when both men were pupils of Rimsky-Korsakov. This possibility seems to be borne out both by the book's complete absence of biographical information and by two or three asides accusing Stravinsky of arrogance in a way that suggests a personal history. In May 1914 Asaf'yev came to Paris for the premiere of *The Nightingale* armed with requests from Stravinsky's friends to admit the critic to rehearsals. But if a meeting took place then, no record of it has emerged, and, to Ansermet, Stravinsky denied ever having known Asaf'yev. Then, too, Arthur Lourié disapproved of this Soviet admirer: "I read Asaf'yev's last article with revulsion, and to think that at one time we almost spoke the same language!" (Letter to Stravinsky, April 14, 1925) Finally, the chapter on *Apollo*, the next-to-last composition that Asaf'yev discusses, is lacking in perspective, expresses fears that Stravinsky could be in danger of losing his way, and compares some of the music to that in Pugni's ballets. Naturally, this would have offended the composer, but it seems doubtful that he read that far.

My explanation differs from these and is based on a trait of Stravinsky's character. He would tolerate no interpreter he could not control—hence his autobiography, and, in conducting, his preference for a mere craftsman over a Bernstein. Whether or not Stravinsky was annoyed that an infidel Marxist, living so far from the center and with only the rarest opportunities to hear the music, had penetrated it so profoundly, the composer freely admitted that Asaf'yev understood him as no one else did, least of all the authors of the French and Italian monographs published at about the same

time and written quite literally under the subject's nose.[5]
In a letter to Asaf'yev, September 6, 1934, Prokofiev wrote:
"We dropped in on Stravinsky, who is writing a concerto for
two pianos . . . and a book about himself. When I asked him
what was the best book about him up to now, he answered,
the Glebov." And on October 26, 1931, Asaf'yev had written
to Miaskovsky: "Have I told you that my book about Stravinsky was very much to his liking and that he was astonished
how, without knowing him personally . . . , I figured out . . .
his creative process?" Asaf'yev does not reveal his source for
Stravinsky's reactions, which are true only in part. It may
have been the composer's friend Jacques Handschin, who
wrote to him from Zürich, February 20, 1931: "I had the opportunity to translate Glebov's Mussorgsky article. . . . I hope
I will have the opportunity to do the same with his book on
you. That would be very interesting." But—to return to
Ansermet's observations—to be completely understood by
anyone is threatening, and who, least of all Igor Stravinsky,
wants an alter ego?

In the spring of 1935, while Stravinsky was on a concert tour
in the United States, his wife's sister, Lyudmila Beliankina,
wrote to him from Sancellemoz that his young American
friend, the pianist Beveridge Webster, had procured a copy

5. This is not true of Herbert Fleischer's 1931 German monograph, published
(in an edition of a thousand copies) by the Russischer Musik Verlag in Berlin.
As Stravinsky wrote to F. V. Weber, September 29, 1931: "A month ago
[Fleischer] wrote me a very kind letter in which he expresses ideas that do
not concur in the least with that article of his in the *Berliner Tageblatt*. . . .
That excerpt from his book had such a negative effect on me because of its
complete misinterpretation of my intentions in, let us say, *Petrushka* and
Sacre; I was utterly bewildered and depressed. And what *is* one to believe,
what he wrote in his letter, or what, to my horror, I read about myself in the
Berliner Tageblatt, where, in his profound German-philosophical language,
he characterizes my work as that of a thoroughgoing pessimist, a nihilist even,
saying that I cannot believe—it is clear to him—in life beyond the grave,
this and other arbitrary fantasies?"

of the book while on a recent visit to the USSR. In it, she says, Asaf'yev dwells at length

> on *Noces*, *Soldat*, and *Mavra*. Up to this time I have not encountered such an interesting and intelligent critique of your music. I was especially struck by how subtly he evaluated *Mavra*. It is amazing that someone who has had no contact with you and no guidance from you understood your work so completely. He analyzed everything himself, and he warmly and intelligently defends you against the academic circle in Russia.

Let me say at once that the *Mavra* essay is a revelation, convincing me, for one, that the work fails in performance only because it demands too much sophistication from its audiences. Being unacquainted with the sources, we in the West fail to relate to the references, not only to such composers as Alyabev, Varlamov, and Verstovsky,[6] but also to Dargomizhsky and Tchaikovsky.[7]

Stravinsky had actually read *Kniga o Stravinskom* years before, having purchased the book through his publishers in Berlin on October 4, 1930. His 1935 Ecole Normale lecture on the Concerto per due pianoforti soli seems to owe something to Asaf'yev's discussion of the etymology of the word "concerto," and the composer's presentation of his aesthetics in *Chroniques de ma vie* might also have been influenced by the Soviet musicologist. In any case, Stravinsky was well aware that Asaf'yev had already disavowed *A Book about Stravinsky* when underscoring lines, inserting question, exclamation, and check marks, and adding comments so consistently deprecatory that when the margins are blank, as in the chapter on *Renard*, the reader interprets the silence as sig-

6. A. A. Alyabev, 1787–1851; A. E. Varlamov, 1801–48; A. N. Verstovsky, 1799–1862.
7. Recently, listening to *Perséphone* with George Balanchine, I was astonished to hear him exclaim "Tchaikovsky" and "Glinka" during melodies that to me seemed purely French.

nifying agreement, if not praise. Stravinsky entered a favorable word—"important"—in only one place, yet this could be taken as a clue to his recognition of the true value of the book, since, if not Asaf'yev, only Stravinsky himself could have written the passage to which the word refers:

> In instrumental music, pitches and rhythms are not used to compose sound complexes that have precise emotional connotations. Nevertheless, the choice of material must be made, and that choice inevitably produces an inner logic of its own and a precise sonorous image . . . a unique complex of intonational "gestures" by which the character and pace of a piece are defined.

Except to correct mistakes in music examples, Stravinsky did not mark the book until the chapter on *The Nightingale*. He probably took exception to some conclusions concerning his three early ballets, but not, I think, to the charge that the unadventurous character of his music before *Fireworks* can be blamed on domination by Rimsky-Korsakov, who, says Asaf'yev, "walked behind his times. . . . Each new work of his represented . . . a *concession* to contemporary demands. . . . The pupil was of necessity behind his times." Asaf'yev's analysis of *Firebird* is conventional, but he was quick to see the technical superiority of the 1919 Suite over the earlier one. In *Le Sacre du printemps*, he seems to have been the first to notice the construction of the melodic ascent toward the end of the piece, from bass A to treble A, A above the clef, then up through C, E, the pivotal F, and rapidly, in the last two measures, to F sharp, G, G sharp, A (the thirty-second-note appoggiatura), and the ultimate A, five octaves above the first one. Needless to say, Asaf'yev regards the music as "tonal" and as resolving from dominant to tonic.[8] More re-

8. In the 1943 score, the final bass note is not D but E. Asaf'yev seems to have used the 1913 four-hand score, but since the sixty-fourth-notes indicated for the flute are not found as shown in his book in any edition, I assume a misprint.

cent studies do not even mention this melodic aspect of the passage, possibly because of distraction by the rhythmic and harmonic considerations.

What must be emphasized is that at a time when it was still necessary to defend the *Sacre* against those who had "not enlarged their ideas about what is permissible in music," and to uphold "the originality that proceeds from organic and natural premises," Asaf'yev had grasped the logic, the substance, and the import of the work, proclaiming that Stravinsky's music is "the child of the era that it has come to define."

For the Westerner, Asaf'yev's most valuable chapters are the ones devoted to the Russian-language theatre pieces, *The Nightingale* not least among them. His analysis identifies not only the opera's specifically Russian features, such as the "Russian rococo" in the Nightingale's aria in Act I, but also those of Stravinsky's music in general. Thus the bell-like sounds that become part of the substance of *Noces* are already present in the texture of *The Nightingale*, in harp and string harmonics, in the timbres of piano and celesta, not to mention the actual bells in the Emperor's court at the beginning of Act II and the funeral gong in Act III. Asaf'yev, who knew that Stravinsky would have heard the great bell of the Nikolsky Sobor in his cradle, could not have been surprised by the continuing evocation of bells in the later music[9]—in the second of the Shakespeare songs, in the setting of Thomas Dekker's *Prayer*, in the *Introitus*, and in *Requiem Canticles*. The mention of the music performed for the composer's funeral in Venice, just before he was ferried to his grave, reminds me of his experiments with notations for the different speeds of the city's bells, since their rhythms absorbed

9. In a talk at the Cleveland Institute of Music in 1968, Victor Babin recalled a visit to Stravinsky in his Hollywood home during which the composer "showed me his *In Memoriam Dylan Thomas* . . . explaining to me how the four trombones sounded like funeral bells. . . ." (From *Victor Babin* [Cleveland, 1982])

him as much as their ring and the percussive articulation of mallet and clapper.[10]

Festive ritual, grotesquery, and the search for the primordial as well as for the new are integral elements of *The Nightingale* no less than of *Fireworks, Firebird, Petrushka,* and *Le Sacre du printemps.* What is new, according to Asaf'yev, is the composer's "growing skepticism" and its "deepening effect on his vital instincts"—remarks, together with some others hinging on the "mature" attitude toward death in the new Russia, that provoke the first of Stravinsky's marginal graffiti:[11] "Very little has changed in this sense since I left Russia twenty years ago." Asaf'yev goes on to say that "the subject of death has always stimulated Russian composers to write deeply felt music," and he includes the Stravinsky of *The Nightingale* in the statement. This seems like special pleading, since the idea of death has produced "deeply felt music" from composers of all times and places. But Asaf'yev argues that "life in Russia is so hard, many regard the gift of it as an unjust accident," a fact he relates to the hysterical reactions (peculiarly Russian, he says) of a Gogol, a Dostoevsky, and a Tchaikovsky. Moreover, nightingales are messengers of Eros, and, in Russia, wedding rites and funeral laments are closely related.

In any event, the Act III death scene gives Stravinsky's opera the human dimension and the depth it would otherwise lack. The struggle between the Nightingale and Death is the opera's dramatic and musical focus, and the Nightingale's aria about the garden in the cemetery is the best and most moving music. The first two acts are mere satire at the expense of the "magisterial stupidity" of the Chinese Emperor and his courtiers, and of the Japanese and their Panasonic nightingale. Moreover, the music after the Emperor's re-

---

10. One of the illustrations in Nathanial Spear's *A Treasury of Archaeological Bells* (New York, 1978) is a photograph of a bell discovered in the 1950s in a Sarmatian (first to second century) burial ground in the Dnepropetrovsky District of Stravinsky's ancestral Ukraine.
11. The originals of these are in Russian.

covery is an anticlimax; his last words, instead of an affirmation of life, are a "puzzled interrogation," and the Fisherman's song is simply a colophon. When the Emperor's temperature returns to normal, Stravinsky's own "nightingale fever"—to borrow Mandelstam's phrase—also disappears, but the emotions aroused by the music of the death scene linger on.

Apart from his stand against the new "mature" Russian attitude toward death, Stravinsky's criticisms of the chapter are picayune. Asaf'yev writes: "The voice of the Nightingale [is] first introduced instrumentally (an ornate improvisation)," and Stravinsky counters: "It is a cadenza and not an improvisation" (as if, traditionally, cadenzas were not improvised). "Kuzmin and Verlaine, Rimsky-Korsakov and Debussy" are among the influences on the opera, Asaf'yev states, and Stravinsky asks, "What is Rimsky-Korsakov doing in this company?" (to which the answer is "Very little," yet Rimsky's influence on the music is undeniable). "In the symphonic poem, *Song of the Nightingale*, the middle section of the [opera's] entr'acte is made over into a new episode," Asaf'yev goes on, and Stravinsky rejoins: "As if no one ever noticed that in the opera this is sung."

In the next chapter, "Toward the New," the smaller works composed between 1913 and 1919 are examined—and illuminated. But Asaf'yev's usually reliable sense of Stravinsky's chronological development is contradicted in the conclusion that "the new style reaches maturity in *Noces*," for we have since learned that much of the composition of that work antedates the *Berceuses du chat*[12] and *Trois Histoires pour enfants*. During World War I, Stravinsky was composing in different styles simultaneously, as is shown by the 1914–17 piano duets. On the other hand, Asaf'yev's remark that the piano accompaniment in *Chicher-Yacher* "suggests orchestral

12. Stravinsky objects to the title *Berceuses de chat*, as Asaf'yev writes it: "Not lullabies *for* the cat but *by* him; it makes a difference."

sonorities" reads like a prediction, since Stravinsky did score the piece, after *Kniga o Stravinskom* had been published.

In "Toward the New," Asaf'yev says that in Stravinsky's concluding chorus for *Khovanshchina*, "the ornate development of the archaic theme is incongruous," and that the composer "desires to be impudent at all costs." Since the piano reduction hardly justifies these reactions, the remarks compound our curiosity to hear the piece—the orchestra score of which remained in Diaghilev's possession after the few performances in June 1913. I should also mention that Asaf'yev writes unenthusiastically about Stravinsky's orchestral *Chant funèbre* for Rimsky-Korsakov, a still earlier lost opus that continues to excite speculation, since it represents the next step beyond *Fireworks*.

In this same chapter, Asaf'yev enumerates the features of the new style, the exploitation of the responsorial principle, the rejection of the large orchestra, of tonic-dominant formulas, and of metrical regularity (or alternatively, the introduction of unequal time-intervals, of figurations with different numerators from those of the meter, and other devices —comparable to the enjambment, dislocated syntax, and so forth of the Russian poets of the time). Most essential, however, is Stravinsky's "new awareness of the functional relationship and interdependence of the various elements composing the texture of sounds." What this means is simply that he has outgrown the rigmarole of academic composition and henceforth will follow only his own artistic logic.

Of Stravinsky's contemporaries, Asaf'yev alone seems to have recognized the importance of the Eight Easy Pieces (1915–17), and that they reveal "the shrewd and incisive intellect of a great artist. [This is music in which] no transplantation of the past can be found, but only contemporary life, with its cinematographic quality." Asaf'yev points out popular elements in each of the pieces that most of us would otherwise miss, in the Balalaika, for example, the abrupt interruptions and turns and the dynamics of the *chastushka,* and in the stretto movement of the Galop, "the sĭxth figure of the quadrille."

The essay on *Renard* is the only one that does the work justice, though this can be blamed on the nonawareness of non-Russians that *Renard* represents the revival of "an authentic old Russian theatre," long suppressed because of its blasphemy, mockery, and anticlerical satire. *Renard,* a seventeen-minute romp that can be described as burlesque, masked buffoonery, mime, is enacted by clowns, actors, acrobats, dancers—anybody but singers. Based on gesture, it stands at the polar opposite of the narrative and descriptive tale of, for instance, Chaucer's Fox and Chanticleer. Stravinsky's singers impersonate the actors with shrieks and howls, measured speech, mock chant, and prayer: the unctuous tone in which the Fox, in nun's habit, confesses the Rooster ("You have wedded, you have bedded, too many wives") is the most delectable lampoon of religious hypocrisy in music. "Laughter is life's real mirror," Asaf'yev says, "its self-criticism."

As for word accentuation, Asaf'yev describes Stravinsky's aim as simply "to preserve the natural flow of the musical speech," which would be inconsistent, of course, with the association of every verbal accent with a point of musical emphasis. It follows, too, that the words must be independent of arbitrary metrical divisions. Near the end of *Renard,* with the arrival of the Cat and the Goat, the accents of the words adhere to the meter, but the dance conforms to a different beat, a counterpoint of accents. But of word setting, more in connection with *Mavra.* The analysis of *Renard* concludes with an out-of-date defense of the work as "a deeply intellectual phenomenon" and the perennially pertinent observation that "this frightens many people."

Asaf'yev's "fertility" interpretation of *Noces* ignited a virtual explosion in Stravinsky, but for all his objections to the obtrusion of the mistaken thesis, he offers no clue to the right

one, simply answering Asaf'yev's statement that the subject of
Noces is "the confrontation of man and his instinct for procre-
ation" with "I do not agree." Asaf'yev repeats his argument:
"One must not forget that *Noces* is the embodiment of the
ancient cult of fertility and reproduction," and Stravinsky re-
bukes him again: "Better to forget, because this has no bearing on it." When the critic reiterates that *Noces* is about
"human beings standing face to face with the act of procre-
ation," Stravinsky objects, this time at greater length:

> I meant nothing of the kind: these statements, which I
> never expected from Asaf'yev, astound me. He has a great
> desire to find an orgiastic tendency that simply is not there.

Next to a remark about the work's "epic forcefulness and
Euripidean rigor,"[13] the exasperated composer asks: "What
is all this deep-thinking nonsense? And I, simpleton, was not
aware of any of this." When Asaf'yev praises Stravinsky's
economy, the compression into four short scenes, the composer jests: "*What?* All of *that* into only four concise
tableaux?"

The sexual interpretation puts the composer so out of sorts
that he chides his champion for using the diminutive "little
berry"—"*Just plain berry*," according to Stravinsky—and at a
reference to the techniques and thought processes of Raphael
and Velázquez, the composer snaps, "As if they were the
same." When a tendency toward symphonism is detected,
Stravinsky exclaims: "This is again your own improvisation,
dear friend: symphonism is not my intention." Seeing Bol-
shevism in a class-war reference to "unfortunates and cap-
tives," the composer wonders "Who?" and further vents his
irritation in a rash of question marks. Asaf'yev's behavioristic
analysis of Stravinsky's irony earns the comment from its
subject: "A curtsy to communists":

---

13. In the English text, "Aeschylean rigor."

It proceeds from pity and from envy . . . of people who, like children, can still find amusement in . . . toys because of the secret mechanisms that make them operate. The curious child breaks the toy open, but he does not uncover a secret thereby: the expert knows that there is no secret but simply a spring adapted to a form. He pities the child and wants to laugh.

Nevertheless, Asaf'yev's essay on *Noces* helps us to understand Russian wedding ritual as both tragic-ironic and grotesque, with threnody and buffoonery as its principal contrasting stylistic elements. On the one side are psalmodic chanting (the murmured *"Chesu, pochesu"*) and the lamentations associated with the loss of virginity, as well as the bereavement of the two mothers. On the other side are the paroxysms, the whooping and shouting—during the ballad of the little swan, for example—the rhythmically notated talk, the clapping, the basso falsetto. The antiphons and responses, of course, derive from peasant music as well as from the church.

That Asaf'yev does not elaborate on the traditions of matchmaking and other rituals is understandable, since he assumed his readers' familiarity with such matters. Nor did Stravinsky ever discuss these elements of the piece, no doubt having despaired of the work's ever being understood in the West. Already in 1923 he had transcribed *Noces* for the pianola—which is to say, eliminated the voices, as he was to do with many of his Russian-text songs. By the time I knew Stravinsky, he was bored with folk music and even more so with the question of its connections to his work. No doubt he interpreted, in a very different way than Asaf'yev intended, the latter's sage remark that *"Sacre* and *Noces,* two of Stravinsky's greatest achievements, are . . . tragedies of race, not tragedies of destiny."

Asaf'yev's observations on *Histoire du soldat* contain flagrant instances of his habit of introducing subjective interpretations, as when he writes of the opening March: "The soldier's head is full of random recollections—flashes of barracks life. . . ." This is the more surprising since he has just said that

> Stravinsky's musical thought is extra-personal, just as his music is extra-sensual (but not sensual-less . . .). . . . The best of his works are not "reflections" of inner life; rather, they incarnate the drive and appetites of life. . . . It is not the inner subjective experiences of people that fascinate him but the styles in which people display themselves.

Asaf'yev considers the Little Concert, with its network of motifs from all of the preceding numbers, as both the musical and dramatic centerpiece and a "synthetic, Lisztian-type" sonata-allegro, the first movement of a symphonic structure in which the Tango is the adagio, the Waltz the scherzo, and the Ragtime the finale. "Dance is the primary agent of form and movement in Stravinsky's art," Asaf'yev concludes, and, "the primary law of all life is rhythm, since all of our senses are rhythmic." In the Soldier's March, "despite the moments of silence, the rhythm is not silenced."

In the Tango, Stravinsky discovered the potentialities of an orchestra of percussion only, composing not just rhythm-lines for these instruments, but rhythm-harmonies as well, layers, or registers, of different timbres and intensities. The "orchestra" of the Waltz suggests a band of street musicians, or a parody of one, through the ornamented, mock-virtuoso violin part. Here, and apropos of the Ragtime, Asaf'yev remarks astutely on Stravinsky's "preference for sudden change, rather than long emotional intensifications and broad crescendi."

In the Chorale, "lines that have been moving toward the limit of individualized utterance" are brought together in tonic cadences that seem to be saying, "Everything comes out well in the end." But the last one is a suspension, a $^6_4$ chord, and Stravinsky's ultimate irony, for the Devil soon leads the doomed Soldier below, to the accompaniment of hot jazz drums. Comparing the death of the Soldier to the "splendors of Isolde's last moments," Asaf'yev decides that the fate of Stravinsky's hero is "the more tragic, by virtue of its simplicity."

The *Pulcinella* chapter abounds in insights, both general ("The instruments are treated as characters in the comedy . . . the doubles of the figures on the stage") and specific ("The strings in the Toccata are used . . . to carry the movement from one *register* to another"). In the 1920s, however, when Asaf'yev wrote, it was not yet known that Stravinsky had not developed "fragments" in *Pulcinella* but, instead, had arranged and orchestrated complete pieces, some by Pergolesi, seven (from the trio sonatas) by Domenico Gallo, and one by Count van Wassenaer.

Turning to *Mavra*, Asaf'yev says that "the whole composition is magnificent, and the melodic line is perfection," which did not stop Stravinsky from scolding him for attributing the "new level of intensity" in the Quartet to qualities of the deceased, for whom the singers repine. "The observation of a fourth-grade schoolboy," the composer writes, though it is one of many helpful evaluations of the musical means with which he delineates character. Thus Parasha, whose prototype was Tchaikovsky's Larina, is portrayed by a gliding melody that avoids "disjunct intervals and temperamental rhythms," and the Hussar by bold entrances and "passionate cadences." Stravinsky's second outburst comes at the end of the analysis, after the statement, "The ingeniousness of reality finds a new and authentic musical utterance." "Only in this?" he demands. "Is it worthwhile, then, to give birth to a musical mouse?"

Mavra's melodic sources and genres, and its "musical speech," occupy a large and, for me, absorbing portion of the essay, but then, I know nothing of Apollon Grigor'ev and Polezhaev, and was only vaguely aware that, like Stravinsky, Tchaikovsky, in *Onegin*, was attacked for his "misplaced accents, ungrammatical word-couplings, pauses in the wrong places, and metrical confusion." Asaf'yev's rebuttal is that "correctness" is not the issue:

> The central problem is to define the music of speech—speech that differs in style according to epoch, rank, society, the personality of the individual. . . . Speech . . . may be filled with interjections, exclamations, interrogations, declarations. The problem is to catch its whole excitement. . . . The critics have applied standards of written style and the pathos of theatrical speech, whereas *Onegin* [and *Mavra*] derive wholly from the music of the speech of the Russian middle class. . . . Words pour out in unbroken melodic lines, commas are ignored . . . and emotional tone and its nuances take precedence over sense. . . .

After the *Mavra* essay, *Kniga o Stravinskom* is less rewarding, both because the subject matter ceases to be Russian and because Stravinsky's 1920s, so-called international-style music quickly attracted a host of younger devotees, including a great many from the Western hemisphere, ready to pore over every note. Yet the final pages contain keen perceptions, both musical—"the reduction in the use of the dominant 7th in cadential formulas helps to unveil the tonic"—and dramaturgical:

> [Creon's] aria proclaims [the] inexorable decree of the oracle in a brilliant and authoritative tone, but . . . in such a way that, though [he] believes he is his own master, to the listener he is made to appear as a plaything . . . which has been set in motion and will go through its mechanical operations.

At the outset, Asaf'yev had distinguished two kinds of composer,

the imitative and the evolving. The imitative preserves—
or, at best, varies—what has been invented by others. The
evolving always struggles to master new methods, new expressions.

One feels that if Boris Asaf'yev had lived as long as his great
coeval, and not been the victim of Soviet mental misprision,
he would have celebrated Stravinsky's glorious evolution
through the music not only of the thirties and forties, the
Concerto per due pianoforti soli and the symphonies, but
also that of the fifties and sixties, *Agon*, Movements, the
Variations. No doubt he would have made the same pronouncement then that he did in his concluding remarks
about *Les Noces:* "Our musical epoch is the epoch of Stravinsky."

Pluralistic Stravinsky

The Apollonian Clockwork[1] is an exhilarating account of a search, external and internal, for Stravinsky, both as a composer and as a man. Following his own example in breaking from the traditional concept of the linear development of musical evolution, the authors suspend chronology and jump "in open form" from one episode to another in the life and the music. One of their chapters is subtitled "Grueling Description of the Numbers 3 and 5 in the Oratorio *Threni*," while another exhibits features of Stravinsky's "style and manner" through the few altered and added notes in his droll arrangement for solo violin of "La Marseillaise."

Messrs Schönberger and Andriessen must be thanked for two acts of iconoclasm performed, respectively, on the myth of Stravinsky's association with C. F. Ramuz and on the musical philosophy of Ernest Ansermet. The young Dutch authors have correctly surmised that the artistic limitations of the librettist of *Histoire du soldat* had begun to dismay the composer even before its premiere, and that Ramuz thereafter became a millstone. As for his book, *Souvenirs sur Igor Stravinsky* (1929), its "tone of pathetic simplicity, sentimental

1. *The Apollonian Clockwork*, by Elmer Schönberger and Louis Andriessen, translated by Jeff Hamburg (Amsterdam, 1983).

unaffectedness, and tormented humbleness, is unbearable"—
a judgment that makes Pierre Suvchinsky's claim, quoted in
François Lesure's *Stravinsky: Etudes et témoignages*,[2] that
Ramuz was *"la plus grande amitié"* of the composer's life
raise doubts about how much this time-to-time Russian friend
really understood about Stravinsky.

Turning to Ansermet's 1961 tome, *Les Fondements de la
musique dans la conscience humaine*, Schönberger and Andriessen attack the "incorrigible school teacher" and "formal-
ist" for setting out to demonstrate "that dodecaphony was
ipso facto nonsense":

> [Ansermet's] blind faith in . . . Husserl left no room for the
> notion that, precisely in art, wrong premises can lead to
> valid consequences. . . . You remember such a book only
> for its rancor, its convulsiveness, its ideological fanaticism
> and its anti-Semitism[3] wrapped up in phenomenological
> terminology.

The Apollonian Clockwork should also be read for its
comments on the *Requiem Canticles*, after which, the authors
say, "Anyone who writes a liturgical requiem for large choir
and orchestra will look like a taxidermist." Stravinsky's
Requiem is not about the Last Judgment, for "that could
only come out positive; the Judgment didn't have to be
feared. Death had already been celebrated too often":

> For the first time since [*Svadebka*], Stravinsky uses real
> clock-bells . . . playing together with two instruments, one
> of which (vibraphone) he had never used before. . . . At the
> end of your life, doing things you have never done before
> —that's conjuring.

---

2. *Stravinsky: Etudes et témoignages*, introduced and compiled by François
Lesure (Paris, 1982).

3. On Ansermet's anti-Semitism, see *Les Fondements*, vol. 1, pp. 235, 423ff.,
534.

In the closing measure, the strokes of the clock and the chord of Death come together for the first and last time, the twenty-third beat of Part B [occurs at the same time] as the thirty-third stroke of the clock. The Hour of Truth? Wasn't there someone who died after 33 years? . . . The twelve strokes that announce Shadow in *The Rake's Progress* are twelve silent strokes in the *Requiem Canticles*: there are twelve beats of silence in the Postlude.

The Apollonian Clockwork is the most ingenious, sharply observed, and original book likely to be written about the composer for a long time, though the authors believe that "the *actual* influence of Stravinsky has just begun." Today's "new music," they write, places serialism as "the furthest consequence of nineteenth-century music, in the mausoleum of the past perfect tense." The new generation, they say, is drawn to Stravinsky, and away from, among others, Boulez and Xenakis.

To turn from Schönberger and Andriessen to François Lesure's thorny centenary garland is to move backward two or three generations to Boulez's essay "Stravinsky demeure. . . ." The book features forty pages of reflections by Suvchinsky and a survey on the texts of the *Sacre* by Louis Cyr. The other contributors include Claude Helffer on the 1924 Concerto, Célestin Deliège on Stravinsky vis-à-vis Schoenberg in 1912, Pierre Boulez's "Balance Sheet?" (in blank verse!), and Stefan Jarocinsky's "Stravinsky as an Apostle of Apollonian Art." Not many of the views are new, and only M. Cyr offers the results of research.

Suvchinsky's Stravinsky is still the Russian émigré of the 1920s and 1930s; or, at any rate, the phenomenal powers of growth and renewal manifested in the later years are not mentioned. Moreover, the composer remains the *"homme simple"* of Ramuz rather than the multiform creative personality re-

vealed by the Schönberger-Andriessen book. Not all of
Suvchinsky's conclusions are mistaken, as when he recognizes
that "Stravinsky was as passionate in his abstract speculations
concerning philosophy and theology as he was remote from
social and political intellectuality" and that "Stravinsky was
no pessimist, but rather an 'anti-optimist' who, with wisdom,
gaiety, humor . . . and profound sadness, accepted the state
of things that one cannot change. . . ." Suvchinsky believes
that a crisis occurred in Stravinsky's life when he discovered
something so frightening that he determined not to think
about it. Suvchinsky neither identifies nor dates the experience, but surely it is related to "the tragic irony of [Oedipus],
of the man who believes himself capable of independent
action, when in fact he is no more than the divinely controlled agent of his own destruction."[4] In any case, with the
creation of *Oedipus Rex* Stravinsky renounced all *sub specie
saeculi* philosophies.

When Suvchinsky assures us that "Stravinsky was indifferent to the pathetic plights of the people in Chekhov," the
present writer can only declare a very different impression,
one of a man who read and reread the stories and letters, and
who would go out of his way to see the plays, even in bad
English translations. (He spent part of an evening in New
York in September 1965 reading howlers in English versions
of Chekhov to Elizabeth Hardwick and Robert Lowell.)

Suvchinsky's factual misinformation is less consequential,
but he should not say that the original title of *Sacre* was "The
Great Sacrifice" (actually "Holy Spring," *Vesna Sviaschen-
naya*), and that Scriabin and Stravinsky, "these two great
musicians"—Stravinsky would hardly have appreciated that

---

4. From "Stravinsky the Litanist," an unpublished thesis (1983) by Edmund
Lee of London University. Stravinsky's religious life from 1926 until he left
Europe in 1939 is an almost totally unknown subject, awaiting the publication
of his letters to the Hieroskhimonakh Gerasim (Mount Athos), the Father
Superior Sergei Zradlovsky (and his assistant, the Superior Igumen, Koz-
lovsky), Archbishop Seraphim (Paris), and, above all, the family cleric, Nikolai
Podosenov (Nice).

—have at last "been assimilated by the Russian conscience." But when did this happen? Actually, most of Stravinsky's music—all of the Biblical kind and even that supreme expression of Russian culture *Svadebka*—is still virtually unknown in the USSR.

Louis Cyr should undertake a full-length critical examination of the *Sacre* texts, if only because his present essay is outdated by the surfacing, in 1982, of the first orchestral draft. Apart from that, Cyr shows good sense, for example in supporting Ansermet's arguments in favor of the restoration of the pizzicati in the Danse sacrale. In revised versions, Stravinsky required the strings to play arco only, for the reason that the rapid switching between bows and fingers was beyond the orchestral technique of 1913; but the alternating modes of articulation are part of his original conception, as well as, so the *Symphony in Three Movements* confirms, an element in his style. The most important chapter in this much-needed book would be a detailed comparison of the Danse sacrale in the earlier and 1943 scores, and a study of the drafts for the latter, including the Kestenbaum manuscript.

Though accurately describing Stravinsky's reactions to questions of performance as "humbly acquiescent" one day and the opposite the next, Cyr mistakenly assumes that the composer was "not interested in a critical edition of his works" or in "establishing definitive versions" of them. (He met with his publishers in Paris in October and November 1968 with no other purpose in mind.) Cyr also suggests that the composer might not have made the two-hand reduction of the complete work, even though "his" piano score is mentioned in letters as having been used during the first rehearsals, and though he had already acquired the habit, in *Firebird* and *Petrushka*, of preparing piano reductions as he composed; but the original manuscript, the scholar's corpus delicti, has not been found. Finally, Cyr does not seem to be aware that before rewriting the Danse sacrale in 1943, Stravinsky had begun a reduced-orchestra version of the entire *Sacre*, of which apparently only a single page survives.[5]

The dust jacket of *Stravinsky on Stage*,[6] a reproduction of Goncharova's backcloth for the "Kolybelnya" set in *Firebird*, is the book's most striking color photograph, but the competition is close and includes a picture of the actual costumes worn by the Chosen One and the Sage in the 1913 *Sacre*; Valentine Gross's pastel impressions of both tableaux in the same production; Bakst's design for *Mavra*; Dülberg's, which looks like an Atari game, for the first scene of the 1928 Berlin *Petrushka*; Barsacq's Chirico-like scene for *Perséphone*; and several of Hockney's designs for the Glyndebourne *Rake*. Among the black-and-white illustrations, the greatest novelty is a selection of Matisse's drawings for *Le Chant du Rossignol* showing his musical notation, including bar lines, accents, eighth-notes, and terminology ("arpeggio"). The last photograph in the book, of Balanchine and Stravinsky, has become deeply poignant.

The presentation of graphic art in *Stravinsky on Stage* is accompanied by valuable information about first performances and "other major productions" of twenty pieces composed specifically for the theatre. Here, perhaps for the first time in book form, Vera Sudeikina, with Nicholas Galitzine, is given credit for the scenery and costumes of the first London staging of *Histoire du soldat*, July 10, 1927. But it should also be noted that the original *Perséphone* (1934) did not run "for only three performances," since the production was re-

5. In the most valuable recording of Stravinsky in rehearsal, the one released (1983) by the Educational Media Association of America, of the composer conducting the *Sacre* in Stockholm in 1961, he tells the lower strings to play the glissando figure beginning at 33 (1943 score) détaché to increase the volume, a revision that should be observed, since the effect he wanted is demonstrated in the recorded performance.

6. *Stravinsky on Stage*, by Alexander Schouvaloff and Victor Borovsky (London, 1983).

vived for three more in the following year; that Rennert's 1963 *Oedipus* was given for the first time not at La Scala but at the Hamburg Opera; and that the unidentified 1949 New York revival of the same work, designed by Frederick Kiesler, took place at the Juilliard School.

One of the most valuable of the papers read at the 1982 Stravinsky symposium in San Diego, Simon Karlinsky's "Stravinsky and Russian Pre-Literate Theater," has appeared in the spring 1983 issue of *19th-Century Music*. At some point during a twelve-year study of "Russian indigenous forms of drama," Karlinsky realized that Stravinsky's stage works from *Petrushka* to the *Soldat* "add up to a compendium of the native theatrical genres of old Russia." Karlinsky became fascinated by the "problem in creative psychology [of] why this musical innovator chose to compose some of his most revolutionary works on subjects taken from archaic and, in his day, mostly defunct pre-literary dramatized folklore." Karlinsky's explanation connects Stravinsky's approach to folklore with that of Symbolist poets and Modernist painters including Khlebnikov, Tsvetayeva, Remizov, and Chagall, as distinguished from the nineteenth-century "hybridization with Western themes" of Pushkin, Glinka, and Rimsky-Korsakov.

The years 1909–17 were a period of new fascination with purely Russian art. Whereas Pushkin had borrowed "The Golden Cockerel" from Washington Irving, and whereas even "Ruslan and Lyudmila" derives from Western elements as well as Russian folklore—like the music of Glinka's opera based on the poem—Stravinsky, in *Svadebka* and *Renard*, turned his back on the West. Karlinsky quotes the pianist Alexei Liubimov on these pieces: "Archaism of melodies and dynamism of rhythms create an extraordinary impression of a natural grasp of the spirit and style of ancient peasant folklore." By this time (1914 to 1917) Stravinsky did not need the actual folk tradition but only the subject matter and the words (in "phonetically transcribed dialect"). The result, Karlinsky writes, was "dazzlingly original Russian music that was free of both ethnography and stylization."

Turning to the *Sacre*, Karlinsky observes that "with the introduction of the disciplines of anthropology and ethnography in the nineteenth century, a wide array of seasonal folk customs and games were easily identified as direct descendants of ancient rituals. . . ." With *Svadebka*, pagan survivals in Christian weddings, officially condemned for at least three centuries, are given permanent artistic form. Karlinsky remarks that when the basses sing the words *"Pod'na svad'bu,"* which amount to a command to the Virgin Mary, we realize "that the mother of the Savior is here replacing some ancient fertility goddess. In monotheistic religions, divinities do not get ordered about, but in *The Iliad* it was quite possible for a warrior to order the goddess off the battlefield." The rituals and ceremonies of the Russian village wedding have been presented as staged theatre performances in the USSR as well as at Harvard University's Russian Research Center (May 1983), culminating in a performance of *Svadebka*.

Karlinsky devotes much space to correcting mistranslations of Stravinsky's Russian texts, a service for which we should all be grateful. But when he says that C. F. Ramuz's French translations of Stravinsky's *skomorokh* (minstrel-buffoon) pieces "deprive them of all connection" with their Russian meanings, we wonder if Ramuz can be blamed for what must have been Stravinsky's intention. After all, the translations are Stravinsky's in substance, and they date from the times of the compositions.[7] Clearly he was not then concerned to hide the anticlericalism of *Renard*, or, forty years later, of *Svadebka*, when he wrote his own, most un-literal English translation of the text, together with his phonetic

---

7. Stravinsky wrote to Nicolas Nabokov, May 10, 1953: *"Renard* is impossible because of a French text that has no value as song and deprives the work of its literary value." The composer's own French translations of his texts not only fit the music better than Ramuz's but are often superior as language. Here

version of the Russian, into the present reviewer's score of the work. (In a 1930s letter, his St. Petersburg friend of the *Firebird* period, the musicologist Jacques Handschin, reminds him that he used to be an ardent "leftist.")

But as Karlinsky points out, Stravinsky's own English titles of his *podblyudnye* choruses belie their sense in Russian, including *Podblyudnye* itself, which the composer translated as "Saucers." ("Dish-divination songs," Karlinsky proposes, though Webster's gives "dish" as both the first and second meanings of "saucer.") One of these choruses, "Ovsen," is called "Autumn" in the English edition—ironically, Karlinsky observes, since the Russian name is that of the first day of spring in the pre-Christian calendar. Yet the piece was first published in German; Stravinsky himself chose, or approved, the title "Herbstlied" (1929 manuscript, now in Mainz); and the English was translated from the German, probably being thought suitable because of a connection with the harvest. In any case, the question—Why, when translating his Russian texts, did Stravinsky deliberately seem to ignore their original meanings?—is not fully answered.

Professor Karlinsky asserts that in the second decade of this century, when Stravinsky "was creating these epochal scores, he was addressing a Russian audience. . . ." Where? By Lac Léman? True, for a moment in 1916 he had hoped for a performance of *Renard* in Russia, even though the piece was commissioned for presentation in a Paris salon. But by the time *Svadebka* was completed, and the *Soldat*—which Karlinsky likens to a folk play described by Dostoevsky as

---

is Stravinsky's translation from one of the passages of his "Cat's Lullabies," followed by Ramuz's revision:

> *Aujourd'hui*
> *Le chat a mis*
> *Son bel habit gris*
> *Pour attraper les souris.*
> > (Stravinsky)
> *Pour faire la chass' aux souris.*
> > (Ramuz)

performed by convicts in a Siberian penal colony—Stravinsky knew that his audiences would be those of the Diaghilev ballet, which had never appeared in Russia and after 1917 no longer aspired to go there.

The piano was the fulcrum of Stravinsky's musical thought, as Charles M. Joseph demonstrates,[8] and though his book naturally focuses on the keyboard works—solo, ensemble, and in transcriptions—it also helps to elucidate Stravinsky's music as a whole. Despite unreliable recent editing, the lack of a critical edition, and the inaccessibility of many of the original sources, Mr. Joseph is a judicious guide from the sketches of the "Tarantella" of 1896 to the last, unfinished, piano piece of 1967. His documentation is extensive, and some of it is new, such as the interview (New York, summer of 1981) with Juilliard professor Adele Marcus, who played the Concerto per due pianoforti soli with the composer several times in the spring of 1940:

> Stravinsky sat very high at the piano. . . . He was especially attentive to matters of rhythmic fidelity. . . . He did not wish to rehearse very much and was nervous about performing. . . . Before a performance, [he] would apply some concoctive paste to the pads of his fingers that would quickly dry and act as a weighting agent. . . . It is known that Stravinsky seemed to be preoccupied with the element of key touch and weight peculiar to any one piano. . . . It would appear that Stravinsky's mysterious adhesive substance was an attempt to counterbalance artificially the resistance of the piano's keys with which he found fault. . . .

One of the most interesting sections in the book concerns the use of "interval vectors" in analyzing the structure of this

8. *Stravinsky and the Piano*, by Charles M. Joseph (Ann Arbor, 1983).

same concerto. Mr. Joseph counts only six possible intervals —major and minor seconds and thirds, the perfect fourth, and the tritone—since he accepts the principle of complementary equivalency (e.g., a major sixth equals a minor third, and so on). But in the first measure, for example, some of us persist in hearing a minor tenth rather than a minor third, and, in the second measure, Piano I, a fifth, not its "complement equivalent" fourth. Nevertheless, the approach enables the musical anatomist to show quickly how the notes in the first two measures, Piano II, comprising the vector 012120, are transposed to other parts of the piece.

Mr. Joseph's coup is his discovery in the autograph piano score of *Firebird*—under our noses in the Morgan Library— of major revisions no doubt undertaken in collaboration with Fokine during the creation of the ballet in the spring of 1910. Thus the six measures at 46, leading to the "Apparition of the Thirteen Princesses," were originally introduced just before the "Apparition of the Firebird"; the "Supplications of the Firebird" was only half as long in the first version; and the passage from 103 to 104 was a late interpolation from Kastchei's "Dance," perhaps to anticipate that movement.

These *Firebird* repairs, probably made during the St. Petersburg rehearsals of the ballet, vivify the description by Brussel, the French critic who heard Stravinsky play the score for Diaghilev and others before the company came to Paris:

> . . . We all met in the little ground-floor room on Zamiatin Perenlokm . . . the composer, young, slim . . . with vague meditative eyes, and lips set firm in an energetic-looking face, was at the piano. But the moment he began to play, the modest and dimly lighted room glowed with . . . radiance. . . . The manuscript on the music-rest, scored over with fine pencillings, revealed a masterpiece.

. . .

The excerpts from twenty-two years of *Modern Music*[9] contain few judgments that have endured, but the book records one important musical insight, in Roger Sessions's "On *Oedipus Rex*" (1928), and provides a gauge of the period as well as of the subsequent conquest of bellettrist criticism by scientific musicology. Thus Robert Tangeman's 1945 article on the Four-hand Sonata does not even refer to its Russian folksong sources, whereas anyone writing about the piece today would be obliged to speculate about the work that Stravinsky had originally thought of basing on them, "Songs Lingering and Quiet" (a note in his hand, in Russian), for which he made a copy of No. 41, music in the character of the title.[10] (The composer found the Jurgenson volume *Russian Ballads and Folk Music*, title in English, in 1942, in a secondhand music store—for $2.50.)

Stravinsky in "Modern Music" reprints two minor classics, Lincoln Kirstein's "Working with Stravinsky" (*Jeu de cartes*) and Frederick Jacobi's "The New Apollo." According to the latter, "The composer indicated his desire that the first scene represent the birth of Apollo; that Apollo be born on the stage, springing full-grown from the womb of his mother. It was thought, however, not advisable to stage it in just this way in Washington." Sessions, following Arthur Lourié, wrote that *Oedipus* is not

> tonal in the ordinary sense of the word. As in nearly all of Stravinsky's works, the shifting harmonies move around a clearly established harmonic axis. . . . To give but one instance: the musical pages which embody the crucial moment of the drama are based on a persistently reiterated D

9. *Stravinsky in "Modern Music" (1924–1946)*, compiled by Carol J. Oja, foreword by Aaron Copland (New York, 1983).
10. The first of Stravinsky's sourcebooks for *Mavra* (1922), especially concerning melodic style, Danilo Kashin's collection of folk music, published by Simeon Selivanovsky in Moscow in 1833, is actually titled "Lingering Songs." Stravinsky edited and rewrote lines of song texts in the Kashin book with a view to using them in *Svadebka*.

minor harmony. The effect of such a style is one of great deliberation and stateliness of movement. Tonality . . . is in no sense a part of the structure of the whole.

This is central to the thesis, more than half a century later, of the most important book so far to appear on the composer, Pieter van den Toorn's *The Music of Igor Stravinsky*.[11] (Those who read Gerald Abraham's superficial review— "Images of Motoric Energy," *Times Literary Supplement*, June 17, 1983—may find this claim extravagant, but since Mr. Abraham writes that the book "evades the problem of describing Stravinsky's harmony in conventional terms" he cannot have understood very much of it, van den Toorn's point of departure being that much of Stravinsky's harmony cannot be described in "conventional terms.") Van den Toorn's statement that in a majority of Stravinsky's works there is "no functional activity to legitimatize any C-scale tonally functional definition of . . . separate keys" simply elaborates, in different, more complicated language, Sessions's observation that the magnetic attractions of harmonies to a triadic center should not be confounded with the larger, functional and hierarchical relationships of keys in the tonal system. This is not true of all of Stravinsky's music, but the point is that he did not think of his triadically pure cadences —"terminating conveniences," van den Toorn calls them— as keys. This is proven by the composer's comments on Paul Collaer's notes on the *Symphony of Psalms* in the original program book (December 1930), which attempts to explain that the first movement "modulates toward G major" and actually ends in this key. Stravinsky vehemently recorded his disagreement in underlinings and question marks.

11. *The Music of Igor Stravinsky*, by Pieter C. van den Toorn (New Haven, 1983).

So, too, twenty years ago, in "Problems of Pitch Organization in Stravinsky," Arthur Berger understood that despite Stravinsky's "congenital orientation" toward "traditional harmony," and the "tonal bias" that obviously "governed the conception" of many pieces, the semblance of "tonal functionality" in the bulk of Stravinsky's work is distinctly parenthetical.

Van den Toorn's analysis of Stravinsky's musical language is on a much higher level than any heretofore attempted, and his grasp of the composer's immense scope extends beyond that of any earlier writer on the subject. At the same time, his conspectus is not as comprehensive as it might have been, since the author concentrates on twenty works which best demonstrate that "octatonic" constructions are at the core of Stravinsky's technique of composition. Thus *Pulcinella, Mavra, Apollo, Le Baiser de la fée, Perséphone,* the piano music, *Jeu de cartes,* the Symphony in C, *The Rake's Progress* are scarcely mentioned, for the reason that they can be discussed in traditional terminology (which appears in this book only in quotation marks—"dominant seventh," "diminished chord," etc.).

Van den Toorn's quest for "consistency, identity, or distinction in pitch organization" in Stravinsky's music led to the discovery that, more than any other composer, he made use of a referential "octatonic pitch collection." The author defines this as "eight pitch classes,"[12] which, exposed in scale form, alternate major and minor seconds in two symmetrical halves:

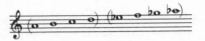

This symmetrical organization might seem to be confining, but when, in *Petrushka* (1910–11), Stravinsky began to com-

---

12. A "pitch class" refers to, for instance, all C's (in any register), whereas "pitch" refers to, for instance, a specific C.

bine triads related through the tritone (in the above example, from *Svadebka*, the interval between A and E flat; in *Petrushka*, the interval between C and F sharp), "a new universe" was opened up, "one that Stravinsky was to render peculiarly his own."

Stravinsky inherited the octatonic collection from Rimsky-Korsakov, who had used it most conspicuously in *Mlada* and *Sadko*. The octatonic scale also corresponds to the second of Messiaen's "modes of limited transposition," and Messiaen was apparently the first (c. 1944) to perceive the extent of Stravinsky's exploitation of it. The term became general currency through Arthur Berger's 1963 essay, though Berger's description did not include the sequence of alternating major and minor seconds. Stravinsky himself never used the word "octatonic," but his own expression *"leit-harmonie,"* in his 1927 analysis of *Firebird*, amounts to the same thing, and the evidence for his awareness of "the octatonic collection as a cohesive frame of reference," and of his "life-long predilection for octatonic partitioning," is irrefutable.

Van den Toorn's observations range widely and are by no means restricted to the theoretical. It seems safe to predict that the book will rock the world of musical analysis as profoundly as, say, Leonid Kachian's *The Polynomial Algorithm in Linear Programming* seems to have changed the world of computer analysis. Thus van den Toorn calls attention to Stravinsky's fondness for the octave and third (without the fifth) and points out a similarity of effect between a harmonic progression in the 1945 Symphony and the traditional Neapolitan sixth—this in a comparison of the conciseness of the *Psalms* with the "sprawling" impression given by the Symphony, in the sense of "abundance and diversity of material, and in the referential implications." In the serial music van den Toorn comments on the simpler rhythms and "tighter delineations" (smaller intervals) in the vocal pieces versus the "looser delineations" (larger intervals) and "poly-rhythmic combinations of great complexity" in the instrumental music (Movements, Variations). In short, van den Toorn is more musician than theoretician, even declaring himself in sympathy with Stravinsky's "suspicion that formal reckoning represented a kind of thinking about music rather than a thinking *in* music . . . that, unlike composition or performance, such reckoning was not fundamentally auditive." More than once a theorist colleague's error is attributed to his having "trusted his eye rather than his ear."

A full chapter and several digressions are devoted to Stravinsky's "metric irregularity as opposed to regular metric periodicity," or, in other words, to "beat" in relation to accent and phrase, and to "off-the-beat/on-the-beat contradictions and reversals." The question has not been studied as thoroughly before, though for some reason van den Toorn does not mention Allen Forte's landmark demonstration that greater harmonic density coincides with metrical stress. Perhaps not all readers will agree with van den Toorn that the horn swoops on the first beats of the $\frac{7}{4}$ measures in the *Firebird* finale remain anacrustic in feeling despite the shifting of the "melodic downbeat" to the second quarter note.

Van den Toorn does not favor the music of any one of Stravinsky's periods or styles, and the book's conclusions about "the startling variety from one context to the next" in the neo-classic music destigmatizes this label. Nor does van den Toorn believe that "serialism . . . could in some ultimate sense threaten the legitimacy of all other processes of musical invention." *Agon*, he writes, is "well-nigh miraculous" because of the music's "vast pluralistic reach in historical reference" and because the synthesis of serialism and "the octatonic-diatonic interaction" works. The author never loses sight of the totality of Stravinsky's music, and if the octatonic perspective is overemphasized, it also provides a unifying view.

For this reader, the most absorbing part of the book is the

last, dealing with the serial music. Van den Toorn traces the composer's development from "untransposed melodic sets" (series)[13] to hexachordal units and transposition by means of a new technique of rotation. But whereas van den Toorn provides a solidly grounded guide for the serial construction of *The Flood*, the one for *Abraham and Isaac* is at sea, in at least two particulars.

Stravinsky began *Abraham and Isaac* (Santa Fe, August 2, 1962)[14] with notations for the original and inverted order of the series, then deployed the pitches partly from right to left, the Hebrew text possibly having suggested this to him. Van den Toorn asserts that "the complete twelve-tone set" occurs in "an ordered rendition only once, at the beginning of the piece." But this first exposition is *not* strictly ordered (the music starts with the second note of the beta hexachord, continuing with the first note and the alpha hexachord in retrograde); the strict version, inverted order, first appears in the vocal part in the—supposedly nonexistent—second statement. Van den Toorn also remarks the "seemingly privileged F identification"; it does not "seem," however, but *is*, for the reason that all rotations of the original and inverted forms of the series begin with F and that four hexachordal sets conclude with it. Nor does the author explain that the F octaves are derived from the combined verticals of the first pitch classes of the original and inverted series.[15]

A result of the "information explosion" is that increasing numbers of the most valuable publications, van den Toorn's

---

13. Actually Stravinsky transposed the first series that he ever used, the "rows" in the Septet.

14. During the next stage of composition, in Venice five weeks later, Stravinsky introduced a unison chorus for the response "Avraham."

15. All three examples in music type for *Abraham and Isaac* contain errors: the clef is wrong in part 1 of example 93; one of the rhythmic quantities in example 94 is a thirty-second short; and in example 95 the sharp is missing before the third sixteenth-note G.

among them, are becoming less accessible to general readers because they are not so much "literature" as manuals of technology. But new and complex phenomena may well require new and complex means of expression, and the vocabulary of Donald Tovey cannot explain the pitch organization of Stravinsky's music. Yet the musically sophisticated reader should not be daunted by the few additions to musical nomenclature required in order to follow van den Toorn's arguments, which deserve to be brought to the attention of the larger public before being sent off to solitary confinement in a journal of music theory.

Having said this, one must admit that the writing also presents unnecessary impediments to communication. Equating such crucial terms as "dissonance" with "friction" (to be "harmonious" is to be "frictionless") is not adequate definition. And many of van den Toorn's sentences are indigestibly long—often more than a jaw-breaking one hundred words. (Could this be a result of word processing? When "the little drummer girl" wonders why her interrogation is not being tape-recorded, Kurtz answers: "The ear selects. . . . Machines don't. Machines are uneconomical.") Furthermore, the language distracts: to describe "diatonic penetration" as "tonally incriminating behavior" is to give moral overtones to what should be a purely musical matter. (The author is at his best when distinguishing the "pulls and attractions" in octatonic progressions from tonally incriminating ones.) Worst of all, approximately half of the hundred or so music examples are marred by wrong pitches, clefs, rhythmic quantities, time signatures. Yet van den Toorn's understanding of Stravinsky's music as a whole rewards the effort of reading the book.

Among forthcoming publications, the most eagerly awaited are the color facsimile of the autograph full score of *Firebird* (Schott and Minkoff); Arthur Comegno's thesis on *Svadebka* (Harvard); *A Stravinsky Scrapbook* (Thames and Hudson's picture-book sequel to *Igor and Vera Stravinsky*, this one focused on the composer's American years); the third volume of the selected correspondence (Knopf); an English translation of Vershinina's *Stravinsky's Early Ballets* (UMI Research Press); and, most important for biographers, selections from Vera Stravinsky's letters and diaries.

Regrettably the list does not include a study of Stravinsky in relation to contemporary musicology. The *TLS* reviewer mentioned above singles out Manfred Bukofzer's "The Neo-Baroque" in *Stravinsky in "Modern Music"*; but it should also be known that Bukofzer had sent his essay "Speculative Thinking in Medieval Music" to Stravinsky in 1942, and that this essay had an effect on him comparable to those of Cingria (*Pétrarque*) and Handschin (*Gregorianisch-Polyphones*) a decade earlier. (Handschin may have given Stravinsky the *Dictionnaire de plain-chant*, in which he entered a *clausula* of his own.) The whole subject of the influence of musicology on the composer, apart from some misunderstood analogies between late Stravinsky and isorhythmic motets and parody masses, is a neglected one. An exordium might be made with a history of his twenty-five-year association with Sol Babitz and his laboratory for "old music" (largely sponsored by the composer), but then even the best of the musical collaborations with Babitz, the violin and piano arrangement of two of the *Pièces faciles*, are unknown.

The book that the present reviewer would most *like* to read would be a memoir of Stravinsky with his poet and painter friends and acquaintances in the Hollywood years, a circle that included Charles Olson,[16] who actually bedded his towering frame on the tiny couch in the Stravinsky den; Theodore Roethke, whose dedication of his *Words for the Wind* —"For Igor Stravinsky, master of finance, from Theodore Roethke, Baron von und zu Gar Nichts, February 1959"— suggests that he might not have been so mad as was once

16. See Olson's poem "Igor Stravinsky" (April 6, 1948).

thought; and Kenneth Rexroth, who, after holding forth on Elgar at the Stravinsky dinner table one evening in November 1957, might have been writing for all of us when he inscribed a book: "What can you possibly say? The thanks of a lifetime."

"Cher Père, Chère Véra"

> As all historians know, our knowledge of the past
> is based very largely on the records of litigation;
> and, as Mantegna was a tireless litigant, we know
> an unusual amount about him at all periods.
>
> Kenneth Clark, *The Art of Humanism*

My title is the salutation that begins most of the letters to Igor and Vera Stravinsky from his three surviving children and their spouses. Similarly, the contents of the correspondence seem to indicate that Stravinsky's children had genuine affection for his second wife. Whatever their true feeling, they must have recognized that their stepmother was responsible for the smoother periods in their relationship with their father, who would do anything for her, and for her alone. Anyone close to the scene knew that Vera Stravinsky regularly interceded in the children's behalf, exhorting their father to continue to provide them with money, or doing so herself when he refused.

On July 7, 1964, for instance, Mrs. Soulima Stravinsky[1] wrote to the composer:

At Ann Arbor [May 3, 1964] I asked Vera if it would be possible for you to help us financially with the work at my home [in France], La Clidelle. Vera's response was so kind

Some of the information in this article comes from files in the New York County Surrogate Court.

1. Françoise, née Blondlat, wife of Soulima ("Svetik") Stravinsky. She had two children by her first husband, M. Bon, a daughter, Hélène Cinqualbre, and a son, Jacques Bon. Françoise Bon married Soulima (b. 1910) in 1946.

and so full of warmth that I now permit myself to broach the subject with you.

Less kindly and warmly, Stravinsky wrote to his publisher in London:

Ashamed to ask me directly, [Françoise] spoke about it to Vera, breaking down into tears. But give the money to the poor girl, since taxes will not allow me to take it to my grave. [July 9, 1964]

And on June 8, 1951, Stravinsky wrote to Theodore, his elder son:

Vera just received the letters from Denise and Kitty.[2] I understand your financial trouble resulting from the trip you are obliged to make to Vichy. As testimony to my sympathy, I enclose a payment order permitting you to withdraw 1,000 Swiss francs from my account in Basel before your departure.

The composer's heirs[3] understood implicitly that they would be wiser to address their requests not to *cher Père*, but to *chère Véra*.

On October 10, 1952, Stravinsky wrote to Theodore, then aged forty-five:

You say that you do not have sufficient money to build the garage and the fence, and you ask me for another 8,000 or 9,000 [dollars]. Although I have already told you how difficult it would be for me to exceed the sum of $15,000, I shall

2. Denise, née Guerzoni, wife of Theodore ("Fedya") Stravinsky, and Catherine Mandelstamm Stravinsky (b. 1937), the orphaned child of the composer's elder daughter, Lyudmila ("Mika") and Yuri Mandelstamm. Kitty lived with Theodore (b. 1907) and Denise in Geneva and was adopted by them in 1952.
3. On December 12, 1979, the *New York Times* published a front-page story, repeated by television, radio, and newspapers worldwide, under the headline

once again explain the state of my finances. . . . If I send
the money you request, I would be reducing to a dangerous
level the small amount that I have put aside for Vera and
myself in the event of my incapacitation. Do not forget, I
am seventy years old. I live modestly, and, if comparatively
comfortably, this is only because I am still conducting.
How long I shall be able to go on conducting without running myself into the ground, I cannot say; but I do know
that without the conducting, it would be difficult to make
ends meet. My earnings as a composer are not enough to
live on, and I will not conceal from you that I live in constant fear of having no security. . . . The greater part of
the savings that I made have been for all of you. I gave
each of you $15,000 to buy or build a house. My own house
cost $13,000.[4]

Despite repeated declarations of this kind from the composer,
he continued to send money, thanks chiefly—as I witnessed—
to Vera Stravinsky, who prevailed upon him not only to help
support his children, but also to give each of them the house
that Stravinsky mentions, and an automobile.

A few excerpts from the myriad letters, covering more than
forty of Stravinsky's later years, are sufficient to indicate that
the flow of money to Theodore was regular and substantial:

Unfortunately, I cannot afford to continue increasing the
sums that I send you monthly. . . . My earnings have de-

"Stravinsky Estate Fight Resolved." The report must have perplexed hundreds
of thousands of readers, for it did not and could not explain the complex
background of the litigation, which is the aim of the following pages.

4. The actual purchase price was $13,607, but Stravinsky was obliged to take
first and second mortgages amounting to nearly $11,000. He paid off the
mortgages at $60 a month, from April 1941 to January 1948. On December 16,
1941, the Stravinskys were forced to move all of their money from a blocked
Hollywood account because he had been a French national (although he
had filed first papers for U.S. citizenship in August 1940). In a letter to
Vittorio Rieti, March 10, 1942, Stravinsky complains of having to "fill in
applications and reports for our blocked account, new applications now to
unblock our account." (Original in English)

creased, especially in the last year, owing to the crisis in [conducting] engagements, which were my principal source of income. In order to help you, I am using the francs in the Basel bank, which do not amount to much and which I had been saving for an emergency. It would be nice to replenish this sum with proceeds from the sale of a manuscript. [June 4, 1950]

I see from your letter that I must immediately provide you with 4,000 francs for your naturalization. Since I do not want to send the money from here, and I do not have enough in Basel at the moment, I have asked [Erwin] Rosenthal, with whom I deal in selling my manuscripts, to send you this sum. [March 14, 1956]

I received your letter and in immediate reply am sending 4,000 Swiss francs. [April 11, 1962]

In each of these instances, Vera Stravinsky was Theodore's advocate. Notwithstanding, neither he nor. his brother, Soulima, or sister, Milene,[5] nor Igor Stravinsky's granddaughter, Catherine, acknowledged the composer's widow at his funeral. And shortly thereafter they retained lawyers to contest her right to inherit much of what he had willed her, an action that, in February 1974, developed into a lawsuit settled (in name only) six years later, to the advantage of no one except the several law firms involved.[6]

---

5. B. 1914. She married Andre Marion in France in 1944.

6. In an affidavit of November 27, 1978, Martin Garbus, Vera Stravinsky's attorney since 1974, felt compelled to remind the court that "litigation does not exist solely for the benefit of lawyers." Each of the lawyers at the depositions in this case received $100 an hour, in addition to $45 an hour for "preparatory study" and a fee for each note taken during the sessions—this in spite of the stenotypist ($600 a day, $2,500 to $3,000 for the transcript, and $500 for the Xeroxes). A two-day deposition—work that Judge Kaufman in a recent article in the *New York Law Journal* described as "mundane," recommending that it be carried on by paralegal aides—cost $9,000. Vera Stravinsky was represented throughout by Mr. Garbus, a member, when the case began, of the New York firm of Emil, Kobrin, Klein and Garbus, but who soon

The documentation for this ugliest and most highly publicized chapter in Stravinsky's biography is found in correspondence and in the depositions taken during the litigation.[7] The latter, on file at the New York County Surrogate Court, are part of the public record.[8] The original language of most of Igor Stravinsky's letters is French, but some are written, partly or entirely, in Russian and English. The quotations from the depositions and from notes and letters entered as evidence follow the official, notarized texts and translations of texts.

Apart from Vera Stravinsky, I was the only person to whom Igor Stravinsky confided extensively vis-à-vis his children and who, at the same time, knew all of the litigants personally: Soulima Stravinsky since June 1948; Milene Marion since July 1948; Theodore Stravinsky and Catherine Mandelstamm Stravinsky since August 1951. Although the aim of this chronicle is to present an unbiased view of a segment of Stravinsky history, I concede that this is not possible; having

---

formed his own firm, Frankfurt, Garbus, Klein and Selz. Another attorney employed by Vera Stravinsky, Helene Kaplan, left Emil, Kobrin at the same time as Mr. Garbus, but continued to work independently. In the first few years of the case, Stravinsky's children and their spouses were represented by Messrs. Cramer, Kunin, and Gleick of the New York firm of Kaye, Scholer, Fierman, Hays and Handler. Later the children replaced these lawyers by James J. Higginson and Francis Wendell of Appleton, Rice and Perrin (New York), by Milton Fisher and G. Bobrinskoy of Mayer, Brown and Platt (Chicago), and, in 1982, as appellants, by Proskauer, Rose, Goetz and Mendelssohn (New York). In addition, Theodore Stravinsky employed the Paris lawyer Jacques Borel and the Geneva lawyer Oliver Dunant.

7. In this article, the excerpts from the letters of Stravinsky's children and their spouses, his granddaughter, and Pierre Suvchinsky are paraphrased; the originals are in French. Theodore Stravinsky's deposition was taken in the Hôtel Mercure, Annemasse (France), November 29 and 30, 1976, by Martin Garbus as counsel for Mrs. Stravinsky, James Higginson, assisted by Oliver Dunant, as counsel for the children. The depositions of Milene Marion and of the nonparty witness Andre Marion were taken at 1888 Century Park East, Los Angeles, April 27 and 28, 1977. The Marions were represented by Higginson, Bobrinskoy, and J. Swanson (a Los Angeles lawyer);

lived with Igor and Vera Stravinsky almost every day for twenty-three years, I am naturally more aware of the perspectives of the elders than of the children. Yet I was fond of the children when I first knew them and felt at times that I was on their "side," partly because we shared the same struggle to preserve our own identities. The children were deeply handicapped, being biologically pre-empted: nature had concentrated all of her power in the awesome father.

Only rarely do great artists make good parents, great art demanding of its creators no less than all they have to give. Stravinsky was no exception to this rule, and it seems to have made him a tyrannical father. During a visit in February 1916, Nijinsky observed that the composer "is like an emperor and his wife and children are his servants and soldiers."[9] Stravinsky's correspondence indicates that his imperiousness with his sons did not diminish when they grew up. Thus Arthur Lourié felt compelled to write to him,

---

Martin Garbus represented Vera Stravinsky. My deposition—like Marion's, that of a nonparty witness—was taken in New York, March 31 and April 1, 1977, by Higginson, Bobrinskoy, and Fisher, and on May 29, 1978, by Bobrinskoy; Garbus represented me on all three occasions. Vera Stravinsky's deposition was taken in New York, March 6 and 7, 1977, by Kunin; Garbus represented her. Some of the transcript of these two days could have been published in an anthology of unintentional humor, so complete was Kunin's and Mrs. Stravinsky's inability to communicate. Here are some excerpts:

KUNIN: I take it you had clothes in your suitcase. . . .
MRS. STRAVINSKY: . . . usually no[t] closed . . . no lock.
      . . .
KUNIN: What kind of a suitcase was it? . . .
MRS. STRAVINSKY: I have twenty suitcases. I don't remember what I had five years ago.
KUNIN: Was it a suitcase?
MRS. STRAVINSKY: A suitcase is a suitcase. . . .
      . . .
KUNIN: You [and your husband] were talking about your birthday, I gather?
MRS. STRAVINSKY: Name day.
MR. GARBUS: Her name day.
KUNIN: Which you say is a birthday.

March 8, 1930: "I am a little worried about [Theodore's] personal affairs. . . . Give him a few kind words of advice, dear friend." And a week later: "I am sorry for [your sons] because even the suggestion that they might be suspected of something bad causes them to despair." In the same year, Theodore wrote to his father: "You hang up the telephone on me, leaving me standing there. . . . I was very hurt by that." Once Stravinsky's wife actually had to remind him that "you were off by an entire month in your birthday cable to Theodore. He was born on March 27, not April 24." (Letter of April 27, 1937) A letter from Stravinsky to Theodore, April 18, 1961, reveals an asperity of a kind more likely to be found in a communication to an errant adolescent than to a man of fifty-four:

> . . . I do not understand anything in your short note of April 14. . . . What exactly is it that has been done "according to my instructions"? . . . I asked you to send the letter I enclosed . . . which you failed to do for reasons unknown to me. . . . And what "documents" are you keeping "here

GARBUS: No, it's better than a birthday, Mr. Kunin. You only have a birthday, Mrs. Stravinsky has a name day.

. . .

KUNIN: "Bapa," is you?
MRS. STRAVINSKY: Vera . . . in Russian . . .
KUNIN: And the next [word] is?
MRS. STRAVINSKY: "Hope," Nadiezhda . . .
KUNIN: Who is that?
MRS. STRAVINSKY: The saint; we have saints in the Russian Church.
KUNIN: That is all that means?
MRS. STRAVINSKY: You know . . . give me the blessings, Saint Vera, Saint Nadiezhda, and there is Charity.
KUNIN: And that is all these things mean?

8. In addition, much tape-recorded testimony of witnesses, among them Lawrence Morton, Nicolas Nabokov, William T. Brown, and Marilyn Stalvey (the Stravinskys' secretary during their last three years in California), has been preserved in the office of Martin Garbus. This material will be made available to future biographers, but has not been used here.
9. *The Diary of Vaslav Nijinsky*, translated and edited by Romola Nijinsky (New York, 1936; Berkeley, Calif., 1968).

for now"? I did not send any documents but only that ill-
fated letter, whose reply I have awaited for three weeks.
Can it really be that you took my letter of instructions to
be a document of some kind? What thoughtlessness! Reply
immediately and explain this stupid misunderstanding.

That holy terror was one of the emotions Stravinsky inspired in his offspring is best shown in an interview by his
daughter in the 1982 London Weekend Television documentary on Stravinsky. There she recalls that when she was a
child, her father would sometimes ask her to join him at the
piano and play a few notes that he could not reach:

He would play the lines for me two or three times so that I
would have an idea [of the music]. . . . It was just a few
notes. Just the fear of not doing it right made me make
mistakes. The first mistake, he was patient. He would say,
"Start over again." Second time, mistake again, and I was
trembling, and then he would show impatience. The third
mistake he would just blow his temper.

Because of the chronic pulmonary condition of Catherine,
Stravinsky's first wife, and because the children were ill so
much of the time,[10] Stravinsky was obliged to repeat the
pattern of his own childhood, entrusting to governesses a
major part of the responsibility for the children's education

10. Their poor health persisted into later life. As Vera Sudeikina, in Paris,
wrote to Stravinsky, in Stockholm, in October 1935: "It is difficult to reach
anyone in your family on the telephone, since everyone is ill: Fedya is in the
hospital practically all the time"—with Denise, who was there for several
weeks—"Katya is unable to come to the phone, Soulima has a feruncle, and
Milene is in bed with a cold." On October 9, 1937, Catherine wrote to Igor:
"My soul grieves for Theodore: he and Denise are always undergoing cures
and with no end to it all." In fact, three of the four children had had
tuberculosis. Catherine's letter of February 28, 1937, states that Dr. V. Nossenko (1882–1929, Catherine's cousin) "did an x-ray of Theodore in Leysin, and
it revealed that there were old scars on his lungs. . . . Apparently his bronchitis
came from an earlier tubercular condition." Mika was severely ill (with
pleurisy) for the first time in January–February 1919, and her TB was dis-

and care.[11] During their formative years, his sudden celebrity as a composer, beginning in June 1910, required frequent separation from the family, at first simply to attend performances of the Ballets Russes, but later to appear as pianist and conductor in hundreds of concerts. After the move from Switzerland to France (June 1920), the family was deprived of his presence for long stretches. In February 1921 he met Vera Sudeikina,[12] and from that year until their marriage (1940) he spent as much time with her as with his family.[13] (Martin Garbus, in an affidavit, described the couple as "common-law man and wife" in the years 1921–39.[14]) Following Stravinsky's emigration to America, he did not see his elder son and granddaughter for twelve years, his younger son and daughter for nine and eight years, respectively. In the thirty-two years from June 1939 to April 1971, meetings between Stravinsky and his children, with the exception of Milene Marion, who remained his Los Angeles neighbor from April 1947 to September 1969, were remarkably rare.

---

covered in 1922. On June 23, 1935, Catherine wrote to Igor: "[The doctor] said yesterday that . . . the little problem [Milene] had was nevertheless the beginning of tuberculosis." In the spring of 1939, a pneumothorax treatment was performed on her.

11. In *Catherine and Igor Stravinsky: A Family Album* (London, 1973), Theodore Stravinsky writes that after the death of the governess Bertha Essert, in April 1917, the Stravinsky home was "a sad place, until Mina Svitalski [1892–1956] came to us as governess." Actually, Mlle Svitalski had been employed by the Stravinskys since March 29, 1916. (Catherine wrote to Igor, March 18, 1936: "I would like to do something at the end of the month for the twentieth anniversary of [Mlle Svitalski's] service with our family—I believe the date is the 29th.") Theodore goes on to claim that Mlle Svitalski "was to stay the rest of her life with one or the other of us," though for five of her seven years in America, she did not live with any member of the Stravinsky family. (Stravinsky wrote to Edouard Svitalski, October 27, 1953: "When my daughter and her husband came to live in Los Angeles in 1947, I asked [your sister] if she would also like to transplant herself. . . . Her experience [here] proved to be negative. For one thing, her life, first in my daughter's house and then in my son's, was contraindicated by everyone involved. . . . She continued to see as 'the children' people who had grown up and were married. From 1949, therefore, she lived alone and earned her living as a dressmaker, quickly attracting a

At Stravinsky's bidding, Catherine Stravinsky and Vera Sudeikina met, in his home in Nice, March 1, 1925. Theodore must have surmised the nature of his father's relationship with Mme Sudeikina later that year when he accompanied them on an automobile trip, but in 1926, Tanya Stravinsky, one of the composer's Leningrad nieces, temporarily living in France, may also have intimated something of the liaison to her cousin, apparently having perceived it after only a few meetings with her uncle and Mme Sudeikina in Paris. Soulima must have discovered the relationship himself by 1928. Mme Sudeikina's 1929 diary mentions lunches with him, and soon both sons were fulfilling errands for their father with regard to her. In a letter of June 21, 1931, Stravinsky instructs Soulima to "call Ranelagh [Mme Sudeikina's apartment was on this street] so that I do not have to repeat this dull account of my illness." In a letter to his father from Sancellemoz, February 9, 1934, Soulima writes: "Perhaps you and Vera could drive here in the automobile." By the mid-1930s, Stravinsky, Mme Sudeikina, and Soulima frequently traveled together,[15] and in 1935, both sons accompanied the couple on an automobile excursion to Venice.[16]

---

devoted clientele.") Mlle Svitalski also did not stay with "one or the other" of the Stravinskys after returning to Switzerland (March 1954) but lived with her brother. (In the early 1950s, I spent many illuminating hours listening to her invaluable recollections and insights about Stravinsky.)

12. Born Vera de Bosset, December 25, 1888, in St. Petersburg, daughter of Artur Efimovich de Bosset and Henriette Malmgren. Vera lived at 3 Troizkaya Ulitsa, St. Petersburg, until 1898, then moved with her family to Kudinovo, near Moscow. For further details see *Igor and Vera Stravinsky: A Photograph Album, 1921–1971*, captions by Robert Craft (London, 1982).

13. "I divide my time between Biarritz and Paris." (Interview in *ABC* [Madrid], March 25, 1925)

14. In this same document, Mr. Garbus says that "the relationship between Vera, Igor, and Catherine, his first wife, exhibited a great deal of mutual understanding never shared by the respondents who now, nearly sixty years later, still hate their father for having left them. . . . Their hatred has grown since the 1920s. And their father's success, their lack of involvement in his life, turned, in the last decades of [his] life, to a deeper hatred that 'justified' the thefts, embezzlements, and blackmail." (p. 34) See, for example, Vera's

The children's letters to their father, written when he was on concert tours in America and elsewhere, mention lunches, dinners, visits with Vera. The letters do not refer to requests to Vera for advice, evidently not available in the straightlaced Stravinsky home. Sometimes Vera's letters to Igor offer glimpses of her role as a surrogate mother, as when, in a letter to Igor of January 18, 1935, Vera reveals that Mika has sought her advice concerning how to deal with an unwanted suitor, the brother of Serge Lifar, as well as support in her determination to study drawing from real-life nudes, the thought of which has nearly provoked apoplexy in Stravinsky's mother. Mika wrote to her father in Scandinavia, October 1, 1935: "Today Yura [Mandelstamm, her fiancé], Fedya, and I are going to Vera's for tea; I called her on the telephone yesterday and wished her a happy name day." Theodore wrote to "Popochka" in New York in February 1937: "Vera is at auntie's all day long and helps out in every possible way." Vera's letters to Stravinsky also mention his family, as in, for example, one dated January 11, 1933: "Give Katya my thanks for the chocolate, and thank the children for remembering me and for their kind wishes on my birthday."

Between November 1938 and June 1939, Stravinsky suffered the loss of his elder daughter (November 30, 1938), his wife (March 2, 1939), and his mother (June 7, 1939)—three

---

letter to Catherine of the end of December 1924 describing Igor's departure for America from Le Havre the day before in *Stravinsky: Selected Correspondence, Volume II*, p. 475.

15. Soulima wrote to Vittorio Rieti, February 14, 1936: "My father asks you to send our railroad tickets, Paris-Rome. Mme Sudeikina will come with us, therefore three tickets with *wagon-lit* are required." On March 18, 1936, Catherine wrote to Igor: "Yesterday I received Vera's letter of the 14th from Barcelona, and today I received Soulima's of the 15th."

16. Catherine's letters to her husband at the time of the trip suggest that she was not aware that her sons were with him.

17. After the Church of Alexander Nevsky (rue Daru) had recognized the primacy of the Metropolitan of Moscow, the Stravinsky family became members of the Cathedral of the Metropolitan Anastasy, on the rue Odessa. Both

funerals in six months, three services in the Church of the Sign of the Holy Mother, 32, rue Boileau.[17] And in mid-March 1939 he himself was obliged to undergo treatment at a tuberculosis sanitarium in Sancellemoz (Haute-Savoie). He was accompanied by Theodore and Denise, probably because Mme Sudeikina could hardly have gone there with him so soon after his wife's death. Following the Paris funeral of the composer's mother,[18] however, Mme Sudeikina returned with him to Sancellemoz and spent the remainder of the summer there.[19] Already at this time Theodore Stravinsky began to show resentment toward Vera, and so noticeably after the composer announced his intention of marrying her that he angrily asked his son to leave. (See Vera's letter to Igor of October 28, 1939, below.) Vera pacified Stravinsky and closed the breach,[20] as she was to do countless times in the future. But in fairness to Theodore and his wife, it must be said that they had recently been prejudiced against Mme Sudeikina by Arthur Lourié, who, it seems, had repeated gossip to them about her life in St. Petersburg before the Revolution. (Though Lourié denied this when confronted by Mme Sudeikina, and though he continued to visit her in the fall of 1939, Stravinsky never forgave his former intimate friend and musical assistant, and during the next twenty-seven years, when they both lived in the United States and most of that time not far apart, they never met.)

Another incident, which took place while Stravinsky was in America in the fall of 1939, can, in retrospect, be recognized as precursory to the rift that occurred twenty-eight years later. On September 14, just before his departure for

---

Lyudmila and Theodore were married there. Then, in 1937, they became members of the diocese of the Church of the Sign of the Holy Mother.

18. At first Stravinsky refused to attend his mother's funeral, finally doing so only at the insistence of Mme Sudeikina.

19. Soulima wrote to his father from Paris, June 17, 1939: "I kiss Vera. . . ."

20. Early in July, Stravinsky and Vera went to Aix-les-Bains to visit Kussevitzky, whom they saw again later in Bourges. At this time Stravinsky was trying to obtain a visa and a *titre de voyage* for Mme Sudeikina to accompany him to America, but his efforts proved unsuccessful.

New York, the composer opened a joint bank account in Paris at the Crédit Commercial in the names of Vera Sudeikina and Theodore Stravinsky, with a cash balance of 139,329 francs. In October, Theodore transferred 112,000 francs of this sum to an account in his name in a bank in Le Mans, where he was living, and withdrew 19,000 francs for himself, his brother, the governess Mlle Svitalski ("Madubo"), and to pay bills. Left with only 5,000 francs, Vera wrote to Stravinsky in Cambridge, Massachusetts, October 28:

I am obliged to tell you about a very unpleasant surprise. Fedya and Denise arrived yesterday from Le Mans. They had drawn all the money from the Paris bank and transferred it to Le Mans. Fedya passed by to tell me that my access to the account, as well as Madubo's, has been cancelled, and that from now on, if I need money I will have to address myself to [Theodore]—and, if he is conscripted, to Denise (!!!). The same is true for Svetik: I can imagine how outraged he will be, since they did not even consult him. Fedya manipulated all this because he had heard that our bank may fail, but I do not see why trustworthy banks should exist only in Le Mans. He could have left the whole arrangement as it was and, if he were really worried about our Paris bank, transferred the money to the Banque de France. Fedya said that, as the oldest, he has the right to arrange things, and that "Papa would have approved my action."

Not being a member of the family, I kept quiet. Also, I did not want to say that the whole thing was manipulated so that Denise could control the money, . . . and everyone would be beholden to her. I hope that they will not do anything foolish and that the money will not be lost under their "management." Nothing can be done now, in any case, since the money has been deposited in their names in Le Mans. . . .

They returned to Le Mans yesterday without waiting for Svetik's arrival on his twenty-four-hour leave. . . .

Forgive me, dearest, for having written you this unpleasant letter. . . . Fedya has nothing to do with all this, and if he had acted alone, I am sure that he would have done so more delicately. . . . I wanted to say: "First ask your father for his permission," since, after all, the money is yours, and you are the only one who can dispose of it; but then I decided not to say anything. . . .

On November 4, Vera wrote to Stravinsky, in response to his cable: "You ask me how much money remains in the Paris bank. I have absolutely no idea; you will have to ask the Theodores. Incidentally, Soulima finds that this story about the money is completely idiotic and that the Theodores behaved with very little consideration for any of us." The remainder of the long letter makes no further mention of the affair.

On November 5, Stravinsky cabled to Vera as follows: "Demand immediate transfer for your needs three-quarters my money Paris Morgan your name and one-quarter remaining Le Mans Theodore's needs." Vera answered on November 13: "Soulima and I decided to transfer the money not to the Morgan but to the Crédit Commercial, where it was before. I do not want to have the account in my name only. I sent Theodore a letter enclosing a copy of your cable. When everything is settled, I will probably send you a cable. In it, '*Tout fait*' will refer to the bank story." On November 16, Vera forwarded to Igor the excuse that she had received from Theodore the day before: "Why did you not tell me right away that you did not agree?" (She had answered: "This money was not mine but your father's; I simply informed him that the instructions he left had been ignored.")

Meanwhile, Stravinsky dispatched an angry letter to Theodore, in care of Vera, with instructions to her to forward it. She did not do so, but wrote to Stravinsky (November 22) defending Theodore and giving her reasons for not delivering the letter:

Dearest Igor,

I have replied to your two letters concerning the money affair and told you that I will forward your letter to Fedya. I have not done this, however, and for the following reasons. When people who are very close find themselves separated and living in nerve-racking circumstances (you because of your own cares and work, we because of the war and constant fears), they should not write such letters: your letter to Theodore was very harsh; I took pity on him. Also, endless explanations would begin, and now, with the termination of the Atlantic Clipper, these could have gone on for a year. Besides, he sent me two apologetic letters: he understood your feelings from your cable. Soulima, too, expressed his opinion to him. Now everything is settled: I have received the money, thanks to your cable, and everything is back to normal. I did not want to upset Theodore all over again with your letter. Consider only that he cannot go to you and explain in person, a terrible situation, and that you would be troubled by a whole month of correspondence. Should something happen to anybody, a life of very bitter feeling would remain.

Forgive me for writing such depressing things, but a war is going on here, and people are perishing every day. . . . A nervous tension exists which we try to hide and to which we become accustomed; still, it is there. I see no point in writing about things that, thanks to your cable, have already been straightened out: so enough of it. If you would write to Fedya that you could not understand his behavior, and that you disagreed with it, but that now everything is arranged—well, that would be sufficient. . . . I think that even you could not explain things at this distance. I hope very much that you will agree with my decision and that you will write to me about it. . . . Either I will forward your letter or burn it. I prefer the latter. If I were to receive even a hundredth part of your criticism of Fedya, I would lose my mind. . . . Fedya is very sensitive and would suffer terribly. He is not stubborn and does not resist, as is shown by his efforts to explain to me and by his sending letters to me. Please, my darling, leave him in peace.

On November 25, Vera wrote that she had deposited the money that Theodore had returned to her in the Crédit Commercial in Paris, adding that "his last letter shows that he realized his blunder." On December 11, Stravinsky wrote to her from San Francisco:

> Only yesterday I received the long-awaited letter from you. . . . Since you never forwarded my letter to Fedya, and in view of your advice to me concerning it, I am inclined to approve, except that I feel the necessity of his answering the two questions I put to him: Why did he remove the money secretly and not tell you? And why did he take it to Le Mans? According to your advice, I agree and do not insist on sending any letter to him: you can destroy it. Still, I will remain unsatisfied until I receive an answer from him to those two torturing questions and an apology for his actions. Without that, it is impossible for me to write to him as if nothing has happened. I feel uncomfortable in my soul, and, not wanting to hurt him, I will write nothing. But I want him to know the reasons for my silence. I received a letter from Denise, but I read it with a heavy heart, for I no longer believe her.

A month later, Vera was in America. She described her impressions in a letter to Soulima: "So far, the hugeness, the lights, the crowds on Broadway depress me; I still have too many ties holding me to Europe. . . . I loved so much to rush out into the street in Paris to buy a newspaper, to exchange a few words with a shopkeeper; but here, from the twentieth floor. . . ." In March, Vera and Igor were married, and in May they moved from Boston to Los Angeles. Though both of them were in their fifties, they began life anew, entering into the spirit and excitement of the California of the time.[21] Thanks to a large refugee population, Los Angeles was a cosmopolitan city, the wartime home of many European musicians, writers, artists, and theatre people, some of them representing philosophies, views, and values to which Stravinsky had theretofore paid little heed. He began to change profoundly as a result of diverse influences in the new environment, which equally stimulated the intellectually liberated, socially popular, open-minded woman who was no longer simply a companion but now his wife. In 1945, after visiting the Stravinskys in Hollywood, Pierre Schaeffer, the promoter of *musique concrète*, published an article portraying the composer's "euphoria" in his life there, adding that the *"sourire éblouissant de Véra . . . [a] aidé Igor Stravinsky,"* and even providing a photo of Mme Stravinsky, *"où figure ce sourire éclatant de joie de vivre, de forte tendresse."*[22] Two decades later the Stravinskys' enchantment with Hollywood had vanished, but not their enchantment with each other, or their *joie de vivre*.

Although Igor and Vera Stravinsky could hardly be described in 1947 as assimilated Americans, they had nevertheless become accustomed to many American ways. The composer's aloofness had given way to an informality in his relations with people, as well as in his habits of daily life, style of dress, and entertaining. He now listened to ideas that he would have rejected outright in the 1930s—such as the Trotskyite polemics of his ex-Viennese physician—and was constantly inspired by the range of knowledge and interests of such friends as Aldous Huxley and Gerald Heard.[23]

21. Stravinsky had wanted to live in California since his first visit there, which began in San Francisco in the early morning of February 13, 1935. On his arrival from Chicago, he was met at the railroad station by a crowd of autograph seekers, and, according to San Francisco's Russian-language newspaper *New Dawn*, "He signed 100 record jackets but refused to be taken to meet a crowd gathered at one of San Francisco's shopping centers." (On the same day, Stravinsky and Samuel Dushkin gave a recital.)
22. *Opéra* (Paris), January 1946.
23. Stravinsky first met Huxley in London with Victoria and Angelica Ocampo in July 1934, Heard in Hollywood in 1950.

Though I can judge the astonishing transformation in Stravinsky only from his correspondence and through those who knew him both before and after the first American decade, it is obvious that while he had once been dogmatic, closed to criticism, contemptuous of colleagues, socially comfortable only with the rich and titled, by 1950 those characteristics had all but disappeared.[24] Now he wore denim trousers, ate hot dogs in diners, and hobnobbed with Hollywood's rank-and-file orchestra players. Moreover, when Russia entered the war his political outlook was quickly reversed, and the rabid anticommunist of the decades before became a supporter of every organization helping the USSR. Most important, he listened to, played, and studied a great deal of new music of diverse tendencies. When, after an absence of twelve years, Stravinsky first visited Europe, he perceived the metamorphosis in himself, everywhere declaring that he felt more American than European.

The composer's three children, meanwhile, had not undergone such a change, or so Stravinsky believed. At the beginning of World War II, Theodore was briefly interned in a camp near Vichy. He lived in France until the spring of 1942, then went to Switzerland permanently. Since he remained in Europe following the war and had not seen his father after 1939,[25] the Americanization of the parent should

24. When I first met the Stravinskys, they were frequent guests of Elsie de Wolfe and Sir Charles Mendl, Atwater Kent, and other society figures, and the composer and his wife invited the likes of Baron de Meyer to their own parties.

25. Eugenio Montale interviewed Theodore in Venice, September 9, 1951: "Theodore Stravinsky, a painter who lives in Geneva, has written a book, *Le Message d'Igor Strawinsky*. . . . Unfortunately, Theodore has not seen his father for the past twelve years and would rather talk to me about his painting. I ask him if he is an impressionist and gather from his start that I have committed a gaffe. Theodore has been profoundly touched by the *esprit de Genève*. . . . When I try to lead him back to the subject, he puts great stress on Stravinsky's religiosity. . . . I pocket the *Message* and take my leave. Aggressiveness has not been as productive as I had anticipated." (*Prime alla Scala* [Milan, 1980])

have been more conspicuous to Theodore than to his brother and sister, yet it was never acknowledged. As for the other children, Soulima served in the French army, was demobilized after its defeat, and, during the Occupation, lived in Paris, where he worked as a musician. Milene lived in the Sancellemoz sanitarium throughout the war and, in 1944, married Andre Marion, another pulmonary patient. Kitty, Stravinsky's granddaughter, lived from January 1939 to August 1946 in the Clinique Les Oiselets, Leysin, where she was treated for tuberculosis.

From the beginning of the war to August 1941, Stravinsky sent money to Theodore through Vittorio Rieti's mother, and Vera sent it to Milene in care of Mrs. E. Schreiber, Zürich. After that date, Mrs. Olga ("Aunt Lyulya") Schwarz, 4, avenue d'Evian, Lausanne, acted as intermediary, and in August 1943, Stravinsky sent $600 for Theodore and Kitty in care of this relative.[26] In 1941, Stravinsky also began to send money to Theodore and Milene by way of Darius Milhaud's mother, in Aix-en-Provence; Milhaud sent cables with the code words "Stravinsky's health good," which meant that she was to forward 30,000 francs to Theodore from her own bank, for which Stravinsky would reimburse his colleague in California. Between June 1942 and November 1943, Milene received $1,800 by this means. Beginning in December 1941, Soulima received his father's French royalties, and after the war Stravinsky transmitted sums to him via returning refugees, among them Vladimir Golschmann.

At the end of the war, Vera Stravinsky invited the Marions

26. Mrs. Max Schwarz, née Nossenko (1872–1953), was a cousin of Stravinsky's first wife. The composer's payments were allowed only after the Bankers Trust Company, New York, applied to the U.S. Treasury Department for a special license on his behalf. On August 6, 1941, he answered an inquiry from the bank saying that Mrs. Schwarz, a Swiss citizen and blood relative, "is taking care of my granddaughter, a four-year-old child." (On October 29, 1951, "Lyulya" wrote to Stravinsky, who was in Switzerland on a concert tour, reminding him that they had not been together since Sancellemoz in the 1930s. She added that she wanted "to see our dear friend from our youth, our 'Gima,' and not just the famous Stravinsky.")

to move to California,[27] looking to the future possibility of Stravinsky's need for assistance if she were to become ill. She persuaded her husband to purchase a house for them nearby.[28] Partly for the same reason, and also to give Soulima a fresh start, Igor and Vera Stravinsky invited him, his wife, and their three-year-old son John to Hollywood, renting a home for them[29] and arranging an American debut as a pianist for Soulima.[30]

Vera and Soulima seem to have had a very friendly relationship in the 1930s, perhaps because she—not Igor—had attended the young man's first recital, in Valenciennes on April 13, 1930. In any case, he spent his first weekend leave from the army with her and Mlle Svitalski. Vera wrote to Igor on November 13, 1939:

> Svetik's visit was a great joy for us. We sat until midnight while he told us about his friends and his daily life. He really is touching in his boyishness, though at the same time you cannot imagine how he has changed, bearing all the difficulties and encouraging everyone else with his good spirits and positiveness. At 6:00 p.m., when he left for the

27. The Marions were obliged to wait more than eight months for U.S. visas. Since both of them had had pulmonary diseases, Stravinsky feared that on arrival in New York they might be detained at Ellis Island and returned to Europe. In January 1947, therefore, he asked for the help of his friend and patron Mrs. Robert Woods Bliss, wife of the diplomat. On January 31, she telegraphed her assurance that special arrangements would be made with the immigration officials to facilitate the Marions' entry into the United States. They were met at the dock, April 7, by the Dushkins, who entertained them and escorted them to the train for California.

28. "We bought a house in Hollywood, which Vera has charmingly decorated," Stravinsky wrote to Mrs. Bliss (January 1947). Before the arrival of the Marions, the Stravinskys used the address as a guest house, for, among others, Katherine Anne Porter and Alexei Haieff. The Marions sold this home, at 146 South La Peer Drive, in October 1980, and moved to 24312 Philiprimm Street, Woodland Hills, California.

29. Whereas the Marions had been French citizens, he by birth, she by naturalization (1934), Soulima did not acquire French citizenship until December 30, 1947. On April 13, 1948, Stravinsky sent the money for the Soulima Stravinskys' trip, Paris to New York, on "French Airlines."

30. At Red Rocks, Colorado, in July 1948.

railroad station, I felt very sad. He asked me to write to
him every day and to send him preserves and chocolates.
Since he is completely free on Sundays, I will be able to
go there and take him to lunch in a restaurant. He is
magnificent.

On November 25, Vera wrote again: "Just this minute I received a charming letter from Svetik. He lovingly thanks me
for my letter, and he is so warm that he makes me happy."
Vera's first letter written on American soil was a lengthy account of her impressions of the United States, sent to "Dearest Svetik" and concluding with: "I am writing this letter at
a desk in Father's sitting room and with your photograph,
from *Vogue*, in front of me. . . . My dearest, I kiss you very,
very hard."

The Marions' transplantation proved to be a mixed blessing. Milene's relationship with her father now depended on
her husband, who began to work as his father-in-law's secretary and thus became dependent on the Stravinskys. The
interests and temperaments of the two men were incompati-
ble, and the Marions took little part in the Stravinskys' social
life, rarely going to concerts, operas, museums, or the theatre
with them. According to the composer, Marion accompanied
him on the train from Los Angeles to Chicago, October
22–24, 1954, without uttering a single word. After one crisis,
Marion asked his father-in-law for $10,000 with which to re-
turn to France, but this was a larger amount than Stravinsky
was prepared to give, and Vera Stravinsky persuaded the
Marions to stay. Finally, in 1954, Marion left his father-in-
law's employ, except as bookkeeper, taking a job in a travel
agency. Nevertheless, the Stravinskys remained the Marions'
chief source of income.[31]

The relocation of the Soulima Stravinskys in California
proved to be a great mistake, and they quickly realized that

31. Stravinsky not only bought their house, furniture, and automobiles for
them but also paid the taxes and upkeep on their property and for their trips
and their medical expenses.

living close to Stravinsky *père* would involve the surrender of whatever professional and personal independence Stravinsky *fils* had attained. The family moved to New York, then to Urbana, where—the composer having exercised his influence through a friend, John Kuypers—Soulima was engaged as a piano teacher at the University of Illinois.[32] Whereas in 1948–49, Stravinsky had procured concert engagements that included his son as piano soloist, the two appeared together after that on only three occasions: in Urbana and St. Louis (March 1950), Hollywood (August 12, 1952), and Chicago and Milwaukee (January 13–15 and 18, 1954). Relations between father and son post-1949 can only be described as remote, and in the last ten years of the composer's life, Soulima saw him during only eleven brief encounters,[33] though meetings in the 1950s had been even rarer.[34]

Perhaps Soulima's potential for conflict with his father was greater than that of the other children simply because music was the younger son's profession. He suffered a crisis on this account when he was twenty-nine, as Pierre Suvchinsky described to Stravinsky in a letter of May 23, 1939.[35] The letter refers to an "aggressiveness" on Soulima's part that may have consisted in his mention of his father's mortality in a letter earlier that month:

---

32. In May 1978, the Soulima Stravinskys sold their Urbana property for $65,000 and moved to Sarasota, Florida.

33. August 16, 1962 (Santa Fe); December 8, 1962 (Hollywood); May 3, 1964 (Ann Arbor); May 12, 1965 (Paris); December 26 and 30, 1965 (New York); October 20–21, 1966 (Hollywood); December 29–31, 1966 (Chicago); January 25, 1969 (Hollywood); May 16, 1969 (New York); August 17, 1969 (Hollywood).

34. December 8–10, 1952 (Cleveland); January 16, 1954 (Urbana); January 16, 1955 (Chicago, between trains); August 1956 (Venice). According to Theodore's deposition, "While [my father] was in Evian [in the summer of 1970], he continuously asked me where Soulima was, and why he was not there. I answered that for me it was easy to come and see him, as I lived in Geneva, while Soulima lived in Urbana." But at that time Soulima was living in France, less than a day's drive away.

35. Suvchinsky had visited Stravinsky in Sancellemoz the month before (i.e., April 1939). Soulima visited his father there immediately after the composer's return from Italy in May, a meeting that left the composer very disturbed.

In the event of your death, not one of us would be able to touch a *centime* unless Kitty's guardianship is established. That is why the matter should be attended to, at your convenience, just to make provisions for the future, because M. Mandelstamm could end up as the guardian.[36]

Of all the Stravinsky children, only Milene saw her father and stepmother with any frequency during the years 1947–68, or, rather, during the six months or so of each year that they spent in California. And since Milene appeared to be close to Vera, successfully appealing to her in every difficulty,[37] the younger woman's behavior after 1968 is less comprehensible than that of the other heirs. Stravinsky's widow was very slow to believe that someone whom she had treated as a daughter, encouraging her talents and lavishing gifts on her, had been a secret enemy long before Stravinsky's death. Milene's deposition conjures a purely fictional Vera Stravinsky, one who asks her husband to "make the record[ings] in London. It brings a lot of money." Anyone who knew Vera Stravinsky in the mid-1960s, the time of this alleged statement, would remember that she bitterly opposed her husband's record making, no matter where, and would recognize that such a remark—unless intended ironically—would be wholly uncharacteristic of her. Precisely her *lack* of interest in money, and therefore in wills, was to cause Vera Stravinsky many difficulties in later life.

Stravinsky's daughter seemed to believe a fabrication to the effect that her father had whispered a message to his lawyer, William D. Montapert,[38] designating "Mr. W. Montapert to

36. Why Yuri Mandelstamm should *not* have been his daughter's guardian is unclear. According to a letter from Vera to Igor, December 3, 1939, referring to an invitation to Yuri's wedding, he remarried in that month.

37. That the Marions perfectly understood the method by which new cars, payments of taxes, and other gifts were obtained is evident from the following remark in a letter from Andre Marion to the New York director of Boosey & Hawkes: "Explain the plan to Mrs. Stravinsky first; you may leave it to her to convince Mr. Stravinsky." (December 18, 1951)

38. Montapert, a graduate of the University of Southern California Law

protect the interests of my children after my death. . . . I want my manuscripts to go to my children, who are so dear to me. My wife will have plenty with the copyrights." Milene did not claim to have seen Montapert's transcription of this message, but Denise, Theodore's wife, was supposedly shown "one complete, crowded, typewritten page (actually a photocopy) . . . definitely signed by *Père*" and worded in the manner quoted above, as she recollected in a letter to Françoise Stravinsky (Exhibit K). Marion further testified that this was "a very good [signature]," which would not have been possible in the summer of 1969, when Stravinsky's handwriting was shaky. When solicited by the court, no such epistle materialized, of course. In this affair, both Milene and Denise displayed extraordinary ignorance of Stravinsky's state of mind, for by this time he deeply distrusted Montapert and would not have shared personal confidences with him. Anyone who knew Igor and Vera Stravinsky would recognize the story as utterly preposterous.

In the mythological tradition of favorite children, Lyudmila, Milene's older sister, was the Stravinsky child to die at a tragically early age. Though she has no direct part in the present chronicle, her influence pervades it. She appears to have had a pleasant nature,[39] good judgment, and talent as a painter, as well as courage, maturity and independence.[40]

Stravinsky seems not to have expected her death, even

School, who also studied law in Switzerland, married another attorney, the niece (d. 1970) of Harold English (d. 1953), a wealthy amateur painter and a friend of Igor Stravinsky for many years. In 1953 Andre Marion became friendly with Montapert, whom the Stravinskys retained as their attorney in February 1959 on Marion's recommendation.

39. On May 19, 1936, Catherine wrote to Igor: "Mikushka writes to me that she keeps feeling happier and happier and is so satisfied with her life."

40. Vera wrote to Igor, January 18, 1937: "Mika, good sport, went on foot to the hospital to have her baby." In May–June 1934, Stravinsky entrusted his twenty-six-year-old daughter—*not* one of her brothers—to go to Germany and bring back assets of his that had been blocked there. She stayed with the

though his correspondence in the months before contains expressions of anxiety about her: [41]

The condition of my married daughter, her health (lungs), distresses me. [Letter to Roland-Manuel, November 24, 1937]

You know that our poor Mika has been in the mountains for three weeks with her child. She has tuberculosis in both lungs and has been separated from her husband for a long while. [Letter to Willy Strecker, February 1, 1938]

Tomorrow evening I go to [Sancellemoz] to bring Mika back home, because the mountains are not doing anything for her. She has a fever all the time, is losing weight, and has just had another bout with pleurisy. According to the doctors here, the brisk mountain air is not indicated for this painful malady, and they insist that as soon as possible

---

Streckers in Mainz, and on May 22 had lung x-rays by a Wiesbaden doctor, L. Fürsteran.

41. Stravinsky conducted a concert in Rome on November 29, the day before Mika's death. (He was to have performed *Perséphone* there with, as narrator, Victoria Ocampo, who made the trip on the same train with him but who became ill at the last moment, forcing a change of program.) Another concert, in Turin on December 2, was canceled. But the letters from his wife and elder son between November 25 and 29 make one wonder why Stravinsky ever left Paris, both Mika and her mother being gravely ill. Catherine Stravinsky, who had a constant temperature of 38.7 Celsius, wrote to Igor in Rome on the 23rd: "All I wanted to do this morning was cry. . . . Mika's pulse is 120." The next day's letter revealed that "Mika is receiving morphine injections and her pulse is 126." The letter of the 25th fills four pages with accounts of treatments and medications, and of the decision to ask Father Vasily to come and give the eucharist to her and Mika. Yet Catherine begins by commiserating with Stravinsky for a "headache" about which he must have complained. On the 26th, she actually apologizes for writing so much: "I am afraid you will scold me for wasting stamps." (Some six months later, Vera wrote to Igor in America telling him that a past due bill had arrived for him from Lanvin for about 3,000 francs.) The next day Theodore wrote: "Mika's pulse is 128 and there is no improvement in her heart condition." He wrote again on the 28th: "There has been no improvement, the doctor is very worried about the heart, and this cannot go on indefinitely. It is disturbing," he adds, "[to think that] you will be traveling even farther away [to Turin]." Catherine's last letter, of November 29, is horrifying: "One of Mika's lungs has collapsed, and she has

she return to Paris, where we can give her more attention than she receives in that sanitarium full of sick people. Poor Mika—I am very sad. [Letter to Willy Strecker, March 20, 1938]

Catherine's letters contain many blunt comparisons between Mika and Milene in which the former appears as a paragon, the latter as a problem-child:

If it had been Mika, she would have spoken with [the young man's] father right then, but of course not Milene. . . . What a difficult child she is for us. [March 30, 1937]

For manifold reasons, Milene's early years do not appear to have been very happy ones, but they may help to illuminate her later conduct. Catherine wrote to Igor, March 10, 1935:

I feel that, *au fond*, Milene is melancholy. Apparently this is her nature, and when I go walking with her I cannot help remembering our walks together in Morges, when she was four, five, and six years old. She was then exactly the way I find her now. Then, just as now, I did not know what to say to the little one, or how to get her out of her solemn mood. . . . But why should her nature be so burdened with guilt?[42] . . . I have seen this in her since childhood, even infancy.

Theodore, who was to become a professional artist, was also compared with Mika, whom her mother clearly considered to be the more gifted child:

---

coughed up part of her bronchiae; her pulse is 134 . . . ; she is having a terrible, terrible time, and tomorrow, God willing, I want her to take the eucharist." But she died at 5:00 a.m. on the 30th, and the family called Vera Sudeikina to get a priest. On reaching Turin, Stravinsky telephoned home from the railroad station and heard the news.

42. Catherine does not explain her assumption that Milene was "burdened with guilt," but it may have been that Milene's birth reactivated her mother's tuberculosis.

Mika . . . was at the home of Grandjean, who asked her to prepare two drawings for him, which he selected from very modest notebook sketches. . . . Mme Normano finds that Mika is very talented and has taste and imaginative ideas. [November 17, 1933]

Theodore, in contrast, seemed to lack conviction. Catherine wrote to Igor, November 3, 1937:

How did you like Theodore's painting of the image of Saint Peter of Panteleimon?[43] . . . Fedya's hesitation in his painting is, I think, a consequence of his nature and character, and probably because of this, he finds it difficult to get on with his work. I think *he* feels this, too.

To return to the 1950s, Theodore saw his father during some of his European concert tours, and, in aggregate, spent considerably more time with him than did Soulima, who lived 5,000 miles closer to "the parents." But Theodore also remained the more dependent, and the composer was obliged to support him all of his life, as well as to meet Kitty's medical and other expenses.[44] When *père* and Vera were away, Milene visited their housekeeper, Yevgenia Petrovna, and sorted the mail. While they were home, the two families occa-

---

43. Stravinsky did not answer the question.
44. Stravinsky was penalized for deducting these sums from his income tax, since the U.S. government does not allow deductions for relatives, even minors, living abroad. He wrote to Theodore, July 21, 1950: "Until now I have deducted part of the costs of supporting Kitty on my annual tax return. . . . But the law requires that the recipient live in the U.S.A. Nothing has been said about this until the present, but now the tax inspectors have demanded an explanation. They do not accept my excuse that Kitty's state of health would not permit her to live in this country . . . and we must provide certification from a Swiss doctor testifying that Kitty has been his patient for ten years, that she is not completely cured, and that she could not risk the fatigue and changes of climate involved in moving here." These certifications were obtained from Dr. Vera Nossenko and Dr. Maurice Gilbert, but still the deduction was not allowed.

sionally dined together. Between 1952 and 1954, Marion accompanied Stravinsky on six short concert tours that Mrs. Stravinsky thought would be too tiring for her. The relationship between "the parents" and Marion was always stiff; that between "the parents" and Milene was affectionate, but in actuality less close than that between the Stravinskys and such friends as Miranda Levy, Lawrence Morton, and Bill Brown.

As for relations between Stravinsky and his sons, these were exacerbated in the mid-1960s by two events and only superficially mended thereafter. Both disturbances, which occurred almost simultaneously, revolved around grandchildren: John Stravinsky, born in France in November 1945, son of Françoise Bon[45] and Soulima Stravinsky; and Catherine Mandelstamm Stravinsky, born in France in January 1937.

After the Soulima Stravinskys moved from California, when John was four years old, the composer rarely saw his grandson. In the last seven years of Stravinsky's life, they had only four significant meetings: in July 1964 (Chicago); on October 4, 1964 (lunch at the Hotel Pierre, New York); on July 26, 1968 (Hollywood); and on November 10, 1969 (at the Essex House, New York).

To borrow John's mother's word, the Chicago encounter was a "disaster." On July 17, 1964, the young man checked into the Ambassador East Hotel in order to see Stravinsky conduct in Ravinia the next night. John had also invited friends, and when he left the hotel after the concert, his charges were transferred to his grandfather's bill. Stravinsky had been in Chicago since the 15th, and his mood could hardly have been worse, as was always the case when his wife was not with him. He was suffering from the heat, had been exhausted by the added strain of traveling back and forth from Chicago to Ravinia for rehearsals, and wanted desperately to rest before a recording session (*Orpheus*), scheduled

---

45. Mme Bon's children by her first husband are a generation older than John.

for the Monday morning after the Saturday-night performance. Practically no time was spent with John. The absence
of Vera Stravinsky was truly unfortunate, for she would have
entertained and looked after the young man, and the painful
aftermath might have been avoided. Three months later,
Stravinsky discussed his grandson with the boy's parents in a
telephone conversation that left the atmosphere charged.

Stravinsky lacked any understanding of the problems that
beset a nineteen-year-old at that time, to say nothing of the
special problems inherent in being *his* grandson. During the
telephone conversation, expressing concern about the boy's
future, the composer criticized John's lack of persistence in
his studies. Although his mother was disturbed by Stravinsky's indifference to the boy and hopelessly old-fashioned notions of discipline and education, she did not express this
when they next met, on May 12, 1965, in the composer's suite
at the Hôtel Plaza-Athénée, Paris. While Stravinsky was traveling to Switzerland, back to Paris, and then to Warsaw, she
wrote him a long letter (June 7) from La Clidelle, elaborat-
ing her feelings, but also, and unhappily, using a tone that
the composer never forgave.

This crucial document in Stravinsky's biography begins by
referring to his "cruel" telephone call of the previous autumn and goes on to explain that the past two years had been
difficult ones for John and that he had been unable to concentrate on his work. She then quotes from a letter that she
and her husband had received from John in which he describes his visit to Chicago to see his grandfather as "a depressing experience." He had been unable even to reach his
grandfather on the telephone, and he concludes: "My grandfather can't be bothered to see his only grandson."

Thus far the letter would not have provoked an irreparable upset, but then John's mother attacks Stravinsky
personally, accusing him of telling people that his grandson
only came to see him to obtain money, and saying that to
learn of such comments has made her "indignant." (Stravin-

sky underlined this statement and wrote next to it, "WHO?")[46] But the conclusion of the letter was even more injurious. Stravinsky's daughter-in-law declines his invitation to come to California and discuss the matter, ostensibly because she and Soulima lack the time, and she encloses a check to cover the expenses of John's "disastrous visit to Ravinia." The letter terminates with the request that Stravinsky speak as little as possible about John in New York and Paris, "where you have already given him a terrible press." The composer was stung to the quick by the insult of the check, and next to the words "a terrible press," he wrote "WITH WHOM?"

Vera Stravinsky answered for her husband, gently reminding John's mother that "Stravinsky is eighty-three, in poor health, and the letter gave him a dangerous emotional shock." A note of apology arrived (June 24), but the incident effectively ended the relationship between Stravinsky and his daughter-in-law, who saw each other only twice more. Twelve years later, in 1977, Milene Marion was to recall that in the summer of 1969 her father said to her: " 'Isn't Soulima's wife a very unsympathetic person?' " Milene then testified that when she asked her father what made him say this, "he answered me in Russian, 'It is a kind of feeling.' "[47]

The other bitter and long-lasting rupture in family relations resulted from a romance between Kitty and Pierre Théus, a married man with two sons. On December 5, 1963, the twenty-eight-year-old woman wrote to Stravinsky to thank him for a check—part of his money from the Sibelius prize. Kitty also says in this letter that she has moved into "a ravishing little apartment"—which is to say, moved out of the Theodore Stravinsky home—and that she feels a need to write to her grandfather directly about her "terrible love affair, in the sense of its unbelievable intensity," which "torments me" because its object, M. Théus, is married.

---

46. Vera Stravinsky's diary, June 2, 1965, reads: "Suvchinsky tells me about a long telephone conversation he had with the Soulimas concerning John."
47. Deposition.

Stravinsky could hardly have been less sympathetic.[48] He wrote a terse reply, but first sent it (December 31) to Theodore, along with a copy of Kitty's letter, asking him for more information. Theodore answered that Kitty lived only for Théus, a wholly inappropriate partner, and that, moreover, she was well aware that he had no intention of divorcing, although she pretended otherwise. Though she had "violently" rejected the advice of Theodore and his wife, they thought that the young woman might listen to her grandfather, whose reply perfectly expressed their own views.

Stravinsky received his son's letter in Philadelphia, January 11, 1964, and sent the following message to Kitty the same day:

Dear Kitty, Happy Birthday and thank you for the Christmas card. I did not reply to your letter of December 5 because I have been *totally* without time. But I must tell you what has been at the center of my heart since then: the urgent and absolute necessity *for you* to dominate your passions and not to allow yourself to be dominated by them. Your grandfather who loves you very much.

The incomprehension, remoteness, and hurried, impersonal tone of this response from the grandfather she worshipped must have hurt the young woman deeply. Having lost both parents in infancy,[49] Kitty was reared first in a tuberculosis sanitarium in Leysin—partly under the care of Dr. Vera

48. A detached slip of paper in Stravinsky's archives, undated but from the 1940s or 1950s, to judge by the composer's Russian script, contains the following characteristic *pensée:* "Musical *Art* must be as indifferent to the element of motive—that which inspires one to compose—as the church is to love in marriage or to any other reasons for which people wed. After all, you do not tell a priest that you are in love. He does not need to know that, and if you did tell him, you would embarrass yourself before God."

49. Her father, Yuri Mandelstamm was deported from Occupied France and is presumed to have died in a concentration camp. A letter from Mandelstamm to Stravinsky, August 10, 1939, indicates that the composer had read his son-in-law's poetry with appreciation. In the same letter, Mandelstamm thanks

Nossenko[50]—and second by her surrogate father and mother, a childless couple themselves. At age twenty, in London to study English and secretarial skills, she was boarded with an elderly couple, Dr. and Mrs. Ernst Roth (he was a director of Boosey & Hawkes), who could hardly have provided very congenial companionship for a young girl. Worst of all, she was still plagued by ill-health; in 1964, after five years as a secretary at the Institut des Hautes Etudes (Geneva), she was obliged to give up her job for this reason.

In August 1964, Kitty wrote to Theodore and Denise accusing them of betraying her, of meddling, of breaking their pledge to remain silent, and of destroying her future with Théus. She sent copies of this declaration of independence to Igor and Vera Stravinsky, to the Soulima Stravinskys, and to the Marions, in each case with a note explaining that she was convinced that the essential motivation in her adoptive parents' behavior was not moral strictness but embarrassment.

This time Stravinsky's response was utterly different. He came to Kitty's defense and ordered Theodore to leave her alone. The composer did not mention his next trip to Europe to Theodore.[51] After it, in California, Stravinsky increased his granddaughter's allowance and made her a beneficiary to his Swiss bank account on an equal basis with Theodore, though denying that the change had anything to do with the "painful development in relations between Kitty and yourself. I have wanted to do this for Kitty for a long time, as I would have done for her mother, and Kitty is more than of age." (September 2, 1964) Theodore was instructed to pro-

---

Stravinsky "for your touching letter and for your offer to pay for my trip to visit Kitinka [Kitty] . . . which I gladly and gratefully accept." But Mandelstamm did not take the trip, because of the international political situation, and he never saw his daughter again.

50. Dr. Nossenko wrote to Stravinsky in October 1939, apparently unaware that he was in America, asking for money to have Kitty tutored in Russian.

51. More than once, Theodore actually wrote to his father in California while he was in Paris. Milene sent a letter to Père and Vera in New York in June 1966: "The fact that Theodore wrote to you here indicates that he does not know that you were in Europe."

cure from Basel whatever papers were necessary to effect the change, and when Kitty signed these, Stravinsky sent them (October 25) to Soulima for his signature as well.

On May 15, 1965, Igor and Vera Stravinsky drove from Paris to the Vevey Palace Hotel on Lake Geneva. Theodore and Denise were waiting for them in the hotel lobby, and the composer, tired after ten hours on the road, did not conceal his irritation at finding them there. The next day Kitty came for lunch—alone—and Vera Stravinsky invited her to visit them in California in the summer (which she did, August 13–27). On May 17, the Stravinskys left Vevey for Basel.[52]

The Stravinskys were in Paris again a year later, in June 1966.[53] Kitty telephoned from Lausanne asking whether her friend, Pierre Théus (alias Carl Flinker, at that stage), could come to see *Vera* Stravinsky on personal business. She agreed, and on June 7 and 8 talked at length to M. Théus, who confided to her that Kitty was pregnant and needed help. Although she privately concluded that marriage would not be a solution for the couple, Vera Stravinsky was sympathetic to Kitty's plight. Then, on June 11, Kitty herself came to Paris, alone (as Stravinsky noted in his diary).

Four months later, on October 10, 1966, Henri Monnet[54] wrote to the composer saying that "Soulima and Françoise" had brought his attention to "the Kitty question" in the hope that, through business connections, he (Monnet) would be able to find Pierre Théus a decent job in Switzerland or France, or anywhere "to get him out of Fribourg." Taking

---

52. In the morning of May 17, Theodore accompanied his father on a visit to "Les Tilleuls," Clarens, where most of *Le Sacre du printemps* had been written.

53. Stravinsky's diary for April 1, 1966, reads: "Sad news from Kitty, we sent Ampenoff a cable to send Kitty immediately $1,000." The "we" means that the decision was Vera Stravinsky's, as I witnessed. Miss Rufina Vsevolodovna Ampenoff was employed by Boosey & Hawkes in London.

54. B. 1896, lawyer. Monnet had known Stravinsky since 1928. In the letter Monnet mentions his home in Asolo and Stravinsky's visit there (September 22, 1957) "while the *savant* Mr. Craft was at G. F. Malipiero's looking for a volume of Monteverdi."

advantage of a sojourn at Peter Ustinov's retreat in Diablerets to become acquainted with Théus, Monnet invited him there and later reported to Stravinsky: "I do not see him as Romeo, but he is a serious and competent man." Monnet also wrote saying that Kitty had telephoned to tell him of the possibility of a quick and amicable divorce for Théus.

Monnet advised Stravinsky to send $6,000 to facilitate the divorce, "not as a gift to Kitty but, rather, as a loan to Théus." Stravinsky replied, October 24, 1966, declaring that he loved Kitty very much and promising to send the $6,000. (The check was sent on November 8, and Monnet acknowledged its receipt in a note of the 11th.) On December 13, Monnet informed Stravinsky that a job had been found for Théus in South Africa, "which I will advise him to accept."

Monnet's next letter, January 8, 1967, is the key document in the relations between the Igor and the Theodore Stravinskys. It discloses that "Kitty, obliged—at least she believed so—to earn her living since the age of eighteen, preferred independent work in Geneva to performing more or less servile tasks for Theodore (or, rather, for his wife)."[55] The composer's indignation on reading this can hardly be imagined. In the same letter, Monnet explained that Théus's wife, learning now that Kitty had the financial backing of Igor Stravinsky, had decided to drive a hard bargain for the divorce; and that Théus, without a decent job, would not be able to support Kitty and also make monthly alimony payments. For this reason, Monnet's advice was to drop divorce proceedings for a time and, instead, use the $6,000 to supplement Kitty's monthly allowance of 500 Swiss francs. She had calculated that her living expenses would come to 1,250 francs a month, and Monnet suggested that an additional 750 francs a month be paid to her out of the $6,000; Stravinsky

55. Vera wrote to Igor, November 4, 1939: "Madubo is happy now in her independence. If she goes to live with Theodore, there will immediately be trouble with Denise, who likes to give orders and who will tell Madubo to 'do this' and 'do that'; in a week's time, she would be the cook, the housekeeper, the laundress."

authorized this in his next communication. On February 2, Kitty gave birth to a daughter[56] (this was announced to Igor and Vera Stravinsky in a cable signed "Pierre"), and on the following day Monnet wrote to say that the godfather was Peter Ustinov. Two months later, Theodore wrote to his father that Théus's wife had finally heard about the baby and was "making a scandal everywhere," and that, consequently, "Kitty is going away for some months." (May 27, 1967) On June 18, Stravinsky received a cable for his eighty-fifth birthday from Neuilly-sur-Seine, signed "Madeleine and Henri, Kitty and Svetlana."

Kitty, who soon became "completely absorbed in the child," as Theodore wrote, spent the early part of the summer with the Soulima Stravinskys at La Clidelle. By this time her letters to California no longer refer to Svetlana's father, and only Stravinsky brought up the subject, tactlessly and icily, in what was to be his last message to his granddaughter: "I am relieved because, like yourself, we do not see any future in a relationship with the father of your child."[57] (August 10, 1967) The composer received Kitty and Svetlana in Paris, December 9 and 10, 1968, and again in Evian-les-Bains, June 14, 1970, but he never forgave his granddaughter for bearing an illegitimate child. In the summer of 1978, Kitty married Michel Yelachich, a distant cousin, who had been in Igor and Vera Stravinsky's home in Hollywood, August 17, 1969, the most infamous date in this chronicle.

To return to the background of the litigation, the Stravinskys and I flew from New York to Zürich, September 27, 1968, for a rest at the Dolder Grand Hotel. The composer's health had improved, and he no longer needed nurses, but the weekly

---

56. The child was baptized Svetlana Marie-Blanche. Blanche was the baptismal name of Théus's mother, Marie that of Denise—chosen as a gesture of conciliation.

57. "Unfortunately, Kitty is seeing Théus again," Theodore's wife wrote to Soulima's wife, March 22, 1973.

analyses of his blood were continued, and a hematologist advised him that the treatment of polycythemia, from which he was then thought to be suffering, was more advanced in the United States than in Europe. This doctor recommended a return to America in a month or two.

The first visitor to the Dolder was Theodore, who arrived on Vera Stravinsky's name day, September 30, in time for her celebration dinner.[58] For the record, the Stravinskys' most noteworthy visitors at the hotel were: October 1–3, Pierre Suvchinsky; October 5–6, Nicolas Nabokov and Dominique Cibiel, his future wife; October 6–11, Miss Ampenoff; October 11, Theodore and Denise; October 17, Hayni Anda (wife of the pianist Geza Anda); October 22, Henri Larese, director of the Museum of St. Gall. (Larese appraised the Picassos that the Stravinskys had brought to Europe, as did Mme Christian Zervos, October 30, in Paris.) Another visitor was Lina Lalandi. Telephone communications were kept up with many friends, including Paul Sacher in Basel, Lilli Palmer in La Loma, and Hermann Dubs in Zürich.

On October 7, Stravinsky expressed the desire to visit his bank in Basel. Ampenoff telephoned for an appointment with Jean-Pierre Puenzieux, one of the directors of the Swiss Bank Corporation, and after lunch the Stravinskys, Ampenoff, and I drove to Basel. M. Puenzieux met the party at the door of the bank, but, to everyone's surprise, would not permit Mrs. Stravinsky to accompany her husband into the inner sanctum. A minute or so later, the banker returned and escorted Mrs. Stravinsky to her husband's side.

When the Stravinskys and Puenzieux emerged two hours later, Ampenoff and I learned what had happened: Stravinsky had been informed that his wife's name did not appear on his account and that, incredible as it sounds, his sole heir was Andre Marion.[59] Hearing this, the composer burst into a

---

58. Theodore, in his deposition, answered negatively to the question: "Did you know when Mrs. Stravinsky's name day was?"

59. Marion did not tell the Theodore and Soulima Stravinskys that he had supplanted them as sole beneficiary in 1965, a fact revealed under questioning

rage, tore up the agreement, and instructed the banker to draw up a new one, replacing Marion's name with that of Vera Stravinsky.[60] Not yet suspicious of Montapert, however, and of the true nature of his relationship with Marion and Puenzieux, Stravinsky, following the banker's advice, did not cancel the lawyer's power of attorney, which the composer had granted on February 12, 1962. Thus Montapert, who should have been dismissed at this first detection of his blatant abuse of his professional duty, continued in Stravinsky's employment.

If Stravinsky had intended to leave his Swiss money in care of any *one* of his children, the choice would naturally have

---

during the litigation. Garbus asked Theodore: "Did you ever receive any letter from [Milene and Andre] concerning the disposition of the assets of your father after his death?" Theodore replied, "No." Marion testified that ". . . prior to their going to Switzerland in October 1968, Mr. Stravinsky stated to Mr. Montapert that Vera Stravinsky and Robert Craft always tried to interfere wherever he would have a chance of talking in private with me, and therefore he was asking Mr. Montapert to see me about taking the necessary steps to protect the money in the Swiss account for the children, because he knew that they were going to take him to Switzerland to try to change the status of the Swiss account in their favor." According to Marion's own agenda in his handwriting, Montapert saw Stravinsky only twice in the month before the Stravinskys left California for New York on September 8, both occasions being dinners at Chasen's with Mrs. Stravinsky, Lillian Libman, and the present writer. But Stravinsky at this time had no intention of going to Switzerland at all; nor did he have business with Marion that he would not have confided to his wife. It must be said that Marion's appointment books for the period agree with Mrs. Stravinsky's and with those of the present writer, from Balanchine's visits in May to those of Alberto Moravia and Maya Plisetskaya, and, throughout the summer, Christopher Isherwood, Miranda, Morton, and Bill Brown.

60. Ampenoff never testified in the case, but merely signed a written deposition of no value to either side (November 23, 1977). If Garbus had subpoenaed her, he intended to ask: (1) Are you of the opinion that Mr. Stravinsky was clear and mentally competent on the day of the bank visit?; (2) If he had not been, do you think he could have negotiated with Mr. Puenzieux for two hours?; (3) Why is your presence at the bank never mentioned in any of the Stravinsky children's hearsay accounts of the visit?; and (4) Why did you take such pains to conceal the fact of your presence in your own correspondence with the children? Ampenoff's letters to the children were later to become exhibits in the suit.

been his elder son, who had been his father's intermediary with the bank for many years; prior to December 1965, a majority of Stravinsky's letters to Theodore contain instructions vis-à-vis the Basel bank. Certainly Stravinsky would not knowingly have left the money to an in-law, especially one whom he only pretended to like for the sake of his daughter.[61]

Had Stravinsky forgotten that both he and his wife had given Marion full power of attorney in 1962? Clearly Stravinsky had not understood the agreement, concocted by Montapert and signed by Vera and Igor Stravinsky, April 1, 1962, which, after his death, would have given the Swiss money to Theodore, Soulima, Milene, and their spouses in equal amounts. This paper had been written in such a way that Stravinsky refers to "Vera and myself" at the beginning but fails to define Vera's position in the event that he should predecease her. Nor could Stravinsky have understood the new dispensation of November 20, 1964, which included Kitty as an equal party, for the text with respect to "Vera and myself" is exactly the same as in the first document.

Marion evidently became the sole beneficiary in December 1965. At any rate, on March 3, 1966, Theodore wrote to the Swiss Bank Corporation asking why, since November 23, 1965, he had not received any of the papers "that you send regularly to my address by understanding with my father." Stravinsky was not aware of this change to his son-in-law's advantage, nor was the composer informed of it by the bank. But from this time, his Basel accountings were received by Marion through Montapert by way of an address in Mexico.

A second event that took place during the Stravinskys' stay at the Dolder was to become an issue in the litigation. On October 9, 1968, Ampenoff presented a letter to the composer for his signature authorizing Boosey & Hawkes to allot, from

61. When Milene defended her husband in a letter to her father (September 6, 1957) as *"simplement un grand nerveux,"* Stravinsky wrote in red pencil next to this phrase, *"un homme assez grossier."*

his royalties, an annuity of £3,000 to Pierre Suvchinsky, "in consideration of [his] work in connection with my archives."[62] Stravinsky thought this sum far too high, saw no reason why he should finance the project, and, in any case, had changed his mind about publishing his papers. He balked until *chère Véra* convinced him that the agreement was simply a way of helping an old friend—one of many good deeds for which she would pay dearly. Ampenoff was discharged from Boosey & Hawkes in the mid-1970s.[63]

Exactly one year before this "Dolder agreement," Stravinsky had been gravely ill with a circulatory ailment that his physician at the time had misdiagnosed as gout. Thinking that her husband, bored because he was unable to work, might be diverted by Suvchinsky's companionship, Vera Stravinsky invited him to Hollywood and accordingly telephoned Boosey & Hawkes to ask them to advance money to Suvchinsky for the trip. Ampenoff, seeing this as an opportunity for Boosey & Hawkes to acquire the publication rights

62. In the book *Stravinsky: Etudes et témoignages* (Paris, 1982), François Lesure states that in a letter of October 9, 1968, to Ampenoff and in an earlier one to Suvchinsky, Stravinsky entrusted the editing of his archives to Suvchinsky. In truth, both letters were written by Ampenoff for Stravinsky's signature. Suvchinsky's letter had to be revised to satisfy him and to include my name as co-editor. Needless to say, Stravinsky did not typewrite letters to Ampenoff in English, nor did he give his California address when he was in Zürich.

63. On the last day of her employment there, at the end of December 1975, she was observed destroying papers from her files. (Personal testimony of W. A. Fell, director of Boosey & Hawkes) One of the difficulties facing future scholars is that she kept as personal property much of Stravinsky's correspondence to her while an employee of Boosey & Hawkes. For example, in June 1962 Jean-Pierre Laubsher of the *Gazette de Lausanne* wrote to Stravinsky in Hamburg proposing that Jean-Luc Godard make a film of *Histoire du soldat*. Stravinsky asked Ampenoff to reply for him and to negotiate a fee of 15,000 Swiss francs. When nothing came of the project, Stravinsky wrote (December 25, 1962) asking her to investigate the matter. Her answer, January 2, 1963, explains that contractual difficulties had arisen with the publisher; but she also requests to be allowed to keep the original of Stravinsky's letter to her since it contains a striking use of a Russian word. On January 8, Stravinsky asked for the return of his notes, since he had no copy, but he never received them. Much of the Boosey & Hawkes correspondence directed to Ampenoff either is still in her possession or has been destroyed.

to Stravinsky's papers, promised Suvchinsky a contract naming him their editor in exchange for securing Stravinsky's signature. Suvchinsky, who was frightened of airplanes and had never been in one, and who had declined earlier invitations by the Stravinskys to visit them, promptly arrived in Hollywood (October 27). He spent two days with the composer, whose condition suddenly worsened. On November 2, he entered Mt. Sinai Hospital. Ampenoff's agreement for the archives arrived the next day, and, on one of two visits to the hospital, Suvchinsky persuaded Stravinsky to sign the paper, after which Suvchinsky promptly returned to Paris (November 9).

Here, for contrast, is Suvchinsky's version of the trip, in his report of a conversation with Vera Stravinsky at the Hôtel Ritz, Paris, March 19, 1974—except that to judge by the style and frequent lapses into the third person, the real author is Ampenoff. "Suvchinsky" says that the purpose of the journey was "to explain in detail his [i.e., my] idea of the archives publication." But at this date Stravinsky was not aware of *any* plan to publish the archives, and, since Suvchinsky had never seen them and had no concrete knowledge of their contents, he could hardly have entertained any "detailed" ideas about editing them. The report does not mention that Stravinsky's acquiescence was obtained while he was ill and hospitalized. In fact, it was I who advised Ampenoff that Stravinsky's hospital signature would not hold up in court, since medical records would show that he was sedated throughout the period of Suvchinsky's California visit. She prepared a new agreement, bringing it to New York herself in October 1969 and obtaining Stravinsky's signature.[64] Neither this nor the hospital contract mentions any payment to Stravinsky himself, yet shortly after his death, Ampenoff held a press conference about the acquisition of the archives. A reporter from

64. The reader must realize that at this time the Stravinskys did not know that Ampenoff had deep feelings of jealousy toward Vera Stravinsky and had sided totally with the children, as her letters to them were to reveal during the litigation.

the *Manchester Guardian* addressed her: "Stravinsky was famous for driving hard bargains. Did Boosey & Hawkes have to pay a large sum for the publication rights to his papers?" Ampenoff replied: "Stravinsky was reasonable." The truth was that he had received nothing at all.[65]

One final incident at the Dolder must be mentioned because of the exaggerated significance attributed to it in the lawsuit. On October 9, 1968, Stravinsky telephoned from the hotel to Theodore, in Geneva, asking him to bring the manuscript of *Le Sacre du printemps* with him when he visited on the 11th. The score had been kept in a Geneva vault since 1962, when the composer received it as an eightieth-birthday present from Boosey & Hawkes. During the litigation, lawyers on both sides endeavored, unsuccessfully, to prove the ownership of the manuscript. Theodore, in his deposition, replied hesitantly to questions concerning the *Sacre* manuscript:

MR. GARBUS: Did you ever tell your father that the *Sacre* was in your name, and not his?

THEODORE: There was trust between my father and me, and there was no need of precisions about that. . . .

MR. GARBUS: Mr. Stravinsky, you did not answer my question: . . . Did you ever write a letter to your father telling him that the manuscript was being held in a safe deposit that was under your name?

THEODORE: I do not remember having written such a letter.

The documents that would have established categorically that Stravinsky did not intend for Theodore to keep the score or the money from its sale were never produced. The first one is a letter from Stravinsky to Theodore, December 7, 1962, giving him the

65. In 1977, Vera Stravinsky bought back the publication rights from Boosey & Hawkes for $90,000.

address of Erwin Rosenthal's son, whose first name is Alby
[*sic*]: 49A Belsize Park Gardens, London NW3. His father
tells me that Alby is going to write to you, Theodore, and
arrange a meeting with you, which might not be so easy,
since you are in Leysin and the [*Sacre*] manuscript (for
which I want to obtain one hundred thousand dollars, to
be deposited in your bank, and then in mine) is in Geneva.

The second document is a letter from father to son, dated
June 1968, asking to have the *Sacre* manuscript microfilmed
and to send the *film* to Boosey & Hawkes for inclusion in the
archives, which is tantamount to saying that Stravinsky did
not consider the *original* to belong with his other manuscripts.

But to return to the incidents that took place at the Dolder
Hotel in October 1968, Theodore duly brought the manuscript, and on the afternoon of the 11th, Stravinsky removed
the brown wrapping paper from the red, imitation-Morocco
volume—in the presence of his wife, Theodore, Denise,
Ampenoff, and myself. Looking at the music, Stravinsky was
suddenly reminded of the premiere. He insisted on rubbing
the Parisian nose in the insults of 1913, and on expressing his
bitterness in writing, on the last page. Ampenoff tried to
dissuade him from doing this, but he took the score and a pen
to my room, which was across the corridor from his. Theodore and Denise then drove Ampenoff to the airport,
whence she took the late-afternoon flight to London. As soon
as they had gone, Stravinsky made a gift of the manuscript to
his wife.

Compare Theodore Stravinsky's testimony concerning
these events. In the first place, he is uncertain whether he
delivered the manuscript to his father on the 10th or the
11th,[66] though his father was not even *in* Zürich until the

66. This confusion is also evident in Theodore's deposition. Thus, on page 21,
he says that he saw the Stravinskys "almost every day during the whole period
of my father's stay in Evian [in the summer of 1970]. . . . They came in July
and left in the first days of September." In fact they came on June 12—
how could Theodore forget his father's birthday party on the 18th?—and re-

late evening of the 10th, having spent the day in Lucerne and at the Wagner house at Triebschen, where Stravinsky's signature can be seen in the visitors' book. In the second place, Theodore recalled:

> When my father asked Miss Ampenoff and myself to help with writing these few words [at the end of the score], he had already worked at it himself. However, I cannot testify as to his doing it a few hours before or on the evening of October 11th. . . . When we finished writing the text, he seemed . . . very much moved. . . . If my memory does not betray me, what was written on the manuscript is exactly what I translated from the Russian text.[67]

At this point, Theodore was interrupted by his own counsel:

> MR. HIGGINSON: Was what was finally written in the manuscript by your father in Russian?
> THEODORE: No. What my father wrote was in French.

What Stravinsky wrote *is* in Russian, as Theodore should have known even though he was *not* present when his father wrote it: the manuscript had been on display in Basel for three years before the date of this deposition. Then, asked who was present when the composer received his manuscript, Theodore answered: "The suite was inhabited by my father, Vera, and Mr. Craft. Miss Ampenoff came in and out, Mr. Suvchinsky also. . . ." In actuality, Suvchinsky was in Paris.

Writing to Soulima's wife three years closer to the event,

---

turned to New York on August 25. Moreover, as the nurses' records show, Theodore saw his father on only seventeen occasions during this seventy-three-day period. A little further on, Theodore says that "the idea of making a book about [Stravinsky] did not come to me before his death." But a letter to Theodore from Ampenoff, written before the death, unmistakably refers to the book.

67. For the original Russian, see the reproduction of the final page of the *Sacre* manuscript in *Stravinsky in Pictures and Documents*, by Vera Stravinsky and Robert Craft (New York, 1978), p. 76.

Theodore's wife describes the return of the *Sacre* score as follows:

> Vera asked us on *Père*'s request to give him back the *Sacre*. Theodore turned it over on October 11, 1968. . . . *Père*, very embarrassed, said that maybe he would sell it to pay taxes (it was obvious that Vera had been working on him).

As for the later history of the manuscript, Mrs. Marion's testimony is wrong in every particular:

> MR. GARBUS: Do you know if the *Sacre* manuscript was in California at any time during 1969?
> MRS. MARION: . . . I learned that it was at Mr. Craft's.
> MR. GARBUS: When did you learn that Mr. Craft had the manuscript?
> MRS. MARION: It was in the summer of 1969.
> MR. GARBUS: When did you learn that Theodore Stravinsky had given the *Sacre* manuscript to Igor Stravinsky in Switzerland in October 1968?
> MRS. MARION: . . . In the fall of 1969.

In other words, Mrs. Marion knew that the manuscript was in Hollywood in the summer of 1969, yet did not find out until the fall of 1969 that it was no longer in Switzerland. But Mrs. Marion's recollections of the summer of 1969 are remarkably selective. Thus she recalls that once "we were sitting at the dining room table, only Robert Craft and myself, and he was talking about travel."

> MR. GARBUS: When was this conversation?
> MRS. MARION: I don't recall. After 1969.

Mrs. Marion never met me "after 1969."

> MR. GARBUS: Was it a practice that each day visitors came and had lunch with [Stravinsky] during that . . . period [July 12–September 15, 1969]?

MRS. MARION: I don't know.

MR. GARBUS: Did you ever have lunch with him [during that time]?

MRS. MARION: I don't remember.

MR. GARBUS: Did you ever have dinner with him during . . . this period?

MRS. MARION: I don't remember.[68]

In fact, Mrs. Marion did *not* dine with her father,[69] but if she remembered this, to admit it would have nullified her efforts to establish her closeness to her father at this period, the more so since he had frequent dinner guests.[70] Mrs. Marion then suddenly came up with "Dr. Edel and the Liebersons" among the friends of her father who came during this period, though Edel's final visit to the house had been two years earlier, and only Mr., not Mrs., Lieberson called on Stravinsky (September 12). But Mrs. Marion shows so little knowledge of her father's activities that she answered Garbus's question "Do you know if he conducted any concerts in 1969?" with "I don't recall," and the follow-up question, "Do you know when the last concert he conducted was?," with "I don't know." (He had stopped conducting two years before.) Mrs. Marion remembers "one instance" when her father was hospitalized in the summer of 1969. "Did you go to visit him?" Mr. Garbus asked. She answered, "No," but

68. The written testimony of Marilyn Stalvey reads as follows: "Milene did her duty, and often complained about that. Once Milene and I had a conversation in my office. She remarked on how time-consuming it was to come to the house . . . and that the visits made her late in getting dinner for Andre which put him in a very bad humor."

69. Mrs. Marion seeks to give the impression (p. 195 in her testimony) that she was the only one who walked with her father in July–September 1969. The facts are that she was with him for a total of about twelve hours during the whole period, almost none of which time was spent in walking. He had nurses and therapists at all times and they helped him to walk.

70. The Stravinskys dined with, among others, William T. Brown on July 11 and August 9 and 21; Lawrence Morton on July 19 and 24, August 22 and 25, and September 3 and 13; Christopher Isherwood and Don Bachardy on August 19 and 26 (Isherwood's birthday) and September 10.

the records show that Stravinsky was hospitalized twice, once at the UCLA Medical Center (July 12) and once at Cedars of Lebanon (July 16–19, for lung tomography), where she *did* visit him, an hour or so after he was admitted.

To conclude the story of the *Sacre* manuscript, Mrs. Stravinsky carried it back to California. It was not "at Mr. Craft's," but, instead, at the First Safe Deposit Company, 210 West 7th Street, Los Angeles, in a vault rented by, of all people, Mr. Montapert. (Mrs. Stravinsky's deposition confirms this and adds the explanation that Montapert had several large bank vaults in which he stored silver dollars.) On April 30, 1970, the score was removed by Mrs. Stalvey and Lawrence Morton, whose brother-in-law, Robert Cunningham,[71] then brought it to New York, where Lew Feldman, a well-known manuscript dealer, showed it to prospective buyers from the New York Public Library.

The Stravinskys left the Dolder on October 23, 1968, and flew from Zürich to Paris. On November 14 they continued from there to New York, and on November 18 from New York to Los Angeles. At home, their first caller was a greatly agitated Mr. Montapert, who warned them that the children were angry about the change in the Basel account. At this, the Stravinskys began to wonder why their lawyer displayed such concern for the children, who, so far as the Stravinskys knew, were not his clients. Moreover, the children could have found out about the change in Basel only from Montapert himself, who nevertheless seemed oblivious to this revelation of his complicity. Marion, however, realized that the Stravinskys had begun to understand the conspiracy, and from this point on his hostility was ill concealed.

Simultaneously, Montapert began to court me, no doubt fearing that I might discover and begin to question his

---

71. Stravinsky had known Cunningham and his wife for many years and, on June 8, 1958, composed a brief piece for them.

schemes. He also invited me to their next business meeting. At this convocation I discovered that the cohorts and their wives were receiving substantial salaries for questionable services in the Stravinskys' Arizona citrus groves and in such ghost corporations as "Verigor International," an abandoned gold mine in the Mojave Desert on which the Stravinskys unwittingly spent $100,000 almost entirely in the form of salaries to the Marions and Montaperts. As the Los Angeles attorney David G. Licht stated in an affidavit:

> In October 1969, I was retained by Igor Stravinsky to prevent the theft or destruction of certain of his manuscripts which were then under the control of Andre Marion. . . . Among other matters which Stravinsky asked me to investigate was the establishment and assets of a company called Verigor Incorporated [*sic*], which appeared to have substantial oil, gas, ore, and mineral leases. Igor Stravinsky knew nothing about the company or its assets, but believed that Montapert and Marion had used the company as a method of diverting Igor Stravinsky's funds for their own use.

Not until the end of the year 1969, when Mrs. Stalvey sent some of Marion's check stubs to the Stravinskys in New York, did they discover the extent to which they had been fleeced.[72] The stubs record the $2,000 "management fees" that Marion paid himself every few weeks, the checks made out to cash, and the checks that he made out to himself for secretarial work that seems to have consisted of little more than writing checks to himself, his wife, and the Montaperts. In 1968, for example, while the Stravinskys were in Zürich, Marion paid $15,000 and $5,000 of their money in one day (October 15),

---

72. Here are some of Marion's stubs for a typical period in 1967:

January 10: $2,100 to Montapert for attorney's fees (unspecified)
January 10: $10,000 to Verigor
January 25: $2,000 to cash
January 30: $1,917.50 to Montapert
February 16: $1,200 to Montapert

the first for the citrus groves and the second for Verigor, both soon to be acquired for himself and Montapert. It goes without saying that the Stravinskys had never seen the books and were never informed.[73]

In March 1969, Montapert urged the Stravinskys to give their Arizona citrus farms to the children, as compensation for the change in beneficiaries in Basel. Not recognizing any such obligation, Stravinsky objected. Since the fruit trees were worth at least $200,000,[74] and nearly as much again in tax deductions, and since his income from conducting and composing had come to an end, he saw no reason to divest himself of such an asset. Yet *chère Véra* finally persuaded him to do just that, and Montapert promptly prepared a deed of warranty—though not the one to which the Stravinskys had agreed. When they were at lunch on April 3, Montapert appeared unexpectedly. He seemed to be in a great hurry, unable to spare even a moment for them to read what they were signing—which, he claimed, simply authorized the gift to which they had already consented. Covering the text with one hand and extending a pen with the other, he induced them to endorse a paper that did not, as they had intended, give their

---

73. Martin Garbus's final affidavit states: "The total amount that the Marions took from Igor Stravinsky in the 1960s will never be known. . . . Montapert had been hired by the Marions to do many things that Igor Stravinsky was not aware of, but was paying for. . . . Montapert made unauthorized visits to the Swiss bank, and Igor Stravinsky never knew how much money Marion and Montapert withdrew from the account." Marion testified that he had been in charge of the entire Stravinsky bookkeeping from January 1955 until October 1969.

> MR. GARBUS: When you paid the monies to Montapert, either in 1966, 1967, or 1968, did you at that time ever tell Vera or Igor Stravinsky that you were making those payments?
> MR. MARION: No, I did not.
> MR. GARBUS: When you were making those payments [to yourself] in 1966, 1967, or 1968, did you at that time ever tell Vera or Igor Stravinsky that you were making those payments?
> MR. MARION: No, I did not.

74. On March 2, 1978, Mrs. Marion sold two parcels of this land, one for $96,000 and the other for $40,000.

property in equal portions to Theodore, Soulima, and Milene, but instead transferred the entire property to the Marions only. Months later, when the other children inadvertently learned about this, they established new standards in gullibility by accepting Mrs. Marion's story that "V[era] being still hostile towards the children, M[ontapert] was able to obtain the gift of these plantations only for Andre Marion and Milene Marion (actually at the time this was done to neutralize [?] Andre)" (deposition p. 111), and showed deep ignorance of the character of Igor Stravinsky, who would never knowingly have made such a gift to one child only.

On April 20, 1969, the Stravinskys flew to New York, intending to stay there a few days, en route to Europe, where Stravinsky had promised to attend a festival of his music in Holland. Then, on May 2, after tests made in New York Hospital, Stravinsky underwent an embolectomy on his left leg, a lengthy operation that, since a second embolism was discovered, had to be performed again twenty-four hours later. He was in intensive care for only two days, however, and the doctors were confident of his recovery. On May 14, Mrs. Stravinsky tried to reach Montapert, rumored to be in Paris, to ask him to sell some of her and her husband's securities in order to pay the hospital, the doctors, the nurses, and the hotel and living expenses; but Montapert could not be traced. (On the 14th, too, John Stravinsky came to the hospital; unfortunately, Mrs. Stravinsky was at the hotel at the time trying to telephone Montapert, and John's grandfather instructed the nurses not to admit him.) On the 17th, Soulima, on his way to France, visited his father briefly. On the 18th, when Mrs. Stravinsky telephoned Mrs. Marion to ask her to have her husband sell some securities, she was informed that Stravinsky's "business manager"[75] of many years knew nothing about such matters.[76] On May 20, Stra-

---

75. Theodore Stravinsky betrayed considerable surprise in his deposition on learning that this was Andre Marion's official title.
76. When the late Arnold Weissberger, Stravinsky's New York attorney at the time, received Marion's account books, in October 1969, it was discovered

vinsky had pneumonia. His wife wrote in her diary that night: "Bob calls Milene and tells her to prepare for the worst." But Stravinsky was back in his hotel in time for his birthday on June 18. Meanwhile, Mrs. Stravinsky had appealed to his publishers to advance part of a semiannual bonus, which they did, but out of which, against the advice of a new lawyer and all of her friends, she kept only enough to pay the most urgent bills, sending the rest to Marion.

On July 9, the Stravinskys and I flew to Los Angeles, where we were met at the airport not by the Marions but by a friend of the Stravinskys, Jack Quinn. In the weeks that followed, the composer's health improved, and he grew steadily stronger. What did deteriorate were relations with the Marions, Milene making a few token appearances and Andre appearing only once in the entire two-month period that the Stravinskys remained in California.

Montapert suddenly materialized, but the Stravinskys were unable to obtain a financial statement from him. Instead, he came again and again to urge Mrs. Stravinsky to remove the money from the Basel bank, arguing that if her husband were to die, the children would block the account. She did not take this bait—which Montapert could have construed as evidence that she intended to keep the money for herself—and day after day he would leave the Stravinsky house in a scarcely controlled temper, unable to fathom such exasperating indifference to money.[77] In truth, few people can have gone through life so utterly guiltless of greed as Vera Stravinsky.

---

that in a recent year in which the income had been $300,000—not including $80,000 deposited in Switzerland—Marion and Montapert had sold $140,000 in securities.

77. Marion actually testified that Mrs. Stravinsky gave Montapert a $10,000 check for his services in transferring the money from the Basel account into another Swiss account under her own name, and that her instructions to Montapert were written. Needless to say, the evidence never materialized. Why Montapert would have accepted $10,000 when, as will appear later in the story, the Stravinsky children had offered him over $200,000 Marion does not attempt to explain.

On July 18, Mrs. Eugene Lourié, whose husband was a long-time friend of the Stravinskys,[78] warned them that Montapert had tapped her telephone and was quite capable of doing the same to theirs. Soon thereafter, Mrs. Lourié, to prove that Montapert was wiretapping, arranged to telephone Vera Stravinsky while she was dining at Lawrence Morton's. On the following day, when Montapert repeated the contents of this call to Mrs. Stravinsky, the composer and his wife finally decided to dismiss "their" lawyer. They telephoned their New York lawyer, L. Arnold Weissberger, who flew to California and, on August 18, met with Montapert, arranged the transfer of limited power of attorney, and then met with the Stravinskys and myself.

But by this time, the main event in this history had already occurred. On August 16, by prearrangement, the Marions and the Soulima Stravinskys (accompanied by Françoise's children by her first marriage, who were touring the United States and Canada) had met in a motel in Cambria, a resort 250 miles north of Los Angeles, long frequented by the Marions. There the foursome made a shocking decision: to sign a contract with Montapert whereby, employing his power of attorney, he would remove the money of Igor and Vera Stravinsky from Basel and divide it 50 percent for himself and 50 percent for the children. On the night of the 16th, after driving to the Marion home in Los Angeles, Milene, Andre, Soulima, and Françoise actually signed the paper. The next day, August 17, Milene, Soulima and Françoise called on Stravinsky; but he did not wish to see them and therefore, to cut the visit short, went to bed, pretending to be ill. None of the three spoke to or even inquired about Mrs. Stravinsky. (Whether or not by coincidence, Michel

78. A letter from Stravinsky to his concert agent, Dr. Enrique Telemaco Susini, February 18, 1932, recommends the "young and very talented Russian painter [Eugene] Lourié, who most recently achieved great success with his work in René Clair's film *A Nous la liberté.*"

Yelachich—Kitty Stravinsky's future husband—a resident of
Paris, paid a call in the afternoon and was received by the
composer in his downstairs living room.) August 17, 1969,
marked the last occasion that Soulima and his wife saw or had
any communication with Igor Stravinsky.

The above description of the hatching of the plot is taken
from the deposition of Milene Marion, who appears to have
had some qualms about her participation.

> MRS. MARION: I said I was against it. I was afraid to do this.
> MR. GARBUS: Why were you afraid? . . .
> MRS. MARION: I felt I shouldn't do it.
> MR. GARBUS: But you did it?
> MRS. MARION: The Soulimas decided to do it, so I followed.
> MR. GARBUS: You made a decision, after discussion with the
> Soulimas, to sign it?
> MRS. MARION: Yes.
> MR. GARBUS: Were you told that any one of the people or
> signatories to that agreement can be charged with em-
> bezzlement?
> MRS. MARION: No.[79]

The continuation of the story comes from the testimony of her
husband:

> MR. GARBUS: Was there no discussion at all concerning what
> would happen to the money after Mr. Montapert re-
> moved it from the Swiss account?
> MR. MARION: I don't remember.

---

79. The Marions' Chicago, New York, and Los Angeles lawyers intervened at
this point, but a letter from Milene to Theodore had already been entered in
evidence. She had written, in October 1969, that "M[ontapert] consulted
lawyers in Switzerland and New York [Samuel Byer, who was one of the
Marions' attorneys as well] and they all agreed that the position was inde-
fensible and that he and Andre were running the risk of being sued for
embezzlement." At another place in her deposition (p. 118), Mrs. Marion

MR. GARBUS: Do you know if Mr. Montapert ever removed the monies from . . . the Swiss account under the name of Mr. and Mrs. Stravinsky?

MR. MARION: . . . Yes.

MR. GARBUS: Do you know what the term embezzlement means? . . . Did you ever discuss with your wife that either you or Mr. Montapert were running the risk of being sued for embezzlement?

MR. MARION: Yes, I did.

. . .

MR. GARBUS: Did you ever have any discussion with Mr. Montapert . . . whereby in exchange for any services that Mr. Montapert would render he would get any fees out of the Swiss account?

MR. MARION: Yes.

. . .

MR. GARBUS: Do you recall signing a document with Mr. Montapert relating to the Swiss account whereby he was to receive 50 percent of the proceeds of that account?

MR. MARION: Yes.

MR. GARBUS: When did you sign that document?

MR. MARION: In August 1969.[80]

. . .

MR. GARBUS: Was Theodore ever told of that conversation?

MR. MARION: Yes, he was.

---

says: "The money was replaced where it was originally, in the first bank. . . ." Mrs. Marion wrote to Theodore, October 20, 1969: ". . . M[ontapert] managed, through a great many acrobatics, to take out of the Basel account . . . the money that was there . . . by combining his own powers of attorney with those of Andre, since the powers of Andre had been taken away from him in October 1968, when [Vera] dragged *Père* to Basel and made him put the account solely in the name of Vera and himself. . . . Andre wanted me to tell you to be very careful when using the above information . . . the reason being that no one must be able to accuse Andre and M. to have plotted together (especially at the time when M. was the parents' attorney)."

80. In Petitioner's Exhibit 37, Mrs. Marion states: "At the time when M[ontapert] embarked upon this matter, Andre had agreed to remunerate him in kind if he were successful."

MR. GARBUS: By whom?

MR. MARION: I do not remember.

MR. GARBUS: Did you tell Theodore?

MR. MARION: I did not.

MR. GARBUS: Did your wife tell Theodore, to your knowledge?

MR. MARION: To my knowledge, she did.

MR. GARBUS: Did she do it in writing or orally?

MR. MARION: In writing.

MR. GARBUS: When you had this conversation with Montapert, was he then Igor Stravinsky's lawyer?

MR. MARION: Yes. Yes, he was.

MR. GARBUS: What happened after you had that conversation with Montapert? Did you agree on your behalf to give him the 50 percent?

MR. MARION: Yes, we did.

MR. GARBUS: And when you say "we did," who is the "we," you and Milene?

MR. MARION: That is right, yes.

MR. GARBUS: And did Theodore and Soulima also agree?

MR. MARION: That is right.

MR. GARBUS: And were any of these agreements written down?

MR. MARION: Yes, they were.

MR. GARBUS: Was there a written agreement between Montapert and the children?

MR. MARION: That is correct, yes.

As Mrs. Marion's testimony shows, Montapert actually did remove the money. Nor did he return it until he was advised that, even though the Swiss account was illegal because of the purposes for which it was being used, he could be extradited and jailed.

Montapert did not go to Switzerland immediately, meeting first with Weissberger, and, once more, on August 20, with the Stravinskys and myself. On the 24th, Marion wrote to Theodore:

Do you intend to remain in Geneva the next two or three weeks . . . because you will have an important visit from a personal representative of ours but not of Vera. . . .[81]

Almost four years later, Theodore's wife, in a letter to Soulima's wife, recollected that

we were in Basel with Montapert, and it was there that we met this man, Puenzieux. [We hesitated in] authorizing power of attorney to Montapert because his methods struck us as a bit odd, [but] we gave Montapert a general power of attorney for Basel. . . . Then Montapert admitted to us that he gets along very well with Craft. "I am playing both sides against the middle in order to help you." Shady character, to say the very least. [March 22, 1973]

Meanwhile, on Weissberger's advice, the composer and his wife decided to go to New York as soon as they could pack. Since one of their nurses from New York Hospital was vacationing in San Francisco, Mrs. Stravinsky asked her to accompany them on the flight, but the presence of this woman does not account for the inaccuracies in Mrs. Marion's testimony concerning the departure:

The persons I recall seeing at the airport besides my father and myself were Vera, Robert Craft, and Rita, the nurse. [Deposition, p. 204]

"Rita, the nurse" is a most peculiar apparition, since she was in Europe and had not even been in California in five months.[82] But then, Mrs. Marion does not mention Jack

---

81. MR. GARBUS: Did you send Theodore a letter prior to the time that Montapert came over to visit him?
MR. MARION: I do not remember.
MR. GARBUS: Do you know if your wife prepared such a letter?
MR. MARION: I do not know. [Deposition pp. 73–74]
82. Mrs. Marion's deposition shows a slightly less hostile feeling toward me than toward her stepmother. For example, she testified that a part of one of

Quinn and Edwin Allen, with whom she rode to the airport in the same car. When Mr. Garbus asked Mrs. Marion whether Mr. Allen had been in the Stravinsky home at any time during the two-month period in the summer of 1969, she answered "Yes":

> MR. GARBUS: How many times was he there, if you recall?
> MRS. MARION: I don't recall.

Mr. Allen *lived* in the Stravinsky home from July 17 to September 14.

The Stravinskys were in New York only three days when Montapert telephoned to Weissberger requesting a meeting with him, Mrs. Stravinsky, and myself. Weissberger consented, though thinking this irregular, since to his knowledge Montapert no longer had any connection with the Stravinskys' affairs. During the meeting (September 19), Montapert openly represented the children against the Stravinskys, negotiating in terms of "what Andre will accept." Marion demanded that no change be made in Stravinsky's will.[83]

After Weissberger left, Montapert requested another meeting, with the Stravinskys and myself alone. The purpose of

---

her letters to Theodore "refers to Bob loving and manipulating the first small sketches that my father wrote when he began to compose *Les Noces*. . . . [Bob] found those little notes upon little pieces of paper made into little booklets were beautiful. . . . It is the first idea that the composer writes down, and [Bob] found that absolutely beautiful, and he expressed it with love, I can say, and admiration." (Deposition, p. 206)

83. In his own interest, Marion should have attempted to have the will changed, but he must have assumed that it was iron-clad, since Montapert had written it. According to the will, the only beneficiaries, after the death of Vera Stravinsky, are the children, grandchildren, and myself. The children who are without issue—Theodore and Milene—cannot bequeath their shares, which must be divided among the surviving direct heirs (of whom, since April 1960, I am one). The new will, written by Weissberger, simply follows Montapert's. It is devoid of specifics (royalty income is not even mentioned!), and it encouraged the suit that the Stravinsky children eventually brought. In lieu of precise stipulations, this final will reduced Vera Stravinsky's lawyers to arguments about "the intent of the testator."

this was to discuss the Swiss account, of whose existence Weissberger had been unaware, Montapert having so terrorized the Stravinskys about the subject that they were conditioned never to mention it. ("I am interested in two payments made by the Hamburg Radio," Stravinsky wrote to Theodore, November 6, 1965. "Ask Basel if these have been received, and write your reply in Russian to Milene's address, taking care not to mention my last name.") At still a third meeting, Montapert brought a letter, addressed to the Swiss Bank Corporation, transferring his power of attorney over the Stravinskys' Basel account to me. His rationale for this was that henceforth he would be too far away from the Stravinskys to work for them, whereas I lived with them and was also frequently in Europe. The Stravinskys signed the paper, which Montapert pocketed. He then left for Switzerland to obtain the signatures of the Theodore Stravinskys on the embezzlement agreement.

Here is Theodore's testimony, after he had confirmed that his conversation with Montapert "was about the numbered account [formerly Secretarial II, 43656, now 47992[84]] with the Swiss Bank Corporation. . . . Mr. Montapert had told me that everything was ready to empty this account":

> From the first time I met Montapert, I felt mistrust towards him. . . . It was not difficult to notice . . . that he was not a trustworthy character. . . . He introduced himself as coming from Milene, Andre, and Soulima, saying that my brother and sister asked me to confide in him. He said "I pretend to be good friends with Bob Craft, but I work with you, for your interests." This already did not please us both [Theodore and his wife]. I let Vera understand that I mistrusted Montapert [two months later, in New York, in November 1969]. [Deposition][85]

84. I do not know the date of the change in number; in a letter from Baden-Baden, October 9, 1957, Stravinsky questioned the identity of a new name, Roger Viollet, in his correspondence with the bank.
85. Milene wrote to Theodore, October 9, 1969: "For the money in Switzer-

On September 28, 1969, I flew to Berlin to conduct a concert (October 2). Montapert telephoned me there from Switzerland, insisting that I meet him in Basel to sign papers without which the New York letter giving me power of attorney would not be valid. Accordingly, at 5:30 a.m., Friday, October 3, accompanied by the aforementioned "Rita, the nurse," I flew to Basel via Munich and Zürich, where I went to the Hotel Drei Könige and waited for Montapert's telephone call. This came in mid-afternoon, and, according to his instructions, I met him in the street outside the bank. Inside, we were ushered into a room where Puenzieux[86] had prepared papers for me to sign, transferring Montapert's power of attorney to me. Much later I discovered that one of them was "a verification of account amounting to more than $400,000." [Letter from Marion to Theodore, November 27, 1969]

As I was leaving the bank, Montapert told me that he had borrowed $10,000 of the Stravinskys' money, that this would show up in the accounting, and that he would return the sum before the end of the year.[87] Why, I wondered, was Marion drawing checks on the Stravinskys' money without informing them, especially since he lived only a few blocks away?

The next day I flew to New York and advised the Stravinskys to repatriate their money immediately. We summoned Weissberger, revealed everthing to him, and I gave him my proxy. After consulting with his partner, Aaron Frosch, Weissberger retained a lawyer with dual, American-Swiss,

---

land, M[ontapert] incurred great risks and could be legally sued for misappropriation of funds. The others have taken away his proxy and given proxy to B[ob]. . . . You should inform yourself there [in Geneva], if you could immediately block the funds in case of the death of Vera or of father. However, B[ob] is very well placed to take a plane the minute this happens and take the whole of the money. . . ."

86. I still had no inkling of the alliance between the lawyer and the banker, even though I knew that Montapert regularly gave Puenzieux $5,000 "tips" from the Stravinsky account.

87. Montapert repaid the sum on December 2, 1969.

citizenship,[88] and sent him to the Swiss Bank Corporation with instructions to purchase United States municipal bonds with all of the money in the account and to send these bearer bonds to New York. Stravinsky did not sign the final authorization for this until November 26—Theodore was in New York and in the room at the time—and the bonds did not arrive until February 1970, at which time they were placed in two vaults in the 57th Street and Park Avenue branch of Bankers Trust Company.[89]

On September 30, 1969, Weissberger served Marion with legal notice that his power of attorney had been canceled, while Stravinsky sent a letter to him demanding the return of his music manuscripts—which were in a vault in the Crocker Bank, Hollywood, in Marion's name—and of Marion's account books. Apparently waiting to consult Montapert, Marion disregarded these instructions until October 12, when he met with Mr. and Mrs. Montapert, the three together drawing up a list of the manuscripts that were to be returned. On October 28, Mrs. Stravinsky wrote to Milene reporting on "father's health"—though she had not inquired about it. Two days later, Mrs. Stravinsky, open-hearted and trusting as always, wrote to Theodore and Denise: "I would like so much to see you, to 'unburden myself.' " (Exhibit 4C)

On November 3, 1969, Stravinsky signed a new will, wit-

88. Elwood Rickless, the protégé of Samuel Pisar, of the Paris firm of Kaplan, Livingston, Goodwin, Berkowitz & Selvin. Rickless was also employed by the Stravinskys to obtain appraisals of their Picassos, which they placed in Geneva in August 1970. The paintings were later brought to New York by a daughter of the basso Andrew Foldi.

89. The Basel money consisted largely of the annual bonuses from Boosey & Hawkes in London. Stravinsky's publishers paid him $25,000 in quarterly installments, which he declared as income; if his music earned more than this, he would receive a bonus, which by the 1960s averaged $150,000 a year. Undoubtedly the sum that had accumulated in the Basel account was well in excess of $400,000, but Stravinsky himself did not keep any accounting of these monies. In 1969, after Weissberger succeeded Montapert as the Stravinskys' attorney, the Boosey & Hawkes bonuses were sent to New York and declared as income.

nessed by Miriam Pollack, William Brown, and Samuel Dushkin. Shortly afterward, Marion refused to return the manuscripts,[90] which he intended to use as leverage in obtaining a general release from his father-in-law and a promise not to prosecute. At this, Stravinsky felt that he had no recourse but to institute legal proceedings. Thus on November 22 (while Theodore was present), the composer signed papers to sue Marion for the return of the manuscripts, an action reported in newspapers and on national television. Stravinsky also decided to make another will and to exclude Marion from it. This was signed on December 9, the same day as Marion's release, which is a litany of the forms of his income from the Stravinskys:

AGREEMENT made this 9th day of December 1969 by and between Andre Marion of Los Angeles, California (hereinafter called "Marion"), and Igor Stravinsky and Vera Stravinsky of New York City (hereinafter called "Stravinskys").

For and in consideration of the delivery by Marion to Stravinskys of the attached list of manuscripts . . . Stravinskys do hereby release and forever discharge Marion individually and as agent and/or employee together with all persons connected with him in any transaction in which said Marion acted individually or as agent or employee for said Stravinskys for and from any and all claims, account damages, demands and causes of action of which the undersigned Stravinskys ever had, now have, or may hereafter acquire or become possessed of by reason of his employment by said Stravinskys as business and investment manager,

---

90. Marion testified that his refusal to return the manuscripts was prompted by Theodore and Soulima:

MR. GARBUS: Did Theodore make that request to you in writing or orally? Did Soulima and Theodore or Theodore or Soulima make that request to you?

MR. MARION: Yes, they did.

MR. GARBUS: Both of them?

MR. MARION: Yes.

holder of various powers of attorney, as bookkeeper, recipient and disburser of funds, as corporate officer and director of Verigor International, Inc., as manager of Stravinskys' farms [citrus groves] and in any and all other capacities or any connection therewith directly or indirectly including but not limited to any claim for salary or fees paid, expenses incurred, obligations undertaken or discharged in their behalf, or their successors in interest, amounts disbursed to himself or others, disbursements or transfers relating to investments, record keeping, acts done under powers of attorney, or otherwise or any claims to damages for anything whatever from 1947 to the present. . . .

Stravinskys hereby expressly waive all benefits of Section 1542 of the Civil Code of the State of California which reads: "1542. A general release does not extend to claims which creditor does not know or expect to exist in his favor at the time of executing the release, which, if known by him, must have materially affected his settlement of the debtor."[91]

Stravinskys hereby warrant . . . that this release is given, based on their knowledge of their business affairs, based on regular periodic review of all records including but not limited to canceled checks, records of disbursements and income, brokerage firm statements, deposit receipts, corporate minutes, bank and check books, and all other records regularly kept by Andre Marion. . . . This is intended as a general release and not a mere covenant not to sue.

The manuscripts were returned three weeks later. When Martin Garbus asked Marion under oath whether he had consulted a lawyer on the issue of the manuscripts, he replied that he had consulted Montapert.

---

91. During Theodore's deposition, his counsel, Higginson, actually volunteered the information, now on the public record (p. 50): "I felt that the general release was at least partially related to the [Swiss] bank account question. . . ."

MR. GARBUS: Did Montapert tell you in August or September of 1969 that he was not free to represent you because he represented Igor Stravinsky?
MR. MARION: I do not remember.

. . .

MR. GARBUS: When did you learn for the first time that Montapert was no longer representing Igor Stravinsky?
MR. MARION: I don't remember.

On arrival at the Essex House on November 18, 1969, Theodore Stravinsky telephoned his wife in Geneva. She told him that his sister had tried to reach him by telephone before his departure in order to explain "a matter of great importance." Vera Stravinsky was convinced that the call her stepson had just missed was to tell him what he should have known six months before, namely, that he had been given one-third of the Stravinskys' citrus groves. She informed him of the gift herself.

During this visit to New York (November 18–23), Theodore kept notes; he later denied this when questioned by Mr. Garbus, but Denise had written on a packet of notes on Essex House stationery: "Summery of the conversations between Vera and Craft during Theodore's stay in New York." The jottings are of interest mainly because of the absence of any expression of concern for Igor Stravinsky. As Mr. Garbus remarks in an affidavit: "When Theodore Stravinsky visited [his father] . . . he reported back to his brother and sister—and made notes not of his father's health, but of the Respondents' shared financial concerns." (no. 69) Mr. Garbus also asked Theodore whether, during this visit, he had questioned his father "about any of his business dealings with Andre Marion. . . ." Theodore answered, "No. My father was in too bad a state";[92] yet one point (no. 46, p. 20) in Higginson's

92. At one point in the litigation, Stravinsky's children seemed to be on the verge of introducing the question of competence, but their lawyers must have advised them that this would only reveal how little they knew about

affidavit of November 27, 1978, reads: "It is apparent that Igor Stravinsky learned about Theodore's mistrust of Montapert from conversations held when Theodore was at the Essex House in November 1969." And at about the same time, Françoise wrote to Milene that John had "found *Père* better." (Exhibit 36) Even Denise was obliged to admit to Milene in a letter sent in the summer of 1970: ". . . I believe . . . that it is true that *Père* is getting better and better. He was definitely on the way lately here [in Evian]." (Exhibit 30) Finally, the nurses' logbook for November 19 reads:

> I.S. fully aware and angry. Says he'd like to "send some people [i.e., Marion and Montapert] to hell." Talking now to son Theodore. Walked four times and played the piano. [Miriam Pollack, R.N.]

Theodore made a note on November 21 or 22 (he could not remember which day): "Vera declares that father alone has access to the Basel account: 'Even I, I cannot touch anything.'" Though this demonstrates exactly how little Vera Stravinsky understood both about the bank transaction and about Theodore's motives, he evidently thought she was trying to deceive him with the statement. But by this time all of the children seem to have had an *idée fixe* about their stepmother's character, as is portrayed in this letter from Theodore's wife to Soulima's wife:

> . . . M. Puenzieux, one of the bank officers, . . . told us the story in a cafe in Basel. . . . *Père* struggled with Vera for a half-hour. Clearly, he did not want to sign a paper to cut off

---

their father and how infrequently they had seen him. Their lawyers surely realized, too, that Weissberger and Garbus would have obtained the testimony of qualified observers. In fact, Weissberger had a written statement from Dr. John S. LaDue: "I examined Mr. Igor Stravinsky on 12/11/69 and found him completely oriented with regard to time, place, recent events, past events and, in a word, in full possession of his mental faculties." And in 1973, Garbus obtained a tape-recording of Dr. Henry Lax testifying that the composer's mind was fully alert in the last fifteen months of his life.

his children from the account that was to be divided at the time of his death. But as M. Puenzieux told us, Vera spoke severely to father in Russian, and finally harassed him to the point of signing. Vera had gotten her way.[93]

This fantasy ignores the fact that the children were not named as beneficiaries, but only Marion and Montapert. (Ampenoff's presence is not mentioned.) In actuality, Vera Stravinsky was wholly *un*interested in the Swiss money, except that she had been disturbed for years about its illegality and wanted her husband to remove it.

On November 23, Theodore flew from New York to Chicago for a meeting with his brother in Urbana, at which time he also conferred with the Marions by telephone. A very different, less communicative Theodore returned to New York (November 25) and left the next day for Geneva. Stravinsky's health continued to improve: on December 5 he posed for photographs for *Time*, and on the 7th he met with Harold Spivacke of the Music Division of the Library of Congress for advice on the disposal of the manuscripts.

The year 1970 was less eventful than 1969. Although the composer was hospitalized (Lenox Hill) on April 6 with pneumonia, he was discharged on the 29th. Dr. Lax advised him to leave New York for the summer, recommending the Hôtel Royal in Evian-les-Bains. The Stravinskys flew to Geneva, June 11, and drove from the airport to Evian. The composer enjoyed the summer there, when the weather was mild enough for him to eat out-of-doors and to take daily rides with his wife driving their automobile, which had been shipped over.

Theodore's Geneva doctor, Della Santa, visited the composer at Evian every few days, and the weekly blood tests

---

93. So much for the confidentiality of Swiss bankers! Puenzieux did not understand Russian, of course; "Vera" was more likely arguing against any change.

were continued at a hospital in Thonon-les-Bains. (When Stravinsky returned to New York, his polycythemia, as it was then erroneously thought to be, disappeared, and no further treatment was prescribed during the remaining seven months of his life.) After Ampenoff had visited him in Evian, she wrote to me saying that she was happy to see him "looking and acting so much better than in New York last October [1969]." Theodore and Denise came from Geneva, too, about every four days, but Stravinsky found their visits fatiguing, and a scouting system was organized with the aid of Marcel, a sympathetic room waiter, who warned the composer whenever the small car with the Swiss license plates approached the parking lot. This was a signal for Stravinsky to take to his bed and feign sleep or illness.

Nevertheless, Stravinsky and I felt that, while we were in Evian, a relationship of trust had been established between ourselves and Theodore and Denise, even if *Père* had been less than eager to spend time with them. The citrus groves, bank accounts, and the suit against Marion to recover the manuscripts were never mentioned, and the only reference to a rift between the parents and the children was in Vera Stravinsky's repeated question: "Why doesn't Soulima come to see his father, call, or send him a letter?" To this Theodore's answer was always the same: "I don't know, and I myself no longer seem able to understand my brother."

Shortly after the Stravinskys had reinstalled themselves at the Essex House on August 26, Mrs. Stravinsky telephoned Geneva, reporting on her husband's improved health and asking for pharmaceutical products not obtainable in New York. A little later I wrote the Theodore Stravinskys a detailed letter, but this was never answered or acknowledged, nor was Mrs. Stravinsky's letter of October 13; and in the remaining eight months of his father's life, Theodore never communicated with him. The autumn was a busy time for Mrs. Stravinsky. Because of noisy remodeling on their floor, the Essex House had become uninhabitable, and a decision was made to move. She personally inspected about twenty apartments until finding one she liked—and purchased, on December 1.

On December 3, a story appeared in the *New York Times* to the effect that Stravinsky's manuscripts and archives were being offered for sale for $3 million, and that the Soviet Union was among the bidders. Scarcely anything in the report was true, though the sale of the manuscripts had indeed been entrusted by Weissberger to the aforementioned Lew Feldman, who had sold the T. S. Eliot collection to Houghton Library at Harvard, and the Evelyn Waugh collection to the University of Texas. In Feldman's opinion, this "advertising" and the establishing of a price would stimulate interest in a sale, though in fact no tangible offer had been made from any quarter, and certainly not from the USSR.

Also on December 3, I wrote to Theodore and Denise explaining the *Times* articles, but apparently Ampenoff had already reached them by telephone and convinced them that a sale was a *fait accompli*. As a result, Theodore retained a lawyer, Jacques Borel, and sent an indignant letter to Mrs. Stravinsky. She answered (December 15) with the help of Arnold Weissberger and myself. The following is a draft of the letter that was sent:

> I am . . . grieved by your breach of faith in consulting a solicitor before speaking to me, and am therefore formulating my reply with the help of my attorney, Mr. Weissberger.
>
> I recall your surprise last year when I mentioned that the remainder of the manuscripts would have to be sold.[94] But what did you suppose Marion intended to do with them? . . . Certainly you know that your father donated fifty-two of them to the Library of Congress, in return for

---

94. Theodore had made a note of a conversation with his stepmother, November 26, 1969, according to which she answers his question "Did you want to sell the manuscripts?" with "If I could, I would frame them, but we need money. . . . Poor, poor father, don't you feel sorry for him?"

tax deductions on which our very limited livelihood depended . . . and you must find it perfectly logical for a man who has sold his manuscripts at every opportunity all his life to continue to do so in his old age, when his needs are greater than ever.

. . . But, perhaps you are not aware of these things, having had so little contact with your father for so many years that you could not have any idea of his true thoughts and feelings. It is sad to have to tell you that not once since his suit to recover his manuscripts from Marion has your father mentioned the name of any of his children. And sad to have to say that Marion's behavior shocked but did not surprise him. . . .

While your father's medical expenses are not likely to diminish, his income from conducting and commissions has ceased. All the same, I am determined to give him as much as I can of the comfort he deserves—and would have if he had not spent $100,000 on, for one example, "Verigor." And, by the way, isn't it more usual for fathers of eighty-eight years to be receiving aid from children in their sixties, rather than the other way around?

. . . But I had better stop before I get into a pique. In fact, one remark in your letter did annoy me: the compliment that you approved of the way I took care of your father. What did you expect me to do, treat him as his children have done? We now hear that your brother excuses *his* neglect of his father with the bogus claim that he felt restricted during his visits to him—of which there have been ten in ten years. He was not restricted, but even if he *had* been, surely this would not have stopped him if he had any real desire to see his father.

Nor is the motive that you give for your own letter consistent, convincing, or ingenuous. . . . In short, I do not believe in this sudden concern about your father's "business affairs" and in the sudden "family feeling" about the fate of the manuscripts. This comes suspiciously late in the day.

Moreover, his affairs and well-being are inseparable from mine; and as I have received no help from his family in the past three years, I feel fully able to continue with my responsibilities alone. Forgive me if in fact I think that this anxiety about the sale of the manuscripts has less to do with your father's welfare than with your own financial future. After all, you did not even ask about his health.

Theodore answered the last criticism, saying that he considered it inappropriate to mention health in a business letter—though he had not sent *any* letters in five months. On February 10, 1971, Mrs. Stravinsky, again with Mr. Weissberger's and my help, wrote to Theodore for the last time. Again, the following is a draft:

First, a misunderstanding. I did not deny your request to see your father in New York Hospital in May 1969. The decision was that of his doctors, who wished to avoid any visit likely to upset him. So sensitive and suspicious a man as your father would have been quick to see a morbid significance in your presence, especially since your brother had just been at his bedside. I hardly need to add that if those visits had not been so rare, the danger of a sinister interpretation being placed on your sudden appearance would have been less likely.[95]

95. Mr. Garbus asked Mrs. Marion to describe the substance of Petitioner's Exhibit 50, and she answered, "The substance is Robert Craft being very worried because my father was very, very bad in the [Mt. Sinai] hospital [November 1967]. . . . Late in the evening Robert Craft and Vera came into our home after visiting *Père* in the hospital."

MR. GARBUS: When was this?
MRS. MARION: In October [*sic*] 1967.
MR. GARBUS: When you say "Bob was worried," do you recall what he said?
MRS. MARION: He said "it looks very bad. This is the end." And then he said, pointing to Vera: "She doesn't realize it."
MR. GARBUS: Do you know if Soulima came to visit [Stravinsky] when he was in the hospital at that time?
MRS. MARION: I don't know.

Second, though no expert on the matter, I am inclined to agree that the state of health of a man of eighty-eight is probably "irreversible." But your father is an exception. His polycythemia has given up on him after a fifteen-year siege, and no sign of an occlusion has been detected in nine months. His only medical ordeals during the past six months were a bone-marrow aspiration, performed on September 11, and, last week, the extraction of two teeth, which he bore extremely well.

I am sure you will agree, on reflection, that the question of your father's awareness or nonawareness of the geography of Evian is trivial. After all, he did not know the town from the past and was transported there directly from a New York hotel room, seeing nothing familiar on the way. To me, it seems natural that the hospital ordeals of May 1969 and April 1970 would disorient him. Yet he has a clear sense of his actuality here in New York. And I know that you will be pleased and grateful to learn that, in order to spare your father any disturbing new adjustment, we have reconstructed his Hollywood studio in the new apartment.

But whether you agree or not, I shall continue to take care of your father, just as I have done these last years (with no help from his children). I have already cut our expenses, above all the astronomical fees that analysis of our books shows he had been paying our former lawyer, Mr. Montapert, and our former business manager, Mr. Marion.

From this time forth, the only communications between Stravinsky's children and their stepmother were a cable from Theodore in August 1971 expressing shock at the death of his cousin Ira Belline,[96] and an announcement of the marriage (August 1978) of Kitty to Michel Yelachich.

MR. GARBUS: Do you know if Theodore came to visit him in the hospital at that time?

MRS. MARION: No.

96. Denise Stravinsky wrote to Françoise Stravinsky: "We could be the ones to bring Ira's things to divide. . . . As far as Ira's account in Geneva is con-

. . .

To most people, Stravinsky's death (April 6, 1971) was probably not unexpected. He was nearly eighty-nine, and his many illnesses since the major stroke that he suffered in Berlin in 1956 had been publicized. Yet the death was a great shock to Mrs. Stravinsky for the very reason that her husband had been ill so often and had always recovered, often against strong odds. At the funeral service in New York she stood on one side of the aisle, the children on the other, and no meeting took place. During the service in Venice, Nicolas Nabokov stood between her and the children, and, in San Michele, he escorted her, at the head of the procession, to the grave— after an awkward fifteen-minute delay in the tiny dock area, during which eyes were averted and no one spoke.

The will was probated in New York in June 1971, and soon after, Mrs. Stravinsky returned to Venice, to be near her husband's grave. But the city oppressed her, and she went to Biarritz until mid-August. While there, she learned from Weissberger that the Marions and Soulima Stravinskys had retained a Chicago lawyer, Milton Fisher, and Theodore a New York lawyer, Francis Wendell, for the purpose of challenging Weissberger's accounting, her ownership of the *Sacre* score, and the inventory of Stravinsky's possessions at the time of his death—three issues that were to constitute the basis of the lawsuit that the children brought against Vera Stravinsky three years later. They contended that everything Stravinsky had acquired before—and nearly everything after —his second marriage belonged not to his widow, but to them. A legal ruling on this was temporarily withheld.

In December 1973, Mrs. Stravinsky sold the *Sacre* manuscript for $220,000, a high price, considering that Ralph Hawkes had failed to find a buyer for it at $12,500 in 1950,

---

cerned, it has not yet been released. . . ." Ira had nothing but contempt for Stravinsky's children, except Lyudmila, and the only member of the Stravinsky family to whom she would have wanted any of her "things" to go was Vera.

and that other *Sacre* scores and sketches exist. Yet the children accused her of accepting a sum beneath the market value.[97] (On February 19, 1970, all of the hundred or so manuscripts together had been assessed by Sigmund Rothschild at $200,000.)

Virtually nothing happened in the case until December 18, 1974, when a deposition was taken from Weissberger. In March 1975, depositions were taken from Vera Stravinsky by Kunin, a man remarkably prone to forget his own questions, as well as wholly unable to communicate with Mrs. Stravinsky (see note 7 above). Had Mrs. Stalvey been her secretary, he asked, and she answered "Yes." Had Mrs. Stalvey been her personal secretary, Kunin went on, and she answered "No," by which she simply meant that her husband and others had also benefited from Mrs. Stalvey's services; yet the record reads as if Mrs. Stravinsky had contradicted herself.

My own depositions were equally unproductive, the first one being spent almost entirely in answering questions about works of art in the Stravinsky home. My attorney, Mr. Garbus, is a trial lawyer, expert at keeping his clients from speaking at all.[98]

As the years went by, countless settlement proposals were drawn up, modified, and rejected. Lawyers' bills mounted, "the children" entered their seventies, and by 1983 Arnold Weissberger, Vera Stravinsky, and Andre Marion had died. On December 18, 1975, Boosey & Hawkes informed Theodore that they would be obliged to suspend work on the

97. When Higginson asked Albi Rosenthal how he had determined a price for the *Sacre*, the answer was: "I took into consideration the sale I made to the Pierpont Morgan Library of the autograph manuscript of Schoenberg's . . . *Moses und Aron*, which was $100,000. I took into consideration the sale of Schubert's . . . *Winterreise*, which was at that time the highest price ever paid for a manuscript. . . . [Also] there was a sale of a Brahms symphony [No. 2] for $75,000. . . ." (July 10, 1978)

98. Higginson's next affidavit asserts (Para. 39) that Garbus had made a "mockery" out of my deposition. Garbus responded that "the deposition of Robert Craft was being conducted by a representative of a Chicago law firm not familiar with New York practice, and, it appeared, not familiar with trial practice." (November 1978)

publication of the archives, since "rising production costs and slackening demand made a project of [this] dimension . . . impossible for anyone other than a richly endowed university." Ampenoff had maintained that the Stravinsky-Ansermet correspondence was ready for publication, but Ansermet's Lausanne lawyer, J.-Claude Piguet, wrote that permission had never been given to publish his client's writings. Moreover, Mrs. Stravinsky vetoed the project on the grounds that, as the first volume of a series, the letters present Ansermet as more important in Stravinsky's life than can be justly asserted, that Ansermet's letters greatly outnumber, and are much longer than, Stravinsky's, and that Stravinsky himself would not have wanted to be coupled with the conductor this way, especially in view of the hostility between them since 1937.

The litigation was brought to a deadlock on November 14, 1977, when Soulima filed a petition in a French court claiming all of his father's royalties from French-speaking countries. A law of July 14, 1819 (Article 2), was cited in support. This "establishes a privilege on account of nationality and derogates from the application of foreign law." In short, the provisions of a will filed in New York State in 1969 counted for little. An injunction, *pendente lite*, freezing the French earnings was entered, and French counsel advised that, however ridiculous the antiquated French law, American law was powerless against it.

Soulima's action provided Garbus with a new weapon, however. Soulima had violated Clause Ninth (K) of his father's will, specifying that anyone who attempted to block any assets that were to go to his wife on his death would be automatically disinherited. The *in terrorem* clause, Article Eleventh, disinheriting Soulima everywhere except in France, could now be invoked, and since the other children would obviously claim a share in Soulima's French royalties[99]

99. On October 13, 1978, Garbus had sworn and deposed for the New York Surrogate Court that "in September 1978, Helene Kaplan, my co-counsel, and

—1 million francs had accumulated at the time of the settlement, and the annual French income was approximately $200,000—Garbus determined to prove that "all of the Respondents would share the funds." This was self-evident, but Garbus was dissuaded from following this course because (a) after six years of largely simulated litigation, the legal fees were already in the millions of dollars; (b) two or three of the Respondents would probably be dead before the case could be decided in the higher courts; and (c) Vera Stravinsky went to court herself in August 1979, prepared to testify, but returned home and instructed Garbus to settle, so horrified was she by the rudeness, vulgarity, and ignorance of lawyers scarcely able to identify the name Igor Stravinsky.

I met with James Higginson. . . . I asked Mr. Higginson . . . whether, irrespective of any settlement, the four respondents had agreed to share in the proceeds of the French proceeding. Mr. Higginson said that all of the respondents would share equally . . . in the French proceedings."

Excerpts from a Diary

1977–1983

*J*uly *12, 1977.* Venice. To San Michele. Loose bricks and stone, cracked walls, eroded *intonaco* facings are more apparent than ever, but restorers are at work at the Zanipolo, and the dome, boxed in wicker scaffolding, looks as if it were being wrapped for shipment. A paludal odor, from the coagulation of refuse in the lagoon, permeates the cemetery island, and the gravel paths have never seemed longer. No trace remains of the "N.A.P.," daubed in red paint on Stravinsky's grave two years ago (August 6, 1975), but the cleaning has dulled the luster of the lapis lazuli. For some reason, too, the letters seem more cramped and in need of the bullet that separates the first and last names; I wonder if Manzù added it because, as we do now, he sensed a miscalculation in the spacing. A newly occupied neighboring plot is marked by a pompous monument framing a passport-like photo of the deceased, as if to identify him at the Resurrection. At Diaghilev's tomb, a toe shoe has been placed beneath the cupola, like an offering on an altar, but this slipper, waterlogged and moldy, seems to symbolize the death of the dance rather than its continuing life.

July 27. Glyndebourne. The performance of *The Rake's Progress* here is dominated, stunningly, by David Hockney's sets and costumes, a rare instance of the decorative dimension determining the perspectives of an opera audience. Hockney has replaced the curtain with a drop that suggests an illustration in a book of nursery rhymes: a man is depicted standing upright, as well as in eight successive positions, falling clockwise and ending upside down. This picture also serves as a program, giving the names of Hogarth, Stravinsky, Auden and Kallman, John Cox, and Hockney. The remaining space is filled with doodles, squares, numbers, a tic-tac-toe board, engravers' lines, a misspelled word and its correction. Clearly Hockney enjoyed himself with his ruler, and his amusement is infectious.

But the drop also frames the individual scenes, and, lowered between them, it clashes with the developing mood. These interruptions are the most serious fault of the performance, for the chatter of the Sussex squirearchy quickly permeates the theatre, and such beautiful transitions as the one from string chords to woodwind trio are covered. At the end of Scene 1, following Shadow's "The Progress of the Rake Begins," *nothing* does for several minutes, during which latecomers are seated.

The principal difference between Cox's staging and that of Ingmar Bergman derives from the Swedish director's distinction that "between an artistic moralist, Hogarth, and a religious moralist, Stravinsky, there is a heaven's distance."[1] Accordingly, Bergman emphasized the supernatural and diabolical, and his Nick Shadow was present even when the libretto neither required nor warranted him to be. Bergman's Sellem resembled a pastor, too, and the crowd at the auction his congregation. The graveyard scene, with three looming shapes gradually emerging as spires, was the most powerful in Bergman's production, whereas the scene at

1. *New York Times,* May 7, 1961.

Glyndebourne is weak, or, at any rate, not the climax that it should be, and the limited histrionic abilities of the singers are only partly to blame. The underlying reason why Shadow's descent into hell fails to strike terror here is that he is not the real devil but only a storybook likeness.

The Glyndebourne stage is shallow, the scale small, the performance intimate. The composer would have been pleased with these proportions, as well as with the limpid singing of the Anne (Felicity Lott), and the even tone, distinct articulation, and absence of heroics in the Rake, especially in his final scene. Bergman, at the other extreme, finding even the large stage of Stockholm's Royal Opera House too small, opened up the wings and the back and extended the apron over the orchestra pit. The effects obtained by this increased depth were both cinematographic and skiagraphic, the actors being momentarily frozen in silhouette before dissolving into darkness.

The Glyndebourne performance follows the two-act division[2] employed by Bergman. The dramatic line is stronger and the apportioning of the music more balanced when the first half of the opera concludes with the unveiling of Tom's wife, Baba, who, at Glyndebourne, has a patriarchal beard and a Mona Lisa (Duchamp's) mustache. (Was Auden aware that "Baba" is a man's name?) At Glyndebourne, moreover, Shadow holds up the broadsheet of Baba for the audience as well as the Rake to see, after which the Rake fixes the picture to the wall. Auden would have objected to this, insisting that the revelation be saved until a moment before the curtain, but Stravinsky feared an emotionally ambiguous response if the audience were not already "in" on the secret.

From time to time the horizontality of Hockney's engraving motif threatens to disorient the viewer, but the idea is

2. The British television film of the Glyndebourne production observes the three-act form of the score.

always imaginatively introduced—in striped stockings, for example—and the black and white lines enhance the colors. Thus Sellem's green jacket and red vest are all the more vivid because the bidders wear black and their faces are whitened, eerily, with greasepaint. No less memorable is Mother Goose's scarlet wig; but, then, the whole of the brothel scene is superbly staged, with Mother Goose, a brief vocal part but an important dramatic role, receiving long-overdue prominence. During the catechism she is virtually alone with Rakewell and Shadow, most of the whores and their clients having retired to cubicles, which helps the audience to focus on the opera's classroom philosophy. She claims Rakewell for her prize while enthroned on a vast, center-stage bed, then strips and lies on top of him, consummating the unholy rites of love in, so to speak, full view.

A feature of the production is the smooth modulation of moods between the Rake's death and the Epilogue, achieved by the simple expedient of not allowing him to complete his dying. As he approaches his straw pallet, and final moment, the drop starts to descend. Then, as it reaches his head, he turns to the audience and walks to the footlights, where the others in the Epilogue ensemble join him from the wings, the drop falling behind them. The pause between the death march and the fast-tempo, moral-drawing quintet is perfectly timed, the audience is not jolted, and the music is not mixed with tentative applause. In addition, the Epilogue is acted, turned into a playlet, the singers bowing to each other as well as to the spectators, and a finale that sometimes seems too long is exactly right.

The Glyndebourne Bedlam scene lacks movement, the Minuet demanding dance, the chorus "Tread softly round his bier" a procession, the Lullaby a change in the position of Rakewell's fellow Bedlamites at each verse. But Hockney has provided brilliant compensations, making the madmen look like fantasy creatures in Bosch and isolating each inmate in a witness box, or cell.

March 4, 1978. London. In contrast to filthy, snowbound New York, still with yeti tracks in Central Park, the grass at Park Lane is green, with purple and yellow crocuses. We go to the *Cherry Orchard*, Peter Hall's well-paced, never-overstated performance—at least in comparison with the recent one in the Vivian Beaumont theatricum anatomicum. Michael Frayn's translation is sprinkled with peculiar words —"litanies," for example, used to describe the singing of peasants at work—which Mrs. Stravinsky writes down, promising to look up Chekhov's originals. The staging is realistic, with the clip-clop of horses, a backdrop of telephone poles leading to a mountain, and Firs (Ralph Richardson) lying down at the end as if he actually were dying. Why, then, is the orchard never suggested visually, since this would be the best way of indicating the change of seasons?

March 5. The magazine of today's *Sunday Telegraph* contains a three-page article about the forthcoming show of paintings by V.A.S., "The Moon Goddess Who Lived History." The director of her London gallery is quoted: "On the very day Madame first called to discuss her exhibition it so happened that Prokofiev also came by with his portfolio." But since Prokofiev died a quarter of a century ago, the reader must conclude either that the arrangements for Madame Stravinsky's exhibition were fixed an unusually long time in advance, or that the Prokofiev in question was not the composer. (It was actually his son, Oleg, who is not mentioned.) The article also fumbles her anecdote about an encounter with swashbucklers on the Black Sea, saying that the ship on which she fled from Baku to Marseille in 1920 "was overrun by Turkish brigands. 'They spoke Russian like Stalin,' Madame recalls." But obviously these cutthroats, like their infamous successor, were Georgians, not Turks.

A more serious misquotation, from another interview, has landed on the front page of the *Guardian* and provoked an international *retentissement,* as we learn from calls to New

York and the Continent. What V.A.S. actually said was that she had burned Stravinsky's love letters at his request before she came to America in 1940. What she is reported to have said is that she intends to burn these letters on returning to America. Messages arrive from everywhere, many of them drawing an analogy between V.A.S. and Clara Schumann, who actually did destroy some of her husband's last compositions as well as correspondence.

June 6, 1979. Paris. The principal novelties in the Bibliothèque Nationale's Diaghilev exhibition are from French sources—"The French Diaghilev" would have been a suitable subtitle for the show—and the displays for *La Chatte* and *Le Dieu bleu,* for example, are larger than they would have been in London or New York. Moreover, Cocteau dominates the scene—ironically, in view of Diaghilev's attitude toward him as an outsider. Cocteau's posters of Karsavina and Nijinsky in *Le Spectre de la rose* fill the walls of the foyer, and a large proportion of the exhibits in the main room are enhanced by those well-known caricatures of the dancers and balletomanes, of the composers and painters, of Diaghilev and his entourage, and of backstage life with the Ballets Russes. Here is the self-portrait in which, by showing his shirtsleeves as too short, Cocteau attempts to make himself look like a gangling youth, and his cartoon of Misia, *chapeau à aigrette,* in her loge with Diaghilev, exclaiming: *"Mais non, Serge, Fokine n'est pas épuisé."*

The most stunning picture is Picasso's 1917 green-ink portrait of Diaghilev, Bakst, and Massine, the most attractive costume design Roerich's delicately colored one (pencil, pen, gouache) for the "third young girl" in Part Two of the *Sacre.* The major pictorial disappointments are Benois's academic sets for *The Nightingale* and *Le Médecin malgré lui,* yet one of the former is reproduced in color in the catalogue, in company with a banal Derain, a Bakst, and an undistinguished Larionov and, ditto, Goncharova.

The *Mavra* artifacts revive V.A.S.'s memories of the private audition of the piece at the Hôtel Continental, which her husband Sudeikin forbade her to attend, thereby precipitating the argument that ended in their permanent separation. (A description of Stravinsky assisted at the piano that night by Nicolas Kopeikin evokes memories in me, as well, Kopeikin having helped me with *Mavra* when I presented it in New York thirty years later.)

For musicians, the highlights of the exhibition are the Satie manuscripts and letters, and the showcases for *Les Biches.*

Photographs are a feature of the show, yet the best of them, such as the 1907 portrait of Rimsky-Korsakov and Saint-Saëns in a gathering of Russian musicians in the Salle Pleyel, are not reproduced in the catalogue, where the space is reserved largely for the familiar. On the credit side, the compilers of the catalogue have attempted to identify the artists who executed the costumes and designs, and not only the names of the designers.

June 7. The Galerie André Pacitti, rue du Faubourg St.-Honoré. About 125 people come to V.A.S.'s *vernissage,* among them members of the Soviet embassy and Boris Kochno, who, like V.A.S., is obviously very pleased to be kissing and making up. Fifty-eight years ago she introduced him to Diaghilev, but, since the latter's death, only one meeting has occurred, in 1951, in Venice, and this involved a shock of nonrecognition. She promises to send a photocopy of Kuzmin's *Kusaja,* which the author inscribed in her album. Lifar comes, too, and Plisetskaya telephones, making the occasion a feast of Russian-speaking. But the Americans buy the pictures.

June 16. Venice. Our last day, and a rainy one. Nevertheless, we walk to the Ponte dei Barretteri (hatters) and to a chandelier shop specializing in glass that looks as if it were wrapped in cellophane.

After several calls from London, each one cut off several times (*"Pronto? Pronto?"*), and some activity in the "corridors of power" there, BEA bounces two passengers from its 6:00 p.m. flight and gives their places to us, the imperative being V.A.S.'s presence at Covent Garden for Monday's gala of *The Rake's Progress*. After a long wait at the airport, we take off in thunder and rain (in rivulets on the airplane window), arriving after midnight at a surprisingly dry Heathrow.

June 18. London. The Covent Garden *Rake* is the best musical presentation that I have heard, thanks to a superb cast and to Colin Davis's conducting. The latter, however, will be criticized as being too expansive and romantic, and his interpretation compared unfavorably with the composer's, even though *this* reflects more about recording conditions (all of the choral pieces taped at one session, all of the recitatives at another, etc.) than about his intentions concerning the performance of the opera.

The principal achievement of Elijah Moshinsky's staging is in the high histrionic quality that the singers attain, the more so in that they are required to perform half-in, half-out of the play. Whether or not he is the first director to notice the similarity between the Rake's philosophy and that of Auden —the program misquotes the essential line, "Have not grave doctors assured us that good works are of avail?" (which should be "of *no* avail")—Moshinsky succeeds remarkably well in projecting the poet's conceits and paradoxes. Indeed, the young director almost manages to neutralize the perversity in the Rake's decision to marry Baba, simply by presenting the matter as a game, "freedom from conscience and freedom from appetite." Baba is dramatically more credible than ever before.

Moshinsky displays a bright imagination in every scene. In

the brothel, for instance, Tom addresses his aria not to the night and the empty space, but to Mother Goose, which focuses the music and provides a dimension that she usually lacks. Yet the scene is almost too turbulent, and the audience becomes apprehensive that people feigning to fall out of balconies might actually do so. The drop curtain for the stage within the stage, a replica of Poussin's *Realm of Flora*, is lowered between the Act I, Scene 3 arias, creating a helpful division—even, in retrospect, a necessary one—but the painting itself is too imposing, and it adds to the confusion in our sense of period, which is not that of Hogarth's engravings (1732), but Georgian. Did Georgian "gentlemen of fashion" smoke cigarettes, as the Rake does here, and would shoppers of the time exclaim, "We've never been through such a hectic day"? Whatever the answer, this *New Yorker* language convinces me that the only feasible temporal transposition of the opera would be to the period of the music, which, despite all the hints of Handel, Mozart, Donizetti, et al., is modern and of the time of the composition. That Auden was concerned about anachronisms—and replaced two of them, pointed out to him by T. S. Eliot—does not matter. "Neoclassicism," Eliot wrote, "is valid so long as the artist always shows an awareness of his own chronological place."

A small diversion brightens the orchestral coda to the duet, Act II, Scene 1, when the Rake and his Shadow break into a music-hall top-hat-and-cane dance routine, a touch of horseplay that would have won Stravinsky's applause. But in this production the act ends with the bread machine—a major error, albeit in accordance with the score and the dramatic time-scale; the feeling of anticlimax is evident from the dim applause and vacant seats at the beginning of Act III.

The main defects in the second and third scenes of Act III are that the harpsichord requires amplification during the card game and that the Bedlamites, moving in a circle like Van Gogh's prisoners, are distracting. Furthermore, the lullaby is paced too slowly, and the pause before Adonis calls to his courtiers is excessive. But the "Sotheby" scene is flawless, making us regret that the auctioneer does not have a part in the Epilogue, and the most astonishing event of the evening occurs here: Baba removes her wedding ring and flings it into the audience, and the thin gold band lands in the lap of . . . Vera Stravinsky. Perhaps it was directed there by the composer himself, on this, his birthday, for the "Baba" did not know where V.A.S. was sitting, and, in any case, could not in a thousand conscious attempts have hit such a target.

I am haunted all night by the memory of Stravinsky singing Rakewell's first graveyard aria and admitting that his inspiration was, of all remote associations, *La Traviata:*

August 24, 1981. London. 12:30 a.m. To Paddington Station, where an all-night Fotomat regurgitates a wanted-dead-or-alive view of me for my Soviet visa. Mr. Cattermole, the clerk, and the station itself—deserted except for memories of a trip with the Stravinskys to Lyme Regis in August 1957—could be raw material for a scene in a Graham Greene novel.

August 28. 8:00 a.m. To Heathrow, with Tony Palmer and his London Weekend Television team, on our way to film the principal Russian locations in Stravinsky's life; to record some of his music performed by Russian orchestras and choruses (singing sacred music!), and to interview on camera a few people who were involved with him or his work. These include Tatiana Rimsky-Korsakov, the granddaughter of his teacher; A. A. Yacovlev, the widower of his niece Xenia and now the custodian of the family archives in Leningrad; and M. S. Druskin, who had known Stravinsky in Berlin in 1931 and who published a monograph on him in 1974.

Part of the feelings of isolation and apprehension at

Shermet'yevo Airport must be attributable to the disproportionately small number of planes for so great a world capital.
Inside the terminal, soldiers check our identities while we
wait behind a gate that locks after each admission. All other
personnel—customs officials, collectors of currency declarations, ticket agents—are women. In the absence of porters, we
drag our baggage and the heavy film equipment to the Philips X-ray machines at the inspection counters. (Why is the
"Philips" so prominently displayed, since this hardly testifies
to the USSR's technological self-sufficiency?)

Inside the customs area, we are met by our official government shepherd, Pavel Kurchagin, soft-spoken, about thirty-
five, wearing a brown leather jacket and (like most Russians)
blue jeans. He is friendly, withdrawn, good-natured about
our complaints, and, I think, more wary of me (has he read
my 1962 Russian diary?) than of the British crew. His boss,
Soviet Minister of Culture Kuharsky, has been astonishingly
cooperative from the planning stage, to the extent of producing Russian footage of Ustilug, which is on the Polish border
and out-of-bounds to us, but vital to the film, Stravinsky having written much of *Le Sacre du printemps* and *The Nightingale* there.

Even considering that it is nineteen years since I traveled
the highway from the airport to the center of Moscow, the
increase in traffic is scarcely believable. Another surprise is
that English is found under Russian on road signs and advertisements, though not under the quotations from Brezhnev
on billboards and overhead passes. The Kremlin seems less
awesome than on my last trip, perhaps because a coat of
bright yellow paint makes it look too new.

The airport for the flight to Kharkov is filthy and mal-
odorous, and the waiting room is crowded with Cameroons
asleep on every bench and over most of the floor. Our plane
reeks of unwashed bodies; nor does the smell dissipate after
takeoff. A stewardess with the build of an Olympics weight-
lifter brings trays of a soft drink, standing by until it is

gulped and she can collect the empties. The "emergency exit" and "no smoking" signs are in English as well as Russian.

Kharkov. 11:45 p.m. Rain. 50 degrees Fahrenheit. We stow our gear and ourselves—ten of us, counting Pavel, the driver, and his guide—into a bus that is decrepit and too small. No one having eaten for twelve hours, I propose that we spend the night here but am overruled, our hotel in Mirgorod supposedly being no more than a two-hour drive away. But with half a ton of cameras, sound equipment, tripods, etc., the bus can barely make the hills, and its maximum speed is only 20 kilometers an hour. The seats are not cushioned, moreover, and the road is a mere topping over dirt. Near Poltava the driver stops, examines the motor, shrugs his shoulders; but we go on through steady rain and, on the treeless stretches, opaque fog. To judge from the picture-language road signs (beds and red crosses) indicating directions to hospitals, as well as from a near-collision of our own and the examples of three on-target ones by others, accidents are by no means infrequent.

Between Poltava and Mirgorod, beginning about 4:00 a.m., people emerge on the sides of the road with suitcases, fardels, baskets, sacks, live geese and turkeys slung in shoulder nets, pails of fish, watermelons, and trussed lambs. Like ourselves, they are going to the fair at Sorochinsk, but they remind me of war refugees in old newsreels. Although at 5:30 a.m. the Mirgorod Hotel is dark, we manage to rouse a young woman (stainless-steel teeth) and a short, fat, and bulbous-nosed old man with the first smiling face I have seen in the Soviet Union. They give us keys for our third-floor rooms, which are small, as cells go, but which have bathrooms of a sort and television. The elevator is nonfunctional, so we must carry our bags. Since breakfast is in two hours and the bus for Sorochinsk—a large one—departs soon thereafter, I go to bed in my clothes and overcoat, just as a cock crows under my window.

August 29. A statue of Gogol marks the turnoff to the fair, where the road abruptly worsens with bulges, craters, and ruts. The country must have looked like this in Gogol's day: wooden cottages with picket fences; windmills; poplar, willow, and chestnut trees; walled cemeteries with ornate crosses. On the roadside the peasants are dressed entirely in black—suits, blouses, skirts, sheepskin caps, kerchiefs, and boots—but at the fair all clothing is in bright colors. Here, as at the airports, the proportion of men in uniform is noticeably high.

Three days of flooding rains have turned the fairgrounds into a vast sty of black mud. This is no obstacle for the booted Russians, but I slip and slide in my thin shoes like a neophyte on a skating rink. Despite the cold, I decide to proceed barefoot, which must be like walking in chocolate ice cream. Duckboards are nonexistent, and the few patches of higher, grassy ground are already occupied. At one place a tractor is being used to raise a car sunk up to its hood.

Itinerant bands of fiddlers, reed-pipers, and accordionists attract dancers from among the onlookers, but except for a grunt produced by rubbing a piece of wood on the drumhead of a tambourine (an effect that Stravinsky used to demonstrate for percussion players), the music is of little interest. More Stravinskyan are the female choruses, in one of which a high soprano wails above a chantlike rhythm in the other voices, recalling *Les Noces.* Many of the songs begin with solo voices or duets, followed by choral responses. A melodic pattern stressing the leading tone, a feature of Stravinsky's music of all periods, is also very evident. But today the suction noises of feet being lifted from the ooze would have delighted him most. A tango blares out, overamplified, and I marvel that any indigenous music has survived the media uncorrupted.

One booth displays a goblin, à la *Petrushka*. On raised platforms, some elderly women demonstrate old-fashioned wheat threshing done by hand, and cloth weaving on treadle looms. Lacquered bowls and spoons are for sale, and pottery made uglier by glazing. The swings and the pole to be shinnied up (and slid down, into a pile of sawdust) are the same as at an American fair, and so is the flavorsome watermelon: no wonder Stravinsky craved it.

After four hours of slithering and sliding, of providing a landing pad for small, light-green frogs, of holding a heavy box of film aloft, I return to the bus with the "London Weekend Television" placard in the window, there to wait for the mire to dry on my feet (in the mistaken expectation of then being able to remove it, like plaster of Paris). Back in Mirgorod, I buy shoes in a grim department store to which I have to walk in my bedroom slippers, thereby attracting looks of disapproval. Luckily, I find a pair of shoes that fit, but unluckily they are ten times heavier than my ruined ones and have plastic soles so thick that I feel as if I am wearing cothurni. The cashier shifts some beads on her abacus and charges me 15 rubles and 80 kopecks (about twenty dollars).

In the hotel restaurant we eat caviar on brown bread, rice, and a tomato salad. Since vodka, tea, and the sugary Russian champagne are served at room temperature, we ask for ice but are told that it cannot be made in less than three hours. While waiting for dinner, Pavel talks about John le Carré and says that his and other Cold War spy stories, though samizdat, are popular in the USSR. Despite Pavel's use of the word "defector," he claims not to have heard of Brodsky, Rostropovich, or even Nureyev, and when asked about Mandelstam, or the work of any of the other writers under a political penumbra, Pavel says: "I have not read it because every new edition is sold out on publication." He clearly believes me to be a CIA mole.

In bed: visions of farmhouses with wood-lace window frames; of geese waddling on grass; of horses with surcingles drawing low carts; of the face of an old man with Taras

Bulba mustache, of Uzbeks with white-beaded hats. What I do *not* feel is any *nostalgie de la boue* (not in Emile Augier's original sense of the term, of course).

August 30. Mirgorod to Kharkov. By daylight, we see that the houses have asbestos shingles, which must be very noisy in the rain. The cornfields, sunflowers, and loam remind me of the American Midwest, as do the police cars with revolving lights, and the size of a queue at a gas station—the only one between Poltava and Kharkov. But the Ukraine is less flat, and the fields are bounded by forests, the road, at times, by walls of trees. The oddest roadside features are the large concrete public lavatories every few miles—in *this* countryside?

We do not see a single grain elevator, or silo, or any machinery—or even any farmers—but only three old women, each one tending a single cow on a rope. In two fields the corn and wheat crops have been harvested, but all the others are rotting, and the apples in the endless orchards have already fallen to the ground. What has happened to the pre-1917 "largest grain exporter in the world"? Our economists write about the "periodic crop failure," but the failure in front of our eyes is that of not reaping.

At least the Intourist Hotel in Kharkov—on Lenin Avenue, a few blocks from Gagarin Avenue—*has* an elevator, but its double doors open in and out so awkwardly that we prefer the stairs; and while the bathrooms are inevitably an improvement on Mirgorod, the showers seem to have been designed for pygmies. The restaurant is a hot, foul-smelling room with disco din and dance floor crowded with girls in tight jeans and Western hairstyles doing the twist. About half of the customers are Africans wearing long robes and crownlike hats.

In bed tonight, I puzzle about the contrast between Stravinsky's hyperacute time-sense—the split-second calculations in his manuscripts, his stopwatches and electric metronomes, his impatience with unpunctuality—and the indifference to the clock of his fellow countrymen today, when nothing occurs at the appointed hour, no one appears as scheduled, and every estimate by Pavel and our drivers is eons off. But then, Pavel is always conducting behind-the-scenes operations, disappearing to make telephone calls to higher-ups, which explains many of the delays and all of the oscillations as to whether appointments will actually take place.

August 31. Kharkov. At breakfast in the hotel restaurant, Brian, our sound technician, says that the woodwork is really a laminated plastic on chipboard that would burn in a few seconds. He alone of the crew withholds no gripe. Nic, our imperturbable cameraman, spends his nonfilming time reading *Lord of the Rings.* Max, his assistant, keeps a tiny phial containing a "stress remedy" so strong that a single drop is reputedly able to pull him back from the brink when he feels about to go into shock. As for Tony Palmer, he thinks and adapts quickly and works even harder than his coolies, editing transcripts of interviews on buses and airplanes, and persisting hour after hour for "yet another piece of the mosaic."

At the airport, we go to a dirty, fly-infested snack bar, in which most of the customers are drinking glasses of sour cream. The adjoining room is a barber shop where a line of small boys and their mothers stretches from the door. "Look at us Russians, we are always waiting," a character in Turgenev remarks; but Russians wait less patiently in airports, and in fact scramble and shove on board the buses and climb the steps into the planes. During our flight to Riga the fortissimo Russian Muzak never lets up. Since the wings are without flaps, the takeoff and landing are bumpy and abrupt, like flying thirty years ago.

Two women meet us at the cold and rainy Riga airport, speaking Lettish between themselves, Russian with Pavel, and English with us. The wooden houses on the outskirts of the town, all with fences and windowsill flowers, are dark reds, blues, and greens. The stone buildings in the center are

Gothic, or, as in the case of the Latvian Theatre, nineteenth-century neoclassical. The city is livelier and the people are better dressed than in any other Russian province we have seen.

Our Hilton-style rooms have practical bed lamps, impractical telephones (a foreign call must be ordered three weeks in advance), large-screen television, notices over the lavatory, wash basin, and bath saying "disinfected." Best of all, the hotel's six elevators are working. In the lobby, the only clue that we are east of NATO is that the kiosk is limited to Soviet-bloc newspapers.

Another innovation is the hard-currency bar, where the money of almost any country except the USSR can buy any brand of hard liquor. As if in further imitation of the United States, the room is over-air-conditioned; and, possibly expressing a criticism of American customs, the bartender asks me: "Would you like too much ice, sir?" From the twenty-sixth floor, where we dine, the streets immediately below form a neon city, including electrically moving Times Square–type signs.

September 1. This morning we film the Latvian Choir in the organ loft of the thirteenth-century Domsky Sobor—a remarkably inappropriate name for this pure Gothic building, with its coats of arms of the Teutonic knights defeated by Alexander Nevsky, its quotations from scripture in German, and its Baroque organ. The German-speaking curator talks to me about her son in Seattle, and she claims that while Riga's Orthodox and Protestant churches have been closed, its Catholic ones are open. Not this one, though, and is a cathedral stripped of its altar a church?

Most of the Dzintars Choir, a bevy of eighty-five braided blondes in Philharmonic Hall, wear headbands like the Adolescents in *Le Sacre du printemps*, and their performance of Stravinsky's *Podbludniye* (*The Saucers*) is the most spirited I have ever heard. During the recording I am interviewed simultaneously by a reporter from Tass and the editor of a newspaper for Latvian refugees abroad. After the session, the choir presents me with a large bouquet of freshly cut flowers. When the director says that he heard me conduct in Leningrad in 1962, I feel ancient indeed.

September 2. 6:00 a.m. Riga to Leningrad. The waiting room in the Riga airport is less dreary than the others—that is, until I begin to read *The Great October Revolution and Mankind's Progress* by L. I. Brezhnev, described as a booklet for "progressive tourists." In Leningrad we are met by an additional guide, Igor Bogdanov, Tass correspondent.

The disparity between the grandeur of St. Petersburg's buildings, parks, and perspectives and the drab and dour-looking inhabitants makes me think of Kierkegaard: "A revolutionary age which is at the same time reflective leaves everything standing but cunningly empties it of significance." In contrast to the deserted walks by the Hermitage and the Admiralty, the lobby of the Astoria Hotel is overpopulated with tourists. Here, porters take our bags to rooms that are spacious, with beds in curtained-off alcoves, and well furnished, except that the refrigerators are purely ornamental (no *elektrichestvo?*).

In the Necropolis of the Great Masters, we film the tombs of Dostoevsky, Mussorgsky, Rimsky-Korsakov (why the elaborately carved Gaelic church stone for an atheist?), Borodin (themes from the Second Symphony and Polovtsian Dances in gold mosaic), and Tchaikovsky (a tortured expression, no doubt aggravated by two female angels, one behind him with a cross, one in front with a book). The monument to Stravinsky's father is superior as sculpture and in better taste than any of the others. Across a canal in the pink, white, and gold Alexander Nevsky Monastery stands some of the finest architecture in the city, as well as, in gates and fences, some beautiful filigreed ironwork. In the brilliant sunlight, we photograph the reflection of a gilded dome in the canal. In contrast to the hordes of sightseers at the graves of the masters, the inner cemetery of the monastery, where children's tombs are shaped like cradles, is deserted. Everywhere pigeons are sunning themselves on the walks and perching on ledges.

In the Astoria's restaurant, a huge and resonant room, a rock band blasts out "Bei mir bist du schön" six times during a "dinner" that takes three hours to order and receive. Though the menu is several pages long, nothing on it is available, and we must wait for one of the maddeningly apathetic waiters to recite the possibilities. Service in the hotel's two hard-currency bars, on the other hand, is prompt, and business there is thriving. Are these bars a CIA stratagem? After all, addiction to Pepsi-Cola might bring about the downfall of the USSR more rapidly than other kinds of chemical warfare, for which the country is no doubt better prepared.

September 3. At the Rimsky-Korsakov Museum, which is in his former apartment, I feel that I am following Stravinsky's footsteps on the four flights of stairs that he climbed for his lessons. The furnishings, including three pictures of the first production of Rimsky's *Mozart and Salieri,* are much the same as at the time of its composer's death, and, following the well-known photograph of Igor and Catherine Stravinsky with Rimsky and his daughter and son-in-law, we are able to reconstruct the scene—or, rather, its props.

The apartment's lived-in feeling is attributable to such details as Rimsky's spectacles on a 1905 Moscow newspaper on his desk, and his fur hat and *shuba* on a coatrack. But it is Tatiana Vladimirovna, bearing a striking resemblance to her grandfather, the composer, who brings the surroundings to life. "This is a national monument," she tells me, in genteel English, pointing to a divan, "but I think we can sit on it."

After describing her meeting with Stravinsky in Moscow in 1962, she says: "Stravinsky was notorious as a pupil for complaining that he had no money, and once my father and aunt and uncle gave him twenty kopecks to arrange and play *God Save the Tsar* as a waltz. Stravinsky accepted and wrote a very witty piece." Of the chorus that Stravinsky composed for Rimsky's sixtieth birthday, she says:

It was prepared as a surprise. The singers, who were the Rimsky-Korsakov children and their friends, gathered in the music room adjoining the one with the dinner table. The chorus, with Stravinsky at the piano, began at the sound of popping champagne corks. My grandfather opened the doors and came in to listen and to congratulate the young composer and the performers. Later that night, my grandfather wrote in his diary: "Not a bad piece."

She adds:

I am not a musician, so I cannot speak about Stravinsky's musical prowess, but I think he has been a much misunderstood figure in this country. I was born in 1915 and did not know him, but I have always been told that he was virtually a member of this family, coming early in the morning and staying until late at night.

The portraits on the walls include two of Wagner, two of Tolstoy, and one each of Schumann, Chopin, and Berlioz. Notably absent is any reference to Tchaikovsky. The showcases contain music notebooks very like Stravinsky's, music manuscripts of the same size as his Rimsky-period songs, and a telegram from him: "How is the health of Nikolai Andreyevich please telegraph. Ustilug [April?] 22, 1908." In these rooms, with their high ceilings and large double windows, the presence of Stravinsky is more pervasive than in some of his own homes.

. . .

In 1981, unlike 1962, the turquoise, white, and gold Nikolsky
Sobor is a functioning church, and in better condition than
most Leningrad buildings, the parquet floors, the icons, the
votive lamps and candle trays being remarkably well kept.
The worshippers are not numerous—technology, not religion, is the "opium of the people"—but we witness two
services at, respectively, the center and side of the refulgent
iconostasis. When the priest, a young man in blue vestments,
raises the gospel to each pair of lips, Pavel flinches.

Like the second story in many Russian churches, this one
is twice as tall as the first. In the pinnacle of the ceiling, the
Eye of Osiris watches from its pyramid, the Freemasonic em-
blem dating, no doubt, from the period of Alexander I. The
gold here, and a gory, life-sized crucifix, remind me of Mexican churches. But the detached bell-tower, a hundred yards
or so closer to the Kriukov Canal, is the Nikolsky's most beautiful feature. While we are filming it, two nefarious-looking
types approach us, furtively unwrap an icon from a newspaper, and offer it for sale. Unlike their counterparts in capitalist countries—Italy, for example—they do not wheedle and
insist, but the speed with which they give up is no less depressing.

Only a few hundred yards separate the Nikolsky Sobor and
the Maryinsky Theatre, itself no more than five hundred
yards from the Stravinsky home. The Conservatory, whose
concert hall was so important in Stravinsky's youth, is just
around the corner. Thus the musical, theatrical, and religious
institutions that to some extent determined the forms of his
life's work were located within two blocks. Although a large
plaque indicates the home of the minor conductor E. F.
Napravnik next door, there is no marker of any kind to identify that of Russia's, and the world's, greatest musician in the
twentieth century. Surely some small slab could have been
spared, even if it had to be quarried from the pedestal of one
of the USSR's several million Lenin statues, one of which is

found at every factory, collective farm, public building, village, town, and city square.

En route to the Theatre Museum, Pavel seems to have been shaken by his exposure to the microbes of religion. At any rate, he informs me, unasked, that he once "took a course in the history of religion and atheism. The difficulty is that atheism and the history of disbelief cannot be presented fairly." Perhaps.

The museum was apprised of our visit months ago, as well as yesterday and this morning, yet nothing is prepared, the curators are hopelessly embrangled, and we wait an hour in a gallery of photographs of actors playing Lenin, before the Stravinsky memorabilia are brought in. These consist of Vasily Shukhayev's portrait of the composer, painted in Paris in 1933; three unidentified Diaghilev-period stage designs by Sudeikin; Golovin's costume designs for *The Nightingale* at the Maryinsky in May 1918; some Benois sketches for *Petrushka*; and, best of all, Bakst's costume design for Pavlova in *Firebird*. The treasure of the museum is Stravinsky's father's notebook of 183 drawings for the costumes that he wore in his 66 roles at the Maryinsky. Four of his other drawings are of Ustilug, three of them being dated "July 1889," "June 19–July 16, 1889," and "1890." A fifth page, "summer 1896, Bad Homburg," contains caricatures of an Englishman (Sherlockian pipe and fore-and-aft cap) and of the Kursaal piano player. "Drawing by daddy," the thirteen-year-old Igor has written at the bottom of the paper, and no doubt "daddy" did it to amuse his son.

September 4. After trying for two days to obtain information about flights from Leningrad to London through *any* connecting city, I have been instructed to appear at eight this morning in the Aeroflot building on Nevsky Prospekt. Knowing that the ticket will not be issued unless I present my passport and visa, just before eight I knock at the door of the office in the Astoria where passports are kept. A girl holds up five fingers, but since five minutes means at least an hour, I pass the time drinking hard-currency espresso and fearing that I will need the *ticket* in order to get the *passport*. When the office finally opens, the clerk insists that she is not allowed to separate my documents from those of the British television crew, but, fortunately, she goes off duty and her successor is unaware of this rule.

Although long lines extend from every ticket window at Aeroflot, the side room for international flights is empty. Despite the involvement of seven girls in my simple transaction —one to calculate the currency exchange, another to take my money, the third to fill out forms, the fourth to write the ticket, and the fifth, sixth, and seventh to pool their English— an hour passes before the ticket is eventually issued. Can the bureaucracy described by Gogol and Dostoevsky have been any less efficient than this? What worries me now is that when my Paddington Station visa photograph is compared with the reality, I may not get through, experiences such as this one having so drastically altered my appearance.

The dining room tonight reverberates with the shouts and laughter of inebriated Finns. According to Pavel, they come to Leningrad in order to drink themselves into a stupor. When this is achieved, they must literally be piled into their returning buses. The puritanical Soviets tolerate this behavior for the sake of the hard currency it brings in.

September 5. On my last day, I arrive at the starting place on the Stravinsky trail, the apartment of A. A. Yacovlev. Here is the huge diary kept by I.S.'s father until the last months of his life, during which his wife made the final entries for him. In this immaculate record, in which every event of every day is entered in detail, including the expenditure of each kopeck tabulated in the right column, the birth of Igor is framed in red ink, and as carefully as if he had done it himself. The book is a history of Igor's first twenty years, as well as evidence of the survival of the habits of the father in the son.

Yacovlev's large collection of photographs from the 1890s to 1912 shows that Stravinsky was a dandy even before adolescence. Whether or not in compensation for his small stature, his clothing and the way he wore it made him stand out in any group. The question is, why would a man in his early twenties choose to wear wing-collars and dress ties in the provincial town of Ustilug, where they must have looked as absurd as the evening dress of the British in India? Whatever the answer, the fact of his abundant wardrobe complicates the dating of the photographs, since ties, scarves, suits, and hats rarely appear more than once.

The most interesting of these pictures are of Stravinsky and Andrei and Vladimir Rimsky-Korsakov; Andrei, wearing the same kind of spectacles as his father, resembles him to an almost confusing degree. A snapshot of Igor with Nadiezhda Nikolayevich Rimsky-Korsakov in Berlin in 1902, at the time of Fyodor Stravinsky's Roentgen treatments there, raises a question about their relationship in the years before their respective marriages, since, to judge from these pictures, the young lady and budding composer were devoted to each other. Also worth noting is that Stravinsky's father, in group portraits, chooses a place in the corner and looks away from the camera, while his most famous son invariably places himself in the middle of the front row and provides the focus of the composition. And Stravinsky junior always looks directly into the camera, where the action is.

Most conspicuous among the ancestor portraits is a large one in oils of Fyodor Ivanovich Engel (1779–1837), who left his considerable wealth entirely to his step-granddaughter, Igor's maternal grandmother. The most attractive art in the apartment is by Dmitri Stelletsky: a bust, some illuminated letters, and a few cartoons of the composer, his classmate.

A sign at the airport reads: "Transporting explosive matters is prohibited" (poems as well as bombs?). My fellow passengers on the Aeroflot to Helsinki are hung-over and still-drunk Finns, some of them carrying huge toy-bear souvenirs.

We land at a speed that frightens me, but the bamboozled Finns applaud. I go directly to the airport restaurant, devour some excellent herring and boiled potatoes, and overtip the waiter for his efficiency, celerity, and affability, qualities totally absent in the acedia of socialism. I then try to decipher Igor Bogdanov's interview with me on the front page of today's *Pravda*, which emboldens a man at the next table to address me in Russian. Understanding that he wishes to borrow the paper, I tell him, with my smattering of Russian, that he is welcome to it. "Thank you," he says in Oxonian, adding, "I am so sorry that you are not one of my fellow countrymen." Many thanks, but *I* am not sorry.

November 22. London. Impressions of the final version of the Stravinsky documentary. First, the film is a delight to the eyes, especially in the views of St. Petersburg's churches, Nevsky Monastery, the Admiralty, the canals, bridges, broad streets, and majestic river. But apart from these and Venice, I do not have much sense of location, and almost none of chronology. Also, the best comments of the interviewees seem to have been edited out. Thus Druskin's important statement that Stravinsky's parents were so opposed to his choice of profession that they forbade him to improvise on the piano has disappeared. And Irina Vershinina is not seen or heard from, though she provides the film's most startling musical moment when two women from her folk chorus sing the original of the Khorovod from *Firebird*. And why is Rachmaninov's 1913 *Otche Nash* used in connection with Stravinsky's baptism, when his own setting is far better music and would have been more appropriate? Gone, too, is the Chinese March, recorded in Moscow in the week of September 7, evidently from the parts that Stravinsky sent from Paris to Petrograd in the summer of 1915, and which are utterly different from those in the score published in Berlin in 1923. The film is open to criticism, too, for overuse of *Firebird* (at the breaking of the ice in the Neva, for "rumblings" foreshadowing the fall of the tsar, in a Royal Ballet performance of the Firebird's Dance, and in views of Stravinsky rehearsing the piece in New York and Warsaw, and conducting it in the 1965 London concert with which the entire film concludes— thereby inevitably placing his first successful opus above all of his later music). It should also be mentioned that Stravinsky is shown leaving an airplane at Heathrow a few days before this concert, raising his hat for a barrage of photographers, but stepping to terra firma at Warsaw. In short, the film has more rigs than Standard Oil.

Palmer wants Stravinsky to be the narrator, but this is not feasible, the composer's recorded commentaries not being sufficiently extensive. Palmer attempts to circumvent the impossible by substituting an actor (George Pravda, not acknowledged in the film's credits) who, imitating Stravinsky's voice, accent, cadence, and idiosyncrasies of emphasis and pronunciation, reads doctored excerpts from the composer's books. The result must shock Stravinsky's familiars and jolt anyone attentive to speech differences. To my ears, not a single word spoken by the actor sounds like Stravinsky.

The device of the "ghost Stravinsky" would be a justified artistic license, perhaps, except that some of his lines are spurious. Also, since Stravinsky's own speech in English can be difficult to follow, the TV audience would certainly prefer clear English narration. Palmer is aware of this problem of intelligibility, since he has had Stravinsky's final speech in the film, recorded by him in 1965, remade more distinctly by the actor. But since Palmer himself reads English versions of the French interviewees (Theodore Stravinsky, Boris Kochno, Lifar, Georges Auric, Jean Wiéner, Cocteau), why did he not narrate for the pseudo-Igor as well? Similarly, native-English–speaking voices would have been preferable to accented Russian ones for the Russian interviewees (Tatiana Rimsky-Korsakov, Yacovlev, Druskin, Krasovskaya, and the Soviet Minister of Culture—whose appearance immediately after a view of Stravinsky's grave provides a nasty shock). Compound these sources of confusion with the French accent of Nadia Boulanger, the differences between British and American dialect, the delay in showing subtitles and in identifying places and speakers, and it is easy to see why the film has problems in communication.

The inauthenticity disturbs me as much as the phony speech of the ghost-Stravinsky. He says:

> My father kept a diary in which all the details of my birth were carefully noted. The diary was kept by my niece, Xenia.

But Stravinsky had long ago forgotten that the diary even existed, far from knowing anything about who kept it. He did not see the book on his 1962 visit to his niece's Leningrad apartment, and he could not have made this anachronistic statement. So, too, he is made to say that

> perhaps the strongest memory of my childhood is of the country fairs I was taken to in the Ukraine. The songs which I heard and the dances which I saw have stayed in my imagination all my life.

Though the statement could be true, Stravinsky did not say it. In the film, it is used to justify the lengthy sequence of the fair at Sorochinsk (not identified), which also has never been linked to Stravinsky. Future Russian biographies of the composer may contradict this, but until then the only certain information that we have about the child Igor's summers is that they were spent with his parents at German spas, Swiss resorts, and relatives' estates in Samara and in Rumania.

Another aspect of inauthenticity is the false impression created by some of the interviewees that they knew Stravinsky. Kyriena Ziloti, filmed in New York, did know him, both at the time of *Fireworks* (1908) and in his American years. Moreover, she is a charming speaker in perfect English, yet for some reason her interview has been left on the cutting-room floor. Kyra Nijinsky, on the other hand, who did not know him and who has nothing to say about him, makes two appearances. We also see, hear, but do not understand ex-dancers Tamara Geva, Alexandra Danilova, and Michel Pavloff, whose acquaintance with the composer was slight in-deed. In contrast to them, a valuable conversation with Lucia Davidova, who observed Stravinsky and Balanchine work to-gether virtually from the beginning, was jettisoned. Serge Lifar and Boris Kochno, though they had a place in Stravin-sky's life, on camera do not even mention him, or *Apollo* and *Mavra*, the works that brought these Diaghilevians within the composer's orbit.

Even the most salient events in a lifetime of nearly ninety years, sixty-five of them in active public life, cannot be touched upon in a three-hour film biography. One hour each is allotted to the Russian, French, and American periods, but there is simply not enough time for adequate presentation of both music and biography. Why, then, spend several minutes on a close-up of a young violinist (no view of either orchestra or conductor), when the viewer wants to see more of Stravin-sky—walking in Venice, for instance, or on his other travels, or even in bed reading, films of which are available, parts of them having been used elsewhere in the documentary? Or if not Stravinsky, why not show more sketches, manuscripts, scores, related objects? Time is also wasted on hackneyed shots of orchestra players, some in full dress (in Moscow, where there is no audience).

The Moscow Symphony's performances of the *Danse russe* and the *Danse sacrale* are stodgy and ragged, betraying the orchestra's unfamiliarity with music that is standard reper-tory elsewhere. The Russian choral performances, by two groups in Riga (not identified), are superior, but the vocal nuggets are the *Kyrie* sung by the Simon Preston Choir in Westminster Abbey, and the minute and a half from *Abra-ham and Isaac* with baritone John Shirley-Quirk. Some of the mating of music and scenery is curious, viz., the *echt*-Russian

Pastorale (1907) for the Eiffel Tower, and the Symphony in C (1940) for the train switchyard at Aigle, a crossroads in Stravinsky's life in 1917.

In what ways does the film distort through improper emphasis? First, not enough has been made known about Stravinsky's religion in his youthful years to make the church a leading motif in his life before 1925. The Nikolsky Sobor, where he was baptized and which is next to his St. Petersburg home, is the symbolic focal point of the film. But in my two decades with Stravinsky, he never mentioned the place, and our visit there in 1962 was at my request, not his. It should also be said that whatever Stravinsky's daily private devotions, he never attended an Orthodox service between 1952 and his death. In statements made at various times in his life, he denied being a "religious composer," calling himself instead "a composer of religious music." In the late 1940s, citing the examples of Bach and older composers, he told a Chilean journalist: "To write religious music is simply to write in a certain form."

The film does not adequately represent Stravinsky's position in the ballet world, though parts of solo dances from the three pop pieces are shown—a horrible rendition of the *Danse sacrale*, and very poor ones of bits of *Firebird* and *Petrushka*. Scenes from *Pulcinella* and *Noces* are included, but there is nothing from any of the masterpieces of choreography, *Apollo*, *Le Baiser de la fée*, and *Agon*. A special difficulty must be acknowledged in Stravinsky's case, however: each work is individual and representative, *Histoire du soldat* no less than the Concerto per due pianoforti soli.

The portrait of Stravinsky the man is balanced and "true to life," but of course he could hardly *not* be himself on camera. Here, in films made between 1957 and 1965, is a sampling of his characteristic gestures: the sudden broad smile, the clenching of the fist, the licking of the thumb before turning a page, the cupping of the left ear, the definiteness in lifting objects. His facility in four languages is also demonstrated, and, in the final and best sequence in the film, his economy of movement when conducting. But, all of this said, the film would have been much better if a lot more footage of old Stravinsky films had been included.

December 23, 1982. Pompano Beach, Florida. On U.S. Federal Highway 1: "Adult Motels," "Adult Films," and Go-Go's advertise such star nudes as "Ms. Illinois" (the Backstage Club) and "Ms. Kansas" (the Centerfold)—though "Ms." hardly seems appropriate in these bastions of male chauvinism. And what about "Wet T-Shirts" (the Playpen)? No matter how torrid the atmosphere, mightn't someone catch cold?

An ad for the Baird-Case Funeral Homes in today's *Sun-Sentinel* offers fifteen combinations of "Sea Burials and Cremation." The customer need only mail in a coupon, placing an "X" next to his/her preference. A "scatter at sea" with "viewing" and a "minimum casket" (knees tucked to chin?) costs $750, a "scatter at sea" without "viewing" and without casket, $625. *"D'incroyables Florides,"* as Rimbaud wrote.

December 25. Walking the beach this morning on the anniversary of V.'s birth does not help me to erase memories of the night of her death. The end was said to be "expected," but is it possible to "expect" the instant transformation of a living person into a motionless image, and can anyone anticipate the beginning of an eternal separation? C. S. Lewis referred to death as "the slamming of the door in your face, and the sound of bolting on the inside."

During that terrible night, September 16–17, the doctor arrived minutes after being notified, looking even more dour than he had in the afternoon, with black suit, black bag, and black expression. He entered the room without a word—not even "I am sorry," though tears were streaming down our faces. When he curtly refused my request to close her eyes, a nurse did so a moment later. After the perfunctory ritual with the stethoscope, he retreated to the living room to write the death certificate ("consequence of a stroke"), then crept out.

Meanwhile, the undertakers appeared as quickly as if they had been waiting in the next room. I kiss her forehead, her hair, her hands, and go out; after the first sight of the lifeless body, the worst shock is the view of the empty bed, where she had been lying for three months. I had gone to her at all hours, holding her hand, whispering in her ear, to which she would respond by opening her eyes and squeezing my hand. Day and night, I waited for the nurse's knock on the wall, a signal that V. wanted to see me. Now the silence in the room will haunt me.

"I haven't hope. I haven't faith": Betjeman's poem speaks for me. "Soul," "spirit," the Buddhist idea of a continuity, a rebirth of minds not connected with a self—even if I understood and believed in these notions, they would not console me. Thinking about death, the mind is unable to imagine something other than life, and I want the resurrection of the person: her face, her smile, her eyes, her voice and accent, her gestures—the way she lighted a cigarette (she smoked until the last days, puffing rapidly, as if it might be the last time). The empty bed is terrible. As the Sudanese (Dinka) chant goes:

> The sun is born, and dies, and comes again.
> And the moon is born, and dies, and comes again.
> And the stars are born, and die, and come again.
> And man is born, and dies, and does not come again.

December 30. She was here in Pompano the night that we waited on the beach for the annual nesting of a herd of sea turtles. They are supposed to emerge from the surf, lay eggs (said to look like Ping-Pong balls and prized as an aphrodisiac), bury them in the sand, and put to sea again. A team of marine biologists was to have come to harvest the deposits, but neither tortoises nor scientists made an appearance, and we left wondering if this year's "egg" might have been filled with cocaine. Every night between eight and eleven, lights in the neighboring condominium have been switching on and off in codelike patterns, signals to a ship, we thought, for the reason that they were visible only on the ocean side. Since this stretch of coast is famed for drug smuggling, we decided to ask the "narcs" to investigate, but our call to the police was so unwelcome that our suspicions were aroused—and confirmed a few minutes later when the semaphoring stopped.

For the last three years, when V. approached my door, walking from her room to the front part of the house, R., the nurse, would call to me: "Look who's here," or "Someone is coming." I would jump up from my desk by the window, run to the corridor, put my arms around V., and kiss her. She was always elegantly dressed and neatly groomed. Until the last three months, she went out every day, sometimes no farther than the bench across the street, from which she would wave to me in my fourth-floor window. Twice a week she was driven to midtown stores and out into the country. In the last year of her life she flew to Florida four times, and once to London. But May 29 was the last time she left the city—for a visit to my sister's in New Paltz. In June, V. attended my orchestra rehearsals with the New York City Ballet, waiting for me in the car after the evening performances. At her last public appearance, for my June 15 New York Philharmonic concert, she was hailed by the audience in her front box.

Last spring, together one evening on the living-room couch, I saw that she was lost in meditation and asked for her thoughts. "They are good ones for me, bad for you. It will be hard for you."

I should be grateful for her death, should have considered it a blessing when the labored breathing stopped, and the relentless pumping of her left knee ended. The truth is that I would have let her pain continue in exchange for even a little more life.

The nurse who was with her at 3:15 a.m. says that she turned to her left side and died looking at an icon that she herself had made in Russia when she was a girl, and which hung on the wall above and behind her head. The icon story is important to R., who adds that immediately after the death, I.S., in the photograph of him next to the bed, "looked happier."

Until the last days, V. recognized R., and when I entered the room the day before the death, V. almost shouted my name. Yet the doctor's argument against the use of artificial life-sustaining procedures is that she had recently shown no sign of recognizing *him*. But she *never* recognized him! And how can he disregard the varying experiences of those who have been with her all the time, and fail to perceive that she could be different according to the hour of the day and night? After more than thirty-four years with her, I knew that she was still too much alive to justify his proposal for an abject surrender, and, on the 15th, I insisted that she be given intravenous feeding, at least for a trial period. He sabotaged this by ordering only a single bottle for the early evening and nothing for the night. Naturally she was weaker the next day, and, in an excruciating decision, I finally consented to cutting the life line. (I felt that R. agreed with me, this once, but a nurse never opposes a doctor.)

Death is inevitable now and must come soon. I sit by the bedside all evening, crying in the dark, except for the flickering light of the nurses' soundless television screen. I.S. died in this same room, in the same kind of hospital bed, and even facing the same way. At 1:30, I take pills to try to sleep. An hour later, I come back and hold her hands for a while. Then, at 3:15, R. calls me: "You had better come!" "Is it over?" "Yes." The forehead and cheeks are still warm, and the silver hair lies behind her on the pillow. When the nurses begin their business of preparing the body, removing her pink woolen socks, I take them, recalling, with a jab, how I used to help her put them on and pull her galoshes over them before she went out in winter.

She was in Pompano in October 1981, on the day that the gulls returned. Another return, this one gruesome: the body of a girl was washed ashore just south of our beach. A two-seater stunt plane, flying at low altitude, had plunged into the sea about a mile offshore and in view of scores of bathers. Helicopters and boats had sped to the scene, but no trace of the plane was found. Not long after, the bodies of thirty-three drowned Haitian refugees were discovered on the sand in front of the wealthiest homes in the area, as if to propitiate Mammon and for a few hours despoil the playground of the rich. *"J'ai heurté, savez-vous, d'incroyables Florides."*

Before dawn, on September 12, 1982, a Roman Catholic priest, at R.'s request, administered extreme unction. I do not believe that this viaticum-passport-stamping meant anything to V., except possibly the confirmation that she was dying; but, then, I cannot imagine a God for whom the last rites would make any difference. Also, I keep remembering that in January 1971, she herself decided to spare Stravinsky the sight of a cleric, believing that it would hasten his death.

R. also arranged for the Russian rites, given the next day by an Orthodox priest who warned me that he would not perform them unless the dying woman was fully conscious. The ceremony took place, nevertheless, and the Russian prayers clearly terrified V., who stared intently at him for a few minutes, then slept while he anointed her forehead, feet, palms of the hands, and pressed the silver cross to her lips (*Svadebka:* "And we kiss now the silver cross"). Since he was not wearing clerical garments, she may have supposed him to be another doctor. Still, to hear *Otche Nash* intoned in her mother tongue at a time when she knew herself to be gravely ill must have alarmed her. The room was hot, and the priest continually mopped his brow.

At 6:30, on the eve of the death, the therapist arrived and, with scarcely believable insensitivity, proceeded to exercise the leg of the semiconscious patient—until I told him to collect his check and leave. Yet V. had been fond of him earlier in the summer, especially when he had helped her from her bed to a chair and, on that glorious day, the high point of the last three months, wheeled her into the dining room, where we applauded her. She smiled, perhaps believing that she would be outside again, taking her daily rides, as I had been assuring her day after depressing day. A week later, when I said the same thing, tears rolled down her cheek.

December 31. New Year's Eve. A year ago we had a party for her in this room overlooking the ocean. She wore the pink dress in which she was buried.

January 2, 1983. I still wake at 3:15 and see myself going to her room. Now I dread sleeping, or, rather, dread the pain of waking, the "Where am I?," and then the realization.

For the first time in my life I have come to understand the desire to turn to spiritualism, even to table-tapping, in the hope of a vision, or the sound of the voice. For I cannot see her face in my imagination, and photographs preserve only one aspect: the whole is unrecapturable. I avoid looking at recent photographs of her, but not those of ten or twenty years ago. The very old woman is the one I so sorely miss, far more than the younger one.

The first music I happened to hear since her death was Stravinsky's *Orpheus*, which was also the first music I heard *with* her, at the New York City Ballet rehearsals in the wonderful month of April 1948. Although this score had not attracted me in the intervening years, now it moves me again as much as anything Stravinsky ever wrote—perhaps because Orpheus is the most human myth. Stravinsky expresses the supreme moment of death with silence. But Orpheus is fortunate, for the Bacchantes soon kill him.

The music I *miss* the most is V.'s very quiet singing. In my twenty-three years with Stravinsky, she sang only one melody in his presence, a mushroom gatherers' song from her childhood that he notated from her in one of his sketchbooks.

After his death, she regularly sang several such songs, especially "Cheezhik" and "Fontanka." If the chatter at dinner ignored her, she would sometimes break in with one of these tunes. Her singing was tape-recorded by R., but I could not bear to listen to it. During the final months, V. did not sing at all.

V. was not in Florida but in New York during hurricane David, but I called her every hour or so, describing how windows were shuttered and storefronts crisscrossed with tape and battened with plywood; how the supermarket shelves were stripped; and how, when the winds began to gust, we crossed the drawbridge to our key, fearing to be stranded on the mainland by an electrical "outage" and to find our elevator service inoperative. "Oh my goodness," she would say.

I also told her how residents of low-lying areas were instructed to evacuate to high schools, and how animals from one zoo were transferred to another one on slightly higher ground, and women in the ninth month of pregnancy were instructed to go to hospitals (since the sudden drop in barometric pressure could induce the onset of labor). But the worst of the experience was in the anticipation, the noise of rattling metal shutters, the falling and bumping of objects, the sirens of the police and fire departments, the electrical wires crackling on the ground like fireworks, the sight of boats in the canals, loosened from moorings and tossing in the waves. After David, many months elapsed before V. returned to Florida.

At 7:00 a.m., September 17, 1982, I receive a representative from the funeral home who happens to be the same man who flew to Italy with us and with Stravinsky's casket in the night of April 12–13, 1971. At 6:00 p.m. we go to a small chapel—next to the one where Stravinsky's casket had lain—

where V.'s body is covered with my blanket of red roses. A young man and woman, dressed in jeans, stumble through the only prayer in Russian, as the priest shakes his censer. One line in the prayers is unbearably poignant: ". . . thy servant Vera, who has fallen asleep."

The Monday-morning service begins with Stravinsky's Three Sacred Choruses, reviving memories of his funeral. Father Gregory, a noble figure, begins by saying: "Vera Stravinsky's passing is that of an era, the civilization of pre-1917 Russia." He explains the meaning of the service and its use of Old Slavonic, then sings antiphons with five superb choristers. After this, each of us kneels by the casket.

We leave New York in the late afternoon, changing planes the next morning in Paris en route to Venice. The magic city is mercifully invisible in a thick haze, and—another piece of good luck—the only available hotel rooms are on the Lido, for me a no man's land without memories. The service is to be at S. Giorgio dei Greci at 10:00 a.m. on the 22nd.

Stepping from a *motoscafo* directly to the canal entrance to the church, I am happy to see close friends. A Stravinskian irony: the casket has not arrived, and V. will be late for her funeral. When the water hearse finally comes, gondolier pallbearers carry the casket to a black and gold carpet, marked by four tall candles, at the center of the church. Behind the iconostasis, the archimandrite dons his black headdress, with drape flowing down the back of his red and gold cassock. Listening to the florid alleluias, the archaic, oriental chant, and the Kyrie Eleison echoed by the sepulchral-voiced old man who participated in Panikheda services for Stravinsky, I think of standing next to V. on this same spot.

From St. George of the Greeks we pass the church of Saints John and Paul, the scene of I.S.'s funeral; V.'s death has brought his back to life. At the dock on San Michele, the casket is lifted to a wagon and wheeled to the entrance of the Reparto Ortodosso, past the pointer marked "Igor Stravinsky." Here all is familiar, the tall, dark cypresses, the old tombstones, and the gravel paths—all except the sight of the newly dug earth. The graveside ceremony is brief, the casket quickly but creakingly lowered, and I sprinkle a handful of dirt over the length of the coffin. Now she and I.S. are to-gether—and only a few feet from Diaghilev, who introduced them to each other fifty-one years ago.

Back in New York, I enter the house filled with the ab-sence of V., into whose room I am drawn, nevertheless, to talk to her just as I did all summer.

On V.'s name day, a letter from Robert Fizdale:

Arthur [Gold] and I have always felt it was one of the great privileges of our lives to be able to feel we were friends of the Stravinskys. You enjoyed that privilege more pro-foundly than anyone they ever knew. Each of them gave us the feeling that they felt it was a privilege for *them* to have *you* in their lives. Vera Arturovna was one of the most beautiful women who ever lived. She was not only born beautiful, but she inspired beauty, created beauty, and lived to make the lives of those around her more beautiful.

Walking the cold winter sand of Florida, I want to believe Joseph Conrad's line: "Life . . . will close upon a sorrow like the sea upon a dead body, no matter how much love has gone to the bottom."

April 27. London to Venice. Low tide. Fish are jumping in the lagoon. A flocculent sky, pall of oil-refinery smoke over Mestre. I can hardly bring myself to look in the direction of San Michele.

I enter the city via the Misericordia. In the last house on the Fondamente Nuove, a young boy sits on a windowsill sunning himself. Weeds sprout from the bridges and coppices in the courtyards of empty palaces. Buildings are flaking, ornaments crumbling, colors fading—the Fondamenta dei Tedeschi, red when I last saw it, is now ghostly white—and the general deturpation seems to have progressed fifty years in the last four. Mercifully, my hotel room is in a wing unknown to me, high over the Alberi Canal and "Bridge of the Oysters."

In the piazza: young girls in miniskirts display hose and shoes in matching scarlet, gamboge, green, indigo, purple; gold-lettered red banners announce an exposition, "WAGNER E VENEZIA." Not Wagner but *Tootsie* is playing at the Cinema San Marco, and I am tempted to go again to see what the film is like dubbed in Italian.

April 28. To S. Giorgio dei Greci, and, half consciously retracing the scenes of last September, to Palazzo Albrizzi.

April 30. George Balanchine dies, a prayed-for release, but also a paralyzing shock. When I first met him, on April 5, 1948, in the Stravinsky suite in the Ambassador Hotel in New York, he was forty-four years old. Thirty-five years have vanished. "We lived ere yet this fleshy robe we wore." Why does Coleridge's line come suddenly to mind?

May 2. I finally go to San Michele, realizing that I cannot leave without visiting the graves. At the flower stall I buy red roses, then follow the path of September 22. A guide (!) at I.S.'s tomb is lecturing some tourists in German. When alone, I plant the roses in the soft mound of earth next to I.S.'s stone. But, turning to walk away, I am drawn back as if by a magnet, and I remain there all afternoon, until the loudspeaker announces closing time.

"A pair of locked caskets," Isak Dinesen wrote, "each containing the key to the other."

May 3. Rome. Adriana and Jane Panni drive me to Ardea to see Manzù about V.'s stone. The maestro, looking younger

than he did twelve years ago, promises to go to Venice himself to measure I.S.'s stone—and, incidentally, to "sign" it,
"Manzù."

May 6. Pompano Beach. Several times during the afternoon
an airplane, just offshore, flies low like a crop duster, trailing
an advertisement for "PLAYPEN SOUTH. FREE DRINKS. LADIES
MUDWRESTLING." Most young people on the beach have radios
plugged into their ears like hearing aids.

June 20. New York. Stravinsky's manuscripts and archives
are offered for sale this afternoon by the lawyers for the Stravinsky Trust, but only one of the two bidders appears, John
Fleming, a New York manuscript dealer representing the
Fred R. Koch Foundation as donor for the Pierpont Morgan
Library (of which Koch is a trustee). The other bidder, Albi
Rosenthal, representing the Paul Sacher Foundation in Basel,
telephones that he will not enter a contest against Koch, because his "oil and pipeline fortune is unlimited." Fleming
quickly states his top price, $4.25 million, and his condition
that he will withdraw it if it is not accepted by 5:30 p.m.
today. My lawyer, Martin Garbus, calls to say: "It is difficult
to walk away from four and a quarter million when Fleming's
previous offer was two million." But Rosenthal knows both
the market and the real value of the manuscripts, and he will
certainly top this figure. Fleming's questions about the contents of the collection, transmitted to me by Garbus, reveal
that Koch is bidding for a prestigious but wholly unknown
property. Garbus *does* walk away from the $4.25 million,
after Fleming promises that he will keep his bid secret.

June 21. Rosenthal rightly accuses the Stravinsky Trust of
dealing unfairly with Sacher, the terms of whose bona fide
offer of $3.5 million, made in London on April 27, were that

the bid would stand for thirty days. The New York Public Library, custodian of the manuscripts since March 26, maintains that it was not properly informed of the Sacher offer. But the second thirty-day period granted the NYPL for a fund-raising campaign, May 17 to June 17, produced a great deal of publicity that worked against the library by attracting other bidders, including Koch. By the end of the afternoon, Stravinsky's children have instructed their lawyers to accept Koch's bid.

June 22. Rosenthal insists that Garbus disclose Koch's offer and that Sacher be allowed to match it. Garbus, well aware that a leak from Fleming or the children's lawyers will occur before long, decides to send an acceptance agreement to Rosenthal for the sale price of $5.25 million. Rosenthal answers that Sacher is away, and Garbus says: "But you know where he is, and a three-minute telephone call to Switzerland can conclude the purchase."

June 23. Rosenthal telephones the children's lawyers and tells them that his top offer is $5 million. The children insist on accepting, but Garbus refuses, on the grounds that in two years the collection will be worth at least twice the amount. Perhaps fearing a postponement, during which Koch would have time to have the materials appraised, Rosenthal, at 2:11 p.m., signs the $5.25 million acceptance agreement.

Stravinsky would have been amused to know that Valium and Librium (the Sacher money comes from the F. Hoffman–LaRoche company) have purchased his manuscripts and that a manufacturer of pharmaceuticals has reimbursed him, or his heirs, for his lifelong expenditures on drugs.

August 17. 12:10 a.m. No sooner does flight 007 leave for Seoul than the stewardesses don brightly colored, flower-patterned kimonos and oriental manners—quick, short bows at every contact—and serve a "heavy snack": hors d'oeuvres (ginseng root), a "starch" course ("France fried potatoes"), *bulgogi* (marinated beef), and *kimchi* (fermented pickle of cabbage). The menu reproduces a Yi-dynasty (1392) embroidery of the mythical bird Bong Hwang, who was "lucky because he foresaw coming catastrophe of the country." The pilot's English is indistinguishable from Korean, but at least the closed-circuit TV advertisement for duty-free products is silent.

The uneventful seven-hour flight to Anchorage ends with a blast of music, shocking at 2:00 a.m. When we are airborne again, a midnight-blue dawn begins to break over the still-shimmering city and harbor lights, but we plunge into darkness for the remaining eight and a half hours. The approach to Seoul at sunrise is a Chinese painting of morning mist, glittering wet land in the low tide along the shores of the Yellow Sea, sinuous rivers, humped mountains with terraced slopes of rice paddies. The valleys, parceled by irrigation ditches, are more intensely green than the summer landscape of the upper New York that I have just left. As we deplane, a stewardess bows and says: "Fank you for frying with us, Mr. Claft."

The drive from Kimpo Airport to the center of the city is in some of the densest traffic I have ever seen, and mammoth trucks threaten to crush my tiny taxi. The road signs here, on the south bank of the Han River, are in Korean and English, and the omnipresent word *dong* (as in the one with a luminous nose), street or area, is probably all the Korean I am destined to learn. The buildings, high-rise monstrosities, are incongruous with the "poetic" willow trees lining most of the road, but we pass a few remnants of an earlier time: one old man pushing a cart, another with a load on his back, a woman carrying a basket on her head. The Han is wide but shallow, to judge from the sandbars and dredging. We cross the last of a dozen low bridges and begin the steep ascent to the Sheraton Walker Hill.

The desk clerk says that I was expected yesterday—the confusion having arisen from my crossing the International Date Line—and have been written off as a no-show. While waiting for a room, I window-shop in the basement, dazzled by the watered silks, lacquer wares, black boxes with inlaid mother-of-pearl, bamboo trays and mats, and elaborately costumed dolls. The fixtures in my room are scaled to the small Korean body, which makes for difficulties in the bathroom. My sixteenth-floor window overlooks the Han, a large new section of the city on the right side, and wooded and farm lands extending to the Chinese-shaped mountains on the left. Immediately below the hotel is an Olympic-size swimming pool and a large red balloon trailing an advertisement for Coca-Cola.

August 19. The English-language *Korea Herald*'s lead story concerns U.S. General Donnelly's declaration that "GIs in Japan are ready for Korean action, the North being capable of invading the South, and the United States committed to defend the Republic of Korea" (along with Chad, Lebanon, and Central America?). The general sincerely "hopes that no situation will develop on the Korean peninsula that will require the use of nuclear weapons," meaning, of course, that they are already there. A sheet inserted in the *Herald*, "Aid to Current English," lists "orchestrate" (nothing to do with music), "break," and "broke" as today's assignments. The examples for the last two include: "Can you break a bill of 10,000 won (pronounced wawn)?," "Give me a break," "The company went broke," and "Someone broke wind." (Why are the Korean translations of the first three sentences the same length as the English originals, while that of the fourth is twelve lines long?) The other English-language newspaper, the *Korean Times*, features "Dear Abby"; an article attributing AIDS to "homosexuals, hemophiliacs and Haitians"; several letters to the editor protesting the false Korea pictured in *M*A*S*H*, and a report from Japan on the displacement of workers by robots, a process that the Japanese Labor Ministry justifies not as economy but as part of "the search for higher precision and quality."

The Romanization of the Korean language follows two radically different systems, so that the Ministry of Education's maps and those published according to the international McCune-Reischauer method do not conform. The M.O.E. replaces *k* by *s*, *p* by *b*, *ch* by *j*, *r* by *l*, and *n* by *r*, and adds the silent English *e* to *o* (Seoul).

August 20. Walter Gillessen, resident director of the Korea Philharmonic, whose two hundred fifty-fifth subscription concert I am to conduct, talks to me about his recent trip in the south. His statement that the country is an armed garrison, on wartime alert, does not surprise me, since a long convoy of soldiers in camouflage uniforms passed beneath my window in open trucks earlier this morning. Moreover, a blackout has been announced for 9:30 p.m. tomorrow, and the midnight curfew is always in effect; foreigners and hotel nightclubs are exempted, but taxis are not permitted to operate during it. Obviously all newspapers are censored, since Rim Young Sam, who advocates democracy, is never mentioned, while President Chun's every word is reported reverentially.

Gillessen, a German, says that the orchestra personnel is now entirely Korean, whereas a few months ago the principal players were European. He advises me to stay away from local inns unless I have a strong sense of adventure, the floor beds and pillows being much too hard for sleeping, and crawlers, including beetles, are abundant.

August 21. To Inchon, returning by way of Chilbo Temple and Suwon. My rehearsal tomorrow has been canceled, and I therefore try to cancel the driver who was to have taken me, but he says he wasn't coming anyway because "tomorrow is my day off." Although willow trees border both sides of the

Seoul-Inchon expressway, they do not conceal the "industrial miracle" of faceless factories and apartment houses behind. The man in the tollbooth bows to me as my driver pays the token.

Unlike the people of Seoul, many Inchonians are dressed in the style of an earlier period, the men in loose white blouses and pants fastened at the ankles, the women in long skirts and turban-like headdresses, carrying their children on their backs. The harbor itself, now supposedly the largest in the world in tonnage as well as area, has only a few docks; the large ships anchor offshore, where they are loaded by smaller ones. The waterfront is lined by a long row of restaurants, the street levels of which are aquariums of squid, eel, crab, lobster, and fish of every size, stripe, design, and color (including green). The customer indicates his choice, which the proprietor scoops out with a net and serves, cooked or raw, in second-story dining rooms.

We climb a steep hill that features a stunning panorama of the harbor and, despite an absurdly heroic statue of General MacArthur, an attractive esplanade, but thick shrubbery and blankets of flowers do not conceal concrete fortifications, guns, and radar. On the edge of the lookout is a large dovecote, an eleven-story wooden condominium for pigeons built more than a century ago. The entrance to each apartment is a different shade of green, red, blue, or yellow, only slightly faded, and the center panel displays the Buddhist vortex, a pinwheel of colors.

In the wine-growing region near Chilbo are clusters of small houses with blue pagoda-shaped roofs. The vines form canopies (to borrow Keats's phrase) "wove in small intricacies." The turnoff to the temple is a mere dirt track, but the slope is 90 degrees. Halfway up is a Christian cemetery whose graves are mounds like the Korean royal tombs. Below the temple, red peppers are drying on tables outside of a farmhouse, presumably the home of the Buddhist priest. On a hill above the temple stands a statue of Miruk, white except for a stylized black pompadour, a tiny green mustache and chin beard, and reddened lips. He wears a kind of mortarboard about a foot above his head, the four corners upturned in the Chinese style, but with eight tassels instead of the graduate's one. Every outer surface of the small temple below is painted with poppies, flying flute-playing Krishnas, and swastikas. Inside, the ceiling is covered with large paper lotus flowers, each with a prayer attached, reminding me that the gold image of a god seated on the altar is Padmapani, the lotus-born. In one corner of the room is a huge bell with a mallet, in another an old scroll, cups, kettles, silver candlesticks, and prayer mats. Every panel is painted or hung with scrolls depicting scenes from the life of Siddhartha Gautama. Climbing back down to the road, I pass four old men, pilgrims, wanderers from temple to temple, with all of their possessions on their backs.

At Suwon, the eighteenth-century wall has been preserved, and this more than any building that I have seen in Seoul helps me to imagine the gates of the old castles.

August 22. To Silluk-sa Temple, south of Seoul, one of the great monuments of the Silla dynasty (50 B.C.–A.D. 935). Bicycles, some with chicken crates on the handlebars, are numerous on this road, and pedestrians bent over from the loads strapped to stepladders on their backs, but the main traffic is military—trucks on the way to army camps.

In contrast to Chilbo, Silluk-sa is a large compound of temples and bowers, of fenced-off stupas and steles. The approach is a long avenue of booths displaying tawdry souvenirs, including plastic Buddha dolls, as well as computers and transistors. Tourists, who arrive here in droves and by taxi, are confronted by placards with historical information in both Korean and a kind of Chaucerian English: "Priest Naong droue a fling dragon away with a mistrious briddle." A flying, fire-breathing dragon is suspended from the roof in one of the pavilions, but whatever the meaning of "briddle," why does this creature have the fins of a fish? And why, too, does it face an immense drum, and a bell six feet high and almost as wide?

The pride of the temple is a stupa enshrining the bones of Ranong, whose epitaph, composed in 1379 by a Confucian scholar, has been inscribed in marble. One house contains twenty life-size gypsum statues of assorted priests and ogres. Another, the monastery's living quarters, is closed to visitors, but a glimpse within reveals such incongruities as an electric coffee percolator on a shelf next to a dozen bowls with chopsticks, and, on the wall, a Westminster clock.

The colors and ornaments in the main temple are almost blinding, from which one deduces that the monks are skilled artisans in preservation. The two birds suspended from the Buddha's betel-shaded altar are like doves of the Holy Spirit in Mexican churches. But his smile strikes me as not exactly that of "anatta." I climb to a rock promontory above the Han River and unintentionally intrude on a man and woman delousing each other's hair.

August 23. The streets around the Korean Broadcasting flagship station, where my rehearsals take place, are lined with bulletin boards containing notices and votive pictures begging for clues and information about relatives missing since the 1950 war. Some three thousand families, out of hundreds of thousands who were separated, have been reunited since June, thanks to television appearances—probably the most constructive achievement in the annals of the medium.

Language is the main impediment in today's rehearsals: only one member of the orchestra speaks English, a Kansas-born Korean-American, but speaks no Korean. While the *Fidelio* Overture is comparatively easy for them, as is the square and simple Prokofiev Second Piano Concerto, *Le Sacre du printemps* is as new as it was to Monteux's musicians in Paris in May 1913.

Between rehearsals, Dr. Kang-Sook Lee, general director of

the Korea Philharmonic Orchestra and an eminent ethno-musicologist, enlightens me on the heterophony and non-metrical, elastic rhythms of Korean music.

August 26. My concert begins with the Korean national anthem, sixteen measures of Western-sounding melody and harmony in which the downbeat seems to be the upbeat. The applause for this, for the Beethoven, for the Prokofiev, and for the Stravinsky is about equal and by no means tumultuous.

August 31. New York. Two weeks to the day of my departure for Seoul, flight 007 is shot down by a Soviet MiG. Baudelaire's words come to mind: "I have received a singular warning. I have felt the wind of the wing . . . pass over me."

A NOTE ON THE TYPE

The text of this book was set on the Linotype in a type face
called Baskerville. The face is a facsimile reproduction of
types cast from molds made for John Baskerville (1706–75)
from his designs. The punches for the revived Linotype
Baskerville were cut under the supervision of the English
printer George W. Jones.

John Baskerville's original face was one of the fore-
runners of the type style known as "modern face" to printers—
a "modern" of the period A.D. 1800.

Composed by Maryland Linotype, Baltimore, Maryland.
Printed and bound by The Haddon Craftsmen,
Scranton, Pennsylvania.

Design by Judith Henry